Witnessing Their Faith

Witnessing Their Faith

Religious Influence on Supreme Court Justices and Their Opinions

Jay Alan Sekulow

ROWMAN & LITTLEFIELD PUBLISHERS, INC.
Lanham • Boulder • New York • Toronto • Oxford

ROWMAN & LITTLEFIELD PUBLISHERS, INC.

Published in the United States of America
by Rowman & Littlefield Publishers, Inc.
A wholly owned subsidiary of The Rowman & Littlefield Publishing Group, Inc.
4501 Forbes Boulevard, Suite 200, Lanham, Maryland 20706
www.rowmanlittlefield.com

PO Box 317
Oxford
OX2 9RU, UK

British Library Cataloguing in Publication Information Available

Library of Congress Cataloging-in-Publication Data

Sekulow, Jay.
  Witnessing their faith : religious influence on Supreme Court justices and their
opinions / Jay Alan Sekulow.
    p. cm.
  Includes bibliographical references and index.
  ISBN 0-7425-5064-8 (cloth : alk. paper)
  1. Freedom of religion—United States—History.   2. Religion in the public
schools—Law and legislation—United States—History.   3. Church and state—
United States—History.   4. Judicial opinions—United States—History.   5. Judges—
United States—Attitudes—History.   6. United States. Supreme Court—History.
I. Title.
KF4783.S45   2005
342.7308'52—dc22   2005016649

Printed in the United States of America

 ∞ ™ The paper used in this publication meets the minimum requirements of American
National Standard for Information Sciences—Permanence of Paper for Printed Library
Materials, ANSI/NISO Z39.48-1992.

This book is dedicated to the memory of my paternal grandfather, Samuel Sekulow, whose voyage to Brooklyn, New York, by way of Ellis Island, made it possible for me to present oral arguments before the Supreme Court of the United States.

Contents

Acknowledgments

$\mathscr{I}$n gathering research materials for this book, I have been greatly assisted by Jeremy Tedesco, Clayton S. Wood, Donn Parsons, and Laura Robertson. Bill Haynes provided valuable assistance as well on the denominational aspects contained in this book.

Cindy Turner and Robyn Archuleta faithfully and cheerfully transcribed drafts and more drafts of this manuscript.

I want to thank my editor, Margaret Hammerot, for her tremendous research and editorial skills. She proved to be an invaluable resource in the preparation of this book.

Finally, many thanks to Jeremy Langford at Rowman & Littlefield, who kept us focused and on track despite a major Supreme Court case developing during the final stages of the preparation of the manuscript.

Introduction

> The Establishment Clause does not license government to treat religion and those who teach or practice it, simply by virtue of their status as such, as subversive of American ideals and therefore subject to unique disabilities.
>
> —Justice William J. Brennan
> *McDaniel v. Paty*, 1978

*W*hen the Founding Fathers of the United States of America signed the Constitution on "the Seventeenth Day of September in the Year of our Lord one thousand seven hundred and Eighty seven," they knew that the document was not quite finished. There were certain gaps that needed to be filled, and therefore Article Five provided a mechanism for amendments to the Constitution. Dozens of amendments had been proposed in the state ratifying conventions, and Congress now undertook the task of sorting and reducing them to a manageable number and sending them back to the states for ratification. Of the twelve sent out, ten were ratified, and these took effect on December 15, 1791. The first nine of these were to guarantee certain basic rights to the people. At the very top of the Founding Fathers' concern was freedom of religion.

The First Amendment to the United States's Constitution guarantees that "Congress shall make no law respecting an establishment of religion, or prohibiting the free exercise thereof; or abridging the freedom of speech, or of the press; or the right of the people peaceably to assemble, and to petition the Government for a redress of grievances."

The opening sixteen words of the First Amendment have two parts that together are referred to as "the religion clauses." The first part with the phrase "establishment of religion" is known as "the Establishment Clause," and the second part with the phrase "free exercise" is known as "the Free Exercise Clause." These provisions are designed to protect against two distinct types of government actions that interfere with religious liberty. The Establishment Clause was designed to draw a line of demarcation in the relationship between church and state by prohibiting the creation of a national religion such as existed in England under the Anglican Church and in the European monarchies under the Roman Catholic Church. The Free Exercise Clause guaranteed individual rights to freedom of religious practices and beliefs without government interference.

It would seem that both clauses are clear and straightforward. However, it is the religion clauses that have resulted in Supreme Court decisions that can best be characterized as confusing, conflicting, and, at times, perplexing. Perhaps no question has so bedeviled the Supreme Court in its history as finding the best way to interpret and apply these two clauses of the First Amendment. How this has come about is the subject of this study.

Much has been written about the faith of the Founding Fathers. There is little doubt that the religious influence on the Founders played a significant role in the majesty of the words chosen in our founding documents. Even in modern times, the Supreme Court in *School District of Abington v. Schempp* (1963) stated: "[T]he fact that the Founding Fathers believed devotedly that there was a God and that the unalienable rights of man were rooted in Him is clearly evidenced in their writings, from the Mayflower Compact to the Constitution itself." There can be little doubt that religion has been closely identified with our national history and government. No one can underestimate the value of understanding the religious influence of the Founding Fathers. Many of that generation went on to be presidents, governors, congressmen, and senators.

In a similar vein of inquiry, this book seeks to examine the impact of the religious faith and practices of Supreme Court justices on their court decisions involving the religion clauses of the First Amendment. Under our constitutional republic, since at least *Marbury v. Madison* (1803), it is the Supreme Court of the United States that has served as the arbiter of constitutional interpretation.

To fully comprehend the religion cases requires an understanding of the background of each of the justices and their religious beliefs and traditions, as well as the theological disputes, in existence at the time their decisions were rendered. In every one of the cases discussed in this book, the opinion of the justices coincided with the official positions held by the religious denomination that had influenced them.

The book is divided into two parts: "Religious Freedom in the Nineteenth Century" and "Religious Freedom in the Twentieth Century." Each chapter is broken into three parts for analysis. First, I look at the cultural/historical context and the controversy surrounding the dispute. The cultural conflicts in existence shaped the actual cases accepted by the Court for review. Next, I look at the justices themselves and how they were raised, their religious tradition and practices, and how they rose to the bench. Finally, I explore the actual case, focusing on the facts of the case, the issues addressed, and the implications of the decision, especially how the individual justice's religious faith played out in the opinions rendered.

I have selected nine justices who represent over 160 years of Supreme Court history—four from the nineteenth century and five from the twentieth. Through this approach, I hope to provide a clear understanding of the effect that religious faith, practices, and experiences have had on the justices and their opinions. Four prominent denominations have had a significant impact on the Supreme Court and its cases: the Unitarians, Baptists, Catholics, and Mormons. For the Unitarians and Southern Baptists, there was a desire to foster a strict separation of church and state, in part, as a reaction to Catholics and Mormons. For the Catholics and Mormons, their practices served as the catalyst for the cultural conflicts.

Justice Joseph Story, who authored the decision in the Court's first case involving government and religion in 1844, was a devout Unitarian. His uncle, a Puritan-Congregationalist minister, also influenced him in his youth. Story was one of the most prolific writers on the religion clauses both on and off the bench. His opinion in the Philadelphia case of *Vidal v. Girard* focused on the issues of public schools and the teaching of religion. Violence and actual riots between Catholics and Protestants were erupting in Boston, New York, and Philadelphia at the time the case was pending and after it was decided. The challenge in *Vidal* focused on a will establishing a college under government trusteeship which specifically excluded ministers from serving as teachers. Concluding that the will was not hostile to Christianity or the laws of Pennsylvania, which mandated Bible teaching in public schools, Justice Story wrote of the importance of teaching the Bible, "without note or comment," in the schools by lay teachers. This practice Justice Story deemed constitutional. The idea of the Bible being taught without note or comment was based on Unitarian theology. One of the Unitarian's primary objections to Catholicism was its annotated Bibles. Thus, the phrase "without note or comment" found its way into the Court's opinion.

With the controversy over slavery galvanizing the nation, the Court found itself involved in a religious dispute of national significance. Across the country, which was expanding ever westward past the Mississippi River to the Pacific Ocean by mid-nineteenth century, Christian denominations began to take formal positions on the issue of slavery. The Unitarians opposed slavery early on, as did the Presbyterians. When *Watson v. Jones* came before the Court in 1871, Associate Justice Samuel Miller authored the opinion. Miller was a Unitarian who served as the president of the National Unitarian Conference for a three-year period. His opinion in *Watson v. Jones* clearly represented the Unitarian stand on the issue of slavery. The Court in *Watson* dealt with a formal split within the national Presbyterian Church over the slavery issue that affected many individual churches before, during, and after the Civil War. A question of the disposition of the church's property was presented in the case. The members of the specific Presbyterian church in Kentucky had split into proslavery and antislavery factions. Justice Miller, siding with the pro-Union antislavery faction, issued an opinion that coincided precisely with the public pronouncements of the Unitarian Church on the slavery issue.

Closely associated, at least from a legal standpoint, with the issue of slavery was the Mormon controversy. The question of state's rights and religious autonomy fueled the slavery debate as well as the controversy over the Mormon religious practice of multiple marriages, or "polygamy." By the 1870s, several federal statutes were passed prohibiting the practice of polygamy in the Utah Territory. Polygamy was a core religious teaching of the Mormon Church. In fact, Mormons believed that men must have multiple wives in order to reach eternal life. The national reaction against polygamy and the Mormons was severe, including comprehensive legislation and violence. *Reynolds v. United States* was a challenge by the Mormons to the federal statute prohibiting polygamy. The case came to the Supreme Court of the United States in 1878 and the Mormons relied on the religion clauses to defend their position. Chief Justice Morrison Waite, an active Episcopalian, authored the opinion, which completely rejected the attempt to use religious freedom to protect the practice of polygamy. The chief justice employed Thomas Jefferson's famous "wall of separation" metaphor (describing, as he understood it, the First Amendment's intention to keep church and state in separate spheres) as justification to uphold the constitutionality of the prohibition. In his ruling, Waite contributed a lasting distinction between "belief" and "conduct." In other words, an individual or a church has the right to freedom of religious belief and doctrine, but if either involves conduct that is injurious to the public safety and welfare, the federal government has the obligation to prohibit the conduct. Justice Waite's position clearly reflected his Episcopalian theological framework: the state may not interfere with religious belief; and religious belief may not interfere with the state. The opinion also defined "marriage" as that between one man and one woman.

As anti-Catholicism continued to fester and the distaste over the polygamy issue grew, so did the political environment change in the last quarter of the nineteenth century. The post–Civil War decades can be fairly characterized as a nation in search of a definition. Who is an American; who is not? Who may come here from foreign countries to work and who may not? Is America a religious or a secular nation? Was the Constitution grounded in Christian doctrine or the secular humanist philosophy of the Enlightenment? Should the Catholic Church have a right to establish their own parochial school system with funds from government tax dollars? All these debates were carried on in the pages of newspapers and filled lecture halls to overflowing with the diversity of points of view. In the mid-1870s public interest had reached what we now refer to as "critical mass" or "the tipping point" and resulted in several proposals for constitutional amendments. The "Blaine Amendment" was an attempt to create a national public school system with government funding, the language of which was designed to exclude Catholic schools. One citizen organization proposed a Christian Amendment to the United States Constitution in order to correct the "Founders' oversight" of not including a specific reference to God in the Constitution. In reaction to that, another organization proposed that all forms of religious language, ceremonies, and traditional practices acknowledging religion in any government activity or utterance be prohibited by constitutional amendment.

Near the end of the century in *Holy Trinity v. United States*, many of these issues coalesced. In a unanimous opinion, the Court chose to reference the Christian character of the nation. Justice David Josiah Brewer, the son of Congregational missionary parents, who was actually born in Asia Minor, authored the opinion. Brewer maintained his Congregationalist ties throughout his life, although he was also heavily influenced by Unitarian teaching. In his 1892 opinion in *Holy Trinity*, it was Justice Brewer who penned the phrase "this is a Christian nation." In rejecting the application of the Contract Labor Act of 1885, which had been invoked to prohibit a church congregation from hiring an English minister, Brewer argued that to apply the Contract Labor Act to restrict the Christian religion would be something the government should not be allowed to do. Throughout Justice Brewer's lengthy opinion, he offers a meticulous review of Christianity and its impact on the national character from colonial times to his present day.

By the beginning of the twentieth century, a growing call for strict separation of church and state was gaining prominence. Still fueled by anti-Catholicism, a majority of the Protestant public was moving toward an absolutist's model of church-state separation. In *United States v. Macintosh* in 1931, a clash of views over proper church-state relations and the constitutional guarantee of the Free Exercise Clause is evidenced in the opinions offered by Justice George Sutherland for the majority, and the dissent by Chief Justice Charles Evans Hughes. It is the dissent of Chief Justice Hughes, a Southern Baptist, that foretells a view of church-state relations that clearly was influenced by the Southern Baptist Convention's formal stands on church-state relations.

The case focused on a Canadian minister who sought U.S. citizenship. The minister refused to take an oath to defend the country, arguing that he would be willing to take up arms for the United States only in the time of a just war. Justice Sutherland was influenced by the teachings of Mormonism in his youth, although he was not a member of the Mormon Church. In his opinion, which sided with the government to deny Macintosh citizenship, Justice Sutherland reasoned that "we are a Christian people" (echoing Brewer's *Holy Trinity* declaration) and, in so being, the will of God is that citizens must defend and protect this Christian nation. In time of war, the church and state, or God and country, are synonymous. Chief Justice Hughes, on the other hand, issued a powerful dissent clearly based on his Baptist heritage arguing for religious freedom. The chief justice would have granted Macintosh citizenship. Hughes wrote, "The essence of religion is belief in a relation to God involving duties superior to those arising from any human relation." These were two distinct views of church-state relations. For Justice Sutherland, the duty that one owes the nation was supreme; and, therefore, the need to subordinate other important rights to that duty was imperative. For Chief Justice Hughes, the right of conscience within the religious sphere was inviolable and constitutionally protected by the Free Exercise Clause.

By the 1940s, the modern church-state separation movement was in full gear. The Southern Baptists and the Unitarians were advocating for a strict separation of church and state. This was still largely a reaction to Catholicism and its growing political power in the United States. Justice Hugo Black, raised in Southern Baptist churches but heavily influenced by Unitarians, became the voice of the separationist movement. Black even served on an early board of directors for an organization that later became known as Americans United for Separation of Church and State.

In the early 1940s the Supreme Court of the United States had ruled that both the Establishment Clause and the Free Exercise Clause were to be applied and made binding on the states. Even though the Court had invoked Jefferson's "wall of separation" phrase seventy-five years earlier, it was Justice Black's opinion in *Everson v. Board of Education* in 1947 that gave it new prominence and almost a life of its own in subsequent decades. In *Everson*, while allowing funds to be used for parochial school buses, Justice Black nevertheless erected a test advocating strict separation of church and state. Justice Black's jurisprudence was adopted as the formal position of the Southern Baptist Convention for almost forty years. Ultimately, the Convention moved toward adopting an accommodationist model of church-state relations.

In part, the denominational shift on behalf of the Baptists could have been foretold by the early 1960s. The school prayer cases brought swift condemnation from religious denominations around the country. While the Court in 1952 recognized that "[w]e are a religious people whose institutions presuppose a Supreme Being" in *Zorach v. Clauson*, some ten years later, it struck down school-sponsored prayer and Bible reading. Justice Tom Clark, a devout Presbyterian, offered the opinion calling for a prohibition on these practices. This began a period of perceived hostility toward religion that existed up until the 1980s, when the Court itself adopted a more accommodationist model to its religion cases.

To bring some order to the confusion that existed over the First Amendment religion clause cases, Chief Justice Warren Burger, a Presbyterian, penned what became known in legal circles as the famed "*Lemon* test," taking its name from the 1971 *Lemon v. Kurtzman* case. Intended to make resolution of cases involving the Establishment Clause clearer, Burger's Presbyterian influence is apparent in his desire to find ways to accommodate traditional church-state relations without violating the First Amendment. This test, however, has never proved satisfactory. Six current justices have criticized the formulation. It has "spooked" Justice Scalia and lawyers around the country. By the 1980s, Chief Justice Burger himself cautioned in a dissent that the *Lemon* test should not be applied too rigidly; and in 1985, Burger prophetically noted that "too rigid an application of the Lemon Test could result in the phrase 'under God' in the Pledge of Allegiance being declared unconstitutional." That very case reached the Supreme Court in 2004.

In the final chapter, "Coming Full Circle," I take leave of the twentieth century and adopt a narrative format to discuss the current state of religion cases in various categories that point to the issues confronting the Court in the twenty-first century.

To be sure, the frustration level of even the most current Court concerning how to best analyze the religion clauses has been very significant and, at times, quite vocal. The state of confusion in which the Court's Establishment and Free Exercises cases languish is the result of a departure from the original intent of the Framers and ratifiers of the First Amendment. The uniquely federal flavor of the amendment was modified over the years, resulting in an application that was never intended by its Founders.

As Chief Justice Burger had warned, the Pledge of Allegiance was challenged in the 2004 *Newdow v. United States* case. Although dismissed on technical grounds, new Pledge of Allegiance cases are now pending. The Supreme Court has also had to deal with the constitutionality of public displays of the Ten Commandments as they relate to the application of the *Lemon* test. The Supreme Court itself has such a display adorning its marble frieze in the courtroom where these cases are actually argued. That depiction has Moses holding the tablets with the words in Hebrew.

In the chapters that follow, I explore how we arrived at such a troubling state of affairs and, in conclusion, offer my hope for a way out. In each case, each justice discussed here has, in his own way, witnessed his faith in rulings or dissent. The effectiveness of this witness has been felt for generations.

Jay Alan Sekulow
Washington, D.C.
October 2005

I

RELIGIOUS FREEDOM IN THE NINETEENTH CENTURY

· 1 ·

The Bible in Public Schools Controversy and the Philadelphia Riots

> The real difficulty lies in ascertaining the limits, to which government may rightfully go in fostering and encouraging religion.
>
> —Justice Joseph Story
> *Commentaries on the Constitution
> of the United States*, 1833

Vidal v. Girard's Executors, one of the Supreme Court's first religion cases with implications for our nation's approach to religious liberty, was decided in the midst of a cultural-theological controversy brewing in the schools and eventually overflowing into the streets of Philadelphia. The controversy pitted Catholics and Protestants against each other in a battle over the proper English version of the Bible to be used in the public-school setting where children of different faiths or denominations were enrolled.

The Protestant-dominated common schools in Philadelphia generally required daily readings from the King James Version, the Protestant-authorized Bible after the Reformation in the sixteenth century. Catholics, by church doctrine, were forbidden to read any English version other than the Catholic Douay Bible. They vehemently rejected the King James Bible and argued that reading from it in the schools was a violation of their conscience and right to control the religious upbringing of their children. In May and July of 1844, the Philadelphia riots erupted out of this controversy—just months after the Supreme Court of the United States rendered its decision in the Philadelphia *Vidal* case, which centered precisely on the issue of religious education and who could teach it.

THE CULTURAL/HISTORICAL CONTEXT

The Philadelphia Bible controversy was one aspect of a much broader debate between Protestants and Catholics that had developed during the first half of the nineteenth century. By the time *Vidal* was decided in February of 1844, this local contest had taken on national dimensions. Concern over the Catholic push for cultural and religious equality through the school Bible issue was at the heart of the schism. This contentious issue played itself out in the classrooms, school boards, and streets of Philadelphia directly preceding and following the Supreme Court's decision in *Vidal*. The first section of this chapter will set forth the nature of the Protestant-Catholic controversies during the first half of the nineteenth century, with special attention on the Philadelphia Bible riots and their significance for understanding the Court's *Vidal* decision.

Anti-Catholic and "nativist" sentiment, which held that the interests of native inhabitants had to be protected against those of immigrants, had been heating up in America for over twenty years preceding the riots. The swell of European immigration, especially a concentration of Irish-Catholic immigrants in Philadelphia, New York, and Boston, awoke anti-Catholic sentiment inherent in a new republic infused with Protestantism.[1] Between 1807 and 1830, the number of Catholic churches and priests increased exponentially. Fervent Catholics considered their church as the "one true church, and . . . prayed . . . that Protestants would some day see the errors of their apostasy."[2] Meanwhile, Protestants and nativists feared the effect of Catholicism on the young democratic society. Contention over "trusteeism" (the debate over whether control of church property and the appointment of priests should belong to the clergy or laymen appointed as trustees by the church body); papal conspiracy theories and dissemination of anti-Catholic rhetoric; the 1834 burning of the renowned Ursuline Convent school in Charlestown, Massachusetts; and the Bible-in-schools debate all combined to intensify religious and cultural differences between Catholics and Protestants.[3]

The conflict between Catholics and Protestants over the concept of trusteeism started as early as the 1820s, impacting the city of Philadelphia and many other cities across the nation.[4] The debate centered on whether Catholic clergy should be permitted to hold complete control over church property, a stalwart Roman Catholic doctrine. Protestants and nativists viewed this doctrine as despotic in nature and adverse to democracy.[5] The majority of Protestant church governance was considered democratic in nature; appointment of clergy and control of church property were powers generally retained by the church body as a whole via elections and laymen appointed as trustees.[6]

The Catholic hierarchy viewed trusteeism as nothing less than "lay interference with ecclesiastical jurisdiction," and became increasingly concerned that American Protestant church influence would divide Catholic immigrants on this question.[7] Baltimore's Archbishop Ambrose Maréchal described American trusteeism and the threat it posed to Catholic Church governance in an 1818 letter to the papal representative at the Vatican:

> [T]he American people clings with the most ardent love to the civil liberty it enjoys. Again it is a primary [*palmare*] principle of civil liberty among them, that absolutely all magistrates, whether high or low . . . should be elected by popular vote. Likewise all sects of Protestants, who constitute the greater part of the people, are ruled by the same principles and accordingly elect or dismiss, at their pleasure, their pastors. Now the Catholics living in their society, are evidently exposed to the danger of admitting the same principles of ecclesiastical rule, and by the artifices of impious priests, who cater to their pride, are easily led to believe that they also have the right to elect and dismiss their pastors as they please.[8]

The pope's response in 1822 exhorted the American immigrant churches to hold firm to Catholic doctrine. Philadelphia in particular did just that; by 1830 the Catholic clergy had prevailed. Nevertheless, the staunch Catholic resistance to a seemingly democratic institution had attracted hostile attention from the entire nation. To most Americans, Catholic doctrines seemed incompatible with the new republic's democratic ideals.[9] The actions of New York City's Archbishop John Hughes best illustrates that trusteeism continued to be a large element in Protestant-Catholic strife for many years. The outspoken Catholic leader wrote a letter in 1842 to Erastus Brooks, editor of the *New York Daily*:

> A system, growing, perhaps, out of the circumstances of the times, has prevailed in this country which is without a parallel in any other nation, or in the whole history of the Catholic Church. That system is, of leaving ecclesiastical property under the management of laymen, who are commonly designated "trustees." We do not disguise, that our conviction of this system is, that it is altogether injurious to religion.[10]

A few state legislatures even went so far as to pass (but later repeal) bills deeming it unlawful for clergy to hold sole control over church property.[11]

To confront the issues surrounding anti-Catholicism, the Catholic hierarchy met together with lay advisors at Baltimore in 1829 for the "First Provincial Council of Catholicity in America."[12] The prestigious ecclesiastical-lay assemblage included Roger B. Taney, attorney general of Maryland at the time, who was soon to serve as chief justice of the Supreme Court of the United States (1836–1864) and thus was at its helm when the *Vidal* case came before the Court.

The most urgent issues on the First Provincial Council's agenda were: (1) trusteeism, (2) the necessity of establishing parochial schools, and (3) the possibility of Americanizing the Catholic Church by replacing foreign-born bishops with native bishops in order to ease nativist concerns.[13] The results of the meeting, however, had the opposite effect. Nativist and Protestant fears were provoked by the language of the "thirty-eight decrees . . . warning Catholics against 'corrupt translations of the Bible,' [and] urging parishes to build parochial schools to save children from 'perversion.'"[14] The council, furthermore, proceeded to condemn trusteeism.[15] Protestants and nativists rose in response to the Catholic resistance to trusteeism, calling it "tyrannical" and "repugnant to our republican institutions."[16]

Over the next decade and a half, anti-Catholic rhetoric was disseminated across the nation through a number of schemes.[17] Protestant preachers used sermons to spread anti-Catholic messages at revivals; thirty anti-Catholic Protestant periodicals were in circulation by 1827; and the New York Protestant Association, formed in 1831, furthered anti-Catholicism through radical debates, including whether Roman Catholicism could coincide with "Civil Liberty."[18] "[S]ocieties, lecturers, newspapers, magazines, churches, ministers, and a political party had all been enlisted in the cause" to beat back the supposed threat to democracy.[19]

Anti-Catholic sentiment among Protestants gained momentum during the 1830s. Influential spokesmen spread papal conspiracy theories, and the burning of Boston's prestigious Ursuline Convent transformed anti-Catholic rhetoric into violent action.[20] The conspiracy theories were published widely and taken to heart. Historian Anson Phelps Stokes vividly describes how Protestants promulgated and embraced such theories:

> The pope, assisted by the Roman Catholic rulers of Europe, was seen
> as trying to capture the Mississippi Valley as the future headquarters

of the Church! Two missionary societies—the "Society for the Propagation of the Faith," formed at Lyons, France, in 1822, and the "Leopold Association" of Austria-Hungary, formed in 1829—because of their active missionary interest in trying to convert the newly settled West to Catholicism and their large contributions to the cause, were specially feared.[21]

The influential nativist leader Samuel F. B. Morse, inventor of the telegraph and head of the American Protestant Union, theorized in 1834 and 1835 publications that immigrants were part of the pope's plan to "convert America." Boston's preeminent Congregationalist preacher, Reverend Lyman Beecher (father of Harriet Beecher Stowe) endorsed the same idea in another publication, theorizing that the pope had plans to subvert the young republic using parochial schools to convert Protestant children. Conspiracy fears even impelled Massachusetts and New York organizations in 1838 to petition Congress to take up the supposed problem.[22]

The 1830s marked an ominous change, from the rhetorical diatribes of the 1820s questioning Catholicism's theological soundness to Protestant and nativist pronouncements on "the immoral nature" of Catholicism. A common charge was that convents were used for evil purposes. Coalescing with the old nativist fears of the effect of Catholicism on democratic society, these new attacks consisted of the publication of ghastly, fictitious tales of physical, sexual, and mental abuse of nuns and children in convents.[23] Other writers theorized that the primary purpose of the convent schools was to convert Protestant children. In the late spring of 1834, the effect of the new propaganda hit hard in the northern Boston suburb of Charlestown—a quiet community of ten thousand, which happened to be the location of the renowned Ursuline Convent school.

"Altogether . . . a most unlikely venue for the nineteenth century's first spectacular outburst of anti-Catholic violence," concludes Charles R. Morris in his 1997 history, *American Catholic*. Charlestown's elite were Unitarians, including leading men of Boston; most of the residents were craftsmen and artisans; but it was also home to some twelve hundred Irish Catholic immigrants, mostly unskilled laborers who lived in the poorest sections. Friction between nativists and these immigrants increased throughout 1833.

Boston's aristocratic Bishop Benedict Fenwick had built the Catholic Ursuline Convent as an elite finishing school for girls. For a steep tuition fee, they could develop the tastes in music, French, and literature expected of a young lady in Boston society. Paris-trained Irish nuns supervised approximately sixty young women, the majority of whom seem to have been Unitarians. There was no effort to convert students to Catholicism; instead, religious services were adjusted to take into account Protestant sensibilities. The convent had no connections to the Irish Catholics in town.[24]

Briefly, in the spring of 1834, when rumors spread of a young nun being abused at the school, Boston and Charlestown papers featured the case of the "kidnapped" nun, and the town's anti-Catholic fervor festered and grew all summer. Finally, the area's Congregationalist ministers joined with nativist leaders through meetings and sermons to incite action against the convent. On Sunday night, August 10, Reverend Lyman Beecher delivered a scathing sermon entitled "The Devil and the Pope of Rome" to a large audience, denouncing the Ursulines. Other ministers followed suit. On the next night, Monday, August 11, throngs of angry torch-wielding mobs stormed the convent and burned it to the ground.[25]

This event had far-reaching effects: anti-Catholicism was elevated to a plane of national importance, the attention of the nation was turned to the "No-Popery" movement, and no Catholic church or property was free from threat.[26]

At the core of this growing religious animosity were two gnawing issues that most incensed Protestants against Catholics: their plan to establish parochial schools and their campaign against the use of the King James Version of the Bible in common (public) schools.

The movement for a strong parochial school system had been authorized at the 1829 First Provincial Council of Catholicity in Baltimore. The purpose of the parochial schools was to insulate Catholic children from anti-Catholicism and Protestant practices in order to instill a strictly Catholic religious education. The effort toward a parochial school system was primarily undertaken in the large eastern cities that contained dense Catholic-immigrant populations. When the Provincial Council reconvened in 1833, it authorized the organization of a campaign to have Catholic textbooks provided in the public schools as well. By the end of the fourth Provincial Council's assemblage in 1840, it had been firmly decided by the hierarchy and lay advisors that Catholic children should no longer be subjected to Protestant religious practices in the public schools.[27]

Philadelphia's Protestant majority controlled most of the city in the

1830s and early 1840s, including the public school system, which concerned Catholics the most. It became clear to them that "public schools in urban America were . . . guilty of evangelizing for Protestantism through a campaign to smear 'popery.'" Catholic children were subjected daily to Protestant teachers, prayers, hymns, anti-Catholic texts, and readings out of the Protestant King James Version of the Bible.[28]

To fully understand the emotional depth of religious feeling on both sides attached to these issues, a brief step back in history is necessary.[29] The Bible battles of nineteenth-century America had deep roots that had begun to spread three hundred years earlier, in 1519, with Martin Luther's protest against the Catholic Church. In the following decades the Protestant Reformation, begun in Germany, spread rapidly. John Calvin established his theological base at Geneva, and many later evangelical Protestant sects derived their structure and doctrine from his formulations; King Henry VIII broke from Rome, confiscating all the Catholic monasteries and lands and established the Church of England under the king's divine sovereignty; the explorations to the New World resulted in Catholic Spain claiming all the lands for the Holy Roman Empire, prompting the British to move quickly to establish colonies for the Protestant king of England.

By mid-sixteenth century the Catholic Church hierarchy at Rome was reeling. What had made the rapid spread of Protestantism possible was the invention of the printing press at Mainz seventy years before Luther. Now the Bible, the Word of God, which for over a thousand years had been in Latin and in the sole interpretive control of the Catholic Church and its priests, could be translated into native tongues and put into the hands of all the people to read for themselves. Luther's translation into German was a powerful tool used to refute Rome and give the people a direct and personal knowledge of God, Jesus Christ, and the Gospels.

The pope convened the Council of Trent (1545–1563) to counter the Reformation. Among the priorities was the authorization of St. Jerome's Latin Vulgate as the official Catholic Bible from which an English translation of both the Old and New Testaments was begun at the English College, Douai, in the Spanish Netherlands (today France), in 1568 by renowned Catholic biblical scholars from Oxford and the Continent, completed and published in 1611. The Douay Bible and its subsequent editions and revisions contained extensive "notes and comments" on Scripture to refute Protestant theological arguments and give Catholic readers Vatican-approved interpretations of Scripture. The Challoner revision of the Douay in the 1750s and its subsequent editions became the authorized Catholic Bible in America.

Meantime, many different Protestant English translations of the Bible had been made until James I of England came to the throne in 1603 and answered the petitions of the dissenting Puritans requesting one true version. King James convened the Hampton Court Conference in 1604 "for the hearing, and for the determining, things pretended to be amiss in the church." Bishops, clergymen, professors, and four Puritan divines assembled to consider the complaints of the Puritans. John Reynolds, the Puritan president of Corpus Christi College, "moved his Majesty, that there might be a new translation of the Bible, because those which were allowed in the reigns of Henry the eighth, and Edward the sixth, were corrupt and not answerable to the truth of the Original." King James resolved "that a translation be made of the whole Bible, as consonant as can be to the original Hebrew and Greek; and this to be set out and printed, without any marginal notes, and only to be used in all churches of England in time of divine service."

From 1604 until the publication of the King James Version of the Bible in 1609–1611 (exactly when the Douay was published), forty-seven distinguished scholars from Cambridge, Oxford, and Westminster labored over every passage from the ancient Hebrew and Greek texts to give the English-speaking world the Word of God translated out of the "original tongues."

In the dedicatory epistle to King James I on the opening page, the translators expressed that they were "poor instruments to make God's holy Truth to be yet more and more known" while at the same time recognizing that "Popish persons" sought to keep the people "in ignorance and darkness." This is the cherished Bible that crossed the ocean on the *Mayflower* and landed at Plymouth Rock with the Puritan pilgrims nine years after its publication.

Throughout the colonial period and until the 1820s, with the beginnings of the public school movement, education of the young was conducted in homes and churches, then sectarian church schools. Literacy was synonymous with the ability to read the Bible and it was from these readings, memorizations, and recitations that children learned their letters and moral lessons as well—from the lips of their mothers and fathers and their church clergy. Both Protestant and Catholic American children also learned how their English and European religious ancestors had been persecuted, tortured, imprisoned, or killed by the other side for their faith and beliefs. Which version of the Bible children were exposed to mattered in every home and hamlet. By the 1830s, it really mattered in Philadelphia.

As early as 1834, at the insistence of Philadelphia's Archbishop Francis Patrick Kenrick, school controllers adopted a screening policy to keep both sectarian and anti-Catholic texts out of the schools. Unfortunately, enforcement of the policy was lacking, causing the problem to simmer unresolved. Complicating matters, the Pennsylvania legislature passed a law in 1838 making school Bible readings—out of the King James Version—mandatory. Whereas individual teachers choosing to read the King James Version did not please Catholic parents or clergy, the new law mandating it seemed malicious in nature.[30] The religious inequality unified Philadelphia's Catholic clergymen, who pointed out that Catholics, like Protestants, paid taxes to fund the schools.[31]

Archbishop Kenrick led the push for equal treatment, focusing foremost on getting the Catholic Douay Bible admitted in the schools, so that Catholic children would no longer be forced to read the King James Version.[32] Explaining the conundrum, Kenrick later wrote to Philadelphia's school controllers:

> [T]eachers shall read and cause to be read, The Bible; by which is understood the version published by command of King James. To this regulation we are forced to object, inasmuch as Catholic children are . . . led to view as authoritative [the King James Version] which is rejected by the Church. . . . [W]e do not ask you to adopt the Catholic version for general use; but we feel warranted in claiming that our conscientious scruples to recognize or use the other, be respected. . . . The consciences of Catholics are also embarrassed by the mode of opening and closing the School exercises which . . . is by the singing of some hymn, or by prayer. It is not consistent with the laws and discipline of the Catholic Church for her members to unite in religious exercises with those who are not of their communion.[33]

Kenrick lobbied for admittance of the Douay Version and exclusion of anti-Catholic texts from 1834 until 1840, without much fanfare, until all eyes were turned to the eruption of the school Bible issue in New York City.[34]

In 1840, the majority of New York City schools were controlled by the Public School Society, a private organization committed to the use of the King James Version of the Bible as a schoolbook, and other sectarian practices such as Protestant hymns and prayers.[35] Anti-Catholic texts were also prevalent in the schools under the Society's administration.[36] The Society supported the public schools with privately raised funds as well as substantial state funds distributed to the Society by the New York City Common Council.[37] As a result, a portion of Catholic tax dollars was being used to fund Protestant-dominated, anti-Catholic schools. Governor William Henry Seward took the issue to the state legislature in January of 1840 in support of parochial schools:

> The children of foreigners, found in great numbers in our populous cities and towns, and in the vicinity of our public works, are too often deprived of the advantages of our system of public education, in consequence of prejudices arising from differences of language or religion. . . . I do not hesitate, therefore, to recommend the establishment of schools in which they may be instructed by teachers speaking the same language with themselves and professing the same faith.[38]

Catholics did not let the opportunity pass. In February, based on the governor's statement, clergy demanded that the New York City Common Council provide Catholics with state funding for parochial schools. The council, undoubtedly influenced by radical, nativist, and anti-Catholic counterefforts, refused.[39] The battle commenced forthwith.

Archbishop John Hughes led the Catholic campaign in New York for school reform in 1840 under his motto, "the school before the church," while the more generally accepted position among Catholics was "the school alongside the church."[40] Because of Hughes's concern over the influence that the Protestant-dominated public schools were having on Catholic students, he thought it would be more important to spend Catholic resources on parochial schools rather than on new churches. He wrote, "Let parochial schools be established and maintained everywhere . . . the school is more necessary than the church."[41] In fact, in a short time thirty-eight new schools were erected in the diocese to accommodate the flood of Irish Catholic immigrants fleeing the ravages of the potato famine in Ireland. Between 1840 and 1850, over one million Irish immigrants arrived and settled in the largest cities of the East.

In comparison to Kenrick's situation, Hughes benefited from New York City's Irish immigrant population which was greater than Philadelphia's in proportion to each city's total population.[42] Behind the support and "fanatical spirit of the times," Hughes lobbied the Common Council to give back to Catholics those Catholic tax dollars used to support the public schools.[43] He argued that Catholic tax dollars should go to fund the few parochial schools rather than the Protestant-dominated public schools.

Hughes's 1840 *Address of the Roman Catholics to their Fellow-Citizens of the City and State of New York* emphatically expressed the Catholic position: "If the public schools could have been constituted on a principle which would have secured a perfect NEUTRALITY of influence on the subject of religion, then we should have no reason to complain. But this has not been done, and we respectfully submit that it is impossible."[44] "Spread it abroad," Hughes preached to New York Catholics in 1841, "that you ask no favor, no preeminence, no boon, from their honors of the Common Council; but that you have rights, and these rights you claim. Let them reserve their favors for those who want them."[45]

Protestant sermons and newspapers produced passionate opposition to the supposed Catholic attempt to take the Bible out of schools and obtain Protestant money. The *American Protestant Vindicator* reported:

> They demand of Republicans . . . to give them funds to train up their children to worship a ghostly monarchy of vicars, bishops, archbishops, cardinals, and Popes! They demand of us to take away our children's funds and bestow them on the subjects of Rome, the creatures of a foreign hierarchy![46]

On the other side, in October of 1842, one Catholic priest went so far as to gather and publicly burn Protestant Bibles distributed by outsiders to his congregation.[47]

Ultimately, Hughes's demand for funds was denied. However, through a series of local political maneuvers, he forced city officials to end school Bible readings in the predominantly Irish-Catholic sectors of the city. Anti-Catholics and nativists became particularly unsettled by Hughes's demonstration of Catholic political influence and predicted Catholic political dominance in the future if no opposition was raised.[48] Their fears were not completely unfounded; Hughes's public pressure achieved results. By 1844, thirty-one schools in Catholic sectors in New York had successfully displaced Bible readings.[49]

Archbishop Kenrick closely followed the school Bible developments in New York.[50] When a Southwark Catholic teacher was removed in 1842 for not obeying a state law requiring the Protestant Bible to be read in school, the archbishop took advantage of the opportunity and confronted the school board, undoubtedly dressed in his full pontifical attire. He demanded that Catholic children be allowed to read their own Douay Version of the Bible and pointed out the continued presence of anti-Catholic texts in the schools, despite school board resolutions to the contrary.[51] In January of 1843, the school board "yielded"—Catholic children did not have to participate in Protestant Bible readings and they could use alternative versions of the Bible as long as they were "without note or comment." This rule effectively excluded the Douay Bible (replete with its doctrinal Catholic interpretations of scriptural passages in the "notes and comments" to each page), without having to name it.[52]

The school board's decision was viewed by Protestants as an unwarranted compromise, however, and was not without consequences.[53] The *North American*, a popular nativist newspaper, argued:

> For years and years the schools have been in operation, planned by Protestants, founded by Protestants, directed by Protestants, and almost wholly supported by Protestants, and now come "the Bishop of New York" and "the Bishop of Philadelphia" to interfere in the management of them, create confusion within their walls and "excitement" without.[54]

Protestants viewed Kenrick's efforts as an attempt to expel faith from education even though his intention was never to completely rid the schools of the Bible: "I do not object to the use of the Bible provided Catholic children be allowed to use their own version."[55] Protestants immediately protested that they, as the long-standing majority, should retain sole authority over public schools.[56]

How did the school board's compromise play out in the classroom with the political tensions between the two sides so strained? In late February 1844, Henry Moore, a Protestant Kensington school director, hastily reported to a packed Methodist church that a teacher, Louisa Bedford, had been ordered by another Kensington school director, Hugh Clark, to stop her classroom Bible reading. Clark also happened to be an Irish-Catholic Philadelphia politician. In truth, Clark had merely suggested that the teacher temporarily postpone readings after the teacher had complained that Catholic children leaving the room during readings caused too much interruption.[57] According to Louisa Bedford's later testimony, the decision to temporarily postpone Bible readings had clearly been left in her hands—it being understood that a later solution to the interruption could be found and, indeed, Bible readings subsequently resumed, in compliance with state law.[58] The truth, however, "was too late to stop the train of consequences."[59]

Protestants and nativists were hungry for anything that could be construed against Catholics in the context of the school Bible dispute. Consequently, news of the incident and following compromise, as interpreted by Moore and the city's nativist bloc, was widely promulgated by religious and nativist newspapers alike. The *Episcopal Recorder* asked, "Are we to yield our personal liberty, our inherited rights, our very Bibles, the special, blessed gift of God to our country, to the will, the ignorance, or the wickedness of these hordes of foreigners, subjects of a foreign despot?"[60] *The Presbyterian* even suggested that the entire public school system was better off wiped out: "The sooner the whole system is leveled to the dust, the better for the common weal."[61] The riots exploded in Kensington only a couple of months after Miss Bedford innocently suspended school Bible readings in her classroom, and Clark was to become a target of nativist reprisal.

During the year just prior to the Philadelphia Bible riots, nativists banded together and established the American Republican Party.[62] They were to play a major role in the violence to come. "[H]atred of Catholicism [and] . . . a fear of the immigrant, not only as a Catholic, but as a menace to the economic, political, and social structure" of America were the two major factors in the creation of this nativist political party. According to nativist thought, immigrants were synonymous with poverty, mob rule, competition for American jobs, and expansion of the suspected antidemocratic institution of Catholicism. Furthermore, immigrants typically voted in blocs whether in support of Democrats or Whigs, which nativists interpreted as control of foreigners by Catholic priests delivering votes in exchange for political favors.[63]

In retaliation, the American Republican Party was officially established as a vehicle for nativist ideals. Those ideals included: (1) longer waiting periods for naturalization, (2) exclusive federal court jurisdiction over naturalization, and (3) the exclusion of foreigners from public office.[64] Leaders of the American Republican Party in New York wrote about the foreign immigrant to America:

[T]here exists on the continent of Europe, in the heart of its most despotic government, a society protected by the crown of Austria, patronized by the most unflinching supporters of civil and religious despotism . . . for the express purpose of exporting to this country, (free America) the abject slaves of their country, who, bound in fetters of civil and religious serfdom, would be incapable . . . of understanding the principles of civil and religious freedom.[65]

Although the party employed considerable subtlety in its anti-Catholic rhetoric, historian Ray Allen Billington noted that even though the entire purpose of the party was not to attack Catholicism, "it is probable that anti-Catholicism was the most powerful single factor in driving members into the party."[66] The editor of the *Native Eagle and American Advocate* articulated the party's stance best when he wrote that a man "may be a Turk, a Jew or a Christian, a Catholic, Methodist or Presbyterian, and we say nothing against it," still, "when we remember that our Pilgrim Fathers landed on Plymouth Rock to establish the Protestant religion, free from persecution, we must contend that this was and always will be a Protestant country!"[67]

Not surprisingly, American Republicans quickly adopted a position on the school Bible issue. They fought for both recitation of the Bible "without note or comment" in schools and separation of church and state.[68] While these two goals seem inconsistent to the twenty-first-century mind, they were considered consistent by American Republicans. The phrase "without note or comment" was viewed by Protestants as preserving the nonsectarian status of the Bibles allowed in the schools.[69] Separation was "endorsed . . . as a constraint on religious groups but not religious individuals" and viewed as a guard against any "[religious groups'] 'pride of sect' and 'desire of propagandism.'"[70] As a result, "Protestants increasingly took for granted that separation of church and state forbade public funding for Catholic education of any sort," legal historian Philip Hamburger noted, "even as it permitted such funding for nonsectarian Protestant teaching." Hamburger further explained:

> [F]rom this perspective, separation allowed the Bible to remain in public schools. The presence of the Bible was desired by many sects and, indeed, by individuals rather than by any one sect. It therefore seemed that Protestants did not act as a church and did not violate the separation of church and state when they formed a majority and placed the Bible in their publicly funded schools.[71]

(As late as 1877, Baptist George C. Lorimer wrote that it was because of the "people" that the Bible was in schools, rather than it being "the result of any union between Protestants and the State; nor was it secured by the political action of one denomination, or of all combined. The Church, as such, did not put it there, and the Church, as such, cannot take it away.")[72]

To many nineteenth-century Americans, the United States was a Protestant, Christian nation and the Bible "without note or comment," which almost always meant the King James Version since all Protestants accepted its infallibility, was considered nonsectarian.[73] In other words, allowing the Bible to be read in schools was construed not as an endorsement of one sect over another, but as a democratic exercise.

The confluence of anti-Catholic sentiment and rhetoric, the establishment of the American Republican Party, and the growing animosity between Catholics and Protestants over the school Bible issue erupted into violence in Philadelphia in 1844.

On Friday, May 3, American Republicans amassed in an antagonistic effort to organize an association in the Third Ward, an Irish-Catholic sector in Kensington. A crowd of three hundred American Republicans and other nativists was quickly broken up by the clubs of angry Irishmen.[74] This opposition, however, only encouraged the group to gather again in Kensington on Monday, May 6—this time three thousand strong. Leading American Republican figures began their nativist harangue in the afternoon following a flag ceremony. One American Republican leader, Lewis Levin, spoke on "immigrant election abuses and religious influence in politics."[75] An abrupt rain forced the rallying throng into the nearby Nanny-Goat Market House, where Irish resistance awaited. Within the energized crowd a pistol rang out, triggering a volley of rifle shots from Irish houses and the open windows of the Hibernia Hose Company, an Irish fire station across the street. A second volley of shots barked down the street, dispersing most of the nativist mob, but a few stayed behind, throwing rocks at the Irish buildings.

Surprisingly, only one young nativist man was killed on the first day of rioting; as many as eleven were injured. Later the same night, nativists invaded the Irish sector again, wrecking Irish houses from which they had been fired upon earlier in the day and making their way to the Sisters of Charity Catholic seminary. Before it could be broken into and torched, the rioters were repelled by gunfire from a group likely defending nearby St. Michael's Catholic Church.

The next day, "excitement in the vicinity of the infected districts was tremendous."[76] Outraged by the events of May 6, nativist periodicals and

American Republicans trumpeted anti-Catholic propaganda throughout the city. The *Native American* ranted, "[t]he bloody hand of the Pope has stretched forth to our destruction. Now we call on our fellow-citizens, who regard free institutions, whether they be native or adopted, to arm. Our liberties are now to be fought for."[77] A mob of three thousand rowdy nativists answered the call from American Republicans to assemble at the State House.

Rallying behind the accusation, among others, that Catholics were trying to rid the public schools of the Bible, the mob again invaded the Irish sector and headed straight for the Hibernia Hose Company, where it was welcomed with gunfire from the upper floors. The mass of armed rioters was quickly pinned down under the Nanny-Goat Market House, seeking cover from bullets shot from the fire station and neighboring houses. The tide turned, however, when nativists sneaked out and set fire to the houses, forcing Irish gunners into the open. At this point, only "poor marksmanship" kept the body count down.[78]

By the time the military arrived and the shooting stopped, the Hibernia Hose Company, Nanny-Goat Market House, and approximately thirty Irish houses were in ashes. At least six nativists were killed and many were injured on the second day of fighting.[79] The second day of riots eclipsed the first in severity, and the *Daily Sun* threw fuel on the fire with its anti-Catholic propaganda: "Armed recruits in aid of the Roman Catholics are pouring in from various neighboring towns! We write at this moment with our garments stained and sprinkled with the blood of victims to Native American rights."[80] Regrettably, the military left only a couple of companies behind to maintain the peace.[81]

By Wednesday, May 8, many Irish had evacuated the suburb to hide in the woods north of Kensington. Father Michael Donohoe, pastor of St. Michael's Catholic Church, fled the area because of his earlier promotion of Catholic equality in the common schools.[82] The outnumbered and hesitant military presence could only stand by and weather nativist heckling until reinforcements showed up in the early evening. Even then, the raucous uprising continued. St. Michael's Catholic Church, the nearby Sisters of Charity Catholic seminary, St. Augustine's Catholic Church, and numerous houses were burned to the ground by nativist fire, while the mayor and police presence outside St. Augustine's did nothing to stop the flames. School director Hugh Clark's house was also endangered and his office vandalized. The following Sunday, Catholic churches were closed by order of Archbishop Kenrick.[83]

The *Pennsylvanian* described the scene:

> Sunday in Philadelphia—soldiers marching and counter-marching in
> the streets, not for display or peaceful purposes, but prepared for actual
> battle . . . with cutlasses, pistols, boarding pikes, and all the appliances
> of war. . . . Religious toleration enforced . . . charity secured through
> dread of "grape and canister."[84]

Irish buildings smoldered in ashes, and the Kensington riots had ended. In all, seven were killed and about twenty-five were wounded.[85]

Yet Philadelphia's violence was only half over. Two months after the Kensington riots, between seventy thousand and a hundred thousand Philadelphians assembled for the city's Fourth of July parade in which families of the nativists killed in the Kensington riots were displayed for the crowd as a tribute to the supposed martyrs. As expected, the day's events sparked nativist passion. On July 5, American Republicans gathered outside St. Philip's Catholic Church in Southwark to protest a rumored cache of Irish guns.[86] A band of nativists subsequently searched St. Philip's, eventually finding nearly ninety loaded Irish guns. By the next morning, word had gotten out about the gun cache, and nativists squared off with the city's military companies guarding the church. Nativist Charles Naylor, a lawyer and former congressman, was arrested by the military and held in the church after he interfered to prevent the soldiers from firing a cannon into the rowdy mob. The nativists pulled out for the night, but vowed violence unless Naylor was released.

True to their word, nativists reassembled Sunday morning with two cannons from a nearby ship, and anger mounted when it was learned that one of the remaining military forces occupying St. Philip's and detaining Naylor was the Montgomery Hibernia Greens, an Irish-Catholic company. The military released Naylor out of fear for their own safety, concerned about the combination of rioters and cannons, but the nativists insisted that the Hibernia Greens leave the church, too. To oblige the growing mob, the Greens were reluctantly led out of the church by two other companies, and military reinforcements arrived on the scene soon thereafter.

Horace Binney, the foremost lawyer in Philadelphia if not the United States, played a leading role in the quelling of the Philadelphia riots. (Only two months earlier he had successfully represented the city before the Supreme Court in the *Vidal* case). On May 9, the day after the burning of St. Augustine's Catholic Church in Kensington, Binney's leadership was called upon by a city committeeman, Mr. McCall. Binney recollected later: "[H]e informed me that the city was in great disorder and agitation from the events of last night, and that I was wanted to advise upon the proper measures for the occasion. . . . Mr. McCall told me that everything depended upon my coming, and that he would not return without me."[87]

Upon meeting with the committee, Binney personally drafted a list of resolutions calling for a citizen-police force to protect the property being burned and the use of whatever physical force was necessary to halt the mobs. His resolutions were presented to the mayor and a crowd of more than ten thousand citizens, who responded with "hearty cheers."[88] He later explained, "The resolutions which I drew up . . . recommended the immediate enrolling of the citizens in each ward under the command of the civil authority of the ward; and they asserted the legal right, for the protection of life and property, to resist and defeat the mob by the use of any degree of force that was necessary for this purpose."[89]

By evening, reinforcements moved in with cannons to protect the church and clear the neighboring streets by pushing forward with bayonets fixed. The nativist crowd, over two thousand strong, did not move quickly enough for the advancing troops, however. The captain and commanding officers in the rear yelled orders to fire, whereupon the soldiers' rifles blasted into the crowd. Four nativists dropped dead, a number were seriously wounded, and the Southwark combat began. By two in the morning, the cavalry captured the remaining nativist cannons. When the smoke cleared, two soldiers were confirmed dead and twenty-three wounded. A Philadelphia newspaper reported ten dead and more than twenty wounded between nativists and bystanders.[90]

The Philadelphia Bible riots were the culmination of two decades of controversy brewing between Catholics and Protestants on all manner of religious and socioethnic issues. The violence that erupted in Philadelphia was symptomatic of a theological division within which the nation itself was deeply entrenched. The perceived Catholic threat to the Protestant-American way of life had aroused bitterness and violence prior to the Philadelphia riots of 1844, but not on so grand a scale. The nuances of this theological and cultural conflict supply the proper context for understanding the Supreme Court's unanimous decision in *Vidal v. Girard*, and the man who wrote the historic opinion.

THE JUSTICE: JOSEPH STORY (1779–1845)

Joseph Story was born on September 18, 1779, at Marblehead, Massachusetts, located on the Atlantic seacoast northeast of Boston. His father, Elisha Story, was a successful doctor and revolutionary patriot. He was among the 150 bold colonists led by Samuel Adams who, on the night of December 16, 1773, had dressed as Mohawks, slipped aboard the English ships, and thrown barrels of English tea into the harbor at the Boston Tea Party. Elisha had seven children by his first wife, who died in 1777. He then married Mehitable Pedrick, the daughter of a wealthy merchant. Joseph was the eldest child of this marriage, followed by ten brothers and sisters.

Joseph greatly admired his father, describing him as "one of the most amiable men I ever knew; kind and indulgent to his children, partaking of all their pleasures, and busy in promoting their innocent amusements. His home was full of cheerfulness." Elisha was a tolerant man, who even spoke charitably of Roman Catholics, which "was almost a deadly sin" at the time. Joseph credited his father's opinions with shaping his love for religious freedom: "I trace back to this source my early and constant hatred of religious persecution, and my love, my inextinguishable love of freedom of opinion and inquiry in matters of religion. They have now become the guiding maxims of my life."[91]

Growing up in a religious home, young Joseph learned the elementary principles of Christianity.[92] He described his father as "a religious man, liberal and charitable in all his views. He was an Arminian in principle."[93] His uncle, on the other hand, was a fiery Calvinist minister at the church Story attended in his youth. Story commented on his religious upbringing:

> [M]y uncle . . . was much inclined in his preaching to dwell on the terrors of the law, upon man's depravity, and eternal torments; and he felt no scruple in mentioning hell, even to ears polite. My earliest impressions, therefore, of God were those of terror, and not of love—of awe, but not of filial affection; and in my secret devotions I approached him as a being whom I was to propitiate, rather than a parent of whom I was to ask blessings.[94]

The tension between his uncle's harsh religion and his father's loving religion was left to Story's contemplation.[95] Story wrote fondly of his father's

Sunday practice of family prayers: "[A]fter the public afternoon service was over, all the family . . . [was] assembled in one room, and he then read a printed sermon of some English divine, and concluded the day with reading a portion of the New Testament, and with prayer. I still remember those meetings with great pleasure."[96] The kindness and toleration of his father, as seen in Story's everyday life, profoundly influenced his later religious opinions.

Despite the economic depression that was afflicting Marblehead following the Revolution, the relative success of his father's medical practice afforded Story significant free time to employ as he chose.[97] The difficulty of the period left little time for education, and Story spent his early days wandering around his native town, observing the natural beauties of the place "in a reverie of delicious indolence."[98] During this time, also, it is easy to imagine the satisfaction in the Story household upon the news that the Constitution of the United States was signed in Philadelphia by the Founding Fathers in late summer 1787, when Joseph was nine years old. It was to become the document to which he would dedicate his life.

The establishment of a school in Marblehead changed young Story's life, and he was soon learning his Latin and Greek grammar. At Marblehead Academy, Story first learned to love English literature, a pursuit that remained strong throughout his life. Story's parents exhorted him to pursue excellence; his mother once said to him, "Now, Joe, I've sat up and tended you many a night when you were a child, and don't you dare not to be a great man."[99] His father likewise instilled within him "an ambition of excellence," which Story heeded and began "to struggle for distinction as a man."[100]

In the fall of 1794, Story was preparing to enter Harvard College when he was severely and unjustifiably disciplined by the instructor of the academy.[101] With his father's permission, Story left the school and resolved to enter Harvard following the January break. He studied diligently, and his uncle took him to Cambridge at the beginning of the break, where he learned that he must be examined on the material covered by freshmen in the fall semester in addition to the regular entrance examinations.

Story was devastated and returned to Marblehead in great disappointment. The following day, however, he determined to spend the six weeks of the break studying the necessary subjects so that he could enter college. For the next three weeks, he recited five lessons each morning and five or six more throughout the rest of the day, preparing in the evening for the next day's recitations. At the end of the three weeks he had learned the material and spent the remainder of the break perfecting his knowledge. He returned to Harvard at the beginning of the spring term, took the examinations, "and without difficulty obtained [his] matriculation."[102]

Harvard College opened a vast, new world to Story. He later wrote, "I seemed to breathe a higher atmosphere, and to look abroad with a wider vision and more comprehensive powers."[103] Story devoted his time to study, and quickly advanced in the class because of his scholarship. While other boys used the yard pump to recover from a night in Boston, Story splashed himself with the cold water so that he could squeeze in one more hour of study before retiring for the night.[104] He graduated second in his class behind William Ellery Channing, who became the leading proponent of Unitarianism.[105]

Story's health suffered in college because of his zeal for books; he later wrote, "I trace back to this cause a serious injury to my health. When I entered college I was very robust and muscular, but before I left I had become pale and feeble and was inclining to dyspepsia."

Following graduation from Harvard in 1798, Story returned to Marblehead and began to study law with Samuel Seward, who later became Chief Justice of the Supreme Court of Massachusetts. Story remained with Seward until his mentor was appointed as a judge in 1801, forcing Story to move to Salem to complete his education with Samuel Putnam.

The study of law at the end of the eighteenth century was tedious work. It required the student first to read *Blackstone's Commentaries*, followed by *Coke on Littleton*.[106] Story was shocked to discover that the study of law was nothing but "dry and technical principles, the dark and mysterious elements of the feudal system, the subtle refinements and intricacies of the middle ages of the Common Law, and the repulsive and almost unintelligible forms of processes and pleadings, for the most part wrapped up in black-letter, or in dusty folios."[107]

Story often spent fourteen hours a day mastering these books, though *Coke on Littleton* nearly broke him: "[A]fter trying it day after day with very little success, I sat myself down and wept bitterly. My tears dropped upon the book, and stained its pages."[108] He did not surrender; his resolve only hardened. At last, he conquered the book: "When I had completed the reading of this most formidable work, I felt that I breathed a purer air, and that I had acquired a new power. The critical period was passed; I no longer hesitated."[109] Story's persistence and dedication carried him through the intricacies of the law, and prepared him for his work as a lawyer and a judge. In July of 1801, he was admitted to the Essex bar and set out to practice law in Salem.[110]

In December 1804, Story married Mary Lynde Fitch Oliver, a Protestant minister's daughter.[111] Tragically, only seven short months after their marriage, Mary suddenly fell ill and died. Story was grief-stricken, and his pain was to increase when he lost his beloved father two months after Mary's death. Recounting these events years later, Story wrote:

> I was new to sorrow, full of hope and ambition, with an ardent enthusiasm, and, perhaps, an almost romantic wildness of imagination. All my hopes were at once cut down and crushed. I remained for a long time like one in a painful dream, and there ever since has been at times on my mind a cloud of gloom, which sorrow, probably, always gathers, and which even the very sunshine of life does not wholly dissolve. . . . I never look back upon this period of my life without feeling a sense of desolation. It left a dark and melancholy train of thoughts behind.[112]

Later that year, Story was elected to the Massachusetts legislature. He served in that body until 1811, interrupted only by serving one session in Congress in 1808–1809 to fill the vacancy that occurred when Jacob Crowninshield, the current representative, died. He refused to seek reelection to Congress, though he would likely have won if he had tried.

Politically, Story was out of place in Massachusetts—a Republican in a predominantly Federalist state. Although he supported the Jefferson presidency, he subsequently alienated Jefferson because of his seemingly anti-Republican positions.[113] In describing the political climate of the day, Story wrote:

> The Republican party then and at all other times embraced men of very different views on many subjects. A Virginia Republican of that day, was very different from a Massachusetts Republican, and the anti-federal doctrines of the former state then had and still have very little support or influence in the latter State, notwithstanding a concurrence in political action upon general principles.[114]

Despite his Republican affiliation, Story at times leaned toward Federalist doctrines.[115] He admired George Washington and favored the federal plan of government: "I never wished to bring the government to a mere confederacy of States; but to preserve the power of the General Government given by all the States, in full exercise and sovereignty for the protection and preservation of all the States."[116] Story left politics after serving for six years, preferring to return to law.[117]

In 1808, Story had married Sarah Waldo Wetmore, the daughter of a judge. Sarah had been a close friend to Story's first wife and "the esteem and affection, which had begun during his previous marriage, now matured into love."[118] The early years of their marriage, however, were fraught with incalculable sorrow. They buried three daughters and a son before any of the children had reached the age of seven.[119]

In January 1811 during his last year as a legislator, Story was elected Speaker of the House of Representatives of Massachusetts. He served at this post for eleven months when President James Madison appointed him to the Supreme Court of the United States. At the age of thirty-two, Joseph Story joined his colleagues in Washington, the youngest justice ever appointed.[120]

In a letter to his long-time friend, Nathaniel Williams, Story described what induced him to accept the appointment:

> Notwithstanding the emoluments of my present business exceed the salary, I have determined to accept the office. The high honor attached to it, the permanence of the tenure, the respectability, if I may so say, of the salary, and the opportunity it will allow me to pursue, what of all things I admire, juridical studies, have combined to urge me to this result.[121]

As a justice on the Supreme Court, Story could devote himself to the study of law, an occupation he greatly relished.

After serving on the bench for eighteen years, Story added a new labor to his already busy schedule: the teaching of law. In 1829, his friend Nathan Dane planned to endow a chair at the fledgling Harvard Law School, but only if Story agreed to fill the position.[122] Story already served Harvard University on its board of overseers and as a member of its corporation but had declined the Royall Professorship of Law the year before, citing concerns for his health and reluctance to move to Cambridge.[123] When Dane pressed Story, however, he agreed, and so began a task that furnished him great joy over the succeeding years.

Harvard Law School technically began in 1817. However, for the first twelve years of its existence, the average student body each year was eight; in 1828, the school boasted only one student.[124] After Story assumed his responsibilities the school blossomed. In October 1829,

Story wrote to a friend: "We have at present twenty-seven students at Cambridge, with a prospect of more. I perceive that there is a vast labor before me."[125] During Story's tenure, 956 students graduated from Harvard Law School, many of whom became leaders in business, politics, and at the bar; all carried with them the principles that Story had so fervently taught.[126]

As a professor, Story immediately began to write treatises on the subjects he taught. He wrote eleven volumes on nine subjects, including his *Commentaries on the Constitution*, begun in 1829 and completed in 1833. While the *Commentaries* were criticized in the South, they were widely accepted in the North; some even compared them to *Blackstone's Commentaries on the Laws of England*. In April of 1833, Story finished an abridged edition for use in colleges and high schools.

Modern scholars have criticized the *Commentaries* as propagandistic, but they served the purpose for which Story wrote them—expositing the Constitution from a conservative, New England perspective, and answering the states' rights claims of southern scholars. [127] We shall take up the main points from his extrajudicial writings after a discussion of his theological beliefs, which later influenced his opinion in one of the Court's first religion cases.

During his time as a student at Harvard, Story firmly settled on Unitarian theology as his personal religious system. The college was in a whirl of secularist fancy. William Ellery Channing, Story's friend and fellow Unitarian, wrote of the atmosphere and experience:

> The French Revolution had diseased the imagination and unsettled the understanding of men everywhere. The old foundations of social order, loyalty, tradition, habit, reverence for antiquity, were everywhere shaken. . . . The authority of the past was gone. The old forms were outgrown, and new ones had not taken their place.[128]

In the midst of this cultural chaos, Story shifted his religious opinions to align more closely with the compassionate and tolerant religion of his father. Story's son William later described his father's conversion at Harvard as being inspired, in part, by the beauty of the Cambridge countryside as opposed to the "sterile rocks and moaning sea of Marblehead." Walking through the "flower-strewn fields, his heart assumed its natural hue of cheerfulness, and he no longer believed in the total depravity of man." Seeing the goodness of God displayed in creation, Story became convinced of divine beneficence. "And from being a Calvinist, he became a Unitarian."[129]

Story's new religion seemingly recognized that no teaching could be heretical. He rejected any notion of bigotry or even proselytism. Instead, he

> gladly allowed every one freedom of belief, and claimed only that it should be a genuine conviction and not a mere theologic opinion, considering the true faith of every man to be the necessary exponent of his nature, and honoring a religious life more than a formal creed. *He admitted within the pale of salvation Mahommedan and Christian, Catholic and Infidel.* He believed that whatever is sincere and honest is recognized of God;—that as the views of any sect are but human opinion, susceptible of error on every side, it behooves all men to be on their guard against arrogance of belief;—*and that in the sight of God it is not the truth or falsity of our views, but the spirit in which we believe, which alone is of vital consequence.*[130] [emphasis added]

Unitarianism made Story focus increasingly on morality and ethics instead of theology; "he disliked 'cant & formal ordinances' and preferred 'unaffected piety & above all religious charity.'"[131] Story described Unitarians as those who "believe in the divine mission of Christ, the credibility and authenticity of the Bible, the miracles wrought by our Saviour and his apostles, and the efficacy of his precepts to lead men to salvation." While Unitarians affirm the place of Scripture, they deny the deity of Christ: "[Unitarians] all agree that he was the special messenger of God, and that what he taught is of Divine authority. In truth, they principally differ from other Christians in disbelieving the Trinity, for they think Christ was not God, but in the Scripture language 'the Son of God.'"[132] One scholar summarizes Story's beliefs: "[Unitarianism's] liberal view of salvation appealed to his romantic idealism. . . . Unitarian emphasis on a learned clergy . . . corresponded with his faith in the articulate 'speaking aristocracy.' Reason was balanced with faith. Life in this world was addressed; life in the next assured."[133]

To understand Story's rejection of Calvinism and acceptance of Unitarianism requires a few words on how Story's religion of choice fit within the predominantly Protestant, Christian values of the early nineteenth century. The key to understanding Christianity during the post–Revolutionary War period was that it was primarily a public expression and was fairly consistent, ethically speaking, among Unitarians as well as orthodox Protestants. Historian Jonathan D. Sassi stated, "The Unitarians advocated many of the traditional prescriptions of the Congregational clergy's public Christianity."[134] Concerning Unitarianism during the post–Revolutionary War period, historian David Walker Howe points out that "Enlightenment rationalism was intermingled with Puritan moralism in Unitarian political views."[135]

Two of the distinguishing characteristics of nineteenth-century Unitarianism were its adherence to the principles of free inquiry and the resultant diversity of religious opinions within the denomination. This freedom occasioned a clash during the early and mid-nineteenth century between the traditional Unitarians and the more progressive Unitarians who were adopting transcendentalism as a theological framework.[136]

While Story's religious opinions were magnanimous, they clearly fall outside the pale of orthodoxy. He believed in the inherent goodness of man and denied the Trinity, as well as the exclusivity of Christ's atonement. Indeed, Story left little room for creeds and confessions, instead emphasizing the sincerity of religious opinion and a moral life.

Story may have embraced heterodox opinions, but he still believed that the principles of Christianity were essential to society. In a letter written in 1801 at the age of twenty-two, Story declared: "I verily believe Christianity necessary to the support of civil society, and shall ever attend to its institutions and acknowledge its precepts as the pure and natural sources of private and social happiness. The man who could subvert its influence will never receive countenance from me."

Years later, a letter from Thomas Jefferson tested Story's resolve on this point. In the summer of 1824, Jefferson wrote to John Cartwright, English parliamentarian (and leading advocate for the abolition of slavery), attacking the idea that the English common law was founded upon Christianity and daring any man to prove otherwise.[137] The letter was published, and Edward Everett, Unitarian pastor and fellow Harvard professor, drew it to Story's attention. In a letter back to Everett, Story wrote: "It appears to me inconceivable how any man can doubt, that Christianity is part of the Common Law of England, in the true sense of this expression, which I take to be no more than that Christianity is recognized as true, and as the established religion of England."[138]

In his inaugural address as Dane Professor of Law at Harvard Law School, Story began publicly to rebut Jefferson's thesis:

> One of the beautiful boasts of our municipal jurisprudence is, that Christianity is a part of the Common Law, from which it seeks the

sanctions of its rights, and by which it endeavors to regulate its doctrines. And, notwithstanding the specious objection of one of our distinguished statesmen, the boast is as true, as it is beautiful. There never has been a period, in which the Common Law did not recognize Christianity as lying at its foundations.[139]

Several years later in 1833, Story continued to refute Jefferson's letter. He published an essay titled "Christianity a Part of the Common Law" in the *American Jurist*, answering Jefferson's arguments point by point.[140] In the same year, Story wrote a letter to Jasper Adams, president of Charleston College and professor of moral and political philosophy, thanking him for sending a copy of his sermon delivered in Charleston on the relationship between Christianity and civil government.[141] Adams had stressed the need for Christianity in civil society, affirming at the same time the need to prevent state recognition of any particular sect of Christianity. Adams declared: "No nation on earth, is more dependent than our own, for its welfare, on the preservation and general belief and influence of Christianity among us." Adams argued that there are only two ways to govern men, either by force or "by religious and moral principles pervading the community." He warned that "[w]e must be a Christian nation, if we wish to continue a free nation. We must make our election—to be swayed by the gentle reign of moral and Christian principle, or ultimately, if not soon, by the iron rod of arbitrary sway."[142]

Story agreed with Adams's sermon: "My own private judgement has long been, (& every day's experience more & more confirms me in it,) that government can not long exist without an alliance with religion *to some extent*; & that Christianity is indispensable to the true interests & solid foundations of all free governments." Story likewise distinguished between the establishment of a particular sect as a state religion and the establishment of Christianity in general, recognizing the latter as the only true foundation for "moral obligation or accountableness."

Story excoriated Jefferson's claim that Christianity is not part of the common law, by saying that "a more egregious error never was uttered by able men." Story felt compelled to answer Jefferson's pernicious letter: "It is due to truth, & to the purity of the Law, to unmask their fallacies."[143] Speaking of the general state of the nation, Story wrote: "These are times in which the friends of Christianity are required to sound the alarm, & to inculcate sound principles. I fear that infidelity is make [*sic*] rapid progress under the delusive guise of the freedom of religious opinion & liberty of conscience."[144]

Story's harsh criticism of Jefferson and his vigorous defense of Christianity's place in law and society dispel any doubts as to his theory of church-state relations. While he upheld freedom of religion, meaning that anyone could practice his faith according to his conscience, he firmly believed that Christianity was the only true foundation for civil order. Without Christianity, moral decay would weaken the nation and threaten to undo all that the Founders had striven so hard to attain.

Story's 1833 *Commentaries on the Constitution* corroborates this analysis. When discussing the First Amendment, he began by positing: "the right of a society or government to interfere in matters of religion will hardly be contested by any persons."[145] Particularly, "it is impossible for those, who believe in the truth of Christianity, as a divine revelation, to doubt, that it is the especial duty of government to foster, and encourage it among all the citizens and subjects."[146] Government support of Christianity did not, in Story's mind, violate freedom of conscience: "This is a point wholly distinct from that of the right of private judgment in matters of religion, and of the freedom of public worship according to the dictates of one's conscience."[147] The difficulty is defining the line between encouragement and coercion.[148]

Story proposed three possible scenarios of government support for religion. First, the government could support one religion generally and let anyone freely adopt another religion. Second, the government could support one particular sect of a religion, again allowing anyone to choose freely another religion. Third, the government could support one sect of a religion and exclude to varying degrees anyone not a member of that religion from public acknowledgment. While these three options may not exhaust the possibilities, they framed Story's analysis. He clearly favored the first option, which had the support of history: "Now, there will probably be found few persons in this, or any other Christian country, who would deliberately contend, that it was unreasonable, or unjust to foster and encourage the Christian religion generally, as a matter of sound policy, as well as of revealed truth."[149]

According to Story, the Framers embraced a similar understanding. Speaking of the time in which the Constitution was adopted, he wrote: "[T]he general, if not universal, sentiment in America was, that Christianity ought to receive encouragement from the state, so far as was not incompatible with the private rights of conscience, and the freedom of religious worship."[150] So widespread was this viewpoint, that "[a]n attempt to level all religions, and to make it a matter of state policy to hold all in utter indifference, would have created universal disapproval, if not universal indignation."[151] The real purpose of the First Amendment "was, not to countenance, much less to advance Mahometanism, or Judaism, or infidelity, by prostrating Christianity; but to exclude all rivalry among Christian sects, and to prevent any national ecclesiastical establishment, which should give to an hierarchy the exclusive patronage of the national government."[152]

Perhaps the most important constitutional conviction that Story held in matters of the relationship between church and state was this: The *national* government was powerless to speak at all on matters of religion; this power was left to the *state* governments. The goal was to enable "the Catholic and the Protestant, the Calvinist and the Arminian, the Jew and the Infidel, [to] sit down at the common table of the national councils, without any inquisition into their faith, or mode of worship."[153] The First Amendment would eliminate the possibility for national religious persecution by "extirpating the power" of the national government over religious issues. (It is worth noting well Story's position here: in chapters 3 and 4 we will see how a dramatic shift placing the *national* government over *state* government took place during and after the Civil War, especially concerning the Mormon Church's beliefs and practices.)

Justice Story did not compose an Establishment Clause or Free Exercise Clause opinion during his tenure on the Court. However, he wrote the opinion of the unanimous Court in *Vidal v. Girard* that laid the foundation for an "accommodationist" view of the religion clauses with an emphasis on equality and governmental neutrality.

In all of Supreme Court history, no justice has written as prolifically on matters of religion, specifically Christianity's impact "upon public and political law," as Joseph Story.[154] Not only did Story write the opinion in *Vidal,* he also wrote extensively off the Court regarding the religion clauses. Story's *Commentaries on the Constitution of the United States* references both religion clauses and serves as a foundational work for constitutional jurisprudence. Concerning the role of Christianity in constitutional analysis, Story wrote:

> Probably at the time of the adoption of the Constitution, and the amendments to it . . . the general, if not the universal, sentiment in America was, that Christianity ought to receive encouragement from the state, so far as was not incompatible with the private rights of conscience, and the freedom of religious worship.[155]

If ever there was the right man, in the right place, at the right time to render judgment on a question of religious liberty in the United States, surely sixty-four-year-old Justice Joseph Story must have felt that he was that man when an unusual Philadelphia case came before him in the opening months of 1844. The expansive, tolerant temperament given to him by his parents, his Unitarian beliefs in freedom of religious conscience, his deep study of the Constitution—its meanings and the relationship between law and religion—all came together in deciding the issue before him.

THE CASE: *VIDAL V. GIRARD'S EXECUTORS* (1844)

The nexus of the *Vidal* case was the will and trust established by Stephen Girard, a native of Bordeaux, France, who made his home in Philadelphia shortly before the colonists' Declaration of Independence in 1776. Born in 1750 the eldest of ten children, Girard took to the sea at an early age, becoming a licensed captain in the French merchant marine. His maritime skills and experience, combined with a keen entrepreneurial instinct for commercial trade and other business ventures, quickly allowed him to own his own ships, conducting overseas trade between Europe and America.

After settling in Philadelphia, Girard became a "citizen" of Pennsylvania in 1778 at the age of twenty-eight and eventually added to his shipping enterprises banking, international trade, construction, coal mining, railroads, and a host of other business investments. In his first decade, he became one of the wealthiest Americans, and he remained so until his death. His generosity and philanthropic activities, both visible and invisible, were extensive. He was extraordinarily grateful to his new country for the opportunities its institutions had afforded him; two examples stand out prominently. When Congress did not renew the U.S. National Bank's charter in 1811, Girard bought the bank (located in Philadelphia) and turned it into a financial powerhouse. When the government incurred catastrophic debt during the War of 1812, he loaned eight million dollars to the U.S. Treasury.[156]

On Christmas Day, 1830, at the age of eighty, Girard signed his last will and testament in Philadelphia, which he had written and rewritten with great care in his final years. He was a widower with no children. One year later—almost to the day—Girard died, on December 26. His will was proved valid five days later, on December 31, 1831. His estate was valued in excess of seven million dollars, a vast amount at that time. He generously bequeathed sums to family, friends, and many charities. Girard was very detailed and specific about the distribution and uses of his fortune, one portion of which became the subject before the Supreme Court of the United States in 1844.

Girard's will provided for the establishment of a college for "poor white male orphans" from the cities of Philadelphia, New York, and New Orleans.[157] The trust document provided for the City of Philadelphia to establish and administer the school. A specific provision of the trust required that no minister or missionary be allowed to teach at the college. The document stated:

> I enjoin and require that no ecclesiastic, missionary, or minister of any sect whatsoever, shall ever hold or exercise any station or duty whatever in the said college; nor shall any such person ever be admitted for any purpose, or as a visitor, within the premises appropriated to the purposes of the said college.[158]

Girard went on to stipulate that

> [i]n making this restriction, I do not mean to cast any reflection upon any sect or person whatsoever; but, as there is such a multitude of sects, and such a diversity of opinion amongst them, I desire to keep the tender minds of the orphans, who are to derive advantage from this bequest, free from the excitement which clashing doctrines and sectarian controversy are so apt to produce; my desire is, that all the instructors and teachers in the college shall take pains to instil into the minds of the scholars the purest principles of morality, so that, on their entrance into active life, they may, from inclination and habit, evince benevolence towards their fellow creatures, and a love of truth, sobriety, and industry, adopting at the same time such religious tenets as their matured reason may enable them to prefer.[159]

The city of Philadelphia took up its duties as trustee of the millions of dollars set out in the will and began the process of acquisition of land and construction plans for Girard's college. Five years later, Girard's niece, Françoise Fénelon Vidal, daughter of his deceased sister, together with his brother, John Girard, and three other nieces by another deceased brother, all citizens of the monarchy of France, instituted a lawsuit in the

Circuit Court of the Eastern District of Pennsylvania challenging the validity of the will. By having the will deemed invalid, Girard's French relatives would gain access to the entire estate. In April 1841, the case came for a hearing in the Circuit Court, which held that the will and all its particulars were, in fact, valid under Pennsylvania law.

The Vidal-Girard families appealed the decision, retaining Daniel Webster and Walter Jones to represent them before the Supreme Court of the United States. Four attorneys presented oral arguments, two for each side, for ten days beginning on February 13, 1844.

Daniel Webster, who was also a Massachusetts senator and had recently served as secretary of state under Presidents Harrison and Tyler, was a close friend of Justice Story. In fact, Story had such tremendous respect for Daniel Webster that he advocated a leadership role for him in the emerging Constitutional Nationalist Movement. Story wrote of the need for statesmen: "We have all at risk . . . and we must always keep on board the ship of state, not only a competent crew to work the ship, but the most cautious of the skillful, as well as the truest of the best."[160] Story thought of his friend Webster as just such a man: "[His mind] is marked by sagacity, caution, accuracy, foresight, comprehensiveness, laborious research, and untiring meditation, as well as by various genius. In short, he possesses that undefinable quality, called WISDOM, in an eminent degree."[161]

Horace Binney, as lead attorney, represented the city of Philadelphia, the governmental entity Girard had named to establish and administer the school.[162] A Philadelphia native, Binney graduated with honors from Harvard a year ahead of Justice Story in 1797. Many considered his argument in the case the best presented. As described earlier, a few months after arguing the *Vidal* case, he was the leader who quelled the riots that broke out between Catholics and Protestants in Philadelphia.[163]

Counsel Walter Jones, representing the appellants with Webster, argued that the "trust would be void, because the plan of education proposed is anti-christian, and therefore repugnant to the laws of Pennsylvania."[164] Jones argued that the trust must be declared void because it would make "a curse to any civilized land; it is a cruel experiment upon poor orphan boys to shut them up and make them the victims of a philosophical speculation. By the laws of Pennsylvania, it is a blasphemy to attack the Christian religion."[165]

Binney in his argument on behalf of the city of Philadelphia asserted that the desire of Mr. Girard was to include the orphan poor of all sects, Jews as well as Christians, and those who had no religion at all. . . . If any clergyman was admitted, he would of course teach the doctrines of his own church. No two sects would agree. Some would adopt one part of the Bible, some another. If they agreed as to what was to be left out as apocryphal, they would differ about the translation of the rest. The Protestant would not receive the Douay Bible.[166]

Binney then presented before the Court an actual controversy concerning the inclusion of the Bible in public school curriculums. He argued that there were existing difficulties "in New York about the introduction of the Bible as a schoolbook. Girard did what was in conformity with the law, and often done practically."[167] Interestingly, in order to establish that the will was not anti-Christian in its content, Binney argued: "the purest principles of morality are to be taught. Where are they found? Whoever searches for them must go to the source from which a Christian man derives his faith—the Bible."[168] He emphasized that Girard's will also specified that laymen must be instructors, "and why cannot they teach religion as well as science?" he asked.[169]

Daniel Webster, who had just celebrated his sixty-second birthday, was in top oratorical form before the Supreme Court, aggressively attacking the clergy prohibition:

[i]n no country in the world is there a body of men who have done so much good as the preachers of the United States; they derive no aid from government, constitute no hierarchy, but live by the voluntary contributions of those to whom they preach. . . . Was there ever an instance before, where, in any Christian country the whole body of the clergy were [*sic*] denounced?[170]

He then directly attacked the assertions of his opposing counsel with regard to the requirements of Christian charity: "The object here is to establish a school of learning and shelter; to give a better education. The counsel upon the other side are right in speaking of charity as an emanation of Christianity. But if this be so, there can be no charity where the authority of God is derided and his word rejected."[171]

In pointing out that the clergy prohibition was derogatory toward Christianity, Webster warned, "The doors of the college are open to infidels. The clause, as it stands, is as derogatory to Christianity as if provision had been made for lectures against it."[172] He concluded:

No fault can be found with Girard for wishing a marble college to bear his name forever, but it is not valuable unless it has a fragrance of Christianity about it.

The reasons which the testator gives are objectionable and derogatory to Christianity; they assume that a difference of opinion upon some religious tenants is of more importance than a Christian education.[173]

On February 27, 1844, Justice Story delivered the unanimous opinion for the Court, upholding the will with the provision prohibiting ministers and missionaries from teaching at the school. Commenting on the arguments of the case, Story said: "This cause has been argued with great learning and ability."[174] In a letter to his wife, he discussed the theological nature of the arguments. "I was not a little amused, with the manner in which . . . the language of the Scriptures, and the doctrines of Christianity, were brought in to point the argument; and to find the Court engaged in hearing . . . expositions of Christianity, with almost the formality of lectures from the pulpit."[175]

In the opinion, Story focused upon the will's "second injunction and requirement [forbidding ecclesiastical teachers] which has been so elaborately commented at bar, as derogatory to the Christian religion."[176] Noting the primary objection to the trust's enforcement, Story declared: "This objection is that the foundation of the college upon the principles and exclusions prescribed by the testator, is derogatory and hostile to the Christian religion, and so is void, as being against the common law and public policy of Pennsylvania."[177] Story acknowledged that "the Christian religion is part of the common law of Pennsylvania," but the way he framed his analysis of Girard's intentions reflects principles of equality and neutrality concerning religion:

Language more comprehensive for complete protection of every variety of religious opinion could scarcely be used; and it must have been intended to extend equally to all sects whether they believed in Christianity or not, and whether they were Jews or infidels. So that we are compelled to admit that although Christianity be a part of the common law of the state, yet it is so in this qualified sense, that its divine origin and truth are admitted and therefore it is not to be maliciously and openly reviled and blasphemed against, to the annoyance of believers or the injury of the public.[178]

In finding the will provision valid, Story said, "Remote inferences, or possible results, or speculative tendencies, are not to be drawn or adopted for such purposes. There must be plain, positive, and express provisions, demonstrating not only that Christianity is not to be taught; but that it is to be impugned or repudiated." Story found that "the testator does not say that Christianity shall not be taught in college."[179] His opinion rested on the determination that laymen were capable of teaching the general principles of Christianity. "Why may not laymen instruct in the general principles of Christianity as well as ecclesiastics? There is no restriction as to the religious opinion of the instructors and officers."[180] Then, regarding the teaching of the Bible, Justice Story noted:

> Why may not the Bible, and especially the New Testament, *without note or comment* be read and taught as a divine revelation in the college—its general precepts expounded, its evidences explained, and its glorious principles of morality inculcated? . . . Where can the purest principles of morality be learned so clearly or so perfectly as from the New Testament? Where are benevolence, the love of truth, sobriety, and industry, so powerful and irresistibly inculcated as in the sacred volume?[181] [emphasis added]

This decision, resting upon the concept that non-clergy could adequately expound the Bible and specifically the New Testament, resonates with Story's Unitarian theology. His Harvard friend, William Ellery Channing, in his famous sermon, *Unitarian Christianity*, said, "We regard the Scriptures as the records of God's successive revelations to mankind, and particularly of the last and most perfect revelation of His will by Jesus Christ. Whatever doctrines seem to us to be clearly taught in Scripture, we receive without reserve or exception."[182] Channing pointed out the importance of and reliance upon the New Testament:

> We do not, however, attach equal importance to all books in this collection. Our religion, we believe, lies chiefly in the New Testament. The dispensation of Moses, compared with that of Jesus, we consider as adapted to the childhood of the human race, a preparation for a nobler system, and chiefly useful now as serving to confirm and illustrate the Christian Scriptures.[183]

This reliance upon the New Testament as a moral source found its way into Justice Story's opinion in *Vidal*.

Justice Story relished the idea of minds left to peruse the New Testament "without note or comment," a position consistent with his view of humanity. Young minds properly nurtured and left to read the divine words of God could make the choice, in his theological understanding, to live productive and meaningful lives and would be drawn to God by His precepts. (This is almost exactly what Girard expressed in his will.) Story concluded:

> Looking to the objection therefore in a mere juridical view, which is the only one in which we are at liberty to consider it, we are satisfied that there is nothing in the devise establishing the college, or in the regulations and restrictions contained therein, which are inconsistent with the Christian religion, or are opposed to any known policy of the state of Pennsylvania.[184]

Thus, the opinion set down three rules: lay teaching of Scripture was satisfactory; the Court would not permit anyone to attack Christianity; and it would allow a school to be established that encouraged Christianity in a nonsectarian manner.

In his opinion, Justice Story set forth principles of equality and neutrality that would later find their way into the Supreme Court's decisions involving the Establishment Clause and Free Exercise Clause of the First Amendment. *Vidal* has been cited in numerous Supreme Court decisions and law review articles because of its enunciations of principles of neutrality and equality among religions. However, it is also interesting to note that Justice Story went out of his way to construe the will so that nothing could be considered "derogatory to Christianity." He specifically notes: "the testator does not say that Christianity shall not be taught in the college." The lasting impact of *Vidal* is still felt even today.

And how enduring have Stephen Girard's last wishes been? Girard College, located on forty-five acres in north Philadelphia, opened its doors on January 1, 1848, to orphaned boys who began studies in the basics of reading, writing, and arithmetic; astronomy and various philosophies; and the French and Spanish languages, as Girard had outlined his curriculum. It has been a remarkable institution of learning for thousands of students ever since. In 1951 Girard's remains were moved from Trinity Cemetery to Founder's Hall at the college; in 1968 the Supreme Court ruled to allow underprivileged students regardless of race, creed, or color to be admitted (and later women were included). Girard College thrives today and is one of the great treasures of Philadelphia—the city whose very name means "brotherly love."

Joseph Story continued in his capacity as Supreme Court justice until 1845, when he retired because the Court had shifted ideologically and he did not wish to be in perpetual dissent.[185] He planned to devote himself fully to teaching and writing at Harvard, but he became ill during the final push to clear his circuit docket. On September 10, 1845, Joseph Story "breathed the name of God, and this was the last word that was ever heard from his lips."[186]

NOTES

1. Ray Allen Billington, *The Protestant Crusade (1800–1860): A Study of the Origins of American Nativism* (New York: Macmillan, 1938), 32–33; Michael Feldberg, *The Philadelphia Riots of 1844: A Study of Ethnic Conflict* (Westport, Conn.: Greenwood Press, 1975), 20.

2. Billington, *Protestant Crusade*, 37; citing J. Salzbacher, *Meine Reise nach Nord-Amerika im Jahre 1842* (Vienna, 1845); Feldberg, *Philadelphia Riots*, 86.

3. *See* Billington, *Protestant Crusade*, 38; and Vincent P. Lannie and Bernard C. Diethorn, "For the Honor and Glory of God: The Philadelphia Bible Riots of 1840," *Hist. of Educ. Q.* 8 (1968), 95 n. 1.

4. Lannie and Diethorn, "Honor and Glory of God," 44; see also Billington, *Protestant Crusade*, 38.

5. Anson Phelps Stokes, *Church and State in the United States*, vol. 1 (1950), 808.

6. Billington, *Protestant Crusade*, 38; Stokes, *Church and State*, 812–13; citing Rev. Patrick J. Dignan, *A History of the Legal Incorporation of Catholic Church Property in the United States, 1784-1932* (Washington, D.C.: The Catholic University of America, 1933), 109–10.

7. Stokes, *Church and State*, 809–12.

8. Stokes, *Church and State*; citing Dignan, *Catholic Church Property*, 109–18, 812–14.

9. Billington, *Protestant Crusade*, 38–39.

10. Stokes, *Church and State*; citing Dignan, *Catholic Church Property*, 166–67, 816.

11. Stokes, *Church and State*, 817.

12. Billington, *Protestant Crusade*, 37; see also J. A. Burns, *The Growth and Development of the Catholic School System in the United States* (New York: Benziger Brothers, 1912).

13. Stokes, *Church and State*, 815–16; Burns, *Catholic School System*, 181; Billington, *Protestant Crusade*, 37.

14. Billington, *Protestant Crusade*, 37; citing Peter Guilday, *A History of the Councils of Baltimore, 1791–1884* (New York: Macmillan, 1932), 89–95.

15. Stokes, *Church and State*, 816; citing Dignan, 145, 156.

16. Billington, *Protestant Crusade*, 40; citing *American Catholic Historical Researches* 11 (1894), 129–32.

17. Billington, *Protestant Crusade*, 43, 209–11, 220.

18. Stokes, *Church and State*, 818–19.

19. Billington, *Protestant Crusade*, 220.

20. Stokes, *Church and State*, 826.

21. Stokes, *Church and State*, 825.

22. Carleton Mabee, *The American Leonardo: A Life of Samuel F. B. Morse* (1969), 162–88; Stokes, *Church and State*, 826–29. See also Samuel F. B. Morse, *Imminent Dangers to the Free Institutions of the United States through Foreign Immigration, and the Present State of the Naturalization Laws* (New York: 1835). Mabee asserted that Morse's initial publication, *Foreign Conspiracy Against the Liberties of the United States*, was a major factor in provoking the 1834 Massachusetts uprising against the Ursuline convent. Mabee, *American Leonardo*, 164.

23. Billington, *Protestant Crusade*, 66–75; Stokes, *Church and State*, 819.

24. Charles R. Morris, *American Catholic: The Saints and Sinners Who Built America's Most Powerful Church* (New York: Vintage Books, 1997), 54–55.

25. Morris, *American Catholic*, 56. Morris notes that court records strongly imply that the ministers knew of the planned attack in advance and "were purposely whipping up tempers."

26. Billington, *Protestant Crusade*, 67–90; Stokes, *Church and State*, 824.

27. Burns, *Catholic School System*, 181–82, 183, n. 6; Stokes, *Church and State*, 823.

28. Feldberg, *Philadelphia Riots*, 23, 89–90.

29. Sources for the narrative historical overview of the Bibles are: Charles Beard, *The Reformation of the 16th Century in Its Relation to Modern Thought and Knowledge* (1883) (Ann Arbor: University of Michigan Press, 1st ed., 1962); Laurence M. Vance, *A Brief History of English Bible Translations* (Pensacola, Fla.: Vance Publications; article online at http://www.av1611.org/kjv/kjvhist.html); *The Catholic Encyclopedia*, vol. 5 (Robert Appleton Company, 1909), online edition by Kevin Knight, 1999; Isaac H. Hall, ed., "History of the King James Version," in *The Revised New Testament and History of Revision* (New York: A. L. Bancroft & Co., 1881); John Henry Newman, "The Rheims and Douay Version of Holy Scripture," *The Rambler* (July 1859), in *The Newman Reader, Works of John Henry Newman* (National Institute for Newman Studies, 2004; online at http://www.newmanreader.org/works/tracts/douayrheims.html).

30. Lannie and Diethorn, "Honor and Glory of God," 48–49.

31. Feldberg, *Philadelphia Riots*, 89.

32. Feldberg, *Philadelphia Riots*, 90.

33. Francis Kenrick, *Letter Ledger* (1842) (on file with the Philadelphia Archdiocesan Archives), 202–204, in Lannie and Deithorn, "Honor and Glory of God," 56.

34. Lannie and Deithorn, "Honor and Glory of God," 50.

35. John W. Pratt, "Religious Conflict in the Development of the New York City Public School System," *Hist. of Educ. Q.* (1965), 5: 110, 112.

36. John R. G. Hassard, *Life of the Most Reverend John Hughes, D. D., First Archbishop of New York* (New York: D. Appleton and Co., 1866), 226.

37. John R. G. Hassard, *Life of the Most Reverend John Hughes*, 225.

38. William H. Seward, *Works*, vol. 2 (1853–1854), G. E. Baker, ed., 215, in Pratt, "Religious Conflict," 112.

39. Pratt, "Religious Conflict," 112–13.

40. Burns, *Catholic School System*, 13.

41. Burns, *Catholic School System*, 160.

42. Feldberg, *Philadelphia Riots*, 91.

43. Burns, *Catholic School System*, 18; Feldberg, *Philadelphia Riots*, 91.

44. Hassard, *Life of Rev. John Hughes*, 232.

45. Hassard, *Life of Rev. John Hughes*, 240.

46. *American Protestant Vindicator*, 5 August 1840, in Billington, *Protestant Crusade*, 148.

47. Billington, *Protestant Crusade*, 157.

48. Feldberg, *Philadelphia Riots*, 91.

49. Stokes, *Church and State*, 829.

50. Billington, *Protestant Crusade*, 221.

51. Feldberg, *Philadelphia Riots*, 91–92.

52. Lannie and Diethorn, "Honor and Glory of God," 57–58.

53. Lannie and Diethorn, "Honor and Glory of God," 59–60.

54. Lannie and Diethorn, "Honor and Glory of God," 59; quoting *North American*, 14 January 1843.

55. Lannie and Diethorn, "Honor and Glory of God," 68; quoting *Catholic Herald*, 21 March 1844.

56. Lannie and Diethorn, "Honor and Glory of God," 59.

57. Feldberg, *Philadelphia Riots*, 93–94.

58. Lannie and Diethorn, "Honor and Glory of God," 65–66.

59. Feldberg, *Philadelphia Riots*, 94.

60. Lannie and Diethorn, "Honor and Glory of God," 67; quoting *Episcopal Recorder*, 9 March 1844.

61. Lannie and Diethorn, "Honor and Glory of God," 66; quoting *Presbyterian*, 16 March 1844.

62. Billington, *Protestant Crusade*, 200. See also J. Thomas Scharf and Thompson Westcott, *History of Philadelphia, 1609-1884*, vol. 1 (Philadelphia: L. H. Everts & Co., 1884), 663.

63. Billington, *Protestant Crusade*, 193–203.

64. Scharf and Westcott, *History of Philadelphia*, 664.

65. Billington, *Protestant Crusade*, 204; quoting "Address of the Executive Committee of New York City," *American Republican*, 26 April 1844.

66. Billington, *Protestant Crusade*, 216 n72.

67. Feldberg, *Philadelphia Riots*, 95; quoting John Hancock Lee, *Origin and Progress of the American Party in Politics* (Philadelphia: Elliot & Gihon, 1855).

68. Scharf and Westcott, *History of Philadelphia*, 664.

69. Lannie and Diethorn, "Honor and Glory of God," 58.

70. Philip Hamburger, *Separation of Church and State* (2002), 276; quoting "Freedom of Opinion," *American Whig Review* (June 1849), 54.

71. Hamburger, *Separation of Church and State*, 228.

72. Hamburger, *Separation of Church and State*, 284; quoting George C. Lorimer, *The Great Conflict: A Discourse, Concerning Baptists, and Religious Liberty* (Boston: Lee and Shepard, 1877), 116.

73. Lannie and Diethorn, "Honor and Glory of God," 62–63. On the Christian character of America at the time, Alexis de Tocqueville wrote in the 1830s that, whether held as a "sincere belief" or not, "Christianity" in the United States "reign[ed] without any obstacle, by universal consent." Alexis de Tocqueville, *Democracy in America*, vol. 1 (1835), trans. Henry Reeve (New York: The Colonial Press, 1900), 309–10. Tocqueville further concluded: "I do not know whether all the Americans have a sincere faith in their religion, for who can search the human heart? but I am certain that they hold it to be indispensable to the maintenance of republican institutions. This opinion is not peculiar to a class of citizens or to a party, but it belongs to the whole nation, and to every rank of society."

74. Scharf and Westcott, *History of Philadelphia*, 664.

75. Feldberg, *Philadelphia Riots*, 102–103.

76. *Philadelphia Public Ledger*, 8 May 1844.

77. Feldberg, *Philadelphia Riots*, 108; quoting *Native American*, 7 May 1844.

78. Billington, *Protestant Crusade*, 225; Feldberg, *Philadelphia Riots*, 109–110.

79. Scharf and Westcott, *History of Philadelphia*, 665–66.

80. Lannie and Diethorn, "Honor and Glory of God," 75; quoting *Daily Sun*, 8 May 1844.

81. Scharf and Westcott, *History of Philadelphia*, 666.

82. Feldberg, *Philadelphia Riots*, 111.

83. Scharf and Westcott, *History of Philadelphia*, 666.

84. Lannie and Diethorn, "Honor and Glory of God," 78; quoting *Pennsylvanian*, 13 May 1844.

85. *Philadelphia Public Ledger*, 14 May 1844.

86. Feldberg, *Philadelphia Riots*, 136–43.

87. Binney, *Life of Horace Binney*, 236–37.

88. *Philadelphia Public Ledger*, 10 May 1844; Scharf and Westcott, *History of Philadelphia*, 667; Binney, *Life of Horace Binney*, 238.

89. Binney, *Life of Horace Binney*, 238.

90. Feldberg, *Philadelphia Riots*, 156.

91. Autobiographical letter from Joseph Story to William W. Story, 23 January 1831, in William W. Story, ed., *Miscellaneous Writings of Joseph Story*, vol. 1 (Boston: Little & Brown, 1852), 1–5 (hereafter *Autobiography*).

92. R. Kent Newmeyer, *Supreme Court Justice Joseph Story* (Chapel Hill: University of North Carolina Press, 1985), 13.

93. *Autobiography*, 5. (The Arminians were within the Protestant Calvinist tradition but they opposed the absolute predestination of strict Calvinism, maintaining the possibility of salvation for all.)

94. *Autobiography*, 10.

95. Newmyer, *Justice Joseph Story,* 13.

96. *Autobiography,* 5.

97. *Autobiography,* 4; see also Newmyer, *Justice Joseph Story,* 17–18. Most children of the time were required to help out on the farm or with the fishing.

98. *Autobiography,* 7, 9. "The general poverty, combined with other circumstances, made the resources of education narrow; and few books were to be found, and few scholars were nurtured on its rocky shores."

99. William W. Story, ed., *Life and Letters of Joseph Story* (Boston: Little & Brown, 1851), 22.

100. Story, ed., *Life and Letters,* 27.

101. *Autobiography,* 11–12.

102. *Autobiography,* 13–14. Writing of his sense of victory at learning the material, Story declared, "The hero who conquers in battle, the orator who triumphs in the senate . . . feels not a more intense delight, than the youth first perceiving, that though born of the dust he is not altogether earth, but that there is something within him of an ethereal and intellectual nature."

103. *Autobiography,* 15.

104. Newmyer, *Justice Joseph Story,* 25.

105. Newmyer, *Justice Joseph Story,* 28. See also Daniel Walker Howe, *The Unitarian Conscience: Harvard Moral Philosophy, 1805–1861* (Middletown, Conn.: Wesleyan University Press; Scranton, Pa.: Harper & Row, 1988), 17–20.

106. Newmyer, 40–42.

107. *Autobiography,* 19.

108. *Autobiography,* 20.

109. *Autobiography,* 20.

110. *Autobiography,* 16–18.

111. *Autobiography,* 25–26.

112. *Autobiography,* 26.

113. *Autobiography,* 33. Jefferson later called Story a "pseudo-republican."

114. *Autobiography,* 27.

115. *Autobiography.* "I was and always have been a lover, a devoted lover, of the Constitution of the United States, and a friend to the union of the States."

116. *Autobiography.* See also Newmyer, *Justice Joseph Story,* 45–72, describing Story's political career.

117. Story wrote: "I cannot disguise that I had lost my relish for political controversy, and I found an entire obedience to party projects required such constant sacrifices of opinion and feeling, that my solicitude was greatly increased to withdraw from the field, that I might devote myself with a singleness of heart to the study of the law, which was at all times the object of my admiration and almost exclusive devotion." *Autobiography,* 30.

118. *Life and Letters,* 169.

119. *Autobiography,* 34–35. Story described his grief: "I have many agonizing recollections on this subject, and some truly pathetic touches of tenderness to tell, but I have neither the heart nor the power to go over them. You will one day learn how difficult it is to bury our sorrows, when they have struck deep into our souls."

120. Henry J. Abraham, *Justices, Presidents, and Senators* (Lanham, Md.: Rowman & Littlefield Publishers, 1999), 67.

121. *Life and Letters*, vol. 1, 201.

122. *Life and Letters*, vol. 2, 2.

123. Newmyer, *Justice Joseph Story*, 165. *Life and Letters*, vol. 1, 533.

124. *Life and Letters*, vol. 2, 23.

125. *Life and Letters*, vol. 2, 23

126. Newmyer, *Justice Joseph Story*, 249, 267–68, 281.

127. Newmyer, *Justice Joseph Story*, 181–94. Newmyer comments: "Let us admit that the *Commentaries* were biased toward nationalism and concede that Story's history was one-sided and in some respects as metaphysical as the states' rights school he criticized for its metaphysics—as when it made sovereignty unequivocally descend on the American people in 1776. Yes, the work is flawed by a lack of symmetry and by an excessively florid style. By modern standards it looks like a great beached whale; but in the nineteenth century it swam majestically in the raging seas of constitutional disputation." (184).

128. William Ellery Channing, *Memoir of William Ellery Channing*, vol. 1 (London: G. Routledge, 1870), 43.

129. *Life and Letters*, vol. 1, 56–57.

130. *Life and Letters*, 57–58.

131. Joseph Story to Sarah Story, 23 February 1827, in Newmyer, *Justice Joseph Story*, 180.

132. *Life and Letters*, vol. 1, 442.

133. Newmyer, *Justice Joseph Story*, 180.

134. Jonathan D. Sassi, *A Republic of Righteousness: The Public Christianity of the Post-Revolutionary New England Clergy* (New York: Oxford University Press, 2001), 159.

135. Daniel Walker Howe, *The Unitarian Conscience* (1970), 207.

136. For an excellent discussion of core "doctrines" of transcendental philosophy, see Conrad Wright, *Three Prophets of Religious Liberalism* (Boston: Beacon, 1961) 19–46, on Channing-Emerson-Parker, analyzing the seminal sermons delivered by Parker and Emerson regarding the Transcendentalist philosophy. For the classic traditional Unitarian response to transcendentalism, see Andrews Norton, *A Discourse on the Latest Form of Infidelity* (1839), reprinted in Sydney E. Ahlstrom and Jonathan S. Carey, *An American Reformation: A Documentary History of Unitarian Christianity* (Middletown, Conn.: Wesleyan University Press; Scranton, Pa.: Harper & Row, 1985), 445.

137. James McClellan, *Joseph Story and the American Constitution: A Study in Political and Legal Thought* (Norman: University of Oklahoma Press, 1971), 118 (hereafter *Story and the Constitution*); Newmyer, *Justice Joseph Story*, 183.

138. *Life and Letters*, vol. 1, 430.

139. *Life and Letters*, vol. 2, 8–9.

140. Joseph Story, "Christianity a Part of the Common Law," *Am. Jurist* 9 (1833), 346; reprinted in *Life and Letters*, vol. 1, 431–33. For further discussion of this article, see McClellan, *Story and the Constitution*, 121–23.

141. Joseph Story to Jasper Adams, 14 May 1833, in *Religion and Politics in the Early*

Republic: Jasper Adams and the Church-State Debate, ed. Daniel L. Dreisbach (Lexington: University of Kentucky Press, 1996), 115–17 (hereafter *Religion and Politics*).

142. Jasper Adams, "The Relation of Christianity to Civil Government in the United States," reprinted in *Religion and Politics*, 39, 40, 51–52. This sermon was delivered to the convention of the Protestant Episcopal Church of the diocese of South Carolina on 13 February 1833.

143. Joseph Story to Jasper Adams, *Religion and Politics*, 115–17.

144. Joseph Story to Jasper Adams, *Religion and Politics*, 115–17.

145. Joseph Story, *Commentaries on the Constitution of the United States*, vol. 3 (1833) (hereafter *Commentaries*), § 1865, photographic reprint (1991).

146. *Commentaries*, § 1865.

147. *Commentaries*, § 1865. Story later confirmed his commitment to religious liberty: "The rights of conscience are, indeed, beyond the just reach of any human power. They are given by God, and cannot be encroached upon by human authority, without a criminal disobedience of the precepts of natural, as well as of revealed religion" (§ 1870).

148. *Commentaries*, § 1866.

149. *Commentaries*, § 1867.

150. *Commentaries*, § 1868.

151. *Commentaries*, § 1868

152. *Commentaries*, § 1871.

153. *Commentaries*, § 1873.

154. *Commentaries*, § 1865.

155. *Commentaries*, § 1868.

156. For an excellent and fascinating account of Girard's life with historical photographs, see http://www.ushistory.org/girard.

157. *Vidal v. Girard's Executors*, 43 U.S. 129 (1844).

158. *Vidal v. Girard's Executors*, 133.

159. *Vidal v. Girard's Executors*.

160. Joseph Story, "Statesmen—Their Rareness and Importance," *New Eng. Mag.* 7 (August 1834): 89, 92.

161. Joseph Story, "Daniel Webster," *New Eng. Mag.* 7 (August 1834): 96, 98.

162. Charles Chauncey Binney, "Horace Binney," in *Great American Lawyers*, vol. 4, ed. William Draper Lewis (Philadelphia: John C. Winston, 1908; photographic reprint 1971), 197, 212.

163. Binney, "Horace Binney," 199, 223–24, 237.

164. *Vidal v. Girard's Executors*, 143.

165. *Vidal v. Girard's Executors*, 146.

166. *Vidal v. Girard's Executors*, 153.

167. *Vidal v. Girard's Executors*, 153.

168. *Vidal v. Girard's Executors*, 153.

169. *Vidal v. Girard's Executors*, 154.

170. *Vidal v. Girard's Executors*, 173.

171. *Vidal v. Girard's Executors*, 174.

172. *Vidal v. Girard's Executors*, 174

173. *Vidal v. Girard's Executors,* 175.

174. *Vidal v. Girard's Executors,* 183.

175. *Life and Letters,* vol. 2, 468.

176. *Vidal v. Girard's Executors,* 184.

177. *Vidal v. Girard's Executors,* 197.

178. *Vidal v. Girard's Executors,* 198.

179. *Vidal v. Girard's Executors,* 199.

180. *Vidal v. Girard's Executors,* 200.

181. *Vidal v. Girard's Executors,* 200.

182. William Ellery Channing, "Unitarian Christianity," in David Robinson, ed., *William Ellery Channing Selected Writings* (New York: Paulist Press, 1985), 70, 71–72.

183. Channing, "Unitarian Christianity," 72 (footnote omitted).

184. Channing, "Unitarian Christianity," 201.

185. *Life and Letters,* vol. 2, 546–48.

186. *Life and Letters,* vol. 2, 546–48.

· 2 ·

The Church-Slavery Controversy

[W]henever the questions of discipline, or of faith, or ecclesiastical rule, custom or law have been decided by the highest of those church judicatories to which the matter has been carried, the legal tribunals must accept such decisions as final, and as binding on them, in the application to the case before them.

—Justice Samuel Freeman Miller
Watson v. Jones, 1871

$\mathcal{N}$othing ran deeper or racked the individual and collective moral conscience of nineteenth-century Americans more than the question of slavery. The Supreme Court's 1871 decision in *Watson v. Jones*, like *Vidal v. Girard*, arose out of a national controversy with theological underpinnings. This time the slavery issue provided the historical context for the Supreme Court's decision: *Watson* involved a schism between the pro- and antislavery factions of the Walnut Street Presbyterian Church in Louisville, Kentucky, and the ensuing battle over rightful ownership of the church's property after the Civil War.

Religion infused the slavery debate. Its most vehement opponents were invariably connected to a Christian denomination. Between the 1830s and the outbreak of the Civil War in 1861, many Protestant denominations issued resolutions denouncing slavery. Although most of these statements characterized slavery as a great evil that was contrary to Christian moral teachings, some constituted outright doctrinal condemnation of the practice as a sin. Religious moralizing from pulpits and in the press about the institution of slavery in the United States drove the question of its legitimacy onto the national scene.

47

Religious doctrine factored prominently in *Watson* because the case grew directly out of declarations issued by the General Assembly of the Presbyterian Church during and after the Civil War condemning slavery and supporting the Union. Whether these declarations, or any other doctrinal statement of a religious denomination for that matter, should be subjected to scrutiny by a civil court was the major issue in *Watson*. The implications of such a question for the freedom of churches to govern their internal affairs were far-reaching.

Associate Justice Samuel Freeman Miller authored the *Watson* opinion. As a dedicated Unitarian, Justice Miller's religious beliefs informed his view of slavery, the Constitution, and our nation's commitment to religious liberty. His personal aversion to slavery, dedication to the Union, and latitudinarian approach to religious opinions were expressed in his decision.

An overview of the development of denominational church opposition to slavery from colonial times to the Civil War will illustrate the depth of religious convictions enmeshed in the slavery debate and *Watson*.

THE CULTURAL/HISTORICAL CONTEXT

Imported slaves first came to the mainland English colonies in 1619 when Jamestown settlers purchased twenty Africans from a Dutch man-of-war.[1] They were servants to be held for a period of years and then freed. Gradually permanent bondage took place in the Virginia colony. In 1697 the slave trade monopoly of the Royal African Company was broken up and the slave trade was opened to English and colonial merchants on a competitive basis. Slave prices went down as a result, and after 1700 there occurred a rapid rise in the number of imported slaves to the colonies.

By 1763, there were in all the colonies approximately 230,000 slaves—16,000 in New England, 29,000 in the middle colonies, and 185,000 in the South. The total population of the colonies was close to two million people. Following the Declaration of Independence and the Revolutionary War, the thirteen newly forming states drafted constitutions. All but South Carolina and Georgia prohibited the further importation of slaves. When Thomas Jefferson and George Washington declared their opposition to slavery, Virginia and other southern states changed their laws to encourage manumission. Pennsylvania passed a gradual emancipation act in 1780 and Massachusetts's highest court held that their bill of rights outlawed the ownership of slaves.

In debating and drafting the Constitution in 1787, the issue between the large and small states regarding representation in the lower house of Congress based on population prompted another division between "free" and "slave" states. Were slaves to be counted in the population figures? Southern delegates argued that they should be included as a strategy to up their number of representatives in the House. At the same time, they argued that slaves should be considered as property, not as persons, in terms of taxation based on state populations. Opposition arose from delegates from states where slavery had disappeared or was expected to disappear. They argued that slaves should be included as persons to calculate taxation but not representation.

The "Great Compromise" occurred on July 16, 1787, when delegates agreed that the states should be represented in the House of Representatives in proportion to their populations, with three-fifths of slaves included for both representation and taxation. The logic of the calculation was that by his labor in contributing to the wealth of a state, the slave was three-fifths as productive as a white man (Article I, Section 2).

The slavery issue came up again in the drafting of legislative power to impose tariffs and conduct commerce. Southern states feared that levying duties on their crops would interfere with their slave trade as well. The delegates to the Constitutional Convention finally agreed to concessions forbidding the legislature to put a duty of more than ten dollars a head on imported slaves and prohibiting the federal outlawing of the importation of slaves until twenty years had elapsed (Article I, Section 9).

Thus, the importation of slaves was outlawed in 1809. But the domestic slave trade and the legalized institution and practice of slavery were left intact. What became known as the "peculiar institution" of slavery in the southern plantation states, so closely tied to the growth of their economy, was established by federal law and regulated in detail by state laws. It was a way of life; and eventually the breeding ground of extreme human misery. From the 1790s to 1860 equal numbers of free states and slave states were maintained as the United States expanded westward. Always, whether a state would be formed as "free" or "slave" state became an increasingly volatile problem to solve.

It was left to the churches, religious spokespersons, and individuals of conscience to address the moral contradiction of the legal practice of human bondage in the land of liberty. In the end, it would require no less than a civil war and the loss of 620,000 lives over four years to finally bring it down.

Opposition to slavery on the North American continent predated the founding of our nation. As early as the late 1600s, there was open opposition to its practice by some churches. The first opponents of slavery were religious leaders and groups in Pennsylvania—Quakers, Mennonites, and Dunkers. The first published protest against slavery in North America was by the Quakers, meeting in Germantown, Pennsylvania, in 1688.[2] In 1758, at their yearly meeting, the Quakers adopted a statement that said:

> After weighty consideration of the circumstances of Friends within the compass of this meeting, who have any negro or other slaves, the accounts and proposals now sent up from several quarters, and the rules of our discipline . . . there appears an unanimous concern prevailing, to put a stop to the increase of the practice of importing, buying, selling, or keeping slaves for term or life . . . if after the sense and judgment of this meeting . . . any professing with us should persist to vindicate it, and be concerned in importing, selling, or purchasing slaves, the respective Monthly Meetings to which they belong, should manifest their disunion with such persons, by refusing to permit them to sit in meetings for discipline, or to be employed in the affairs of Truth, or to receive from them any contribution.[3]

The Pennsylvania Quakers went further: they expelled those who did not emancipate their slaves. Before the end of the century, slaves of Quakers had practically all been set free.[4] The Quakers continued to take the lead in the abolitionist cause and became the first to petition Congress to end slavery in 1790.[5]

In the first half of the 1800s Christian denominations became more involved in the antislavery movement. Two Presbyterian bodies adopted resolutions in 1830 and 1831, which, according to historian Anson Phelps Stokes, "were highly significant as showing public opinion at this time."[6] Two of the Associate Reformed Synod's resolutions in 1830 stated:

> RESOLVED, I. That the religion of Christ Jesus requires that involuntary slavery should be removed from the Church, as soon as an opportunity, in the providence of God, is offered . . .
>
>   . . .
>
> 4. That the practice of buying or selling of slaves for gain, by any member of this Church be disapproved, and that slave-owners under

the jurisdiction of this Synod, be, as they hereby are, forbidden . . . of the evils of slavery. . . .[7]

The second Presbyterian statement came a year later by the Synod of the Associate Church. This group had long opposed slavery. Their statement read:

> RESOLVED, I. That as slavery is clearly condemned by the law of God, and has been long since judicially declared to be a moral evil by this Church, no member thereof shall, from and after this date, be allowed to hold a human being in the character or condition of a slave.[8]

At an international level from the 1820s on, slavery was subjected to ever mounting condemnation, not only from the northern churches but also from Latin American countries, where it had become illegal. Then, in 1833, the English government abolished slavery throughout the British Empire. The South, then, was an area of Western civilization (not a nation but a minority section of a nation) that cherished an institution at variance with the culture of the civilization of which it was a part. The world let the South know it disapproved.[9] American Protestant denominations, especially those with missions abroad, could not help but be responsive to the world consensus that was building against slavery on religious grounds. The South was now the only area of the Western world, with the exception of Brazil and Cuba, where slavery existed.

In 1834 the Congregational Association of Illinois adopted the following resolution:

> I. Resolved that this Association earnestly & solemnly renew their purpose by all proper means to effect the total overthrow of the system of Slavery as it prevails in the United States . . .
>
> . . .
>
> IV. That we will bear our testimony against the sin of slavery in public and private on all suitable occasions and lend our aid in the circulation of information through the medium of the press.
>
> V. That we will ever maintain the right of free description and of petition and that we recommend to the community to withhold their support from all candidates for office who deny these rights.
>
> VI. That we remember the cause of the oppressed slave in our public prayers in the sanctuary and will not knowingly admit slaveholders into our pulpits.[10]

During this period other Protestant churches were not "prepared to go as far as these Presbyterian groups" and the Congregational Association.[11] Along with William Lloyd Garrison and his New York *Liberator* newspaper, begun in 1831, much of the abolitionist work was carried on by individual preachers rather than by official pronouncements from the denominations. The clergy in the churches in the northern states, in particular, increasingly identified with the antislavery cause.[12]

During the twenty years before the outbreak of the Civil War in 1861, the slavery issue heated up to a boiling point, causing divisions in several denominations. The Methodists (1844), the Baptists (1845), the Presbyterians (1858 and 1861) all tore apart over their positions on slavery in one fashion or another. The Roman Catholic Church felt the strain but, because of its organization and structure, it did not divide. The split in the Presbyterian Church ultimately led to the church property contest entertained by the Supreme Court in *Watson v. Jones*.[13]

Although there was an increasing antislavery sentiment in the northern churches during this period, according to historians John McKivigan and Mitchell Snay, "only the traditionally antislavery denominations (including the Quakers and Freewill Baptists and a few new 'comeouter' sects founded by abolitionists) condemned all slaveholders as sinners and refused to share religious fellowship with them before the beginning of the Civil War."[14] The reaction of other churches to slavery largely depended on their openness to evangelical doctrines:

> The degree to which evangelical doctrines affected a denomination generally determined its receptivity to abolitionist arguments. For example, the liturgical churches, such as those of Catholics and those of Episcopalians, and liberal churches, such as the Unitarians, all objected to one or more aspects of abolitionists' evangelically inspired claim that slaveholders were inherently sinners and that the churches had a moral obligation to purify their communions by expelling them.[15]

Thus, it was religious doctrine—the degree to which slavery was accepted or opposed and on what grounds—that caused deep fissures within individual churches and whole denominations. Three prominent Protestant denominations faced the slavery issue head-on in the years directly preceding the Civil War. The Methodists, Baptists, and Presbyterians took varying stances at their national conferences, the effects of which rippled back to individual churches within each denomination.

The Methodists, at the 1836 general conference held in Cincinnati, were forced to consider abolitionism. After discussion it was evident that very serious differences of opinion were represented in the body. However, they adopted the following resolution against abolition of slavery by a vote of 120 to 14:

> *Resolved* by the delegates, That they disapprove in the most unqualified sense the conduct of the two members of the General Conference who are reported to have lectured in this city, Cincinnati, . . . in favor of modern abolitionism.
>
> Second, That they are decidedly opposed to modern abolitionism, and wholly disclaim any right, wish, or intention to interfere with the civil and political relation between master and slave as it exists in the slave-holding States of this Union.

On the general subject of slavery the conference resolved that "it is inexpedient to make any change in our book of Discipline respecting slavery, and that we deem it improper, therefore, to agitate the subject in the General Conference at present."[16]

In the same year, the Methodists' Baltimore conference declared itself "convinced of the great evil of slavery" but opposed to the abolitionists.[17] In 1838, the Philadelphia, Pittsburgh, and Michigan conferences followed suit by declaring that it is "incompatible with the duties and obligations of Methodist preachers to deliver abolition lectures, promote meetings in the interest of that movement, attend its conventions, or circulate its publications."[18] Stokes captures the tension: "the 'irrepressible conflict' was now on in earnest within the Methodist Church. . . . Feeling ran high. Methodist antislavery conventions were held annually from 1837 on in the North, and the Southern Methodists were equally vocal in supporting their right to hold slaves if they wished to, and condemned Northern interference."[19]

In 1860, the Methodist Episcopal Church took important action on the issue of slavery after receiving memorials signed by over 45,000 people urging a change in the book of Discipline on the subject.[20] The action involved this question and answer:

> *Question.* What shall be done for the extirpation of the evil of slavery?
>
> *Answer.* We declare that we are as much as ever convinced of the great evil of slavery. . . . We, therefore, affectionately admonish all our

preachers and people to keep themselves pure from this great evil, and to seek its extirpation by all lawful and Christian means.[21]

The Baptists from both the North and the South, at their 1841 triennial convention in Baltimore, decided simply not to discuss slavery. This was an attempt to prevent friction in the convention that was obviously brewing between participants from the two sections of the country within their denomination. To this end, the convention adopted a neutral resolution:

> Resolved, That in cooperating together as members of this Convention in the work of Foreign Missions, we disclaim all sanction, either express or implied, whether of slavery or of antislavery, but as individuals we are perfectly free to both express and promote our own views on these subjects in a Christian manner and spirit.[22]

One of the southern leaders, Dr. Richard Fuller of South Carolina, a Harvard-educated pastor, stated during the discussion of this resolution that although he thought slavery to be a "great evil" and "hoped and prayed" that it would be done away with, he felt it was not a personal sin.[23] This inconsistency was not lost on the opponents of slavery.

The slavery issue was brought to a head in 1844 when the Baptists' Alabama state convention challenged the Foreign Mission Board's authority to refuse to appoint slaveholders as missionaries. Part of their challenging resolution read:

> Whereas, The holding of property in African negro slaves has for some years excited discussion, as a question of morals, between different portions of the Baptist denomination united in benevolent enterprise . . . Resolved, That our duty at this crisis requires us to demand from the proper authorities in all those bodies to whose funds we have contributed, or with whom we have in any way been connected . . . avowal that slave-holders are eligible, and entitled, equally with non-slave-holders, to all the privileges and immunities of their several unions; and especially to receive any agency, mission, or other appointment, which may run within the scope of their operations or duties.[24]

An officer of the Foreign Mission Board replied, in a spirit of conciliation, but refused to acknowledge the right of anyone to appointment as a missionary. In his response he said:

In the thirty years in which the board has existed, no slaver-holder, to our knowledge, has applied to be a missionary. And, as we send out no domestics or servants, such an event as a missionary taking slaves with him, were it morally right, could not, in accordance with all our past arrangements or present plans, possibly occur. If, however, any one should offer himself as a missionary, having slaves, and should insist on retaining them as his property, we could not appoint him. One thing is certain, we can never be a party to any arrangement which would imply approbation of slavery.[25]

The board's decision led to the formal withdrawal of various Southern Baptist state conventions and auxiliary foreign mission societies from the national body. At the suggestion of the Foreign Missionary Society of the Virginia Baptists, the Southern Baptists met in Augusta, Georgia, in May of 1845 to set up the Southern Baptist Convention (SBC).[26]

The Presbyterians split in 1837–1838 into two groups that were called "New School" and "Old School" Presbyterians, respectively. This parting of the ways was based purely on theological, doctrinal differences, and not related to the issue of slavery. "In the years immediately following the schism neither branch wished to take a definite action on slavery."[27] But this was to change within a decade.

In 1846 at the New School Presbyterian General Assembly held in Philadelphia, a declaration was adopted to the effect that slavery was wrong, and it urged the church to do way with the evil.[28] Four years later, they adopted a stringent position calling for action:

> We exceedingly deplore the working of the whole system of slavery as it exists in our country and is interwoven with the political institutions of the slave-holding States, as fraught with many and great evils to the civil, political, and moral interests of those regions where it exists . . .
>
> . . .
>
> That, after this declaration of sentiment, the whole subject of slavery, as it exists in the church, be referred to the sessions and presbyteries, to take such action thereon as in their judgment the laws of Christianity require.[29]

The Old School Presbyterians, dominated by southern churches, had the issue arise at their 1845 General Assembly. They refused to accept the call of the antislavery delegates and stated the following:

The question which is now unhappily agitating and dividing other branches of the church, and which is pressed upon the attention of the Assembly is, whether the holding of slaves is, under all circumstances, a heinous sin, calling for the discipline of the church.

The [C]hurch of Christ is a spiritual body, whose jurisdiction extends only to the religious faith, and moral conduct of her members. She cannot legislate where Christ has not legislated, nor make terms of membership which he has not made. The question, therefore, which this Assembly is called upon to decide, is this: Do the Scriptures teach that the holding of slaves, without regard to circumstances, is a sin, the renunciation of which should be made a condition of membership in the church of Christ.[30]

The assembly went on to say, "It is impossible to answer this question in the affirmative without contradicting some of the plainest declarations of the word of God."[31] The members of the assembly, however, did not wish to be on record as saying there was no evil in the practice of slavery; hence, they added a caveat to their resolution:

In so saying, however, the Assembly are not to be understood as denying that there is evil connected with slavery. . . . Every Christian and philanthropist certainly should seek by all peaceable and lawful means the repeal of unjust and oppressive laws . . . so as to protect the slaves from cruel treatment by wicked men and secure to them the right to receive religious instruction.[32]

Southern Presbyterians, like the Baptists, suffered from biblical misunderstandings as they attempted to make the culture of their day justify their support for the institution of slavery. Southern Christians, who felt threatened and angered by the northern abolitionist movement, struggled to justify their economic way of life and white supremacist culture with biblical Scripture that would support the institution of slavery.

And so it came to be that, on the brink of the Civil War in 1861, northern and southern denominational factions and churches generally lined up with their respective states as Union or Confederate. But some states, like Kentucky, were caught in the middle between the two sides. Because the *Watson* case derives from a Presbyterian church in Kentucky and was decided after the Civil War, it is important to understand the cultural and historical context of Kentucky's experience.

In the first half of the nineteenth century, Kentucky was primarily a state of small farms that were not adaptable to large-scale use of slave labor. Slavery thus declined, and from 1833 to 1850 the importation of slaves into the state was forbidden. But in 1850 the legislature repealed this restriction, and Kentucky became a huge slave market for the lower South.

Antislavery efforts had begun in the state in the late eighteenth century within the churches and continued into the nineteenth. After 1850 Kentucky was torn by conflict over the slavery issue between radical abolitionists, an extremist proslavery faction, and a moderate group working valiantly for an acceptable compromise.

At the outbreak of the Civil War, Kentucky attempted to remain neutral, to no avail. Confederate forces invaded and occupied part of southern Kentucky until September 1861, when the state legislature voted to rid Kentucky of the Confederates and Ulysses S. Grant crossed the Ohio River and took Paducah, thus securing the state for the Union. After battles in Mill Springs, Richmond (the hometown of Justice Miller), and Perryville in 1862, there was no major fighting in the state, although Union-Confederate skirmishes continued throughout the war.

For Kentucky it was truly a civil war, as neighbors, friends, and even families became bitterly divided in their loyalties. Over thirty thousand Kentuckians fought for the Confederacy; another sixty-four thousand served in the Union ranks.

A majority of Kentuckians supported the southern Democratic Party during the Republicans' Reconstruction programs after the war (1865–1877), which was one of the bitterest periods in the annals of victors and vanquished. We will see shortly how bitter it became in Kentucky; resolutions from each Presbyterian faction immediately after the war in 1865 compelled the Supreme Court of the United States to finally resolve their church-slavery conflict in 1871.

At the outset and for the duration of the Civil War, the northern Protestant churches, almost without exception, expressed allegiance to the Union and condemnation of slavery. The southern churches, "with at least equal fervor and unanimity," supported the cause of the Confederacy.[33] Most northern denominations adopted resolutions forcefully condemning slavery after the commencement of the Civil War. A sampling of these resolutions demonstrates the unanimity of the northern churches.

In November of 1861, the Synod of New York and New Jersey, Old School Presbyterians, passed the following:

> *Resolved,* That, while we do not feel called upon to add any thing to the repeated testimonials of our Church on the subject of slavery, nor to offer any advice to the Government on the subject, still, fully believing that it lies at the foundation of all our present national troubles, we recommend to all our people to pray more earnestly than ever for its removal, and that the time may speedily come when God, by his providence, shall in his own good time and way bring it to an end, that nothing may be left of it but the painful record of its past existence.[34]

The possibility that President Lincoln would soon issue an Emancipation Proclamation to free the slaves loomed large throughout 1862, and Protestant denominations registered their support. In May of 1862 the Evangelical Lutheran Synod passed the following resolution:

> *Resolved,* That it is the deliberate judgment of this Synod that the rebellion against the constitutional Government of this land is most wicked in its inception, unjustifiable in its cause, unnatural in its character, inhuman in its prosecution, oppressive in its aims, and destructive in its results to the highest interests of morality and religion.
>
>   . . . .
>
> *Resolved,* That, whilst we regard this unhappy war as a righteous judgment of God visited upon us because of the individual and national sins of which we have been guilty, we nevertheless regard this rebellion as more immediately the natural result of the continuance and spread of domestic slavery in our land, and therefore hail the proposition of our Chief Magistrate . . . to initiate a system of constitutional emancipation.[35]

In the same month, the Black River Methodist Conference in New York resolved:

> That we recognize slavery as the cause of the present rebellion and civil war, and are more than ever convinced that either slavery or the nation must perish; and therefore we hail with joy the recent emancipation of the slaves in the District of Columbia by Congress.[36]

The president issued his formal Emancipation Proclamation on January 1, 1863, freeing all slaves in the rebellious states of the South, but it did not apply to the border states or to parts of Confederate states by then under Union control. Slavery continued to be legal in Kentucky, for example. But the proclamation psychologically now transformed the war to preserve the Union into a war for freedom. By the end of the war, over two hundred thousand black soldiers and sailors fought for the Union as liberators.

Four months after the proclamation, in May of 1863, the General Assembly of the New School Presbyterian Church issued a declaration:

> *Resolved*, That the system of human bondage, as existing in the slave-holding States . . . is not only a violation of the domestic rights of human nature, but essentially hostile to the letter and spirit of the Christian religion; that the evil character and demoralizing tendency of this system, so properly described, so justly condemned, by the General Assembly of our Church, especially, from 1818 to the present time . . . that the Assembly beseech Almighty God, in his own time, to remove the last vestige of slavery from the country, and give to the nation, preserved, disciplined, and purified, a peace that shall be based on the principles of eternal righteousness.[37]

The Unitarian Church had been somewhat silent in making any pronouncement related to slavery prior to the outbreak of the war. In June of 1863, however (while Justice Samuel Miller served as an associate justice of the Supreme Court of the United States and was an active Unitarian), the Western Unitarian Association met in Toledo, Ohio, and passed a resolution calling for the enforcement of Congress's emancipation of the slaves that year:

> *Resolved*, That we hail with gratitude and hope the rapidly growing conviction among the loyal masses of our countrymen that the existence of human slavery is inconsistent with the national safety and honor, as it is inconsistent with natural right and justice, and that we ask of the Government a thorough and vigorous enforcement of the policy of emancipation, as necessary alike to military success, to lasting peace, and to the just supremacy of the Constitution over all the land.[38]

Thus, the northern churches, one after another, universally condemned slavery as an institution contrary to Christian morality or asserted that its abolishment was the only sure way to preserve the Union.[39]

Confederate churches answered their northern counterparts in the form of a group declaration titled, "An Address to Christians Throughout the World."[40] In April of 1863, ninety-six ministers representing the

Methodists, Baptists, Episcopalians, Presbyterians, Lutherans, German Reformed, and other church groups signed the statement on behalf of their respective religious bodies.[41] The address served to justify the position of the Confederate government. It stated: "The recent Proclamation of the President of the United States, seeking the emancipation of the slaves of the South, is, in our judgment, a suitable occasion for solemn protest on the part of the people of God throughout the world."[42] This statement fairly well sums up the attitude of the churches in the southern states. None had taken a stand against secession, nor would they take a stand against slavery.

The internecine conflict within and between denominations regarding the propriety and morality of slavery undeniably impacted state and national debate over the issue and vice versa. The public declarations adopted by various denominations drove wedges between Christians in the North and the South. On a local level, acceptance or rejection of these resolutions generated lasting, personal animosities between members of individual churches. *Watson v. Jones* (1871) implicated both the national and local levels of the denominational dispute over slavery. The Supreme Court's affirmation of the Presbyterian General Assembly's resolutions condemning slavery, in essence, validated the rightfulness of the national antislavery movement. At the same time, it dealt locally with a division between the members of an individual church that occurred as a result of denominational disagreements over slavery.

It fell to Associate Justice Samuel Freeman Miller to render the decision in the *Watson* case.

THE JUSTICE: SAMUEL FREEMAN MILLER
(1816–1890)

Samuel Freeman Miller was born in Richmond, Kentucky, on April 5, 1816, the eldest of the ten children of Frederick and Patsy (Freeman) Miller.[43] Samuel grew up working on the family farm and attended school at an academy in Richmond. He excelled at school and was typically positioned at the head of his class.[44] Unfortunately, Samuel's father proved to be irresponsible in the support of his family, causing young Miller to quit school at age fourteen to help his mother raise his nine younger siblings and work the farm. He also took a job at a local pharmacy. His mother left an important impression on his life. In a letter to his brother-in-law in later years, Miller reflected on her, saying: "I think you know how much I value her, how dearly I loved, and how much of the success which has attended my life I attribute to her example, her instruction, and the qualities I have inherited from her."[45]

Miller's rise to the Supreme Court is unique because he did not originally practice law. In fact, he did not enter the profession until the age of thirty.[46] Instead, he started his professional life as a doctor. While clerking at Dr. Leverill's pharmacy in Richmond, Miller diligently studied medical texts with Leverill's guidance and encouragement. He then went on in 1835 to begin medical studies at Transylvania University in Lexington, the first college west of the Appalachians. He received his medical degree in 1838 at the age of twenty-two.[47] Miller spent the next ten years of his life practicing medicine in the backwoods of Kentucky—a lifestyle, historian Charles Gregory depicted as "riding day and night, with his drug store in his saddle bags, over the rough mountain roads of that sparsely settled region, to minister to the sick, where none were rich and most were very poor."[48]

Miller's eventual decision to give up medicine to commence the practice of law was due in part to his involvement in a spirited debating society in the small Kentucky town of Barbourville, southeast of Richmond.[49] He participated in organizing this society and was its most prominent and vocal member during its lifetime.

In this society, Miller discovered his natural ability for effective public speaking. Even more important, it drew "the mind of a country doctor in a mountain hamlet into the current of national thought and afforded him a means of relating himself to the great public questions of the day." The topics of debate ranged from mundane questions concerning the utility of public railroads to highly emotional and moral issues, for example: Is it a crime to keep slaves? It is an interesting and little-known fact that this debating society, which drew its participants from a town of only two hundred, contained among its members many future statesmen, including a Supreme Court justice, a governor of Missouri, a member of Congress, a state judge and legislator, and one of the most respected lawyers of the Southwest.[50]

It was also in Barbourville that Miller met and courted Lucy Ballinger, whose family members included several lawyers who may have had an influence on his interest in a law career. Samuel and Lucy were married in 1839, and, upon marriage, Lucy received from her father five slaves who became Miller's property under Kentucky law. Simultaneous with his involvement in the debating society and his duties as a country doctor, Miller engaged in study of the law at a local attorney's office and served as a justice of the peace. He was admitted to the Kentucky bar in 1847. He also campaigned to serve as a delegate to the Kentucky Constitutional Convention, but relented upon the request of his debating society partner, Silas Woodson, on condition that Woodson would argue the case for the gradual emancipation of the slaves. The convention voted to reject emancipation in 1849.

Disappointed that emancipation would not become a reality in Kentucky, Miller chose to leave his boyhood state—his aversion to slavery so strong that he could no longer live where slavery was legal. Thus, in 1850, he emancipated his slaves and moved to Keokuk, Iowa, a place he would call home from that point forward. Iowa had been admitted to the United States as a free state in 1846.[51]

Miller quickly climbed the professional and social ladder in Keokuk. Upon arrival, he entered into a law partnership with Lewis R. Reeves.[52] Through his activities in this practice, Miller rapidly gained respect throughout the Iowa legal community.[53] He rose at an equal pace within the political circles of Keokuk. He started out as a member of the Whig Party as he had been in Kentucky, but with its dissolution in the mid-1850s, he found that he identified more with the new Republican Party's philosophy and immersed himself in state party politics.

In 1854, Miller endured a double tragedy. Lewis Reeves died in a cholera outbreak, and Miller's wife, Lucy, passed away from consumption. Miller found himself a widower trying to run a successful law practice by himself while raising three young daughters. In time his friendship with Reeves's widow, Elizabeth Winter Reeves, grew into love; they were married in 1857 and went on to add a son and a daughter to their family.

Throughout the 1850s Miller served in many capacities within the Iowa Republican Party. These included county convention delegate, president of the Republican Party in Keokuk, candidate for state senate, organizer of rallies for 1860 presidential candidate Abraham Lincoln, and aspirant to the governorship of Iowa.[54]

Miller's ultimate place of public service, however, was not to be at the state level, but, instead, at the federal level, as a Supreme Court justice during the most internally turbulent and anguishing time in the history of the United States.

President Lincoln's appointment of Samuel Freeman Miller to the

Supreme Court in July 1862 could be characterized as extraordinary, especially considering the fact that, beyond his outstanding reputation in Iowa, Miller was relatively unknown to the rest of the nation.[55] In fact, in a revealing anecdote, when President Lincoln was asked by a supporter to consider "Mr. Miller" from Keokuk, Iowa, for the Supreme Court vacancy, Lincoln believed the request to be on behalf of another Keokuk lawyer named Daniel Miller.[56]

Two factors overcame Miller's lack of a national reputation: the zealous and unanimous support Miller received from the Iowa State Bar and, even more unusual, the overwhelming support Miller received from Congress.[57] In both House and Senate, petitions were passed for members to sign recommending that Lincoln appoint Miller. Miller received twenty-eight of thirty-two signatures from the Senate and three-fourths of the House signatures. After his appointment, Lincoln remarked that such a show of support had never occurred concerning the appointment of a justice to the Supreme Court.[58] Miller was the first candidate west of the Mississippi to be appointed to that high office.

As destiny would also have it, Miller's appointment to the Supreme Court in the turbulent second year of the Civil War put him quite literally in the middle between two fellow born-and-raised Kentuckians—U.S. President Abraham Lincoln and Confederate President Jefferson Davis.

After several years of distinguished service on the bench, Miller became a candidate for promotion to the position of chief justice. The overwhelming support that Miller received from legal journals and national newspapers served as a testimony to his quick rise to national prominence and respect.[59] However, he was passed over by President Ulysses S. Grant for Morrison R. Waite, who was sworn in on March 4, 1874.[60]

This particular episode, while disappointing to Miller, serves as an example of his character. Of the rumors of his potential appointment even before the vacancy occurred, Miller wrote to his brother-in-law, "I confess to you that it is the first time in my life that I have felt a serious and uncomfortable distrust of my capability of properly discharging the duties of a place to which I might possibly be called."[61] Miller rarely lacked in self-confidence, as this remark suggests. Indeed, it appears the only thing that seriously rattled him professionally during his lifetime was the possibility of appointment as chief justice of the Supreme Court of the United States.

From his earlier days in the Barbourville debating society, Miller's public sentiments demonstrated a clear opposition to the practice of slavery.[62] In his speech accepting the Iowa Republican Party nomination for state senator in 1856, Miller declared that slavery was the paramount and overriding issue of the day.[63] He said his observations of the practice of slavery during his many years in Kentucky had resulted in

> a conviction that both to the white man and the black it is full of evil. The institution of African Slavery as it exists in the United States, is in my judgment the most stupendous wrong, and the most prolific source of human misery, both to the master and the slave, that the sun shines upon in daily circuit around the globe.[64]

In the same speech, and very importantly for the Supreme Court decision he would render fifteen years later, Miller characterized slavery as "a creature alone of local statutory law," and thus needed to be removed, if at all, by the states themselves.[65] Miller did not consider himself an abolitionist, and he actually criticized that movement because its most radical adherents, such as William Lloyd Garrison, characterized the Constitution as a "compact with hell" that had legalized slavery from the outset.[66]

The abiding concern undergirding Miller's opposition to slavery was one of his core political beliefs: his love for the Union and the Constitution and his desire to preserve them.[67] He certainly found the practice of slavery abominable, but he also feared that the slavery issue would divide the country irrevocably. In an 1854 letter to his Kentucky brother-in-law, William Ballinger, Miller wrote: "I feel for the first time in my life that there is real danger that you and I shall live to be citizens of different nations."[68] Miller possessed an unmatched love and loyalty for this country and its founding documents, and he did not want to see the slavery issue destroy them.

Giving voice to his patriotism, Miller emphasized in his acceptance speech as a candidate for state senator that the Republican Party was dedicated to the preservation of the Union at all costs.[69] In a stirring conclusion, he declared that if the Union should be dissolved, the Republican Party would "wrap itself in the mantle of the principles of the Declaration of Independence and of the Constitution," and "fall like Caesar at the base of its pillar of eternal truth, clinging to the wreck so long as a fragment of the great temple remains."[70]

Further evidence of Miller's reverence for our nation and its founding documents is contained in his speech titled "The Formation of the Constitution." Throughout this speech, Miller calls attention to the brilliance of the Constitution and its unique approach to governance. He remarked that many of the great successes of the United States should be attributed to the American form of government as embodied in the Constitution.[71] In fact, the Constitution enabled the United States to become "the most remarkable, if not the only successful, happy, and prosperous, federated government of the world."[72] Miller characterized it as his "profound belief" that "the wisdom of man, unaided by inspiration," had never before produced a writing "so valuable to humanity."[73]

Another of Miller's later political beliefs was his vehement anti-socialism and related positions regarding personal autonomy and private property. His address to the graduating class of the State University of Iowa in 1888, entitled "An Address on the Conflict in This Country between Socialism and Organized Society," provides an excellent insight into Miller's views concerning these subjects. In the speech, the justice espoused Adam Smith's *Wealth of Nations* approach to the proper order of human affairs, commenting that "[m]an is essentially a selfish creature" and that "egoism, rather than altruism, is the controlling principle of human nature and the mainspring of its action."[74] He then attributes most of our "great steps onward in the march of progress" to man's desire "for gain or profit to himself."[75] In fact, according to Miller, the products of man's selfishness made the world more civilized, progressive, and happy.[76] He believed the egalitarian system of socialism would work to destroy man's motivations and thus create a society of laziness and indolence.[77] Indeed, Miller said that socialism would "deprive the industrious man of the rewards appropriate to the efforts which he puts forth," and thus "take away from him his main incentive to exertion."[78]

While Miller's political beliefs are easy to identify from his frequent engagements in public discussion, classifying his personal beliefs presents a greater challenge. Perhaps biographer Charles Fairman best described Miller when he referred to him as a "free thinker."[79] Fairman believes evidence of this characterization exists in Miller's experiences in the Barbourville debating society, where he learned that the best way to solve the political issues of the day was through "original thinking and public discussion." At one of the Barbourville debates, the question presented to the panel was whether there was any evidence of the existence of a Deity apart from revelation and human tradition. Miller argued that no other evidence existed, which placed him in the minority vote.[80]

Miller's close association with the Unitarian Church tends to support the characterization of Miller as a free thinker as well. A lifetime member of the Unitarian Church, he was one of the founders of the Keokuk Unitarian Church and provided his legal expertise in drawing up its articles of incorporation. He retained his membership in the Keokuk Church throughout his life and is buried in Keokuk.[81] In addition, Miller served as the president of the National Unitarian Conference for a three-year period in the mid-1880s.[82] Fairman believes the Unitarian's tolerant approach to religious views were congenial to Miller's highly critical habits of thought.[83]

However, it should be noted that some of Miller's writings demonstrate evidence of a respect for Scripture. For example, in his speech on socialism, Miller made numerous references to the Bible. He directly quoted Proverbs 30:8, "give me neither poverty nor riches," when discussing the proper goals to set for one's life. He quoted 1 Kings 20:10, "One who puts on his armor should not boast like one who takes it off," in reference to the intellectual and moral conflicts that the world would present to the graduating students. In discussing the unique capacity of the American form of government to establish a peaceful, prosperous, and secure society, he alluded to 1 Kings 4:25, which discusses the security of Judah and Israel during Solomon's reign.

Regarding his long lifetime, Miller said it had "now extended beyond the three-score years and ten allotted to man by the psalmist," which is a direct reference to Psalm 90:10. Miller also said that "it has always been considered a curse denounced upon man that he should earn his bread by the sweat of his brow," an assertion clearly based on the curse God placed on Adam in Genesis 3. In addition to these direct references to Scripture, Miller also argued that Christianity was largely responsible for the present state of the world. He stated that the Protestant Reformation "revolutionized the civilized world," and that it not only reformed religion but "carried with it the revival of learning, the increased study of the classics and poetry, the introduction of modern scientific research, and marvelous improvements in the arts."[84]

Miller's affiliation with the National Unitarian Conference (NUC) may also shed some light on his theological beliefs. Henry Bellows, who served the Union during the Civil War as president of the United States Sanitary Commission, formed the NUC in 1865.[85] His vision was to bind together, through the formation of a national institutional body, the very independent, theologically diverse, and thoroughly anti-institutional Unitarian churches across the country.[86] He believed that unity and cooperation were essential to the present and future propagation of the Unitarian Church.[87] Bellows's underlying purpose was to establish an organization that would bind churches together on the "basis of *work*, not of creed" [emphasis added].[88]

Seemingly contradicting this professed purpose, the NUC adopted a constitution, the preamble of which contained arguably evangelical terminology. The preamble stated: "Whereas the great opportunities and demands for Christian labor and consecration at this time increase our sense of the obligations of all disciples of the Lord Jesus Christ to prove their faith by self-denial and devoted service."[89] Although the presence of such phrases alienated some of the radical elements at the conference, it appeared to be representative of the majority of Unitarian churches present.[90] Indeed, the constitution was passed by an overwhelming vote of 10 to 1.

Despite the Christian nature of the preamble, initially "most of the radicals stayed within the fold." They stayed for two important reasons that revealed the true spirit of the conference. First, they were encouraged by the convention delegates' refusal to "affix a dogmatic or theological meaning" to the preamble. Second, they were convinced that the convention embodied a broader vision of harmony, conciliation, and freedom that would ultimately lead to a far more liberal and inclusive NUC in the future. To the radicals' disappointment, proposals to remove the Christian terminology from the preamble were rejected at the second annual meeting of the NUC. Because of this refusal and other conservative tendencies of the NUC, the most radical elements decided to withdraw and formed their own organization, the Free Religious Association.

The NUC was certainly not a paragon of Christian orthodoxy, despite its refusal to remove the evangelical language from its constitution. At its inception in 1865, the NUC theological spectrum ranged between a conservative wing that believed that "Christianity was of divine origin . . . and that Jesus Christ, though not a person of the Trinity, was divinely authorized to proclaim the way of salvation to erring men," and a radical wing that believed in "a wholly naturalistic interpretation of religion, which allowed no specially privileged place for Jesus."[91] As the nineteenth century progressed, so did Unitarian theology. Toward the end of Miller's life, the most influential thinkers within the Unitarian fold, such as James Freeman Clarke, demonstrated the convergence of the disparate theological views represented at the inception of the NUC into one, highly inclusive doctrinal statement.[92]

Clarke's Five Points of "the theology of the future," included: (1) The Fatherhood of God, (2) The Brotherhood of Man, (3) The Leadership of Jesus, (4) Salvation by Character, and (5) The Continuity of Human Development in all worlds, or the Progress of Mankind onward and upward forever.[93]

Unfortunately, it is difficult to pin down Miller's precise theological beliefs. The lack of direct statements by Miller regarding his faith forces speculation. However, this brief excursion into Unitarian history does help to shed some light on Miller's religious sentiments. First, it is probably a fair statement that Miller espoused the Unitarian Church's equivocal stance on theology. He did not go as far as to align himself with the radical elements of the church, but any affiliation with the Unitarian faith tends to indicate a disaffection with the traditional tenets of orthodox Christianity and, as Fairman put it, a more latitudinarian approach to religion.[94] The fact that he acted as president of an organization whose purpose was to unite Unitarians on the basis of action and not doctrine is a strong indication of a less stringent view of theological imperatives. However, perhaps Miller tended toward the more conservative wing in the Unitarian Church, given his frequent allusions to Scripture in some of his speeches and the evidence of his biblical view of the nature of man and property.

Finally, Miller's service as president of the NUC makes sense in light of his great love for the Union and his desire to preserve it. Serving as president of an organization with national unity as its overriding purpose probably gave Miller a great sense of satisfaction. He was given the opportunity to be actively involved in an effort to bring unity and reconciliation to a nation struggling to define itself in the crucial decades after the Civil War.

Miller never attained the historical notoriety of Chief Justice John Marshall (1801–1835), but he was consistently compared to him in regard to his preeminence as an interpreter of the Constitution. Upon Miller's death on October 13, 1890, at the age of seventy-four, the *Springfield Republican* gave him high praise: "When the history of constitutional interpretation for the quarter of a century succeeding the rebellion comes to be written, the most influential of all the minds engaged will probably be regarded as that of Samuel F. Miller."[95] Adding support to this view, historian Charles Gregory concluded his 1907 biographical sketch of Miller with these words:

The two chief guides to the due understanding of "that constitution" are, and must forever remain, the opinions of Chief Justice Marshall, of Virginia, and Associate Justice Miller, of Iowa. More than any others, they have written its glossary and share what we hope is the immortality of that great charter of our rights, that precious epitome of our fundamental and paramount law.[96]

THE CASE: *WATSON V. JONES* (1871)

In 1871, Justice Miller wrote the opinion in *Watson v. Jones*.[97] He had made up his mind on the slavery issue early in life—he was adamantly opposed to it. Miller's opposition to slavery grew out of several factors, including religious and moral teachings of the Unitarian Church. Yet nothing compelled him so forcefully into the antislavery camp than his love for the Union and his desire to preserve it. It comes as no surprise, then, that this Unitarian justice, born and raised in Kentucky, delivered an opinion that awarded the church property at the center of the dispute in *Watson v. Jones*, located in Kentucky, to the pro-Union members of a Christian denomination deeply divided over the issue of slavery.

In granting certiorari and deciding to hear the case on the merits, the Supreme Court was taking an unprecedented step into the area of religious liberty, a realm almost universally understood at the time to belong solely to the states.[98] Miller's decision impacted the nation's view of religious liberty. It could be argued that the Court's decision in this case was its first pronouncement regarding the meaning of the First Amendment religion clauses. While Miller did not make explicit reference to these clauses in discussing the Court's decision, the theoretical principles underlying these clauses served as the key rationale for the Court's declaration that religious bodies were to remain autonomous of civil authority.[99]

It may be recalled that in 1863, the Presbyterian General Assembly, the national governing body of the Presbyterian Church, made a public declaration condemning slavery and supporting the Union. This sent shockwaves throughout Presbyterian churches in the South, dividing many, including the church involved in *Watson*, into proslavery and antislavery factions.[100] After the war, in 1865, the factions at the national level split even wider, leaving local churches with a mixture of members from each faction in conflict. Local church property disputes multiplied.

In *Watson*, the Court had to determine, first of all, which religious body was in control of the Walnut Street Church. The case had been going through the Kentucky courts for several years with conflicting opinions as to which national Presbyterian Assembly (Old or New) had jurisdiction over the church property.

Watson arrived at the Supreme Court as a result of an ongoing struggle within the Louisville Walnut Street Presbyterian Church between the proslavery Watson faction and the antislavery Jones faction over ownership of the church and its property. The Walnut Street Church had been organized in 1842 as part of the Presbyterian Church in the United States. The church was and remained affiliated with the denomination up until the time that the conflict arose. At the time that the Walnut Street Church was affiliated with the Presbyterian Church U.S.A., the denomination's General Assembly had passed a number of resolutions condemning the practice of slavery. The *Watson* Court summarized the resolutions in its opinion by noting that: "From the beginning of the war to its close, the General Assembly of the Presbyterian Church at its annual meetings expressed in Declaratory Statements or Resolutions, its sense of the obligation of all good citizens to support the Federal government in that struggle; and when, by the proclamation of President Lincoln, emancipation of the slaves of the States in insurrection was announced, that body also expressed views favorable to emancipation, and adverse to the institution of slavery." At a national denomination meeting held in Pittsburgh in May of 1865, instructions concerning the slavery issue "were given to the Presbyteries, the Board of Missions, and to the Sessions of the churches," pertaining to applicants for employment from southern states. Specifically, the instructions stated that applicants for missionary positions, ministerial positions, or church membership should be required to state their sentiments concerning loyalty to the federal government and their position on the subject of slavery. The instructions also stated that "if it was found that they had been guilty of voluntarily aiding the war of the rebellion, or held the doctrine announced by the large body of the churches in the insurrectionary States which had organized a new General Assembly, that 'the system of negro slavery in the South is a divine institution, and that it is the peculiar mission of the Southern church to conserve that institution,' they should be required to repent and forsake these sins before they could be received."

In September of 1865, the Presbytery of Louisville, under whose immediate jurisdiction was the Walnut Street Church, rejected the denomination's instructions and published a pamphlet titled "A Declaration and Testimony against the erroneous and heretical doctrines and practices which have obtained and been propagated in the Presbyterian Church of the United States during the last five years." This declaration rejected the action of the General Assembly and, instead, declared their intention to refuse to be governed by that action. The declaration also "invited the co-operation of all members of the Presbyterian Church who shared the sentiments of the Declaration, in a concerted resistance to what they called 'the usurpation of authority' by the Assembly."

The General Assembly of 1866 responded to the declaration by offering Louisville Presbytery an opportunity for repentance and conformity or else face dissolution. The Presbytery in Louisville divided over the General Assembly's position, and those who adhered to the declaration and testimony obtained admission into "the Presbyterian Church of the Confederate States." This organization had already formally withdrawn from the General Assembly of the United States.

By January of 1866, the Walnut Street Church itself was deeply divided into two factions, both claiming authority over the church and its property. The Synod of Kentucky became divided over the issues as well.

On June 1, 1867, the General Assembly declared that the Synod recognized by Watson and his party were "in no sense a true and lawful Synod and Presbytery." They were permanently excluded from connection with or representation in the Assembly.

In *Watson*, the proslavery faction considered the General Assembly's proclamation a violation of the Presbyterian Church's constitution, which prohibited the meddling of the church in the affairs of the state.[101] That faction refused to comply with the proclamation and claimed rightful ownership of the church building and its property.[102] The Court, thus, was required to decide what level of respect civil government should give to a proclamation made by the highest authority of a hierarchically structured church.

Before addressing the *Watson* decision, it is important to briefly review how state courts were resolving this same issue. Typically, the state courts resolved these church schisms caused by the slavery issue in favor of the "dominant political tradition of the community in which the court sat."[103] For example, the Kentucky Court of Appeals decided the 1868 *Gartin v. Penick* case in favor of the proslavery political majority of its state.[104] In deciding so, it made the problematic and unprecedented statement that church constitutions should be treated as civil contracts, to be interpreted and enforced by the courts.[105] Taking this line of reasoning further, the court said that the General Assembly was not only bound by its own constitution but also was "subordinate to the political sovereignty of the civil union, which is as supreme over members of churches as over any other citizens."[106] The court then stated the logical conclusion of its argument: the General Assembly could not exercise authority outside the bounds of its own constitution or the constitutions of the state and federal governments.[107]

The state court, having arrogated to itself extraordinary authority over ecclesiastical matters, not surprisingly decided that the General Assembly's proclamation "signalized the Assembly as an intermeddling and revolutionary partisan in an unconstitutional, unholy, and bloody work of abolition by armies, and even servile war and insurrection."[108] Specifically, the proclamation was in violation of the provision of the church's constitution, which stated that "[s]ynods and councils are to handle or conclude nothing but that which is ecclesiastical, and *are not to intermeddle with civil affairs which concern the Commonwealth*" [emphasis added].[109] The court found that the appellants, who represented the proslavery faction, must be allowed to retain the church's property because the General Assembly's proclamation was unconstitutional and thus unenforceable.[110] The court argued that the General Assembly could not divest the proslavery faction of its right to possess the church based on a proclamation that violated not only its own constitution but also the principle of separation of church and state.[111]

Paradoxically, the majority's reasoning was contrary to its appeal to the principle of separation, since the effect of the state court's decision to treat ecclesiastical constitutions as civil contracts was to inject the civil government into nearly any ecclesiastical matter. Indeed, the concurring opinion warned that, although this decision provided the proslavery faction their desired result, it also meant that the civil courts would likely become "the Trojan horse" that would develop into "a most devouring enemy to the . . . churches of all denominations."[112]

The Supreme Court decided *Watson* just three years after *Gartin*. Justice Miller's decision in *Watson* demonstrated the Supreme Court's appreciation for the dangers to religious freedom posed by decisions like *Gartin*, the very dangers of which the concurring opinion in that case had warned against. In entertaining essentially the same issue that faced the Kentucky court—that is, how much deference civil courts should give to decisions made by the governing body of a hierarchically structured church—Miller arrived at a completely opposite conclusion. He rejected the meddlesome approach embodied in *Gartin* and announced a new rule to apply when a court is asked to decide an issue that implicates the decisions and declarations of ecclesiastical bodies:

> [W]henever the questions of discipline, or of faith, or ecclesiastical rule, custom, or law have been decided by the highest of these church judicatories to which the matter has been carried, the legal tribunals must accept such decisions as final, and as binding on them, in their application to the case before them.[113]

This rule was a major victory for religious freedom. It provided churches the greatest possible freedom within which to pursue their goals and conduct their affairs. Mark DeWolfe Howe commented that this rule represented the Court's belief that "a federal court would repudiate the nation's commitment to religious liberty if it allowed the lawfulness of a decree of [a] church's highest authority to be questioned."[114] Indeed, religious freedom for churches would be illusory if civil courts had the authority to pass on the propriety of church decisions pertaining to doctrine, discipline, and faith.

Justice Miller provided several reasons for his decision. First, he counseled hesitancy when issues involving ecclesiastical matters came before civil tribunals. He explained that hierarchical churches, like the Presbyterian Church in *Watson*, had developed complete bodies of constitutional and ecclesiastical law, exclusive of the civil law.[115] For even "the ablest minds," becoming familiar with these intricate laws and rules presented a significant challenge.[116] In addition, where civil courts were the experts on state law, ecclesiastical courts were the experts on their respective bodies of church law.[117] Based on this view of church authority and autonomy, Miller asserted:

> It is not to be supposed that the judges of the civil courts can be as competent in the ecclesiastical law and religious faith of all these bodies as the ablest men in each are in reference to their own. [Appealing the decision of a church tribunal to a civil court] would therefore be an appeal from the more learned tribunal in the law which should decide the case, to one which is less so.[118]

According to Miller, and the majority of the Supreme Court in *Watson*, civil courts should take great care not to invade the spiritual realm in which churches exercise ultimate authority when presented with a dispute that implicates matters of church doctrine and faith.

Hesitancy in ecclesiastical matters was an important aspect of Miller's decision, but the overriding rationale behind his opinion were the principles of religious liberty and freedom of association. Admittedly, Miller did not explicitly mention the First Amendment religion clauses; nevertheless, the rule he pronounced was inspired by the principle of religious liberty enshrined in those clauses. Appealing to the religious freedom that "lies at the foundation of our political principles," Miller asserted:

> In this country the full and free right to entertain any religious belief, to practice any religious principle and to teach any religious doctrine which does not violate the laws of morality and property, and which does not infringe personal rights, is conceded to all. The law knows no heresy, and is committed to the support of no dogma, the establishment of no sect.[119]

Miller argued that there is an unquestioned right within this nation to organize voluntary associations in order to promote religious doctrines and to govern the affairs of a church and its members.[120] These essential rights of free association and religious liberty make it imperative that a religious society be free from civil authority. Miller argued that religious authority would be completely subverted if a member of a religious society, who is displeased by one of its decisions, could have that decision overturned by a civil court.[121]

Miller pointed out that this type of subversion is exactly what had been happening in the Presbyterian schism cases decided by the state courts.[122] He viewed the decision that led to the appeal in *Watson* as a prime example. There, according to Miller, the Court of Appeals of Kentucky had engaged in "an elaborate examination of the principles of Presbyterian church government, and ended by overruling the decision of the highest judicatory of that church in the United States . . . substituting its own judgment for that of the ecclesiastical court."[123] As outlined above, the Kentucky court had done the same thing in *Gartin v. Penick*.[124] To Miller, this type of judicial review of ecclesiastical decisions deprived churches of the right to construe their own laws and was antithetical to the principles of religious freedom that were and are so dear to this nation.[125]

Miller found plentiful support for his position in other state court decisions. He quoted extensively from the South Carolina Court of Appeals noting that:

> It belongs not to the civil power to enter into or review the proceedings of a spiritual court. The structure of our government has, for the preservation of civil liberty, rescued the temporal institutions from religious interference. On the other hand, it has secured religious liberty from the invasion of the civil authority. The judgments, therefore, of religious associations, bearing on their own members, are not examinable here. . . . When a civil right depends upon an ecclesiastical matter, it is the civil court and not the ecclesiastical which is to decide. But the civil tribunal tries the civil right, and no more, taking the ecclesiastical decisions out of which the civil right arises as it finds them.[126]

Miller also approvingly quoted language from the Supreme Court of Pennsylvania to support this position of church autonomy:

> The decisions of ecclesiastical courts, like every other judicial tribunal, are final, as they are the best judges of what constitutes an offence against the word of God and the discipline of the church. Any other than those courts must be incompetent judges of matters of faith, discipline, and doctrine; and civil courts, if they should be so unwise as to attempt to supervise their judgments on matters which come within their jurisdiction, would only involve themselves in a sea of uncertainty and doubt which would do anything but improve either religion or good morals.[127]

The language Miller chose from these decisions reveals the religious liberty considerations upon which his decision so squarely rested.

Although *Watson* dealt with the narrow issue of a church property dispute, Miller's opinion had much broader implications. As Miller himself recognized, if civil courts were permitted to inquire into ecclesiastical decisions,

> the whole subject of the doctrinal theology, the usages and customs, the written laws, and fundamental organization of every religious denomination may, and must, be examined into with minuteness and care, for they would become, in almost every case, the criteria by which the validity of the ecclesiastical decree would be determined in the civil court.[128]

Essentially, opening ecclesiastical decrees regarding church property to review by civil tribunals would necessarily open all ecclesiastical decisions to similar review. Such a course of action would undercut the emerging concept of religious liberty in America.

In his analysis, Howe is very cautious in not ascribing to the Court's decision in *Watson* more significance than it actually deserves.[129] The Court itself recognized other forms of church governance to which the rule it announced would not apply. Both the congregational form of government and situations where property had been donated to a particular church and intended for the promotion of a particular faith were outside the scope of the *Watson* rule.[130] Nevertheless, the decision suggested that the ruling of a church's highest authority, whether arrived at by majority, pope, or assembly, should be respected by civil government.[131]

The Court did not propose that its decision in *Watson* was based on the First Amendment. However, it appears that the religion clauses, and the principles behind them, were the underlying justification for the decision. This contention can be supported by the fact that words from the First Amendment "make rather frequent appearances" in the text of *Watson*.[132] The decision serves as an affirmation of the First Amendment principle that government should exercise no power over religion, or, to put it in the terms of Rhode Island founder, Roger Williams, that government should not tread in the garden of the church.[133]

Watson certainly does not, as Kurt T. Lash argues in his 1995 book on the subject, signify that the Court was developing a principle of "nonestablishment." Lash defines this concept as the progression from the original understanding of the Establishment Clause as a restriction on the federal government to the modern view that the clause embodies a personal right of immunity from state establishment of religion.[134] Nothing in the language of *Watson* lends itself to reading the opinion as an embodiment of that very twentieth-century view of the Establishment Clause. In fact, the language of the opinion evinces, more than anything else, an understanding that churches possess a unique "institutional freedom" in our society that "no other collegiate body" enjoys; in other words, that churches in the United States possess an inalienable liberty to govern themselves.[135]

Howe, on the other hand, contends that the Court was in part influenced by its observation of the affect of state court approaches to this same issue. He believes *Watson* was an attempt to rectify the limiting effects these approaches were having on churches, and thus demonstrates the

Court's concern with protecting the institutional freedom of churches, not personal freedom.[136] A brief review of state court decisions regarding the proper allocation of church property sheds some light on Howe's contention.

The state courts were attempting to achieve religious liberty by treating religions equally. The means the states employed to achieve this end can be boiled down to two very different approaches. The first involved the imposition of congregational government on all churches, which negated the ecclesiastical authority of hierarchical churches and upset the intent of donors who intended their property to be used for the promotion of a particular faith.[137] The second involved the application of the doctrine of implied trust, which embroiled courts in deep theological issues and often ignored the progressive spiritual inclinations of a state's citizenry.[138]

Seeing the frustration and injustices that resulted from both of these approaches, the *Watson* Court likely drew the conclusion that Howe suggests logically follows from the experiences of the states, "liberty is not necessarily the by-product of equality."[139] Thus, the Court affirmed this nation's commitment to religious liberty by providing a rationale that recognized the right of a church to adopt the form of church government best suited to its purposes and that required civil authorities to treat ecclesiastical decisions from these organs of church government as final.

In addition, Howe refers to the 1952 *Kedroff v. St. Nicholas Cathedral* case that points not only to the motivating force behind *Watson* but also to its lasting effect in the area of religious liberty. First, as to motivation, the *Kedroff* Court characterized the *Watson* rationale as one that affirmed the importance of religious freedom for churches.[140] The Court noted that *Watson* "radiates . . . a spirit of freedom for religious organizations, an independence from secular control or manipulation—in short, power to decide for themselves, free from state interference, matters of church government as well as those of faith and doctrine."[141]

It is important to emphasize, therefore, that while the *Watson* opinion resolved the Kentucky church dispute by affirming the lower state court's ruling, it was not binding on all the states when it was decided in 1871. Even though the Fourteenth Amendment to the United States Constitution guaranteeing individual liberties and due process had been passed and ratified in 1868, it did not contemplate the concept of incorporation of the First Amendment Establishment Clause. However, when *Kedroff* was decided incorporation had become a reality, and the Court's adoption of the religious liberty rationale of *Watson* acted to bind the states with a rule of federal constitutional law.[142]

Kedroff also demonstrates the legacy of Miller's decision in *Watson*. The *Kedroff* Court, relying on *Watson*, found a New York statute concerning the administration of the Russian Orthodox Church unconstitutional.[143] The Court argued that the statute unconstitutionally wrested control of the Russian Orthodox Church of America away from the church's central governing authority located in Moscow and gave it instead to the governing authorities of the Russian Church in America.[144] As the Court said, "[f]reedom to select the clergy, where no improper methods of choice are proven, we think, must now be said to have federal constitutional protection as a part of the free exercise of religion against state interference."[145] The Court declared that the statute prohibited the free exercise of religion by allowing "the power of the state into the forbidden area of religious freedom."[146]

The *Watson* decision developed into a concept that was aptly titled the "deference doctrine" by Arlin M. Adams, a judge who served on the United States Court of Appeals for the Third Circuit.[147] In tracking the development of the deference doctrine, Adams points out the lasting influence *Watson* has had in the area of religious liberty. For example, in *Serbian E. Orthodox Church v. Milivojevich*, in 1976, the Court relied on the *Watson* rationale to overturn an Illinois court's deep probe into a church's doctrine and constitution. The Court reasoned, employing language reminiscent of the *Watson* decision, that

> where resolution of the disputes cannot be made without extensive inquiry by civil courts into religious law and polity, the First and Fourteenth Amendments mandate that civil courts shall not disturb the decisions of the highest ecclesiastical tribunal within a church of hierarchical polity, but must accept such decisions as binding on them, in their application to the religious issues of doctrine or polity before them.[148]

Similar to the court in *Watson*, the *Milivojevich* court pronounced that the Illinois court's interpretation of church doctrine had resulted in the substitution of "its interpretation of the Diocesan and Mother church constitutions for that of the highest ecclesiastical tribunals in which church law vests authority to make that interpretation."[149]

Recently, *Watson* was threatened by the development of the so-called neutral principles of law approach to settling church property disputes.[150] However, the Supreme Court has never expressly struck down the deference doctrine in favor of neutral principles, leaving the lower courts to decide which approach to adopt.[151] Some courts have strictly adopted the deference doctrine.[152] Others have relied on it only as a secondary approach if neutral principles cannot be applied to the specific situation at hand.[153] Either way, the deference commanded by the Court in *Watson* impacts First Amendment law to this day.

Miller's approach in *Watson* can be explained in several ways. First, he was dedicated to preserving the Union and the Constitution. In fact, his love of country was one of the paramount beliefs of his life and influenced many of his decisions, politically and legally. The *Watson* decision can be understood as an expression of this belief. One need only recollect Miller's words regarding the importance of preserving the Union and the value of our form of government to understand why, as Howe puts it, the post–Civil War Court "was eager to support the nation-wide authority of any church which had so organized its polity as to make its jurisdiction continental."[154] Miller was motivated to decide this case as he did, at least partly, to protect the Union and encourage the exercise of forces that would unify a divided nation.

Second, in terms of the religious liberty aspects of the decision, Miller's religious philosophy compelled his decision in *Watson*. As a Unitarian, Miller subscribed to an approach of broad tolerance for all religious beliefs and believed that churches should be allowed to operate in freedom in order to develop their own doctrines and approaches to the religious experience. Indeed, the arguably conservative National Unitarian Conference that he presided over for three years as president in the 1880s existed for the main purpose of bringing together churches that represented a wide range of theological viewpoints.

In regard to personal religious influence, it is also noteworthy that Miller referred to 1 Corinthians 13 in his *Watson* decision. His reference to this popular chapter came in the context of explaining why the Court had held back issuing its decision for an entire year:

> we have held [our decision] under advisement for a year; not uninfluenced by the hope, that since the civil commotion, which evidently lay at the foundation of the trouble, has passed away, that charity, which is so large an element in the faith of both parties, and which, by one of the apostles of that religion, is said to be the greatest of all the

Christian virtues, would have brought about a reconciliation. But we
have been disappointed. It is not for us to determine of opportion [*sic*]
the moral responsibility which attaches to the parties for this result.
We can only pronounce the judgment of the law as applicable to the
case presented to us.[155]

Third, as already noted, by 1863 Unitarian churches had publicly
condemned the practice of slavery and sought to end the evil practice by
lawful means. In a sense, the decision in *Watson* sought to condemn the
practice of slavery while upholding religious freedom concepts.

Miller's reputation as a preeminent expositor of the Constitution
should be remembered, especially in light of the lasting impact *Watson* has
had in the area of church property disputes. Miller could not frame his
1871 decision as a constitutional mandate upon the states. But the *Kedroff*
decision nearly a century later, in adopting Miller's rationale as a proper
expression of the principles underlying the First Amendment religious
clauses, made that interpretation binding upon the states, and demonstrated that Miller's preeminence as a constitutional scholar was not misplaced by the commentators of his time. Even more, it demonstrated that
the First Amendment religious clauses were certainly intended to preserve
the right of religious organizations to operate in freedom by rendering
governments virtually powerless in the area of religious disputes. The
Court's decisions in both *Watson* and *Kedroff* mainly speak of the inherent
right of churches to govern their own affairs—a right they found at the
core of the First Amendment religious clauses.

Justice Samuel Freeman Miller's attainment of a position on the
Supreme Court was extraordinary. He did not begin the practice of law
until the age of thirty, yet quickly ascended the professional ladder and
arrived on the Supreme Court after only sixteen years in practice. His primary motivations for becoming involved in public life were his opposition
to slavery and his love for the country and the Constitution. It is not difficult to imagine his feeling of justice finally rendered when the Thirteenth Amendment to the Constitution abolishing slavery was passed and
ratified in 1865. In his distinguished twenty-eight years of service on the
Supreme Court from 1862 to his death in 1890, he participated in more
than five thousand cases.

Miller's opinion in *Watson v. Jones* was clearly inspired by his deep
reverence for this country, its commitment to religious liberty, and a fervent desire to heal the wounds so deeply inflicted by the Civil War and its

aftermath. He left a legacy and a hope for future generations that these United States would truly become one nation.

NOTES

1. Richard N. Current, T. Harry Williams, and Frank Freidel, *American History: A Survey*, 2nd ed. (New York: Alfred A. Knopf, 1966). The brief factual background covering the period of slavery in the colonies to the adoption of the Constitution is based on this work.

2. Anson Phelps Stokes, *Church and State*, vol. 2, 121.

3. *A Brief Statement of the Rise and Progress of the Testimony of the Religious Society of Friends, Against Slavery and the Slave Trade* (Published by Direction of the Yearly Meeting, Philadelphia [April 1843]), microformed on LAC No. 40077 (Libr. of Am. Civilization).

4. Stokes, *Church and State*, vol. 2, 123.

5. Joseph J. Ellis, *Founding Brothers: The Revolutionary Generation* (New York: Vintage, 2000), 96–97.

6. Stokes, *Church and State*, vol. 2, 143.

7. Robert Ellis Thompson, "A History of the Presbyterian Churches in the United States," in *The American Church History Series*, vol. 6, ed. Philip Schaff et al. (New York: The Christian Literature Co., 1895), 368–69.

8. Thompson, "A History of the Presbyterian Churches," 369.

9. Current, Williams, and Freidel, *American History*, 346.

10. William W. Sweet, *Religion on the American Frontier 1783–1850: The Congregationalists*, vol. 3 (Chicago, Ill.: University of Chicago Press, 1939), 201.

11. Stokes, *Church and State*, vol. 2, 144.

12. Stokes, *Church and State*, vol. 2, 144.

13. *Watson v. Jones*, 80 U.S. 679 (1871).

14. John R. McKivigan and Mitchell Snay, eds., *Religion and the Antebellum Debate over Slavery* (Athens: University of Georgia Press, 1998), 13.

15. McKivigan and Snay, *Religion and the Antebellum Debate*, 10.

16. J. M. Buckley, "A History of Methodists in the United States," in *The American Church History Series*, vol. 5, (1896), 378–79.

17. Buckley, "A History of Methodists in the United States," 386.

18. Buckley, "A History of Methodists in the United States," 386.

19. Stokes, *Church and State*, vol. 2, 159.

20. Buckley, "A History of Methodists," 500.

21. Buckley, "A History of Methodists," 501.

22. Albert Henry Newman, "A History of the Baptists of the United States," in *The American Church History Series* (1894), 444–45.

23. Newman, "A History of Baptists," 445.

24. Newman, "A History of Baptists," 446–47.

25. Newman, "A History of Baptists," 447.

26. Stokes, *Church and State*, vol. 2, 170.

27. Stokes, *Church and State*, vol. 2, 172.

28. Stokes, *Church and State*, vol. 2, 172.

29. Thompson, "A History of the Presbyterian Churches," 372–73.

30. Thompson, "A History of the Presbyterian Churches," 369–70.

31. Thompson, "A History of the Presbyterian Churches," 370.

32. Thompson, "A History of the Presbyterian Churches," 370–71.

33. Stokes, *Church and State*, vol. 2, 203.

34. Stokes, *Church and State*, vol. 2, 204.

35. Stokes, *Church and State*, vol. 2, 205.

36. Stokes, *Church and State*, vol. 2, 206.

37. Stokes, *Church and State*, vol. 2, 207–208.

38. Stokes, *Church and State*, vol. 2, 208.

39. The Catholic clergy in America, on the other hand, had a different reaction to emancipation. In 1862 New York Archbishop John Hughes, fearing that millions of freed slaves would flee northward, declared that "we Catholics, and a vast majority of our brave troops in the field, have not the slightest idea of carrying on a war that costs so much blood and treasure just to gratify a clique of Abolitionists." Cited in James M. McPherson, *Battle Cry of Freedom: The Civil War Era* (New York: Ballantine Books, 1989), 507.

40. Stokes, *Church and State*, 242.

41. Stokes, *Church and State*, 242.

42. Stokes, *Church and State*, 242.

43. Charles Fairman, *Mr. Justice Miller and the Supreme Court: 1862–1890* (Cambridge, Mass.: Harvard University Press, 1939), 4.

44. Fairman, *Mr. Justice Miller*, 4.

45. Fairman, *Mr. Justice Miller*, 4; quoting a letter from Justice Miller to his brother-in-law, William Pitt Ballinger, 24 October 1872.

46. Charles Noble Gregory, *Samuel Freeman Miller*, in *Iowa Biographical Series*, ed. Benjamin F. Shambaugh (1907), 4.

47. Fairman, *Mr. Justice Miller*, 5.

48. Gregory, *Samuel Freeman Miller*, 4.

49. Gregory, *Samuel Freeman Miller*, 4.

50. Fairman, *Mr. Justice Miller*, 7–17.

51. Gregory, *Samuel Freeman Miller*, 5.

52. Gregory, *Samuel Freeman Miller*, 5.

53. Fairman, *Mr. Justice Miller*, 19.

54. Fairman, *Mr. Justice Miller* (discussing Miller's numerous political activities and quoting directly from some of Miller's political speeches), 28–36.

55. Samuel F. Miller, "Address Delivered Before the Iowa State Bar" (13 May 1879), *Alb. L.J.* 20 (1879): 25.

56. Fairman, *Mr. Justice Miller*, 49.

57. Miller, "Address to Iowa State Bar," 25.

58. Fairman, *Mr. Justice Miller*, 50; quoting *Iowa Historical Record*, vol. 7 (1891), 88.

59. Fairman, *Mr. Justice Miller*, 250–57 (outlining the numerous journals, magazines, and newspapers that argued that Miller was the most qualified candidate for elevation to the position).

60. Gregory, *Samuel Freeman Miller*, 57.

61. Fairman, *Mr. Justice Miller* (quoting a letter from Justice Miller to his brother-in-law, William Ballinger, 15 October 1876), 251.

62. Fairman, *Mr. Justice Miller*, 16 (describing Miller as "an active emancipationist" during his days in Kentucky).

63. Fairman, *Mr. Justice Miller*, 31; quoting Samuel F. Miller, "Address to Voters of Lee and Van Buren Counties," *Gate City*, 17 July 1856.

64. Fairman, *Mr. Justice Miller*, 30.

65. Fairman, *Mr. Justice Miller*, 30..

66. Fairman, *Mr. Justice Miller*, 31.

67. Samuel F. Miller, *The Formation of the Constitution, Address Delivered as Part of Celebration of the One Hundredth Anniversary of the Promulgation of the Constitution of the United States* (17 September 1887), reprinted in Gregory, *Samuel Freeman Miller*, 112. "The Constitution," he said, "is the first successful attempt, in the history of the world, to lay the deep and broad foundations of a government for millions of people and an unlimited territory in a single written instrument, framed and adopted in one great national effort."

68. Fairman, *Mr. Justice Miller*, 27; quoting a letter from Justice Miller to William Ballinger, 19 March 1854.

69. Fairman, *Mr. Justice Miller*, 32; citing Samuel F. Miller, "Address to Voters."

70. Fairman, *Mr. Justice Miller*, 32.

71. Miller, *The Formation of the Constitution*, 117 (arguing that the Constitution should not be given sole merit for the wonderful condition of our country, but admitting that such a contention could be supported).

72. Miller, *The Formation of the Constitution*, 114.

73. Miller, *The Formation of the Constitution*, 118.

74. Samuel F. Miller, "An Address on the Conflict in This Country between Socialism and Organized Society," a commencement speech delivered at the State University of Iowa, 19 June 1888, 10.

75. Miller, "An Address on the Conflict," 11.

76. Miller, "An Address on the Conflict," 11.

77. Miller, "An Address on the Conflict," 12.

78. Miller, "An Address on the Conflict," 12.

79. Fairman, *Mr. Justice Miller*, 14.

80. Fairman, *Mr. Justice Miller*, 14

81. Fairman, *Mr. Justice Miller*, 14

82. Fairman, *Mr. Justice Miller*, 58–59.

83. Fairman, *Mr. Justice Miller*, 14.

84. Miller, "Address on Socialism and Organized Society," 4–14.

85. Sydney E. Ahlstrom and Jonathan S. Carey, *An American Reformation: A Docu-*

mentary History of Unitarian Christianity (Middletown, Conn.: Wesleyan University Presss, 1985), 371.

86. Conrad Wright, *The Liberal Christians: Essays on American Unitarian History* (Unitarian Universalist Association, 1970), 85–88. Wright discusses the factionalism and diverse viewpoints represented within the Unitarian faith and the problems they posed for unification.

87. Wright, *The Liberal Christians*, 88.

88. Wright, *The Liberal Christians*, 94; quoting a letter from Henry Bellows to his son, R. N. Bellows, 12 December 1863, preserved by the Missouri Historical Society.

89. Joseph Henry Allen, *Historical Sketch of the Unitarian Movement since the Reformation*, in *The American Church History Series: A History of the Unitarians and the Universalists in the United States*, vol. 10, Joseph Henry Allen and Richard Eddy, eds., (New York: The Christian Literature Co., 1894), 227.

90. Wright, *The Liberal Christians*, 83–107.

91. Wright, *The Liberal Christians*, 83.

92. David Robinson, *The Unitarians and the Universalists* (Westport, Conn.: Greenwood Press, 1985), 105.

93. Robinson, *The Unitarians and the Universalists*, 105.

94. Fairman, *Mr. Justice Miller*, 14.

95. Fairman, *Mr. Justice Miller* (quoting the *Springfield Republican*), 426.

96. Gregory, *Samuel Freeman Miller*, 65.

97. *Watson v. Jones*, 80 U.S. 679 (1871).

98. Mark DeWolfe Howe, *The Garden and the Wilderness* (Chicago: University of Chicago Press, 1965), 70.

99. Howe, *The Garden and the Wilderness*, 82–84.

100. Howe, *The Garden and the Wilderness*, 74–75.

101. Kurt T. Lash, "The Second Adoption of the Establishment Clause: The Rise of the Non-Establishment Principle," *Ariz. St. L.J.* 27 (1995): 1115.

102. Lash, "The Second Adoption of the Establishment Clause," 1115.

103. Howe, *The Garden and the Wilderness*, 75–76.

104. *Gartin v. Penick*, 68 Ky. (1 Bush) 110 (1868).

105. *Gartin v. Penick*, 115, 191–200.

106. *Gartin v. Penick*, 115.

107. *Gartin v. Penick*, 116.

108. *Gartin v. Penick*, 130.

109. *Gartin v. Penick*, 119 (quoting the *Fourth Section of the 31st Chapter of the Confession of Faith*).

110. *Gartin v. Penick*, 136.

111. *Gartin v. Penick*, 119.

112. *Gartin v. Penick*, 150.

113. *Watson v. Jones*, 727.

114. Howe, *The Garden and the Wilderness*, 83.

115. *Watson v. Jones*, 729.

116. *Watson v. Jones*, 729.

117. *Watson v. Jones*, 729.
118. *Watson v. Jones*, 729.
119. *Watson v. Jones*, 728.
120. *Watson v. Jones*, 728–29. "The right to organize voluntary religious associations to assist in the expression and dissemination of any religious doctrine, and to create tribunals for the decision of controverted questions of faith within the association, and for the ecclesiastical government of all the individual members, congregations, and officers within the general association, is unquestioned."
121. *Watson v. Jones*, 729. "[I]t would be a vain consent and would lead to the total subversion of . . . religious bodies, if any one aggrieved by one of their decisions could appeal to the secular courts and have them reversed. It is of the essence of . . . religious unions, and of their right to establish tribunals for the decision of questions arising among themselves, that those decisions should be binding in all cases of ecclesiastical cognizance, subject only to such appeals as the organism itself provides for."
122. *Watson v. Jones*, 734.
123. *Watson v. Jones*, 734.
124. *Gartin v. Penick* (see preceding discussion).
125. *Watson v. Jones*, 733.
126. *Watson v. Jones*, 730–31, quoting *Harmon v. Dreher*, 17 S.C. Eq. 87 (Speers Eq. 1843).
127. *Watson v. Jones*, 732, quoting *German Reformed Church v. Seibert*, 3 Pa. 282, 291 (1846).
128. *Watson v. Jones*, 733.
129. Howe, *The Garden and the Wilderness*, 85.
130. *Watson v. Jones*, 723–27; discussing the situations of the congregationally structured church, the implied trust doctrine, and the different legal rules that applied to these situations.
131. Howe, *The Garden and the Wilderness*, 85.
132. Howe, *The Garden and the Wilderness*, 83.
133. Howe, *The Garden and the Wilderness*, 90.
134. Lash, *The Second Adoption*, 1114–18, 1131.
135. Howe, *The Garden and the Wilderness*, 90.
136. Howe, *The Garden and the Wilderness*, 86.
137. Howe, *The Garden and the Wilderness*, 41–42, 47; discussing the experiences of South Carolina and New York in imposing congregational rule on all churches, no matter their preferred governmental structure, and the impact such imposition had on church property disputes.
138. Howe, *The Garden and the Wilderness*, 46, 48–53; commenting on how judicial enforcement of religious trusts involved judges in the intricacies of church doctrine and belief and prevented churches from being able to grow and evolve theologically.
139. Howe, *The Garden and the Wilderness*, 60.
140. *Kedroff v. St. Nicholas Cathedral*, 344 U.S. 94 (1952).
141. *Kedroff v. St. Nicholas Cathedral*, 116.
142. Howe, *The Garden and the Wilderness*, 89.

143. *Kedroff v. St. Nicholas Cathedral*, 107.

144. *Kedroff v. St. Nicholas Cathedral*, 107.

145. *Kedroff v. St. Nicholas Cathedral*, 116.

146. *Kedroff v. St. Nicholas Cathedral*, 119.

147. Arlin M. Adams and William R. Hanlon, "*Jones v. Wolf*: Church Autonomy and the Religion Clauses of the First Amendment," 128 *U. Pa. L. Rev.* 1291 (1980).

148. *Serbian E. Orthodox Church v. Milivojevich*, 426 U.S. 696, 709 (1976).

149. *Serbian E. Orthodox Church v. Milivojevich*, 721.

150. Adams and Hanlon, "Church Autonomy," 1332. The authors go on to point out: "Under this approach, the aim of judicial inquiry is to ascertain the body in which the parties mutually consented to place ultimate authority over the property, so as to decide the controversy in accord with the intentions of the parties."

151. Adams and Hanlon, "Church Autonomy," 1333. Adams and Hanlon elaborate: "Despite its strong endorsement of 'neutral principles of law,' the Supreme Court indicated . . . that this approach to the resolution of church-property disputes represents merely an optional, not a required, mode of decision. Apparently, civil courts are free . . . to avoid an inquiry into the parties' actual intent and to decide church-property disputes instead on the basis of the *Watson v. Jones* fiction of an implied consent by associated churches to the authority of the general church."

152. Adams and Hanlon, "Church Autonomy," 1313.

153. Adams and Hanlon, "Church Autonomy," 1313.

154. Howe, *The Garden and the Wilderness*, 87.

155. *Watson v. Jones*, 735.

· *3* ·

The Mormon Controversy

[T]here has never been a time in any State of the Union when polygamy has not been an offense against society . . . it is impossible to believe that the constitutional guaranty of religious freedom was intended to prohibit legislation in respect to this most important feature of social life.

—Chief Justice Morrison Remick Waite
Reynolds v. United States, 1878

The great magnet of religious freedom in the United States of America attracted increasing numbers of religious dissidents to leave the conditions of their home countries in the early part of the nineteenth century. By the 1820s, a religious revival was occurring as a concentration of new, out-of-the-mainstream Christian sects was forming in upstate New York. One of these sects, founded by a dynamic, charismatic leader claiming to have received divine revelation directly from God, gained followers from America and from missionary excursions abroad. Eventually this group became the powerful Church of Jesus Christ of Latter-Day Saints—the Mormons.

In the first thirty years of the Mormons' existence, they continually moved ever westward from New York, being rejected and persecuted time and again by local communities and law enforcement authorities for their unorthodox religious beliefs and practices and their isolated communal living arrangements. One of the Mormon religious beliefs remained secret until 1852, when they were securely established in the Utah Territory: In order to obtain eternal life with God and be saved from damnation, male Mormons were obliged to engage in multiple marriages. At law, having a second wife while the first is still living was called "bigamy" and was a crime punishable by death in some states. Having multiple wives—

polygamy—encompasses bigamy.[1] It was especially this belief and practice of the Mormons, once it became known, that brought the wrath of the legal, theological, and political forces of the nation down upon them.

Reynolds v. United States was the most significant of the polygamy cases that came before the Supreme Court in the second half of the nineteenth century.[2] It was the seminal case directly dealing with the First Amendment's Religion Clauses and it has retained a lasting presence in the area of Free Exercise jurisprudence ever since. Chief Justice Morrison Waite wrote the opinion in *Reynolds* in 1878. He firmly believed that Christianity was of paramount importance in shaping America's moral and, to some degree, legal foundations. The *Reynolds* opinion was primarily rendered in opposition to the marital and sexual arrangements of Mormons in the Utah Territory.[3]

THE CULTURAL/HISTORICAL CONTEXT

Appreciating the history and religious tenets of Mormonism and the national reaction against this religious group is essential to understanding the Supreme Court's decision in *Reynolds*. As Sarah Barringer Gordon, historian of the nineteenth-century Mormon controversy, noted, "legal history occurs outside the confines of law books, out in the world of popular culture, political cartooning, and sermonizing, and even in outbreaks of violence."[4] While this assertion does not apply to all legal issues, it is certainly applicable to Mormonism.

The Church of Jesus Christ of Latter-Day Saints (the Mormon Church) had its beginnings in the 1820s when, as Mormons believe, God "periodically communicated with Joseph Smith." Smith, the founder of the Mormon Church in western New York, recorded these divine revelations in the Book of Mormon.[5] Based on these revelations, Mormons believed that polygamy was a duty of male members of the church.[6] Mormon polygamy officially commenced on April 5, 1841, the date of Smith's first plural marriage. Mormons did not, however, openly proclaim their belief in and practice of polygamy until eleven years later after they settled in Utah.[7]

Initially, it was because of their other known heterodox doctrines that Mormons met with swift, and at times violent, opposition from mainstream American religious society. Joseph Smith, a mesmerizing, fiery speaker, claimed to be the true Prophet of God who was given the final revelations in the Golden Plates that he transcribed into the *Book of Mormon*. God gave him the mission to proclaim these revelations to the world. Ordinary Christians found all of this blasphemous.

Smith decided to move with his followers from New York to Ohio but was met with an even harsher reaction. There he was beaten, tarred, and feathered in 1832.[8] The Mormons pulled up stakes again and moved to Missouri. Seventeen Mormons were massacred there in 1838 after the governor ordered all Mormons "'exterminated' or expelled from the state."[9] Smith called on the national government for protection "in the name of religious freedom." Such protection was not forthcoming, however, due to the principle of federalism then understood to be enshrined in the First Amendment: the federal government cannot interfere in supporting one religion over another. As Gordon explains, nineteenth-century Americans generally thought that the Constitution "guaranteed only that the *federal* government must respect the religious freedom of its citizens; the states were not affected by constitutional provisions aimed explicitly at the national sovereign" [emphasis in original].[10]

When Smith realized that the federal government was not going to provide protection for Mormon religious freedom, and in order to escape further persecution, he decided to move the "Saints" to Illinois, to a town he would later rename Nauvoo, meaning "the Beautiful." There he established a Mormon military and adopted for himself the "imposing rank of Lieutenant General."[11] Moreover, Smith set out to create a new theocratic government: "His was a vision of a reunited church and state, a 'Kingdom of God.'"[12] In 1844 Smith even ran for president of the United States.[13] One historian noted of this decision: "The logic behind Smith's actions in 1844 may have been a desperate one; yet, in view of his sense of mission and in view of the destiny which he believed God had in store for him and for the kingdom of God, this logic was also inevitable."[14]

Most problematic from a cultural perspective, however, was that Smith made polygamy essential to the attainment of his vision.[15] Polygamy, known as "celestial marriage" among Mormons, "was instituted for the purification and edification of the world. The children of Mormon patriarchs would usher in the Millennium."[16] Polygamy directly correlated with salvation, according to Smith, and "family quantity" was a necessity for "elite status in heaven."[17]

Americans of social conscience confronted with the issue of polygamy had an immediate and negative response. They feared that a loosening of sexual standards would result in a breakdown of society.[18]

Therefore, polygamy "proved to be the real sticking point in the Mormon relationship with their Gentile antagonists. . . . [I]t became morally intolerable to the cultural, religious, and political leaders of America."[19] Smith paid the ultimate price for his unorthodox approach to religion, marriage, and government. In 1844, Illinois officials arrested him for leading the destruction of an anti-polygamy newspaper's printing press. An angry mob attacked the jail where Smith was being detained and killed him.[20]

Smith's death, extensive persecution, and belief in his prophecies that the Saints would "become a mighty people in the midst of the Rocky Mountains" persuaded Mormons that a "Promised Land" awaited them elsewhere in the country. Under the new leadership of Brigham Young, the Mormons headed west from Illinois.[21]

Brigham Young (1801–1877) was born in Whittingham, Vermont, the ninth of eleven children.[22] His strict, religious family moved frequently to various communities throughout upstate New York where religious fervor was in full swing. It was in the town of Mendon in 1830 that he first came in contact with the teachings of the newly formed Mormon Church. Young was baptized into the Mormon Church in 1832 after other members of his immediate family had joined. He found Mormonism attractive for its emphasis on Christian primitivism, its millennialistic orientation, authoritarianism, and certain Puritan-like beliefs. But most of all Mormonism offered him an opportunity to achieve status and recognition through its lay priesthood.

Young's commitment to Mormonism strengthened when he met Joseph Smith, whom he believed to be a true prophet of God. He threw his full energies into promoting Mormonism through highly successful recruitment expeditions in America. He rose quickly through church ranks, being appointed to the Council of the Twelve Apostles in 1835. It was Young who took charge and led the Mormons from Missouri to Illinois in 1838. In 1840 he traveled to England, where he was in charge of missionary efforts, supervising the dramatic growth of Mormonism in that country. When he returned to Nauvoo, Illinois, in 1841, he embraced Smith's still secret religious belief in the practice of polygamy. (Accounts differ but his eventual marriage to as many as fifty-five women produced fifty-seven children by sixteen of his wives.)

Two years after Smith's assassination and amid continuing extreme anti-Mormon violence in Illinois, Young emerged as Mormonism's principal leader. Through careful planning and preparation, he organized the mass Mormon migration to the West. Together with his twelve thousand emigrants, Young arrived at the Great Salt Basin on July 24, 1847. It was one of the epic mass migrations in American history. Shortly, Young was elected president of the Mormon Church and governor of the provisional state of "Deseret" in 1849; he was appointed governor of the new federal territory of Utah by Congress in 1850.

Under Young's driving leadership, the Mormons prospered through successful engagement in agriculture, thriving home industries, and a profitable trade with emigrants on the way to California. Over the next thirty years, Young would go on to bring thousands of new Mormons to settlements in Utah, Nevada, Idaho, Wyoming, Arizona, and California through his Perpetual Emigrating Fund Company. As a pioneer business-man, Young had a wide variety of successful enterprises that he engaged in by himself or in partnerships. He had a wagon express company, a fer-ryboat company, and a railroad. He processed lumber, wool, sugar beets, and iron. His greatest success in the vast territories of the West was in real estate. When he died in 1877, his personal fortune was calculated at $600,000, making him the most successful Utah businessman up to that time.

Young established the theocratic kingdom of Smith's vision: "[B]etween 1847 and the mid-1880s the Utah Territory—its economic, social, and political life—was under the nearly absolute domination of the centralized hierarchy of the Church of Jesus Christ of Latter-Day Saints."[23] The hierarchy established its first government in 1847, led by John Smith (uncle of Joseph Smith) and a few select men, which yielded power to a legislature known as the "Council of Fifty" in the winter of 1849. Both governments were essentially a unification of church and state: the Council of Fifty considered itself to be "guided by divine revelation." Its purpose was to "provid[e] a congenial environment for the practice of . . . plural marriage." Thus, polygamy became legally enshrined in Utah. It was only a few short years later that the Mormons officially declared to the rest of the nation their belief in polygamy.[24]

This 1852 Mormon declaration set off an immediate national reac-tion that matched and became entwined with the passionate attacks against slavery. The Mormons could not have chosen a worse year to so proudly go public with their religious practice of polygamy. Harriet Bee-cher Stowe's *Uncle Tom's Cabin* was hot off the Boston publishing house press on March 20. Vividly portraying in novel form the real horrors and injustices of the institution of human bondage as practiced in the Ameri-can South, Stowe impassioned Christian moral sensibilities to a level not previously thought possible. By June, *Uncle Tom's Cabin* was selling at a rate of ten thousand copies a week. By October, over 150,000 copies were sold in the United States alone.[25] While the Mormons doggedly defended polygamy as one of the central tenets of their faith, the rest of the nation vilified it as debasing to women and dangerous to the nation.[26]

Mormons claimed that polygamy offered society many benefits. It provided the cure for prostitution, they said. Polygamy protected women from the "'adultery, and hypocrisy' of the rest of the country," and "in Utah all women understood that they could be united with a responsible and proven man, who would openly acknowledge his relationship with her and his paternity of her children." But most importantly, Mormons emphasized, it enabled men to replicate the marriages of the biblical patriarchs.[27]

Anti-polygamists responded to these arguments with harshness and derision. One cartoonist attached a slogan to the Mormons that stuck, "I don't care how you bring 'em, just Bring 'Em Young."

Francis Lieber, the renowned southern intellectual and father of political science, made arguments that were representative of the anti-polygamy response.[28] Lieber wrote, "The family cannot exist without marriage, nor can it develop its highest importance, it would seem, without monogamy. Civilisation, in its highest state, requires it as well as the natural organisation and wants of man."[29] Lieber renounced Mormonism as "a repulsive fraud" and "a wicked idea."[30] Other opponents made the "powerful and appealing" argument that polygamy "constituted the abuse of women." Only in a monogamous society, the argument went, could "legal protection for women be best realized." In contrast, polygamous societies engendered "rape, incest, and other crimes against women."[31]

Christianity and its moral teachings played a prominent role in America's rejection of polygamy. Not only did it produce colorful commentary, such as the remark of one Chicago pastor that "Mormonism ought to be dynamited," it also provided the moral and theological foundation for the rejection of polygamy.[32] Mormon revelation was almost universally contrary to the doctrines of orthodox Christianity. This was especially true where polygamy was concerned. The Mormons taught that polygamy was justified not only because of the practice of the Hebrew patriarchs but also because God and Jesus practiced polygamy.[33] This assertion was "a shocking blasphemy to most Christians."[34]

In addition to the moral repugnance with which the nation viewed polygamy, it also appreciated and feared the political power of the Mormons. Even though other religious eccentrics were espousing deviant sexual practices contemporaneously, none were as well organized and powerful as the Mormons: "They were the largest, the most powerful, the most explicitly political, and the best organized. They also had their own territory, and they claimed the rights of government there. They personified the power and the instability of religious innovation."[35]

Magrath explains further that the Mormon Church controlled Utah's territorial legislature and the local courts. When President Buchanan in 1857 refused to continue the practice of appointing Brigham Young as territorial governor, the Mormons set up a "ghost government" to control Utah: "Each year until 1870 the ghost government conducted a one-day session after the official legislature had adjourned, listening to a message from 'Governor' Young and ratifying the laws passed during the session." An increasing concern was the Mormon military, the Nauvoo Legion, some thirteen thousand strong by 1870.[36] Because of the country's revulsion toward polygamy and fear of Mormon political power, anti-polygamy and anti-Mormon sentiment rose to the level of a national commitment. Anti-polygamists were so successful in getting their message across that within only a few years, "it was clear that no respectable American could openly support polygamy."[37]

Prominent spokespersons against polygamy linked the practice to slavery. These individuals argued, "Polygamy was a new form of slavery, this time focused explicitly and exclusively on women."[38] Not surprisingly, Stowe put polygamy on the same level as slavery.[39] She condemned the "degrading bondage" of polygamy as vigorously as she once blasted Negro slavery.[40] The bondage to which she referred was the bondage of women trapped in a polygamous society.[41] According to Stowe, polygamy was "a cruel slavery whose chains have cut into the very hearts of thousands of our sisters" and had to be terminated.[42]

Gordon explains the analogies drawn between the practices of slavery and polygamy:

> By the late 1850s, it was commonplace to allude to the sexual exploitation of slaves and to stress the sensuality and self-indulgence of slaveholding men. The sexual abuse of women, the argument went, produced tyrants like slaveholders, incapable of governing themselves or participating in democratic government. The graphic violence that novelists argued was a corollary of polygamy catered to audiences that had been trained in the humanitarian tradition of antislavery fiction.[43]

The Republican Party quickly capitalized on the polygamy-slavery connection. The party's 1856 platform strongly rebuked polygamy and put its evils on the same level as the evils of slavery.[44] The Republicans stated that Congress has the "right" and the "imperative duty" to end "those *twin relics of barbarism*" [emphasis added], polygamy and slavery, in the territories of the United States.[45] Southerners, especially state-rights Democrats, understood the implications of the analogy; if the federal government could intrude into local affairs in Utah by outlawing polygamy, it could do the same in the South in regard to slavery.[46] While most southerners were disgusted by polygamy, they argued against the authority of the federal government to outlaw it.[47] They "blocked any action against polygamy as the first step toward emancipation" of the slaves throughout the 1850s.[48]

The southerners' fears came to fruition. Prior to the Civil War, the Democratic Party's argument that the federal government was precluded from intruding in the domestic relations of states or localities had been successful.[49] But upon the commencement of the Civil War in 1861 and the subsequent secession of the southern slave states, this argument became moot. The path to Union federal control over U.S. territories thus cleared, the Republican majority in Congress passed the Morrill Act in 1862 at the same time that President Lincoln was preparing his Emancipation Proclamation. The Morrill Act made invalid all Utah laws that "establish, support, maintain, shield, or countenance polygamy."[50] In addition, it "'punish[ed] and prevent[ed] the practice of polygamy in the Territories of the United States.'"[51] In line with the southerners' prediction, "federal legislation on polygamy was a prelude to action against slavery. Only three months later, Lincoln resolved that slaves in the Confederacy should be emancipated at the first opportune moment."[52]

It was one thing to have an act of Congress outlawing polygamy on the books, but it was quite another to actually enforce it. The Civil War finally ended in 1865; a bitter, humiliating Reconstruction period followed to bring the Confederate states back into the Union under military force and upon the terms of the Republican majority in Congress. In short, the Morrill Act, as it pertained to the Mormons, was not immediately put into action.[53]

By the 1870s, however, Republican president Ulysses S. Grant, the very Union general who had brought the South to its knees, and now eager to solidify the requirements necessary for the western territories to become states, sought additional legislation against polygamy. The

Republican Congress passed the Poland Act of 1874.[54] This new legislation took jurisdiction away from Mormon-controlled probate courts and granted jurisdiction in important cases to the federal territorial courts.[55] Brigham Young's thirty-year theocracy and economic empire was now under direct, enforceable, attack. Undaunted, Young responded to the challenge with a unique legal strategy. He died one year before the Supreme Court of the United States rendered its definitive answer to his challenge.

The question at hand in 1878 was as simple as it was complex: Were the Morrill and Poland Acts constitutional in terms of the First Amendment's guarantee of freedom of exercise of religious belief? That fundamental clause was about to be tested and defined for the first time. The Supreme Court justice who would write the historic opinion was a northern Republican who was nominated to the Court by President Grant and sworn in as chief justice in the same year the Poland Act became federal law.

THE JUSTICE: MORRISON REMICK WAITE
(1816–1888)

Morrison Waite was born on November 29, 1816, in Lyme, Connecticut.[56] Lyme had a rich and proud history, to which Waite's accomplishments would eventually add. In fact, Waite's own family played a part in the development of Lyme's history. One of his ancestors, Judge Marvin Waite, served as an elector for George Washington in the first presidential election. His mother's grandfather, Colonel Samuel Seldon, was an accomplished Revolutionary War officer. His father, Henry Matson Waite, was an attorney who would later serve as chief justice of the Connecticut Supreme Court. Waite's pedigree indicated the potential for great accomplishments, and he would not disappoint.[57]

The Waite household was dominated by political and religious activity. In politics, Waite inherited his father's preference for the Federalist and Whig Parties.[58] His father's lifetime involvement in Connecticut politics exposed a young Waite to the leading political figures of his state.[59] The political aspirations of his father rubbed off on Waite, who later ran for several political offices during his years in Ohio.

In religion, Waite grew up a low-church Episcopalian.[60] Some early anecdotes indicate that the religious influences of his childhood were quite strict. For example, Waite's great-grandmother "forbade cooking or sweeping on the Sabbath and 'always entered church at the precise and proper moment.'"[61] Waite's parents brought their children up in a less severe, though no less devout, atmosphere.[62] Waite's religious training during his childhood left an indelible mark upon him throughout his life, a mark that is most conspicuously captured in the manner in which he dealt with others. In addition, Waite's opinion in *Reynolds* was clearly influenced by his sincere Christian beliefs.

Waite demonstrated a penchant for the practice of law at a young age.[63] His aptitude for the law was cultivated by his extremely close relationship with his father. This fortunate circumstance gave Waite access to discussions about the law and the legal profession almost daily, and thus made his decision to practice law the natural and obvious choice.[64]

Waite received his education at some of the best eastern schools, including Bacon Academy in Colchester and eventually Yale College. While at Yale, he was actively involved in the Brothers-in-Unity debating society, an experience he cherished.[65] In a letter to a friend at Yale, he extolled the value of debating society training by saying that it is "felt by every student who availed himself of the privileges they afforded. . . . I cannot express myself too strongly in their favor."[66] Waite graduated from Yale in 1837, returned home to Lyme, and studied law for one year at his father's office in preparation for his entrance into the legal profession.

Upon completing his legal training, Waite decided to leave Connecticut to travel west. His uncle lived in Maumee, Ohio, and Waite decided to explore the possibilities of starting a law practice there. He arrived in Maumee in November of 1838 and obtained a job in the law offices of Samuel M. Young, whom he would remain intimate friends with throughout his life. Young was immediately impressed with Waite's legal abilities and offered him a partnership in just five months. By 1850, the Young & Waite partnership was so successful that Waite was asked to open a satellite office in Toledo, Ohio. Six years later, Young decided to quit the practice to pursue his business interests. Waite brought on his younger brother, Richard, and the firm was reorganized as M. R. & R. Waite. Waite's law practice was highly remunerative and was considered one of the Midwest's leading law firms.[67]

Contemporaneous with building his legal practice, Waite involved himself in state politics with the Whig and Republican Parties. His first involvement in state politics came at an Ohio state Whig convention, where he served as a delegate. He then ran for a congressional seat under the Whig name, but was soundly defeated by his opponent. Next, he ran for and won a seat in the state legislature, where he served only a single term. In 1862, he would again be called upon to run for a congressional seat, this time as a pro-Lincoln, Union candidate, a race he would lose by just over a thousand votes.[68]

Waite "unquestioningly accepted" the three basic propositions that the Jacksonian Democracy movement popularized: "all the people . . . should rule without suffrage restrictions; government should serve all the people; and the average person had sufficient ability to fill positions of responsibility in . . . government."[69] He also espoused a dislike for the practice of slavery, and engaged in many activities during the Civil War in support of the Union.[70]

Waite's most conspicuous service before being elevated to the Supreme Court was his appointment as one of four attorneys to represent the United States's interests before the Geneva Tribunal. The Geneva Tribunal was provided for in 1871 in the Treaty of Washington as an international board of arbitration set up to rule on the claims the American government made against the British government concerning Britain's role in covertly aiding and supporting the South during the Civil War.[71] In the course of tackling the formidable task set before him, Waite seized an opportunity to defend President Grant against a political attack concerning his handling of the Geneva arbitration. This defense of Grant against his political foes, which Waite engaged in with no urging from Grant, along with the success of the Geneva Arbitration (which secured an award of over $15 million), placed Waite in President Grant's good graces.[72]

Waite came back from Geneva to a hero's welcome. Not only was a parade organized in his honor in his hometown of Toledo, but he also received an honorary doctorate from Yale and was overwhelmingly selected by the delegates to the 1873 Ohio Constitutional Convention to serve as its president. Toward the end of the convention, President Grant surprisingly nominated Waite to be the next chief justice of the Supreme Court of the United States.[73]

Morrison Waite was a devout Christian. Evidence of his Christian faith exists both in his dedicated service to the Episcopal Church and in numerous anecdotes from his life. Waite began his religious adventure in the Congregational Church, but switched his allegiance to the Episcopal Church, in which he retained membership for the rest of his life.[74] He regularly attended church services and served as a vestryman for several Episcopal churches throughout his life.[75] Despite his lifelong Christian commitment, Waite spoke little of his faith publicly and did not "wear his religion on his sleeve."[76] Nevertheless, he was considered a "devout" Christian, who "never wavered in his personal religious commitment."[77] Waite's grandson characterized his grandfather as "a religious man, a true Christian, not ostentatiously, but quietly, deeply and sincerely."[78] Further commenting on his grandfather's faith, he said that Waite regulated his daily life by "the truest religion," and that "his highest ambitions and inspirations were drawn from it."[79]

In addition to his lifelong commitment to the Episcopal Church, personal anecdotes from Waite's life shed a great deal of light on his religious convictions. One such anecdote arose from his service as chancellor of the Smithsonian Institution. The Smithsonian was considering, for the first time in its history, opening its doors on Sunday.[80] Joseph Henry, a highly regarded nineteenth-century scientist, wrote Waite an emphatic letter in opposition, calling the proposed Sunday opening "irreverent."[81] Waite informed Henry that he would not vote against the policy to open the Smithsonian on Sunday, saying:

> I will go as far as anyone to promote the observance of the Sabbath, and to make it a day of holy thoughts, but I am by no means certain that the opening of the rooms of the Smithsonian . . . may not conduce to that end. All people will not attend church, and as Sunday is a day of rest, they are very likely to go to some other place. That place will probably be worse than the Smithsonian. My idea is, if you cant [*sic*] make people as good as you wish, make them as good as you can. Education at the Smithsonian may send some to Church. At any rate it is not likely to make anyone who wont [*sic*] go there worse.[82]

Waite's refusal to vote against the Sunday opening should not be interpreted as evidence of his own irreverence, but instead that he was not legalistic in his approach to Christianity. Waite utilized Sunday as a day of rest out of religious motives and necessity.[83]

All who came in contact with him remarked on the chief justice's outstanding character. His most conspicuous personal qualities were his kindness and humility, self-sacrificing nature, and servant attitude. The former ambassador to Russia, reminiscing about the innumerable social activities at the Waite residence, commented on Waite's humility, saying:

While his parlors were thronged with the famous people of the capital at his receptions, there were always found in the same circle many persons of merit occupying the lower ranks of society; and for these he had as warm and hearty a welcome as for the great and titled. He was the same plain and unassuming gentleman to all with whom he came in contact and had for everyone, high or low, the same frank and cheerful greeting.[84]

Waite dealt in this unassuming manner with almost everyone he came in contact with, and as a result was liked and respected by nearly everyone he knew. Indeed, his kindness and humility were major elements of his character, and were commented upon by people throughout his lifetime.[85]

Waite was also self-sacrificing. He frequently subordinated his own desires to the interests of others. He clearly conducted himself in this manner in regard to his own family. For example, Waite's friends, the Bissells, had invited his daughter, Mary, who was nicknamed Nany, to accompany them to Europe.[86] Waite's first inclination was to decline the invitation, since he did not have enough money to pay for her trip. However, his love for his daughter soon overcame this first inclination, and he permitted her to go, admitting to his friends "I have not the heart to disappoint Nany," and that "it always gives me the greatest pleasure to gratify the wishes of Nany and her mother."[87] Here, Waite placed his daughter's desire to travel to Europe over his legitimate interest to keep the embarrassing state of his financial troubles hidden. Other examples of Waite's self-sacrificing nature abound, most of which are similarly related to the well-documented historical fact that Waite consistently found himself in financial trouble.[88] Waite's financial trouble, however, did not curb his self-sacrificing nature. As the following examples illuminate, he continued to generously give to those in need.

Historian Bruce Trimble recounts one occasion where a stranger wrote to the chief justice asking if he would send him an overcoat.[89] Waite kindly informed the gentleman that he did not have an overcoat to spare, but dutifully sent the man a check, saying, "enclosed is a mite which I hope may be of some service."[90] In addition, Waite undertook the financial burden of educating the daughter of his boyhood friend, J. Alexander Hart, who could no longer provide for her education because of serious physical and financial problems. This duty came at a high cost, since she was a voice major who spent four years in Rome studying under the musical luminaries of the day.

The ultimate example of Waite's self-sacrifice and service to others was also, ironically, the primary cause of his death. In March 1888, his coachman drove Waite to the home of Senator Hearst for a reception. During the reception, Waite's coachman became ill and fell from the carriage. Waite immediately undertook the care of his coachman, exposing himself bareheaded and in his evening clothes to the cold night air. He returned to the reception, but soon felt ill and retired early; the next day he awoke with a severe cold.[91]

The chief justice contracted pneumonia in just a few short days. Waite died within a week, his death a consequence of the way in which he lived his life, occurring as a result of his willingness to serve others. Beyond Waite losing his life, ultimately, through taking care of the needs of his coachman, another aspect of the circumstances surrounding the chief justice's death is worth noting. Even though deathly ill, he insisted on attending the sessions of the Court that began just days after he had contracted his illness. Waite's motivation for doing so had nothing to do with self-interest. His concern was for his wife, who was on vacation in California. He was certain that she would become worried when she read the papers and saw that he was not in attendance. Thus, until the very end, Waite placed the concerns and needs of others above his own.[92]

Morrison Waite's life was a fine example of Christian character at work. He was a devout Episcopalian who attended church weekly and served his denomination in several official capacities. Equally indicative of his Christian faith was the manner in which he conducted his life. His personal qualities of humility, self-sacrifice, and a caring attitude toward others show the deep impact his upbringing in the Christian faith had upon him. In summing up Waite's life, historian C. Peter Magrath relates a set of "rules for life" written by Waite's brother, George, that could have easily been penned by Waite himself:

> I must practice in economy in every profitable way. . . . I must make every honorable effort to get business. I must do in private as I would in public. . . . I must improve every opportunity to speak in public. I must endeavor to make myself sociable and popular among my associates. I must improve every opportunity to cultivate the art of conversation. . . . And lastly, though by no means the least, I must do nothing of which I would be ashamed, if the whole world should find it out, keeping also in mind that passage of Scripture which says: "Know ye that for all these things, God shall one day bring thee to judgment."[93]

THE CASE: *REYNOLDS V. UNITED STATES* (1878)

Brigham Young and the Mormon Church hierarchy decided to challenge the constitutionality of the anti-polygamy laws after the passage of the Poland Act in 1874. They chose George Reynolds for the test case.[94] Reynolds was selected because his superiors "trust[ed] him to stay loyal, [and because] he was young, handsome, and the husband of only two wives. Reynolds belied the stereotype of the grizzled patriarch who married ever-younger women as he grew old and fat."[95]

Reynolds's trial on the charge of bigamy in the territorial court was hampered by Mormon obfuscation. As Gordon notes, "All the named witnesses experienced sudden gaps in their memory of George Reynolds and his reputation for having married more than one woman."[96] The prosecution attained a conviction only after bringing in Reynolds's "very pregnant second wife, who had not been coached and openly admitted that she had married him."[97] Reynolds appealed his conviction and the Supreme Court heard the case in 1878.

The Court's deliberation is historically intriguing from two vantage points. First, as Gordon aptly sets forth in her article, *Reynolds* and the Mormon controversy redefined how our nation understood the relationship between federal and local governments. Indeed, the decision to eradicate polygamy "rested on the conviction that federal control of local affairs was the only appropriate response to a violation of rights as fundamental as polygamy."[98]

Second, and more importantly, *Reynolds* demonstrates how the cultural history of the twin relics of barbarism, slavery, and polygamy were woven "into the institutional and doctrinal history of the Court."[99] Of the several polygamy cases in the last quarter of the nineteenth century, *Reynolds* most clearly shows the impact of the analogy drawn between polygamy and slavery. The Mormons relied on the infamous 1857 slavery decision in the *Dred Scott* case, "as the deciding precedent" in their appeal.[100] But the Court distanced itself from that opinion. It used "the language of bondage and tyranny" to frame the polygamy issue, arguing that the practice of polygamy "would 'fetter' the people in 'stationary despotism'" and "ultimately compromis[e] democracy."[101] The Court's argument reflected the connection that had been made between slavery and polygamy culturally in the previous decades. It also showed that by 1878 the Court held slavery and polygamy in equal disdain. Moreover, the

Court's polygamy decisions reflect the universal Christian condemnation of polygamy.

In *Reynolds v. United States*, the Supreme Court was presented with its first opportunity to seriously construe the First Amendment Free Exercise Clause. *Reynolds* presented the novel question whether the Free Exercise Clause required the creation of an exemption for an individual whose religious beliefs compelled him to engage in behavior that was contrary to a duly enacted law of the United States. The specific law in question was passed by Congress in 1862 (the Morrill Act) making the practice of polygamy illegal in the United States and its territories. The act subjected those violating the law to fines and imprisonment of up to five years.[102]

Reynolds requested an exemption from the anti-polygamy law on the basis that his religion required him to practice polygamy.[103] He demonstrated that, according to Mormon doctrine, failure to practice polygamy would result in eternal damnation.[104] In deciding that an exemption would not be granted, the Court, through Chief Justice Morrison Waite, did two important things: it provided the legal definition of the word "religion" and it outlined the belief/conduct distinction, which has had lasting impact in Free Exercise jurisprudence.

Waite argued that the Court had to define the term "religion" in order to determine whether the anti-polygamy law in question violated the constitutional guarantee of religious freedom.[105] He endeavored to define the term "religion" by engaging in an historical analysis of the Free Exercise Clause.[106] Of paramount interest to Waite's historical inquiry was the experience of the state of Virginia.

Waite appealed to the writings of James Madison and Thomas Jefferson in order to develop an understanding of the religion clauses. Madison's *Memorial and Remonstrance* provided a preliminary definition of religion by stating that religion was "the duty we owe our Creator," and that it "was not within the cognizance of civil government" to regulate.[107] Waite spent little time on Madison's writings, however, as he found Jefferson's writings a more authoritative source for the meaning of the term "religion." Consequently, Waite next turned to the 1786 Virginia Religious Freedom Act, penned by Jefferson. This act began by declaring the principle, "Almighty God hath created the mind free."[108] The act then stated the logical extension of this principle, "that to suffer the civil magistrate to intrude his powers into the field of opinion, and to restrain the profession or propagation of principles on supposition of their ill tendency, is a dangerous fallacy, which at once destroys all religious liberty."[109]

Thus, the Virginia Religious Freedom Act placed religious opinion outside the competence of governmental control. However, it also provided that civil government could regulate religiously motivated conduct, declaring that "it is time enough for the rightful purposes of civil government, for its officers to interfere, when principles break out into overt acts against peace and good order."[110] After analyzing this act, Waite turned to Jefferson's famous 1802 reply letter to the Danbury Baptist Association for more evidence of the meaning of religion and the First Amendment.

In quoting passages from Jefferson's letter, Waite treated it as definitive theoretical and legal authority for the definition of "religion" within the First Amendment.[111] Of particular importance were the following words:

> Believing with you that religion is a matter which lies solely between man and his god; that he owes account to none other for his faith or his worship; that the legislative powers of the government reach actions only, and not opinions,—I contemplate with sovereign reverence that act of the whole American people which declared that their legislature should "make no law respecting an establishment of religion or prohibiting the free exercise thereof," thus building a wall of separation between church and state.[112]

Based on the Danbury letter, Jefferson's Religious Freedom Act, and Madison's *Memorial and Remonstrance*, Waite concluded that "religion" could be defined as "mere religious belief and opinions."[113] This definition of religion meant that the area of religious freedom protected by the Free Exercise Clause was fairly narrow. In other words, it gave civil government considerable authority to regulate religious conduct.[114]

Waite's definition of religion led the Court to announce its legally significant corollary, the distinction between belief and conduct. Waite succinctly summarized this historically maligned principle when he said that the effect of the First Amendment was to deprive Congress "of all legislative power over mere opinion," but that it was "left free to reach actions which were in violation of social duties or subversive of good order."[115] Applying his definition of religion and the belief/conduct distinction to the case at hand, Waite determined that Reynolds's claim amounted to a request for an exemption for religious conduct that was subversive of good order and thus refused to grant it.[116]

While this was likely sufficient reasoning to support the law outlawing polygamy, Waite offered further justification for his opinion. First, he recounted the historical legal treatment of polygamy, noting that at common law and from the earliest history of England polygamy was considered offensive by society.[117] Even more, all the American colonies had adopted statutes similar to the statute passed earlier by James I that made polygamy an offense punishable by death.[118] Waite also considered it significant, in light of Virginia's leadership in the area of religious liberty, that the legislature of Virginia enacted an anti-polygamy statute, death penalty included, subsequent to passing its statute regarding religious freedom.[119] Waite summarized his brief historical legal analysis by declaring that

> there never has been a time in any State of the Union when polygamy has not been an offense against society, cognizable by the civil courts and punishable with more or less severity. In the face of all this evidence, it is impossible to believe that the constitutional guaranty of religious freedom was intended to prohibit legislation in respect to this most important feature of social life.[120]

Waite next focused his attention on assessing the practice of polygamy, and why that practice could not be tolerated in America, where monogamous marriages were preferred. He defended the institution of monogamous marriage on primarily sociological grounds, contending that marriage was a fundamental building block of society.[121] Using this contention as a stepping stone, Waite argued that the type of government a society adopted was largely dependent upon the form of marriage it adopted.[122] Relying on the writings of Francis Lieber, the eminent nineteenth-century legal philosopher, Waite argued that polygamy was based on a principle of patriarchy, and that when that principle was applied to large societies, it necessarily fettered "the people in stationary despotism."[123] Implicit in Waite's commentary is the contention that monogamous marriages cultivate attitudes that favor democratic institutions and forms of government.[124] Waite was concerned about the danger the practice of polygamy posed to the prevailing social order, and because of this danger reasoned that there could be no doubt that civil government had the authority to determine whether polygamy or monogamy would "be the law of social life under its dominion."[125]

Waite further explained why government could legitimately prohibit immoral, or what he called "odious," religious practices by giving examples of other religiously motivated practices that would warrant proscription.[126] He presented two hypothetical situations, one of a religion that required the practice of human sacrifices and the other where a wife believed it her religious duty to burn herself alive at her husband's funeral, and concluded that in both situations the civil government could prevent these religious adherents from carrying their beliefs into actions.[127] Waite's overriding concern was that granting exemptions to every religious objector would inevitably lead to making "the professed doctrines of religious belief superior to the law of the land, and in effect . . . permit every citizen to become a law unto himself."[128] Such an approach to the Free Exercise Clause would result in a government that would wield little to no authority over the conduct of its citizens.[129]

The private nature of Waite's religious beliefs resulted in scant evidence in his public or private statements to explain his motivations for deciding *Reynolds* as he did. However, one passing reference Waite made to his opinion indicates that his religious beliefs played a role in his disposition of the case. He mailed his decision in *Reynolds* to his former pastor, Reverend Walbridge, and in an accompanying letter said, "I send you enclosed my sermon on the religion of polygamy. . . . I hope you will not find it poisoned with heterodoxy."[130] This is a very revealing comment. First, it appears to indicate a humble attitude in Waite regarding the proper view of serious religious matters. Waite was admitting to Reverend Walbridge that he was not a theologian, and thus hoped that the clergyman would not find anything in his decision contrary to the orthodox teachings of Christianity.[131] Second, it demonstrates that Waite recognized the serious religious matters implicated by *Reynolds*, and that his decision was as much an expression of Christian orthodoxy as it was binding legal precedent.

Waite's letter to Walbridge offers the only conspicuous evidence that his decision was influenced by his religious beliefs. As a result, *Reynolds* has engendered numerous commentaries in legal journals regarding the underlying motivations behind its decision. Interestingly, scholars have come to strikingly different conclusions on what motivated Waite to decide *Reynolds* as he did, ranging from completely divorcing his decision from any religious motivation at all to arguing that it was based almost completely on Protestant Christian theology. A brief survey of these views will help to demonstrate the probable sociological and theological motivations for Waite's refusal to grant an exemption to the Mormons. Even more, it will underscore what Waite's letter to Reverend Walbridge implied—that Waite viewed his decision in *Reynolds* as an expression of his orthodox Christian faith.

Waite's sociological reasons for refusing to grant the Mormons an exemption were analyzed extensively in an article written by Maura I. Strassberg.[132] His opinion admittedly lacks depth on this point, and Strassberg's article helps to flesh out the sociological argument, especially concerning Waite's reference to Francis Lieber's writings. Strassberg explains that Waite's dependence on Lieber's writings demonstrated his belief that monogamous marriages were an essential foundation for the development of a democratic state.[133] According to Strassberg, Lieber believed the family was essential to the development and perpetuation of democracy,

> because it recreates the primitive conditions of human "sociality," for example, the need of human infants for extensive, long-term care, but also because the family promotes the development of sociality beyond these primitive physical origins to include the possibility of mutual dependence, division of labor, and the transmittal of acquired knowledge.[134]

A reading of Lieber's writings on the family confirms this characterization of his viewpoints. In his *Manual of Political Ethics*, Lieber states that the affections and relations that develop within a family unit enlarge "into affections for a wider society." The family member begins to feel "mingled" with this larger society's recollections, history, and destiny. According to Lieber, the progressive nature of the relationship between man, family, and larger society eventually "becomes a distinct and ardent devotedness to his country."[135]

Lieber opposed polygamy because its practice involved the implementation of a patriarchal principle within family relations that became easily translated into an "acceptance of absolutism and tyranny" by civil authorities.[136] The likely confusion between patriarchal authority and state authority is explained by noting the "inherent internecine conflict and competition" within a polygamous family that creates "distinctly less affectionate and altruistic family relationships."[137] Thus, the despotic nature of parental authority in polygamous marriages plants the seeds in the hearts of family members for the legitimacy of political despotism, just as monogamous family relationships plant the seed for democratic institutions.[138]

This brief description of Lieber's views on the sociological impacts of different forms of marriage helps us to understand Waite's reference to Lieber's writings in his *Reynolds* opinion. Clearly, Waite was convinced that monogamous marriage benefited our society because it laid the foundation for the preservation of democratic institutions. Also, like Lieber, he believed that polygamy fostered familial relationships and attitudes contrary to our social structure. Strassberg takes this sociological view too far, however, endeavoring to completely divorce Waite's opinion from the religious origins of the marital relationship, thus failing to fully account for his motivations.[139] In fact, in the process of analyzing Lieber's perspective on marriage, Strassberg was forced to ignore some of Lieber's own references to the sacred nature of marriage.

An example of Lieber's understanding that the marital relationship had a religious foundation can be found in his book, *Manual of Political Ethics*. Lieber noted that laws that provide for civil marriage are simply acknowledgments of the "sacredness of matrimony."[140] Even more indicative of Lieber's religious view of marriage was an article he wrote in 1855, in which he vehemently opposed the proposal that the territory of Utah be elevated to statehood.[141] In that article, he argued, "Monogamy is sanctioned by our religion, indeed, as everything pure and holy is, but monogamy goes beyond our religion. It is 'a law written in the hearts' of our race."[142] Lieber speaks of the ills of polygamy in categorical moral, not sociological, terms, calling the practice defiling, immoral, obscene, and brutal.[143] Moreover, in a footnote to his moral diatribe against polygamy, Lieber criticized the Mormons' approach to biblical interpretation, saying he would not be surprised if the Mormons also sanctioned the practice of polyandry (women having more than one husband),

> since the followers of Smith have on several occasions used the mere absence of a prohibition in the Bible as a positive permission, they may use the argument that polyandry is . . . prohibited in direct terms nowhere in that book. [Justifying polyandry in this way] would be so Mormonian, in logic as well as in morals.[144]

Lieber was opposed to polygamy for both sociological and moral reasons. And while it is true that his writings dwell more on the sociological depredations of the practice of polygamy, they also evince a religious, and even Christian, justification for opposing the practice.

While not explicitly stated, it appears that Waite viewed marriage through a Christian moral lens similar to that of Francis Lieber. Such a proposition is not difficult to defend, given the language of his opinion and the overwhelming evidence that he was a devout Christian. For instance, the chief justice echoed Lieber's remarks regarding the religious nature of marriage in his opinion when he stated that "marriage . . . from its very nature [is] a sacred obligation."[145] Waite's Christian faith informed him that polygamy was morally and sociologically repugnant, and thus he dutifully delivered "one of the most scathing indictments of what he considered an immoral practice which he ever delivered from the bench."[146]

Other commentators have interpreted *Reynolds* with a mind toward the religious undertones of the opinion. In fact, Marci A. Hamilton asserts that the *Reynolds* distinction between belief and conduct closely mirrors the Christian faith's distinction between faith and works.[147] Specifically, Hamilton proposes that the Court's doctrine closely resembles what she calls the Apostle Paul's "Preconversion Paradigm."[148] This paradigm juxtaposed two potential paths to salvation, one through faith and the other through the law.[149] According to Hamilton, under this paradigm faith and the law were mutually exclusive concepts.[150] Thus, faith was "an inward state of the individual soul," while works were "purely external."[151] Even more, works were considered "superfluous to salvation," while faith was the "antithesis of all formal concrete fulfilling of the law, for it is rooted solely in the heart's confident trust in God's grace; it is in no way a human achievement or ability."[152]

Based on this brief description of Pauline theology, Hamilton argues that "the descriptions of belief [in *Reynolds*] and faith [according to Paul] are virtually indistinguishable: each is individual, interior, private."[153] Equally similar are the descriptions of conduct and works. Both the opinion in *Reynolds* and the Apostle Paul considered conduct worldly and external, thus subjecting religiously motivated conduct to the control and regulation of civil authorities.[154] Both the belief/conduct and faith/works paradigms approach these related concepts as exclusive and independent of each other.[155] Hamilton deplores the Christian influence on this area of the law, but nevertheless recognizes that Christian theology has had and continues to have a pervasive impact on Free Exercise jurisprudence.[156]

Hamilton makes a compelling argument that Protestant theology impacted the development of the law in the area of free exercise. In fact, several other scholars support her overtly Christian interpretation of

Reynolds. For example, Harold J. Berman, in his 1986 article, analyzed the Christian nature of American society during its first hundred-plus years of existence.[157] After briefly commenting on the influence of Christianity upon the founding of our country and analyzing numerous declarations from governmental bodies that Christianity was its favored religion, Berman concluded that prior to World War I "[i]t was generally assumed that America [was] a Christian country, and more particularly, a Protestant Christian country, and that the first amendment was intended to protect Christianity by freeing it from any governmental interference . . . and by giving all denominations equality before the law."[158]

Berman's conclusion lends credence to Mark DeWolfe Howe's proposition that a "*de facto* establishment" of the Protestant Christian religion existed in America throughout the nineteenth century and into the early twentieth century.[159] In fact, Howe explicitly cites the *Reynolds* decision as a stark example of the tendency of nineteenth-century governmental bodies to officially favor the Christian faith over others.[160]

Howe viewed this implicit governmental sanction of Christianity as an expression of an evangelical theory of separation. Under this theory, the First Amendment was passed so as to secure and protect the prominent position religion occupied within American society.[161] Howe argued that the evangelical theory of separation found its origin in the writings of Roger Williams, founder of the Providence, Rhode Island, settlement in 1635, who is remembered for his admonition to protect the garden of the church from the corrupting influence of the world. A more in-depth analysis of Howe's contention that *Reynolds* was a clear example of the evangelical theory of separation will demonstrate the intimate connection between Williams's theories and the *Reynolds* decision.

The rule of law that Waite presented in *Reynolds* as the meaning of the Free Exercise Clause could be said to be the embodiment of Roger Williams's evangelical theory of separation.[162] Williams had a deep concern for the freedom of religious expression, and he was especially aware of the harm that coercive governmental pressure had on both believer and nonbeliever.[163] Indeed, he was diametrically opposed to any attempt by civil authorities to force religious compliance.[164] Despite Williams's view of the elevated status of religious liberty, he nevertheless believed that some areas of legislation overrode matters of religious conscience.[165] Included in these areas were "legislation intended to preserve the peace, legislation to prevent harms by one individual to another, legislation to enforce what he perceived to be universally recognized moral norms and legislation to provide for the financial support and military defense of government."[166]

With these words, Williams had essentially expounded the distinction between belief and conduct that Waite adopted in his decision in *Reynolds*. In fact, based on this synopsis of Williams's theory of separation, one commentator concluded that Williams would unquestionably have supported Congress's decision to outlaw polygamy, even though it did not provide for religious exemptions.[167] Williams himself justified the punishment of other immoral conduct, like adultery, on similar grounds to those the Court used to justify Congress's prohibition of polygamy.[168]

Further evidence of the connection between the developing evangelical theory of separation and Waite's rule of law in *Reynolds* exists. For example, Waite's idea that religious liberty was protected so long as religiously motivated conduct was not "in violation of social duties or subversive of good order" closely resembled the language of Rhode Island's first charter of 1663, largely the embodiment of Williams's theories:

> [N]o person within said colony, at any time hereafter, shall be any wise molested, punished, disquieted, or called in question, for any differences in opinion in matters of religion, and do not actually disturb the civil peace of our said colony; but that every person and persons may . . . freely and fully have and enjoy his and their own judgments and consciences, in matters of religious concernments . . . they behaving themselves peaceably and quietly, and not using this liberty to lycentiousness and profaneness, nor to the civil injury or outward disturbance of others.[169]

The rule Waite enunciated in *Reynolds* is remarkably similar to Roger Williams's theory of religious liberty as embodied in Rhode Island's charter. Waite's definition of religion, and his distinction between belief and conduct, both clearly evident in Williams's Rhode Island Charter, indicates the extent to which the evangelical theory of separation had influenced nineteenth-century thought regarding religious liberty.

Polygamy did not end in the Utah Territory as a result of *Reynolds*. Anti-polygamy laws encountered the same resistance after the case that civil rights laws encountered after 1964.[170] "In a territory where three-quarters of the population were Mormon, bigamy prosecution became a farce: polygamists went into hiding in the 'Underground,' key witnesses disappeared, plural wives refused to testify against their husbands, and sympathetic juries would not convict."[171]

Nevertheless, the federal government's persistence in squashing polygamy was more powerful than the Mormon resistance. The federal government had won the legal battle; indeed, Mormons could no longer "plausibly claim that they had the Constitution on their side."[172] As a result, the federal government implemented "an array of legislative invigorations of antipolygamy law" which, combined with vigorous enforcement, eventually led to the prosecution of 2,500 criminal cases.[173]

Congress took two steps that effectively ended the acceptance of polygamy in the Mormon Church. First, William M. Evarts, President Hayes's secretary of state (1877–1881), sought the support of foreign governments "to discourage Mormonism and to prevent Mormon migration to America."[174] Second, Congress enacted the Mormon Control Acts.[175]

The Mormon Control Acts consisted of two legislative enactments that were harsh responses to the Mormon's resistance to the Morrill Act.[176] The first, the Edmunds Act of 1882, made it a crime to even cohabitate with more than one woman, let alone marry more than one.[177] The law also prevented those who favored polygamy or cohabitation from serving on juries in a polygamy or cohabitation case.[178] When combined with the Supreme Court's decision in *Reynolds*, the law ensured that polygamy would be found illegal in all future cases.[179] The second legislative enactment, the Edmunds-Tucker Act of 1887, was a direct attack on the resisting Mormon Church. Under this law, the statute that granted the incorporation of the Church of Jesus Christ of Latter-Day Saints was revoked, causing the corporation to be dissolved and much of the church property to be escheated.[180]

The Supreme Court upheld the Mormon Control Acts.[181] By the late 1880s, the success of these laws was evident. The will of the Mormons to resist federal anti-polygamy laws was waning. Thousands of men, including many church leaders, had either been imprisoned for violating the anti-polygamy laws or were hiding from federal authorities.[182] Additionally, in 1885 President Grover Cleveland strengthened the federal troops in Salt Lake City; the result was the taking of valuable church property under the Edmunds-Tucker Act.[183]

On September 24, 1890, shortly after the Supreme Court upheld the Edmunds-Tucker Act, Wilford Woodruff, the president of the Church of Jesus Christ of Latter-Day Saints, issued a "Manifesto" saying, "I now publicly declare that my advice to the Latter-day Saints is to refrain from contracting any marriage forbidden by the law of the land."[184] The Mormon Church and the federal government then reconciled. Presidents

Harrison and Cleveland issued proclamations of amnesty and pardon that ended the punishment for convicted polygamists.[185] The Utah Territorial Assembly passed an anti-cohabitation law, and the Mormon-controlled constitutional convention "adopted irrevocable provisions forever outlawing polygamy in Utah."[186] Congress passed resolutions regarding the return of church real estate, and the territorial courts subsequently interpreted the Edmunds-Tucker Act so that remaining church property could be returned.[187] With the support of polygamy ended, Utah was finally granted statehood in 1896.[188]

The nineteenth-century Mormon controversy significantly impacted the development of the Supreme Court's religious liberty jurisprudence. It is not possible to fully comprehend *Reynolds* or other Supreme Court decisions regarding Mormonism and polygamy without appreciating the cultural response to the Mormon religion. The Supreme Court's treatment of the polygamy controversy demonstrates how Christian moral and ethical teachings pervaded late nineteenth-century America. Because of the moral teachings of Christianity, both the Supreme Court and the nation were committed to protect marriage based on "an unambiguous constitutional principle: one man, one woman."[189] Accordingly, marriage was returned to its monogamous roots, which strengthened the family and nation.[190]

NOTES

1. 11 *Am. Jur. 2d*, "Bigamy" § 1 (1997).

2. *Reynolds v. United States*, 98 U.S. 145 (1878).

3. The following section on the history of the Mormon religion depends heavily on an article that appeared in 2003, Sarah Barringer Gordon, "The Mormon Question: Polygamy and Constitutional Conflict in Nineteenth-Century America," *J. Sup. Ct. Hist.* 28 (2003): 14. Gordon's article superbly details the American cultural reaction to Mormonism and its practice of polygamy.

4. Gordon, "The Mormon Question," 14.

5. C. Peter Magrath, "Chief Justice Waite and the 'Twin Relics': *Reynolds v. United States*," *Vand. L. Rev.* 18 (1965): 507, 514.

6. At his original trial, Reynolds proved the following: [T]hat it was an accepted doctrine of that church "that it was the duty of all male members of said church, circumstances permitting, to practice polygamy; . . . that this duty was enjoined by different books which the members of said church believed to be of divine origin, and among others the Holy Bible, and also that the members of the church believed that the practice of polygamy was directly enjoined upon the male members thereof by the Almighty God, in a

revelation to Joseph Smith, the founder and prophet of said church; that the failing or refusing to practice polygamy by such male members of said church, when circumstances would admit, would be punished, and that the penalty for such failure and refusal would be damnation in the life to come." *Reynolds*, 161.

7. George D. Smith, "Strange Bedfellows: Mormon Polygamy and Baptist History," in *Free Inquiry*, 22 March, 1996, 41; Magrath, "Chief Justice Waite," 514–15.

8. William Alexander Linn, *The Story of the Mormons: From the Date of Their Origin to the Year 1901* (New York: Macmillan Co., 1923), 133–34.

9. Jan Shipps, *Mormonism: The Story of a New Religious Tradition* (Urbana: University of Illinois Press, 1985), 158–59.

10. Gordon, "The Mormon Question," citing Kenneth R. Bowling, "'A Tub to the Whale': The Founding Fathers and Adoption of the Federal Bill of Rights," *J. of the Early Republic* 8 (1988): 16.

11. Klaus J. Hansen, *Quest for Empire: The Political Kingdom of God and the Council of Fifty in Mormon History* (East Lansing: Michigan State University Press, 1970), 50.

12. Gordon, "The Mormon Question," citing B. Carmon Hardy, *Solemn Covenant: The Mormon Polygamous Passage* (Urbana: University of Illinois Press, 1992), 16.

13. Hansen, *Quest for Empire*, 74–78.

14. Hansen, *Quest for Empire*, 79.

15. Gordon, "The Mormon Question," 16, 18.

16. Gordon, "The Mormon Question," 18.

17. Richard N. Ostling and Joan K. Ostling, *Mormon America: The Power and the Promise* (San Francisco: Harper, 1999), 67.

18. Tyson Gibbs and Judith Campbell, "Practicing Polygamy in Black America: Challenging Definition, Legal and Social Considerations for the African American Community," *W. J. Black Studies* 23 (1999): 144; quoting D. Buice, "A Stench in the Nostrils of Honest Men: Southern Democrats and the Edmunds-Tucker Act of 1882," *A Journal of Mormon Thought* 21 (1981): 100.

19. Magrath, "Chief Justice Waite," 541.

20. See Linn, *The Story of the Mormons*, 290–301, and 305–307 for an in-depth discussion of this incident.

21. Leonard J. Arrington and Davis Bitton, *The Mormon Experience: A History of the Latter-Day Saints* (Urbana: University of Illinois Press, 1992), 95–101; quoting from B. H. Roberts, ed., *History of the Church of Jesus Christ of Latter-Day Saints: History of Joseph Smith, the Prophet, by Himself and Apostolic Interregnum*, vol. 5 (1957), 85.

22. This brief account of Brigham Young is based on the following sources: Newell G. Bringhurst, *Brigham Young and the Expanding American Frontier* (Boston: Little, Brown, 1986); Utah History Collections, http://www.media.utah.edu/UHE; and Richard N. Current et al., *American History: A Survey* (New York: Knopf, 1966), 377–78.

23. Magrath, "Chief Justice Waite," 517.

24. Hansen, *Quest for Empire*, 68–69, 123–24.

25. Ann Douglas, "Introduction," to *Uncle Tom's Cabin* by Harriet Beecher Stowe (New York: Viking Penguin, 1981), 9.

26. Mormon sincerity over the centrality of polygamy to the practice of their faith is

unquestionable. It was, in many ways, the fundamental tenet of their religion. As Peter Magrath explains:

> According to the Mormon faith, life on earth is a transitional stage where man, who has a pre-worldly existence as a spirit, takes possession of his human body. If he leads a holy life, he can look forward to afterlife in a resurrected body containing a clean spirit. Heaven in the Mormon view is made up of millions of worlds, and each man who attains godhood may aspire to inhabiting his own world solely with the members of his family. But before a spirit can make the migration from pre-existence to a heavenly state, it must first be brought to earth—hence the biblical command to "replenish the earth." As a consequence, there exists a sort of reverse population pressure: the devout Mormon desires many children . . ., since he can thereby provide more earthly bodies for the spirits and at the same time guarantee himself many heavenly companions in his future world. Obviously, the more wives one had, the more children one could father: polygamy was a part of God's grand design. Magrath, "Chief Justice Waite," 515.

27. Gordon, "The Mormon Question," 19–20.

28. Magrath, "Chief Justice Waite," 514.

29. Francis Lieber, *Manual of Political Ethics: Designed Chiefly for the Use of Colleges and Students at Law*, vol. 1 (Boston: Little & Brown, 1838), 155.

30. Francis Lieber, *On Civil Liberty and Self-Government* (Philadelphia: J. B. Lippincott & Co., 1859), 320.

31. Gordon, "The Mormon Question," 21; citing Sarah Barringer Gordon, "'Our National Hearthstone': Antipolygamy Fiction and the Sentimental Campaign against Moral Diversity in Antebellum America," *Yale J. L. & Human.* 8 (1996): 295.

32. Magrath, "Chief Justice Waite," 514; quoting Ray B. West, *Kingdom of the Saints: The Story of Brigham Young and the Mormons* (New York: Viking Press, 1957), 322.

33. Smith, *Strange Bedfellows*, 41.

34. Magrath, "Chief Justice Waite," 515.

35. See Gordon, "The Mormon Question," 20, mentioning other nineteenth-century religious minorities and their unorthodox sexual teachings.

36. Magrath, "Chief Justice Waite," 517.

37. Gordon, "The Mormon Question," 20–21.

38. Gordon, "The Mormon Question," 20–21.

39. *See* Magrath, "Chief Justice Waite," 518.

40. Magrath, "Chief Justice Waite," 518; quoting Fanny Stenhouse, *Tell It All, The Story of a Woman's Life in Polygamy* (Whitefish, Mont.: Kissinger, 1890), vi.

41. Magrath, "Chief Justice Waite," 518. Brigham Young, president of the Mormon Church, said in 1859 that the majority of Mormon women "could not be more adverse to [polygamy]" but that "they generally accept it . . . as the will of God." "Horace Greeley

Goes West, Meets Brigham Young on Overland Journey," *Salt Lake Tribune*, 15 August 1993, D1.

42. Magrath, "Chief Justice Waite," 518.

43. Gordon, "The Mormon Question," 21–22.

44. Republican Platform of 1856, in Donald Bruce Johnson, comp., *National Party Platforms 1840–1956* (Urbana: University of Illinois Press, rev. ed. 1978) vol. 1, 27. The Republican Party platform included the following statement: "*Resolved*: That the Constitution confers upon Congress sovereign powers over the Territories of the United States for their government; and that in the exercise of this power, it is both the right and the imperative duty of Congress to prohibit in the Territories those twin relics of barbarism— Polygamy, and Slavery."

45. Johnson, *National Party Platforms*, 27.

46. Gordon, "The Mormon Question," 22.

47. Gordon, "The Mormon Question," 22.

48. Gordon, "The Mormon Question," 22.

49. Gordon, "The Mormon Question," 22.

50. Magrath, "Chief Justice Waite," 520; quoting Act of 1 July 1862, ch. 126, § 1, 12 Stat. 501.

51. Linn, "The Story of the Mormons," 590.

52. Gordon, "The Mormon Question," 23.

53. His attention demanded by the Civil War, Lincoln said, "You tell Brigham Young if he will leave me alone, I'll leave him alone." Jessie L. Embry, *Mormon Polygamous Families: Life in the Principle* (Salt Lake City: University of Utah Press, 1987), 8; quoting Gustave D. Larson, *Government, Politics, and Conflict, in Utah's History* (Provo, Utah: Brigham Young University Press, 1978), 244.

54. Magrath, "Chief Justice Waite," 521; citing Kimball Young, *Isn't One Wife Enough* (New York: Holt, 1954). Kimball Young was a professional sociologist who was a direct descendant of Brigham Young. "Chief Justice Waite," 515, n.41.

55. Magrath, "Chief Justice Waite," 521; citing Act of 23 June 1874, ch. 469, § 3, 18 Stat. 253.

56. Benjamin Rush Cowen, "Morrison Remick Waite," in *Great American Lawyers: A History of the Legal Profession in America*, vol. 7 (Philadelphia: John C. Winston, 1909), 89 (William Draper Lewis, ed., Rothman Reprints, 1971).

57. C. Peter Magrath, *Morrison R. Waite: The Triumph of Character* (New York: Macmillan, 1963), 24; discussing the history of Lyme, including its close association with the Mather, Buckingham, and Griswold families and the town's role in the Revolutionary War.

58. Bruce R. Trimble, *Chief Justice Waite: Defender of the Public Interest* (Princeton: Princeton University Press, 1938), 10; discussing the active political life of Waite's father.

59. Magrath, *Triumph of Character*, 25.

60. Magrath, *Triumph of Character*, 25. The term "low-church" is not pejorative. It is simply a theological term of art for a style of worship that tends to "minimize the impor-

tance within the Church of episcopacy, priesthood, sacraments and ceremonial richness as against the more biblical and personal notes of individual conversion, the preaching of the Gospel, and salvation by faith"; Paul Kevin Meagher et al., eds., *Encyclopedic Dictionary of Religion*, vol. 2 (Philadelphia: Sisters of St. Joseph of Philadelphia, 1979), 2170.

61. Magrath, *Triumph of Character,* 25; quoting Martha Lamb, "Lyme," *Harper's Magazine* 52 (1876): 317.

62. Magrath, *Triumph of Character*, 25.

63. Trimble, *Chief Justice Waite*, 18. "As a boy he showed no extraordinary traits except an early inclination to study law. He would have been an unusual lad had he decided on any other profession. [I]t was the only profession about which he knew" (citing Martha Lamb, "Lyme").

64. Trimble, *Chief Justice Waite*, 18.

65. Magrath, *Triumph of Character*, 27–29.

66. Trimble, *Chief Justice Waite,* 21; quoting a letter from Morrison R. Waite to W.L. Kingsley, Washington, D.C., 16 June 1887.

67. Magrath, *Triumph of Character*, 31–46.

68. Magrath, *Triumph of Character*, 56–70. Throughout the 1840s and 1850s, Waite served in various capacities as secretary at meetings, president at conventions, and stump speaker for party candidates.

69. Magrath, *Triumph of Character*, 57–58.

70. Magrath, *Triumph of Character*, 70. On the subject of slavery, Waite said, "every friend of humanity will desire to see every invidious distinction abolished, and a perfect admission of equality to every class of the human race." Magrath, *Triumph of Character*, 66; quoting *Ohio State Journal*, 13 and 14 February 1850.

71. Magrath, *Triumph of Character*, 75–77.

72. Magrath, *Triumph of Character*, 85. Waite penned a shrewd defense of the Grant administration's handling of the Geneva Arbitration and sent it to a well-known journalist.

73. Magrath, *Triumph of Character*, 87–90.

74. Trimble, *Chief Justice Waite*, 18.

75. Trimble, *Chief Justice Waite*, 18. While in Washington, "he served as a vestryman of the Church of the Epiphany and represented his diocese at Episcopal conventions," Magrath, *Triumph of Character*, 306.

76. Trimble, *Chief Justice Waite*, 18.

77. Trimble, *Chief Justice Waite*, 18. Waite "never gave vent in later life to the sort of religious moralizing that characterized his contemporary, Stephen J. Field," Trimble, *"Chief Justice Waite,* 25.

78. Morrison R. Waite, "Morrison R. Waite," *W. Res. L.J.* 1 (1895): 93, 98. On file with author.

79. Waite, "Morrison R. Waite," 97–98. Although Waite was a man of "untiring diligence and orderly method" whose library was considered his sanctum, he nonetheless devoted a large portion of his time to his family.

80. Magrath, *Triumph of Character*, 305.

81. Magrath, *Triumph of Character*, 305.

82. Magrath, *Triumph of Character*, 305–306; quoting a letter from Morrison R. Waite to Joseph Henry, 26 October 1874.

83. Magrath, *Triumph of Character*, 305–306.

84. Trimble, *Chief Justice Waite*, 278–79; quoting Martha Lamb, "Lyme."

85. Magrath, *Triumph of Character*, 303–305; discussing several examples of Waite's exceeding kindness and humility in dealing with others.

86. Trimble, *Chief Justice Waite*, 279.

87. Trimble, *Chief Justice Waite*, 279; quoting a letter from Morrison R. Waite to Dr. A. F. Bissell, 21 October 1877.

88. Trimble, *Chief Justice Waite*, 280–86. Waite's financial condition reflects the conditions under which a justice of the Supreme Court had to live at that time. In reviewing correspondence from Waite to his friends concerning his financial woes, it is evident that Waite's financial condition required him to reluctantly turn down requests for aid and also required him to constantly request money from his friends, especially his former law partner, Samuel Young.

89. Trimble, *Chief Justice Waite*, 281.

90. Trimble, *Chief Justice Waite*, 281; quoting a letter from Morrison R. Waite to "My Dear Will," 21 November 1878.

91. Trimble, *Chief Justice Waite*, 286–97.

92. Trimble, *Chief Justice Waite*, 296–97.

93. Magrath, *Triumph of Character*, 32; quoting Mrs. John B. Waite, "The American Ancestry and Some of the Descendants of Henry Matson and Marie Seldon Waite" (unpublished manuscript).

94. Ostling and Ostling, *Mormon America*, 70.

95. Gordon, "The Mormon Question," 23.

96. Gordon, "The Mormon Question," 23.

97. Gordon, "The Mormon Question," 23–24.

98. Gordon, "The Mormon Question," 26.

99. Gordon, "The Mormon Question," 24. The same assertion applies to the Court's subsequent Mormon polygamy decisions.

100. Gordon, "The Mormon Question," 24.

101. Gordon, "The Mormon Question"; quoting *Reynolds*, 166.

102. Act of 1 July 1862, 12 Stat. 501.

103. *Reynolds v. United States*, 161.

104. *Reynolds v. United States*, 161.

105. *Reynolds v. United States*, 162.

106. *Reynolds v. United States*, 162.

107. *Reynolds v. United States*, 163; quoting James Madison, *Memorial and Remonstrance against Religious Assessments* (1785).

108. Va. Code Ann. § 57-1 (2001).

109. Va. Code Ann. § 57-1 (2001).

110. Va. Code Ann. § 57-1 (2001).

111. *Reynolds v. United States,* 164.

112. *Reynolds v. United States;* quoting *Jefferson's Works,* vol. 8, 113.

113. *Reynolds v. United States,* 166.

114. For a thorough critique of the *Reynolds* decision as it relates to this point, see Marci A. Hamilton, "The Belief/Conduct Paradigm in the Supreme Court's Free Exercise Jurisprudence: A Theological Account of the Failure to Protect Religious Conduct," 54 *Ohio St. L.J.* (1993): 713.

115. *Reynolds v. United States,* 164.

116. *Reynolds v. United States,* 166–67.

117. *Reynolds v. United States,* 164.

118. *Reynolds v. United States,* 165.

119. *Reynolds v. United States,* 165.

120. *Reynolds v. United States,* 165.

121. *Reynolds v. United States,* 165. While Waite recognized that marriage is a sacred institution, he also considered it a civil contract that may be regulated by the state: "Upon [marriage] society may be said to be built, and out of its fruits spring social relations and social obligations and duties, with which government is necessarily required to deal."

122. *Reynolds v. United States,* 165–66.

123. *Reynolds v. United States,* 166.

124. *Reynolds v. United States,* 166.

125. *Reynolds v. United States,* 166.

126. Waite commented, "polygamy has always been odious among the northern and western nations of Europe," *Reynolds,* 164.

127. *Reynolds v. United States,* 166.

128. *Reynolds v. United States,* 167.

129. *Reynolds v. United States,* 167.

130. Trimble, *Chief Justice Waite,* 244 n18.

131. Waite's use of the word "heterodoxy" is helpful in coming to this conclusion. Heterodox is defined as "contrary to or different from an acknowledged standard, a traditional form, or an established religion," *Merriam-Webster's Collegiate Dictionary,* 10th ed. (Springfield, Mass.: Merriam-Webster, 1993), 544. Thus, it appears Waite's hope that his former pastor would not find his opinion "poisoned with heterodoxy," was a hope that Rev. Walbridge would find that his opinion was in conformity with Christian teachings.

132. Maura I. Strassberg, "Distinctions of Form or Substance: Monogamy, Polygamy and Same-Sex Marriage," *N.C.L. Rev.* 75 (1997): 1501.

133. Strassberg, "Distinctions of Form or Substance," 1509–10.

134. Strassberg, "Distinctions of Form or Substance," 1518–19.

135. Lieber, *Manual of Political Ethics,* 112–13.

136. Strassberg, "Distinctions of Form or Substance," 1522.

137. Strassberg, "Distinctions of Form or Substance," 1522.

138. Strassberg, "Distinctions of Form or Substance," 1522.

139. It should be noted that the ultimate goal of Strassberg's article is to lay a founda-tion for the acceptance of homosexual marriage by making the argument that *Reynolds* explained "the traditional Western prohibition against polygamy as arising from a view of polygamy as a social offense 'subversive of good order,' rather than as a religious offense." "Distinctions of Form or Substance," 1562. According to Strassberg, this leaves the door open for same-sex marriage because "the monogamous nature of same-sex marriage, together with the fundamental personal, religious, political, ideological, and geographic diversity of homosexuals, prevents same-sex marriage from being a threat to our political ideals in the way Mormon polygamous marriage was." (1594). Strassberg, however, failed to understand that Waite's notion of "good order" had both moral and sociological aspects that found their foundation, ultimately, in Protestant political theory.

140. Lieber, *Manual of Political Ethics*, 152.

141. Francis Lieber, "The Mormons: Shall Utah Be Admitted into the Union?" *Put-nam's Monthly* 5 (March, 1855): 225.

142. Lieber, "The Mormons," 234.

143. Lieber, "The Mormons," 233.

144. Lieber, "The Mormons," 233 n.t.

145. *Reynolds*, 165.

146. Trimble, *Chief Justice Waite*, 244.

147. Hamilton, "The Belief/Conduct Paradigm," 771–87; discussing Pauline theology as a motivation for Waite's opinion in *Reynolds*. Hamilton is an associate professor of law at Benjamin N. Cardozo School of Law.

148. Hamilton, "The Belief/Conduct Paradigm," 775.

149. Hamilton, "The Belief/Conduct Paradigm," 775.

150. Hamilton, "The Belief/Conduct Paradigm," 776.

151. Hamilton, "The Belief/Conduct Paradigm," 776.

152. Hamilton, "The Belief/Conduct Paradigm," 777; quoting H. J. Schoeps, *Paul: The Theology of the Apostle in the Light of Jewish Religious History* (London: Lutterworth Press, 1961), 212.

153. Hamilton, "The Belief/Conduct Paradigm," 784.

154. Hamilton, "The Belief/Conduct Paradigm," 784.

155. Hamilton, "The Belief/Conduct Paradigm," 784.

156. Hamilton argues that the belief/conduct distinction "places no restrictions on the Protestant Christian's capacity to commune with the divine." However, the distinction impinges this capacity for Peyotists, because for them "communication with the divine does not occur as it can for the Christian, through unspoken communication from the soul, but rather takes place through the activity of taking peyote," "The Belief/Conduct Paradigm," 786–87.

157. Harold J. Berman, "Religion and Law: The First Amendment in Historical Per-spective," *Emory L.J.* 35 (1986): 777.

158. Berman, "Religion and Law," 777–83.

159. Mark DeWolfe Howe, *The Garden and the Wilderness* (1965), 11–12; arguing that the de facto establishment led to a "host of favoring tributes to faith" by government enti-

ties. By using the phrase "*de facto* establishment," Howe suggests that the religious institution as a whole is a social reality and not "maintained and activated" by forces kindled directly by government.

160. Howe, *The Garden and the Wilderness*, 102.

161. Howe, *The Garden and the Wilderness*, 19.

162. *Reynolds*, 164. "Congress was deprived of all legislative power over mere opinion, but was left free to reach actions which were in violation of social duties or subversive of good order."

163. Timothy L. Hall, "Roger Williams and the Foundations of Religious Liberty," *B.U.L. Rev.* 71 (1991): 455, 474. Hall summarizes the major tenets of Williams's political theories.

164. Hall, "Roger Williams," 469–70. "Persecution for cause of conscience was the 'bloudy tenet' that robbed the world of peace and delivered the souls of men over to a "Soule or Spirituall Rape," more abominable in the eyes of God than 'to force and ravish the Bodies of all the Women in the World.'" (Quoting Roger Williams, "The Bloudy Tenet, Of Persecution," in *Complete Writings of Roger Williams*, vol. 3, ed. Russell and Russell [New York: Russell & Russell, 1963.])

165. Hall, "Roger Williams," 523.

166. Hall, "Roger Williams," 523

167. Hall, "Roger Williams," 519.

168. Hall, "Roger Williams," 519.

169. Hall, "Roger Williams," 477; quoting *Sources of Our Liberties: Documentary Origins of Individual Liberties in the United States Constitution and Bill of Rights*, R. Perry and J. Cooper, rev. ed. (Chicago: American Bar Foundation, 1978), 170.

170. Magrath, "Chief Justice Waite," 534.

171. Magrath, "Chief Justice Waite," 534.

172. Gordon, "The Mormon Question," 25.

173. Gordon, "The Mormon Question," 25, 29 n.29.

174. Magrath, "Chief Justice Waite," 534.

175. Magrath, "Chief Justice Waite," 534.

176. Magrath, "Chief Justice Waite," 534.

177. Magrath, "Chief Justice Waite," 535; citing Act of 22 March 1882, 22 Stat. 31.

178. Magrath, "Chief Justice Waite," 535.

179. Magrath, "Chief Justice Waite," 535.

180. Magrath, "Chief Justice Waite," 535; citing Act of 3 March 1887, 24 Stat. 635.

181. See *Late Corporation of the Church of Jesus Christ of Latter-Day Saints v. United States*, 136 U.S. 1 (1890), upholding the escheating of the church's property; *Clawson v. United States*, 114 U.S. 477 (1885), upholding the exclusion of those favoring polygamy or cohabitation from juries that were to hear such cases.

182. Magrath, "Chief Justice Waite," 538.

183. Magrath, "Chief Justice Waite," 538.

184. Magrath, "Chief Justice Waite," 540; citing Young, *Isn't One Wife Enough?* 376–77.

185. Magrath, "Chief Justice Waite," 540; citing Young, *Isn't One Wife Enough?* 376–77.

186. Magrath, "Chief Justice Waite," 540–41.

187. Magrath, "Chief Justice Waite," 540–41.

188. Magrath, "Chief Justice Waite," 540–41.

189. Magrath, "Chief Justice Waite," 534.

190. See Lieber, *Manual of Political Ethics*, 155–60.

· 4 ·

The Christian Nation Debate

This is a Christian nation.

—Justice David Josiah Brewer
Holy Trinity v. United States, 1892

The Civil War, for all time to come, was America's defining moment. It transformed the United States from a Union of independent states with a weak central government to a nation in which the Constitution was the supreme law of the land and the federal government took precedence over the states.

During the course of the war, President Lincoln reflected the dramatic psychological shift in America's self-perception in his speeches. Civil War historian James McPherson detected the subtle transition: In his first inaugural address in 1861, just months after the attack on Fort Sumter, Lincoln used the word "Union" twenty times and the word "nation" none. In his first message to Congress in July 1861, he referred to "Union" thirty-two times and "nation" three times. At Gettysburg on November 19, 1863, he did not use the word "Union" at all but spoke only of the "nation," five times, "to invoke a new birth of freedom and nationalism for the United States." And finally, in his second inaugural address on March 4, 1865, Lincoln thought back over the past four years and spoke of one side seeking to dissolve the *Union* in 1861 and the other accepting the challenge of war to preserve the *nation*.[1]

Lincoln had always been dedicated to the principle that from its founding, the United States was indivisible—no state could withdraw at will—and he never spoke of the "Confederate States" or the "Confederacy." The Civil War was the result of a rebellion that had to be put down by military force. The triumph of the North was a triumph for the concept of the United States as a national state composed of a single people irrevocably bound together. To make that concept a permanent reality, Lincoln determined that it was time to amend the Constitution.

Eleven of the first twelve amendments to the Constitution limited the powers of the federal government. In 1864, Lincoln initiated the process of centralizing authority that would apply to all the states so that, as he said at Gettysburg, "government of the people, by the people, for the people, shall not perish from the earth." After he was assassinated on April 14, 1865, Congress passed and the states ratified the program Lincoln had begun. In rapid succession from 1865 to 1870 three new amendments were added to the Constitution. The Thirteenth Amendment (1865) abolished slavery within the United States and its territories. The Fourteenth Amendment (1868) made it clear that all persons born or naturalized in the United States were citizens and as such could not be deprived by any state of "life, liberty or property without due process of law," and due process was to be interpreted by the Supreme Court of the United States. This amendment gave the country its first national definition of citizenship. The Fifteenth Amendment (1870) gave all citizens the right to vote regardless of race, color, or previous condition of servitude.[2]

The idea that the Constitution could be changed and was the ultimate instrument that could heal the wounds of a divided nation and bind the people together prompted two citizen's groups and a congressman to propose three other amendments in the decade after the Civil War. One organization interpreted the Constitution through the lens of Christianity and wanted the United States to be defined in those terms. The second organization interpreted the Constitution as a secular document that deliberately kept religion out of government control. The congressional proposal endeavored to create a national educational system to once and for all resolve the controversy between public and sectarian schools and to more uniformly educate its burgeoning population.

These three amendment efforts came before Congress in the mid-1870s. Although none of them met with successful passage, continuous public debates over the issues permeated the thirty-five years after the Civil War to the end of the century. As native-born and foreign-born residents of the various states grew accustomed to the notion that they were equal citizens of a democratic nation and therefore had a voice in its governance, they began to think deeply about the question: What *kind* of nation is the United States of America?

Near the close of the nineteenth century, the case of *Church of the Holy Trinity v. United States* came before the Supreme Court. It involved a foreign-born clergyman who had been contracted by a New York church to perform duties as pastor and rector. The issue was whether or not hiring a foreigner violated the federal Contract Labor Act of 1885. Justice David Josiah Brewer, foreign-born himself and son of Congregational missionary parents, wrote the unanimous opinion in favor of the clergyman. In his lengthy opinion reviewing the intentions of the Framers of the Constitution and the historical laws and traditions that were embedded in American culture, he gave final definition to all the debates that had taken place in the preceding decades by declaring: "This is a Christian nation."

THE CULTURAL/HISTORICAL CONTEXT

The National Association to Secure the Religious Amendment to the Constitution was formed in 1864.[3] Its purpose, apparent from its title, was to propose the following change to the preamble to the Constitution (in brackets):

> WE, THE PEOPLE OF THE UNITED STATES, [recognizing the being and attributes of Almighty God, the Divine Authority of the Holy Scriptures, the Law of God as the paramount rule, and Jesus, the Messiah, the Savior and Lord of all,] in order to form a more perfect union, establish justice, ensure domestic tranquility, provide for the common defense, promote the general welfare, and secure the blessings of liberty to ourselves and to our posterity, do ordain and establish this Constitution for the United States of America.[4]

This organization changed its name in 1875 to the National Reform Association (NRA), the name by which it is known to this day.[5]

The NRA proposed this amendment in order to rectify what they called the "religious defect" in our Constitution, namely, that it "contained no acknowledgement of God, or the Christian religion." The NRA believed this omission constituted "a dishonor . . . to the God of nations."[6] In light of these views and of the Christian character of the United States, the NRA believed the "Constitution ought to contain explicit evidence of the Christian character and purpose of the nation which frames it."[7]

The NRA's amendment received strong support from Protestant-dominated nineteenth-century America. The organization's membership roles included many prominent citizens, including the governors and ex-governors of several states, sitting and retired state and federal court judges, public school administrators, church officials, presidents of universities, university professors, and many other pastors, lawyers, and concerned citizens.[8] Associate Supreme Court Justice William Strong served as the third president of the NRA from 1867 to 1873. During three of those years, he was also an associate justice of the Supreme Court of the United States. The social status and prominence of the NRA's members and officers shows that it indeed had become "mainstreamed" by the 1870s.

The NRA's Christian Amendment was considered twice by Congress: once in 1874 and again in 1894. The House Judiciary Committee rejected the amendment on both occasions. (In its second attempt, the NRA naturally took Justice David Brewer's declaration that this is a "Christian nation," written in his 1892 *Holy Trinity* opinion, as a show of support for the amendment, at least from Justice Brewer, if not the whole Court, since the decision was unanimous.)[9]

The NRA espoused goals in addition to its Christian Amendment. It was also devoted, in the words of its general secretary, to "the preservation of the Christian Institutions of this country; such as our civil Sabbath, the Bible in the public schools; the securing of a uniform marriage and divorce law, conformed to the law of Christ; the retention of the oath in our courts; [and] chaplains in our army and navy."[10]

It is interesting that the NRA advocated both the Christian Amendment to the Constitution and the separation of church and state. David McAllister, NRA general secretary, addressed this apparent contradiction in a short article he wrote on the history and progress of the NRA in 1874. He explained that two theories of the proper relationship between church and state prevailed in our country. The first "maintains that government has nothing to do with religion but let it alone. . . . It separates not only the church, but all religion from the state."[11] The other, "while rejecting church establishments, holds that civil government has a proper and necessary connection with religion."[12] Among adherents of these two theories, McAllister asserted, there was no dispute that church and state should remain separate: "All are agreed that the civil establishment and endowment of any ecclesiastical body would be an evil."[13] The real dispute was over the "relation of religion and the state, not of Church and State."[14]

Many speakers at the National Convention of the NRA in 1874 addressed the charge that the NRA's goals violated the concept of church and state separation. Then president of the NRA, Felix Brunot, expounded on this point. His lengthy commentary on the roles of the state and the church illuminates the NRA's position on freedom of conscience and church-state separation:

> The civil law of the State has to do with the acts of men, and its penalties concern their bodies; it has nothing to do with their souls. Religion, on the other hand, is a matter of the soul, of conscience, of faith. You cannot make one believe by a penalty upon his body. . . . His religion must be a matter of inward conviction produced by reason. The State controls men's actions for the good and safety of society by acting from without. The Church controls men's acts for the salvation of their souls by acting from within. Their functions and modes of operation are separate and distinct; hence no State can rightly attempt to compel the consciences of its citizens with a particular religion, and, as we believe, no particular religion can rightly attempt to use the State to compel men's consciences to its belief. This principle is an essential element of Protestant Christianity.[15]

Members of the NRA referred frequently to the persistent demands of the "enemies of our Christian institutions" to eradicate all vestiges of religion from public life.[16] Such epithets referred to the National Liberal League and spokesman Robert Green Ingersoll. The National Liberal League's platform of 1870 called for the

> [t]otal separation of church and state, to be guaranteed by amendment of the national Constitution; including the equitable taxation of church property, secularization of the public schools, abrogation of Sabbatarian laws, abolition of chaplaincies, prohibition of public appropriations for religious purposes, and all measures necessary to the same general end.[17]

The Liberal League existed to eradicate everything the NRA desired to maintain. To achieve its goals, the Liberal League, like the NRA, proposed an amendment to the Constitution called the Religious Freedom Amendment. It had a twofold purpose: to extend to the states the prohibitions of the national Constitution concerning establishments and free exercise of religion, and to impose a radical, absolute separation of church and state on the federal and state governments.

Robert Ingersoll was one of the most prominent secularists of the nineteenth century. He was closely associated with the Liberal League, exemplified by his selection as its presidential candidate in 1880. Later, in 1885, Ingersoll founded the American Secular Union.[18] Yet Ingersoll's reputation was grounded in his oratorical skills more than in his connection with any organization or cause.[19] According to one biographer, Ingersoll's adeptness at public speaking had made him so popular that "[i]f he had been willing to let religion alone, he could have had anything in the gift of the American people. He could have walked in and out of the White House to suit himself.[20]

Ingersoll employed his skill at oration for the furtherance of many causes, one of them being the separation of church and state. His most salient work concerning church-state views in late nineteenth-century America was an article he wrote in 1890 castigating the NRA's proposition that the Constitution needed to be amended so as to recognize God, Jesus, and Christianity. In this article, Ingersoll addressed the purpose of our founding fathers concerning the relationship between religion and government in strict separationist terms:

> In 1776 our fathers endeavored to retire the gods from politics. They declared that "all governments derive their just powers from the consent of the governed." This was . . . a renunciation of the Deity. It was in fact a declaration of the independence of the earth. It was a notice to all churches and priests that thereafter mankind would govern and protect themselves. Politically it tore down every altar and denied the authority of every "sacred book," and appealed from the Providence of God to the Providence of Man.[21]

Based on this premise, Ingersoll rejected any attempt to amend the Constitution to include references to God. Doing so, he said, "would be the destruction of religious liberty," since it would require the protection of the God mentioned in the Constitution.

While the NRA and the National Liberal League were garnering public support for their opposite positions and vying for the attention of Congress, a third effort toward constitutional change emerged—this time from the president and Congress.

In the 1870s, nativist sentiments escalated in response to the growing immigrant populations. At the same time, the Reconstruction period after the Civil War under President Grant's administration had created a legacy of bitterness in the South. The Republicans needed a platform for the

1876 election that would positively affect the greatest number of voters. One solution, proposed by President Grant in 1875, was to focus the attention of the nation on the issues of education and school funding. By uniting the entire nation in the common cause of improving education, the Republicans could redirect the focus of the country from the failures of Reconstruction to the hope of rebuilding the nation. One of the 1876 presidential hopefuls, Congressman James G. Blaine, recognized the political promise of the school issue and proposed a constitutional amendment in 1875. The Blaine Amendment stated that:

> No State shall make any law respecting an establishment of religion or prohibiting the free exercise thereof; and no money raised by taxation in any State for the support of public schools, or derived from any public fund therefor, nor any public lands devoted thereto, shall ever be under the control of any religious sect, nor shall any money so raised or lands so devoted be divided between religious sects or denominations.[22]

The Republican Party's calculated decision to stress education in order to divert the nation's attention from the failure of Reconstruction was successful. The party's school agenda, coupled with the Blaine Amendment, served well as a vehicle for political gain. One of the main reasons this strategy worked was the anti-Catholic animus that undergirded the public school issue during the latter half of the nineteenth century. Because Protestant principles were at the core of the common school system, many Catholics sent their children to parochial schools in order to educate their children according to their beliefs. The Blaine Amendment's main purpose—to prohibit government funding of sectarian schools—directly hurt the Catholic community since most sectarian schools at the time were Catholic. The Blaine Amendment also rekindled anti-Catholic sentiments and suspicions among Protestants. These sentiments motivated the subsequent incorporation of variations of the Blaine Amendment in different state constitutions of 1889. The inclusion of Blaine-like amendments in these states' constitutions is highly relevant today. Washington, one of the several states that came into the Union in 1889, adopted a Blaine-inspired Establishment Clause into its Constitution. (That amendment and its implications were at the center of the *Locke v. Davey* case decided by the Supreme Court in 2004 that will be discussed in chapter 9.)

With a twenty-year career in Congress before serving as secretary of the cabinet and secretary of state, Maine Republican James G. Blaine was one of the most influential politicians of the second half of the nineteenth century. Interestingly, Blaine's mother was a strongly devoted Catholic and, according to one of Blaine's biographers, an upstanding citizen and extremely virtuous woman. While Blaine likely attended Mass as a child, he associated more closely with the Presbyterian faith of his father, Ephraim L. Blaine, an affluent prothonotary and Protestant of Scotch-Irish descent.

A successful man with political aspirations of his own, Ephraim's attempt to run for public office failed, in part due to accusations that he was a Catholic himself. He later had a priest certify that "Ephraim L. Blaine is not now, and never was a member of the Catholic Church, and furthermore, in my opinion he is not fit to be a member of any church."[23] Despite these remarks, Ephraim Blaine was ultimately buried in a Catholic cemetery.[24]

James G. Blaine served fourteen years in the House of Representatives, spending the last three terms as Speaker of the House. In June of 1876, he left the House and was appointed to the Senate, where he served six years. Once in the Senate, Blaine concentrated his efforts on his ultimately unsuccessful presidential campaign. His charisma and good record in Congress made him an extremely appealing candidate. The School Amendment, ultimately known as the Blaine Amendment, was an ideal proposal to launch Blaine's campaign for the presidency.

Meanwhile, President Grant had delivered a speech at a military convention for the Society of the Army of Tennessee in Des Moines, given on September 29, 1875. This served as the catalyst for the ensuing national debate over funding for sectarian schools, and later the Blaine Amendment.[25] Grant's speech expressed his desires and goals for the nation. Rather than a separation between North and South, Grant predicted the new divide "between patriotism and intelligence on one side, and superstition, ambition and ignorance on the other."[26] Grant predicted the new division in the country would be between the Protestants and all others of different faiths, particularly the Catholics. He exhorted the nation to "encourage free schools, and resolve that not one dollar appropriated for their support shall be appropriated to the support of any sectarian schools."[27]

In order to "effectuate President Grant's political vision for public education," Blaine formally proposed his amendment to the House on

December 14, 1875.[28] The fact was that the Republican public school agenda expressed the sentiments of much of mainstream America. Indeed, public schools in the nineteenth century, "apart from providing a free education in basic subjects, were used to assimilate immigrants and their children into American society by enculturating them with American values and attitudes."[29] As professor Steven Green explained, the American values taught were based almost exclusively in Protestant Christianity:

> In all levels of education . . . the moral teachings of the Bible were taught and, to varying degrees, religious services were conducted. But public schools did more than act as surrogates for church instruction. The entire curriculum centered on general assumptions of God's existence, the sense of His universe, and the "spirituality" of human nature. Schools were the primary promulgators of this Protestant way of life.[30]

Because much of American society equated "civic virtue" with "Protestant religiosity, the Protestantism of the common schools was seen as a defense of democratic values, rather than the values of a particular religious tradition."[31] Thus, any attack on the inclusion of Protestant teachings and practices in the common schools was elevated to an attack on American political values, not just on the dominant religious values of the country.

The Blaine Amendment decisively passed the House 180–7 without significant debate.[32] It was only slightly altered from its initial state, and all members of the Judiciary Committee agreed that the underlying principles of the amendment exemplified the spirit of the age. One of the most significant changes made by the Judiciary Committee was adding the clause that explicitly endorsed the use of the Bible in public schools: "*This article shall not be construed to prohibit the reading of the Bible in any school or institution*; and it shall not have the effect to impair rights of property already vested" [emphasis added]. [33]

The Protestant-Catholic controversy strongly influenced the national legislature's debate over the Blaine Amendment. Indeed, Protestant control over public schools, the creation of Catholic parochial schools, the use of the Bible in the common schools, all impacted the debate. Despite garnering a majority of the votes in the Senate, the Blaine Amendment failed to gain the two-thirds needed for it to be passed to the states for ratification.

The defeat of the Blaine Amendment did not stop leaders in the

Republican Congress from attempting to influence the school funding issue in the states and territories. In the 1880s Republicans realized that they could use federal aid for schools as a tool to manipulate public policy. As a condition of statehood, the western territories were "required to incorporate Blaine-like provisions into their new constitutions." The requirement was contained in the Enabling Act of 1889 that granted statehood to Washington and Montana and divided the Dakotas into two separate states: The Enabling Act mandated that the public schools be free from sectarian control. Of the seventeen states with the most restrictive constitutional provisions prohibiting state aid to religious educational institutions, fourteen are in the West, where new states were admitted during the era of the Blaine Amendment.[34]

The state of Washington's attainment of statehood in 1889 serves as an excellent example of the phenomenon of the federally defunct Blaine Amendment becoming incorporated into state constitutions. The state's delegation to the Republican National Conventions in 1876, 1880, 1884, and 1892 championed Blaine for president and supported his views on public schools.[35] Further, Washington's Constitutional Convention of 1889 had a Republican majority.[36] Public opinion in Washington State evidently favored an Establishment Clause that mirrored the Blaine Amendment. The *Portland Oregonian* printed an editorial on "religious instruction" in public schools, which concluded:

> In order that liberty of conscience may remain inviolate as intended by our constitution builders, there must be absolute separation of church and state, religion and public schools; and in order to guide the public school system onward to the fulfillment of the mission that called it into existence, it is necessary to keep the public schools free from religious influences, from theological disputes and sectarian teaching.[37]

On July 25, 1889, just days after the rash of editorials and letters on religious instruction in public schools, the Constitutional Committee submitted its amended report to the convention, which included a restriction on state funds for religious instruction.[38] The final version of the Washington Establishment Clause passed the convention without debate, and provided: "No public money or property shall be appropriated for, or applied to any religious worship, exercise or instruction, or the support of any religious establishment."[39]

Religious liberty and church-state separation were important issues on the national political level during the latter half of the nineteenth century. The foregoing analysis reveals that three main approaches to such issues were vying to capture the American mind during this time. The National Reform Association emphasized the Christian character of our nation and advocated amendment of the Constitution in such a way that the United States would be permanently and officially aligned with Christianity. The National Liberal League championed an absolute separation between church and state. The Republican Party's agenda and the Blaine Amendment were predicated on protecting the de facto Protestant domination of our culture and schools while at the same time suppressing minority religions, especially Catholicism.

It is interesting, for historical purposes, to note that the Blaine version of separation garnered the most support among Americans in the last quarter of the nineteenth century. This amendment, unlike those of the NRA or the Liberal League, was seriously considered in both houses of Congress and fell just a few votes short of being passed to the states for ratification. The NRA's amendment had broad support from many prominent citizens, yet failed to ever make it out of the House Judiciary Committee. The Liberal League's amendment and cause received the least support of all. This tells us much about the attitude of Americans at this time concerning church-state separation. They generally supported a narrow view of separation that affirmed the separation of church and state, but not of religion and state. The relative success of the Blaine Amendment, a pro-Protestant, anti-Catholic measure, showed that Americans wanted to maintain and protect their Protestant-infused culture and its many Protestant-inspired practices. The general lack of support for the Liberal League indicates, according to Hamburger, that the "Liberals had made themselves unpopular with their secular vision of separation [and] their anti-Christian beliefs." The ongoing debate concerning these proposals culminated in the Supreme Court of the United States in 1892. The case decided by Justice Brewer declared America to be a "Christian nation."

Justice David Brewer's life, beliefs, and opinion in *Holy Trinity v. United States* provide the perfect framework to analyze how a late nineteenth-century jurist viewed the issues being debated in the culture contemporaneously. Brewer was a prolific writer and speaker off the bench. The United States's connection with Christianity and the implications of that connection for our nation's customs and laws were a frequent topic of Brewer's articles and speeches. A devout Christian, Brewer drew deeply from his religious beliefs to decide all manner of questions, including constitutional ones. As we will see, his religious beliefs impacted the development of his views on religious liberty, church-state relations, and, ultimately, his entire constitutional philosophy.

THE JUSTICE: DAVID JOSIAH BREWER
(1837–1910)

David Josiah Brewer was born in Smyrna, Asia Minor (now Izmir, Turkey), on June 20, 1837.[40] His father, Josiah Brewer, a Congregationalist missionary and pastor, spent the early years of his ministry overseas spreading both the Gospel and the Protestant religion among the Jews and the Greeks.[41] His mother, Emilia Field, was a member of a highly regarded family from Haddam, Connecticut. When Emilia was growing up, her father, David Field, was a Puritan-minded Congregationalist minister who occupied the same pastorate in Stockbridge, Massachusetts, that Jonathan Edwards had occupied nearly a century before. One of David's maternal uncles, David Dudley Field, was a prominent New York lawyer who codified the laws of New York. Another uncle, Stephen J. Field, would later serve as associate justice on the Supreme Court of the United States and was joined on the Court by his nephew, David, in 1889.

Despite Josiah's passion for international ministries, the Brewer family returned to America soon after David's birth and made Wethersfield, Connecticut, their permanent home. As a child, David had a great enthusiasm for education. At the age of fourteen he entered Wesleyan College. Two years later he transferred to Yale, where his father had graduated as valedictorian. He had a distinguished academic career at Yale and actively participated in the school's forensic societies. He graduated in 1856, finishing fourth in his class. At commencement, he delivered an essay titled "The Estimate of Life: A Criterion of the State of Civilization." In his speech, Brewer asserted: "Christianity increases the value of life not alone by adding a richer beauty to all its varied scenes but by conditioning the character of immortality upon it. Here appears the full sublimity of Christianity as the most important agent in civilization. Christianity came and with it the assurance of an immortality and the connection between this life and that immortality, and under its light the soul is slowly toiling up to a full realization of the value of life. Eternity gives infinite value to life."[42]

Brewer's path to the Supreme Court was rich with legal experiences.

He began his legal career by moving to Albany, New York, to read law at the offices of his uncle, David Dudley Field. He also enrolled at Albany Law School. In 1858, with the missionary zeal of his forebears, twenty-one-year-old David Brewer set out west for Leavenworth, Kansas Territory, to begin his career as a lawyer.

He had chosen to go straight into the violent storm of "Bleeding Kansas"—the prelude to the Civil War—where proslavery and antislavery brigands of ruffians fought against each other to win Kansas as either a slave or a free state. During the first years of Brewer's arrival, no less that three conflicting constitutional conventions had met; three territorial governors had been appointed but soon went back East; and the fate of Kansas was the main issue in the presidential election of 1860. After the start of the Civil War, Kansas was admitted as a free state in 1861. But the violence continued for many years.

Two other historic and happier events occurred in Brewer's life in the fall of 1861. On October 3 he married Louise R. Landon (who would be his devoted wife until her death in 1898). On October 24, work on the transcontinental telegraph line culminated at the Western Union office in Salt Lake City as wires strung from opposite coasts were joined. The first cross-country telegram sent over the span was a message to President Abraham Lincoln in Washington from Brewer's uncle Stephen Field, chief justice of the California Supreme Court, pledging his state's loyalty to the Union.[43]

Brewer had great success in Kansas, and served in many legal capacities while there, including county probate judge, judge of the First Judicial District of Kansas, county attorney, and associate justice of the Kansas Supreme Court. In addition to these official duties, Brewer engaged in private law practice as time allowed. Due to his quick rise to the Kansas Supreme Court, his rich legal experience, and the support of Senator Benjamin Plumb, Brewer was appointed to the Supreme Court of the United States by President Benjamin Harrison on December 4, 1889, and was confirmed two weeks later by the United States Senate on December 18.

Brewer believed strongly in the civic responsibilities of being an American citizen. As part of discharging his civic duties, Brewer also promoted universal education. He served as an elected member of the Leavenworth school board, and later served as its vice president and president. He also served as a member of the Board of Examiners, which certified public school teachers. In addition, he became the superintendent of the Leavenworth school system in 1865.

Brewer's most important belief was his abiding faith in Christianity. He was closely associated with several Congregational churches throughout his life. While in Leavenworth, he helped establish the First Congregational Church and devoted "considerable time as Bible class teacher and Sunday school superintendent."[44] During his years as a Supreme Court Justice (1889–1910), Brewer was a member of the First Congregational Church of Washington. There he regularly taught Sunday school as well, his favorite topic being the life of Christ. He even wrote an article for the *Sunday School Times* in 1897 discussing his suggestions on how to conduct a Bible class.[45]

Brewer's support of Christian organizations determined to spread Christianity throughout the world also indicates his devotion to his faith. He was a lifetime member of the American Bible Society, a group that translated the Bible and distributed it throughout the globe. He was a corporate member of the American Board of Commissioners for Foreign Missions. In addition, he supported American military actions in China during the Boxer Rebellion, departing from his anti-military stance; his sole basis for that support was the threat the rebels posed to American missionaries.[46]

The mainstay of liberal Protestantism of the late nineteenth century was its emphasis upon "God's love for humanity and the ethical teachings of Jesus Christ."[47] Liberal Protestants also "believed that, under God's guidance, humanity would progress until it brought about God's kingdom on earth as foretold in the Bible."[48] As a result, liberal Protestants tended to downplay or abandon traditional, orthodox doctrines like human depravity, Christ's atonement, and eternal damnation. Justice Brewer certainly shared many of these liberal Protestant beliefs.

Brewer minimized Christian creeds and stressed Christian morality in his words concerning Jesus as well. According to Brewer, Christ was not significant because of his atonement for our sins, but because "His life, supreme in all its attributes, will be the great appeal to humanity to come up higher."[49] Christ's life and words had taught us "to measure the religious character of a man not by the clearness of his intellectual convictions, . . . but by the purity of his life and the sweetness of its touch upon others."[50]

In light of these views, it is not surprising to find that Brewer tended toward universalism. He often spoke of a "redeemed humanity" and on one occasion said that more ecumenism in the twentieth century would bring a "keener and more just appreciation of the means [moral growth] by which alone humanity can become fit to enter the new Paradise which one day shall dawn upon the earth."[51] Linda Przybyszewski noted that Brewer "once went so far as to look forward to the 'cooperation of all, Gentile or Jew' in moral reform projects, so that they could all look forward to being welcomed into heaven by Christ."[52] Despite Brewer's liberal Protestant leanings, his break with orthodoxy was not complete. Brewer's continued allegiance to the orthodox doctrine of the Trinity is the most compelling evidence of the incompleteness of his break. In his *Twentieth Century* speech he emphasized two truths Christians in the next century must embrace to promote greater Christian unity. The first was "that back of the visible and material world is an infinite being, one whose height and depth, whose length and breadth no man can fathom."[53] Brewer's formulation of the second truth captured his Trinitarian beliefs:

> Christ of Nazareth was the incarnation of the infinite, the envoy extraordinary from the unseen world, bearing to us the messages of peace and hope and the promise of eternal life. He will be to us and for us, if I may so express it, *the seen Jehovah, the visible God.* [emphasis added]

Someone who rejected the Trinity would likely not have uttered such a clear statement of the deity of Jesus.

In addition, Brewer maintained a respect and desire, albeit somewhat diluted, for orthodox doctrine. While Brewer clearly minimized the importance of creeds, he nevertheless affirmed their significance. As he said in his *Twentieth Century* speech: "I am not here to condemn creeds, nor to pour out contempt upon the efforts to ascertain the absolute truth in reference to all the facts about Christianity."[54] Brewer reiterated this statement in his advice to Yale divinity graduates concerning appropriate topics for sermons:

> [G]ive us not too much theology, and yet certainly some. . . . We like to have the good old doctrines of the church placed before us in all their fullness with clearness and with power. . . . It is a great mistake to suppose that theology is out of date; that we care not what our fathers believed, nor what is the creed of the church today.[55]

In Brewer's mind, doctrine was still important as the foundation of ethics and morality. He submitted the nation's Puritan forefathers as a prime example of the benefits of devotion to religious doctrine: "[The pilgrims] believed earnestly. They defined their beliefs in a creed, and their lives were lived in intense effort to make that creed the universal and controlling fact in society. This may have led to some harshness. . . . [Yet] who would strike from our history the glories which attended their lives of intense convictions."[56]

Brewer maintained an unwavering belief that God had predestined America to greatness and world leadership. The confluence of the Gutenberg press, the Protestant Reformation, and the discovery of America was no accident. To Brewer, these events suggested

> that in the councils of eternity it was thought out long before man began to be, that here in this Republic, in the Providence of God, should be worked out the unity of the race—a unity made possible by the influences of education and the power of Christianity. . . . [T]o me it is a supreme conviction, growing stronger and stronger as the years go by, that that is the purpose of Providence in the life of this republic.[57]

Brewer also asserted that our nation was "baptized from its infancy into the gospel of the Prince of Peace," and he compared the faithful actions of the pilgrims with those of Abraham: "Just as Abraham obeyed God's command to seek out Canaan, so 'did the pilgrims leave country and kindred and homes in the faith that God was leading them to a second Canaan, where should be the homes of themselves and their children forever.'"[58] Brewer's beliefs that God had foreordained America's greatness and would guide its steps were clearly inspired by the Puritan faith of his father.

Despite Brewer's many statements concerning Christianity, some commentators have nevertheless questioned his dedication to the faith. Legal historian Steven Green paints Justice Brewer as a marginal Christian who thought "other religious viewpoints could also be correct" and believed "God could be called by different names or be revealed in different manifestations."[59] To support these assertions, Green cited a section of Brewer's *Twentieth Century* speech where he listed different names by which the "infinite being" may be referred. Among these names were the Omnipotent, the All-wise, the Infinitely Lovely, the All-merciful, and the Absolute Justice.[60]

Two points undermine Green's dependence on this section of Brewer's speech to question the devoutness of his religious convictions. First,

Christians would arguably use all of these names to describe God. This is clearly how Brewer understood them. He listed these alternate names for God while denouncing the denominational strife that had been a hallmark of the nineteenth century. Second, in the sentence immediately following these names, Brewer says that the most fitting name for the "infinite being" is simply "God."

Brewer's 1904 article titled "A Plea for the Bible" helps to clarify his position on the supremacy of the Christian faith. He argued that while other religions have rules similar to Christianity's Golden Rule, there is still a "worldwide difference" between them. He treated Confucianism's Golden Rule, "Do not do to others that which you would not have them do to you," as a prime example. He argued that one could follow this rule and yet ignore all the suffering and sorrow of one's fellow man. Brewer said, "You can pass by the man in the pit and thus not do him any direct injury, yet you are avoiding doing what you would have him do to you."[61] He argued that the Christian statement of the rule is superior because it requires an affirmative act in the face of another's plight.

In this same article, Brewer attested to his belief in the truth of the Bible. His main reason for believing in the truth of the Bible was "that it most satisfactorily answers the question, 'What of the life beyond?' The glory of this Book . . . comes from the . . . revelation of future life." He rhetorically asked, "Who has ever read unmoved the parting words of the Master in that upper chamber: 'In my Father's house are many mansions, if it were not so, I would have told you. I go to prepare a place for you.'" Brewer's words demonstrate both his belief in the superiority of Christianity and his hope in its promise of eternal life.

He also believed that Christianity was the only religion that offered humanity a satisfactory answer to the problems of this world. One such problem, according to Brewer, was "the inevitable failure of justice in this life."[62] Yet the failure of justice in this life, in his mind, assured us of a life to come. He explained his point of view to one audience with these moving words: "[O]ut of my judicial experience, and looking through the glass of my life-work, I have learned to see in the cross the visible symbol of faultless justice, and in the resurrection of Christ the prophecy and truth of its final triumph."[63] Clearly, Brewer believed in the ascendancy of Christianity and felt it offered suffering humanity its only hope of ultimate comfort and justice.

Brewer's speeches and writings demonstrate the earnestness of his religious convictions. He was convinced that the future success and greatness of America depended on its people embracing and advancing the Christian faith:

> If you want to build [American character] wisely, you must put into that character religion. It matters not what other elements there may be, if religion is left out of the future life of this country you may be sure that it will go down. It will be numbered like the nations that have been before it, and will pass away like them. It will only endure when there has entered into the national life as a potent and controlling force, religion, and there is no religion like that of Christ.[64]

Nearly all commentators who have analyzed Justice Brewer's life and jurisprudence have concluded that his constitutional philosophy developed out of his religious beliefs.[65] Joseph Hylton provided the clearest and most emphatic statement of this conclusion:

> Brewer's religious views were an integral part of his intellectual makeup. Because he started with his religious beliefs and then worked out a compatible theory of the Constitution, he was literally incapable of deciding any case without being influenced by those views. To describe David Brewer's view of the United States Constitution without taking into account his religious beliefs would be to describe a book without looking inside its covers.[66]

Historian Michael Brodhead, who has written the only full-length biography of Brewer, remarked: "Brewer's concern for individuals stemmed not so much from any economic theory as from his religious convictions. Indeed, his responses to the public questions of the day were to a great extent shaped by the Christian beliefs of this son of a missionary."[67]

Brewer left no doubt concerning the impact his religious beliefs had on his view of the law. In several speeches he specifically connected his Christian faith and the law. Addressing the congregation of his Congregational church in Washington, D.C., Brewer "announced his belief that 'the law and the gospel ought always to go together.'"[68] In a speech delivered in 1904, Brewer observed, "A lawyer in the pulpit may seem out of place, and perhaps a preacher on the bench would be out of place, but it occurs to me that if there were more Gospel on the bench and perhaps more Law in the pulpit it might be better for us all."[69]

Justice Brewer also based his belief in personal liberty and responsibility on the Bible, and specifically the teachings of Christ:

> The great thought of the Master was that over the human soul there was no earthly sovereign. There is no truth which shines more clearly through the gospels and the epistles than that of the independence of the human soul. In that great forum where are settled the destinies of time and eternity each one stands alone with his conscience. "Work out your own salvation with fear and trembling."[70]

According to Hylton, Brewer believed that "Christ's emphasis on the individual rather than the state had 'laid a foundation of a truer and nobler republic.'"[71] God intended to limit the power of "democratic majorities" over human freedom "since 'the Almighty is wiser than even such majority, and He has decreed it best for man to leave each free to work out his own salvation.'"[72]

From these statements it appears that Brewer's constitutional philosophy was principally based on the theory of natural rights. Brewer believed our nation's founding documents embodied this theory of law. To him, both the Declaration of Independence and the Constitution protected fundamental, God-given rights. As he said in one of his speeches, the Declaration affirms that the rights to life, liberty, and property are "unalienable rights; anteceding human government, and its only sure foundation; given not to man by man, but granted by the Almighty to every one; something which he has by virtue of his manhood, which he may not surrender, and of which he cannot be deprived."[73] In a sense, the Declaration of Independence represented for Brewer the enshrinement of his biblically based constitutional philosophy.

The connection Brewer drew between Christianity and the Declaration is evident in his writings. On one occasion, he connected God and the principles enshrined in the Declaration of Independence: "The Good Father has planted this Republic here . . . [and] is calling upon you and every citizen of the United States to join Him in upholding those immortal principles laid down in the Declaration of Independence."[74] Perhaps Yale Law professor Owen Fiss best captured Brewer's view of the interrelationship between Christianity and our nation's founding documents by observing that Brewer "did not draw sharp lines between the Constitution, the Declaration of Independence, Holy Scripture, and *The Wealth of Nations*."[75]

Brewer noted that the Constitution failed to reaffirm the principles of the Declaration, yet found this no bar to judicial enforcement of its standards. He viewed the Declaration as "the foundation upon which the Constitution was built. . . . I read into the one the affirmation of the other, that some truths are self-evident, existing before and superior to constitutions, and, therefore, unnecessary of mention therein."[76] To solve the problem of judges hesitating to enforce the standards of the Declaration, Brewer advocated a constitutional amendment that would "re-write into our Constitution the affirmations of the Declaration of Independence . . . in . . . clear and peremptory" language.[77]

The key to understanding Brewer's view of church-state relations is to recognize that it flowed from his religious beliefs. Brewer thought that America's commitment to disestablishment was "one of its highest credentials to the title of a Christian nation."[78] He argued that there is a separation between church and state in America precisely because Christianity is the chosen religion of this country, "for a peculiar thought of Christianity is of a personal relationship between man and his Maker, uncontrolled by and independent of human government."[79] Brewer's allegiance to separation was based on the Protestant principle of freedom of conscience.

Simply recognizing Brewer's allegiance to church-state separation, however, does not disclose the approach to separation he favored. Some commentators have intimated that Brewer's beliefs resembled a more modern understanding of the relationship between church and state, one in which the state should be neutral toward religion. However, a closer reading of Brewer's comments related to church-state relations demonstrates that he ascribed to an accommodationist's approach, not one of complete separation.

Justice Brewer's decision as a member of the Kansas Supreme Court in the 1883 case of *Wyandotte v. First Presbyterian Church of Wyandotte* provides the first evidence that Brewer favored government accommodation of religion.[80] This case involved a challenge to the county of Wyandotte holding property in trust for the benefit of the First Presbyterian Church. In the course of rejecting the separation claim that was advocated, Brewer declared:

> We have no state church, and the settled rule in this country is of entire separation between state and church; and *yet that separation is not so complete that the state is indifferent to the welfare and prosperity of the church. This is a Christian commonwealth.*[81] [emphasis added]

Further indicating his preference for accommodation, Brewer discussed some intersections between religion and government that his version of church-state relations would allow. In his 1905 *Christian Nation* speech, he supported the continued civil enforcement of Sunday-closing laws:

> [Sunday] is a day consecrated of old, a day separated by law and religion as well as by the custom of the church for ages, and ought not to be turned into a day of public frivolity and ga[i]ety. While it may be true that all are not under obligations to conform to the higher and better uses of the day, yet at least they owe that respect to Christianity to pursue their frivolities and gaieties in such a way as not to offend those who believe in its sacredness.[82]

Brewer recognized that Sunday's "separation from the other days as a day of rest is enforced by the legislation of nearly all if not all the States of the Union."[83] Interestingly, Brewer supported such legislation not only because it was physically and socially beneficial for citizens to have a day of rest, but because of the Christian teaching that Sunday was sacred.

In addition, Brewer noted without objection the prevalent practice among public schools of using the Bible as a textbook: "In the common schools the Bible has been as much a text book as the New England primer."[84] Brewer observed that some objection had been made to its continued use, but that such objection "sprung as much from differences between the Catholic and Protestant denominations concerning the version to be used as from opposition to the book itself."[85] The lack of denunciation in Brewer's words leads to the reasonable conclusion that he did not object to the use of the Bible in public schools.

Brewer's support for Sabbath closing laws and the use of the Bible in schools can be reconciled with his professed allegiance to church-state separation. His discussion of Sabbath laws is demonstrative. Individuals who did not view Sunday as sacred, according to Brewer, were "not under obligations to conform to the higher and better uses of the day, yet at least they owe that respect to Christianity to pursue their frivolities . . . in such a way as not to offend those who believe in its sacredness."[86] Apparently, freedom of conscience was maintained, and the principle of separation not violated, so long as the nonconformist was not forced to participate in the religious aspects of Sabbath observance.

Despite all evidence to the contrary, commentators still attempt to argue that Brewer favored the strict separationist model of church-state relations. Two main points have been put forward to support this assertion—that Brewer was against both religious involvement in politics and religiously based legislation. The former point is based on the following words Brewer imparted to the students of the Yale Divinity Department in 1897:

> [T]he moment [a minister] presents himself in the city hall, or where the legislature of a state is convened, or beneath the great dome of the Capitol where Congress meets to determine the welfare of the nation, and assumes to say that "because I am a minister I have a right to prescribe the terms, the limits and the character of legislation, city, state, or national," that moment the common sense of the community says to him most emphatically, "go back to your pulpit and leave matters of . . . legislation to those who are trained therefor."[87]

Green cited these words as proof that Brewer "spoke against religious participation in the political process."[88] Taken out of context, that seems a reasonable construction of Brewer's comment. However, a brief look at the context in which he made this remark reveals that it was not motivated by anticlericalism.

The first half of Brewer's speech to the Yale divinity students was about the changing role of ministers in our society. A generation ago, Brewer explained, "the extent of human knowledge . . . was restricted."[89] Ministers were one of the only educated classes and were highly respected in their communities, and thus were naturally looked to for leadership in all aspects of life. But "[n]ow all this has been changed. The range of human inquiry has become vast, and no man can hope to walk all its various ways with any hope of attaining proficiency therein during the limits of a single lifetime."[90] The present age called for specialists in each field. Ministers were wise in theology and religion, but could not, because of the exponential growth in human knowledge and pursuits, lead in other areas. Thus, Brewer's admonition against ministerial involvement in politics was not motivated by anticlericalism, but by his belief that ministers, like all other professionals, should stay within the field of knowledge they knew best.

Brewer's negative words concerning sumptuary legislation have also been relied upon to argue that he favored strict separation of church and state. Green has suggested that Brewer opposed "most religiously-based legislation" because of his allegiance to the principle of separation, yet this is hardly the case.[91] Admittedly, Brewer did denounce the idea that a statute could reform a person, but most Christians would agree with this sentiment. Brewer was simply stating what common sense tells us, that "[n]o man is reformed by a statute—made good by an ordinance."[92] Brewer's denunciation of sumptuary legislation is better understood as a product of his belief that only God can change the heart of a man, not, as Green purports, a belief that laws should not be based on Christian principles. As Brewer aptly said, "The Master taught a more excellent way" to reform man—by filling "the empty chambers of the soul" with the "new and better spirit" of Christianity.[93]

Hylton observed that Brewer "did not believe in an inactive state." In fact, Brewer believed that government "had a responsibility to facilitate" the "process of moral self-development." He believed so because the Declaration of Independence, in its guarantees of life, liberty, and the pursuit of happiness, "had . . . made the protection of the individual's right to pursue his own destiny the cornerstone of American constitutionalism." Hylton argued that Brewer elevated "support of individual moral development . . . to a constitutional standard" of "legislative legitimacy."[94]

In light of this philosophy, Brewer was more apt to approve government regulation in the area of morality than in any other area. As Hylton notes, "Brewer was willing to grant the state broad authority to regulate morals. Bans on gambling, lotteries, and prostitution were legitimate exercises of state power, as were the prohibition of the sale of alcoholic beverages, the criminalizing of polygamy, and the enactment of Sunday closing laws."[95] Hylton explains how Brewer's philosophy permitted such expansive regulation: "Statutes that facilitated the right of moral self-development were valid because they made it more likely that man, or woman, could obtain the salvation which was the purpose of their earthly existence."[96] Hylton's observations demonstrate how Brewer's Christian-based constitutional philosophy necessarily led him to approve morally and religiously based legislation. Even more, it casts doubt on Steven Green's contention that Brewer generally rejected religiously based legislation on separationist grounds. Brewer's very philosophy required the infusion of Christian moral principles into his decision-making.

THE CASE: *CHURCH OF THE HOLY TRINITY V. UNITED STATES* (1892)

In 1892, Justice Brewer decided the *Church of the Holy Trinity v. United States* case. This case is important to consider because it demonstrates the way in which Brewer, and probably the majority of nineteenth-century jurists, viewed the relationship between religion and government.

Holy Trinity involved the right of a foreign clergyman to come to the United States to serve as a pastor and rector of a church. The only issue presented to the Court was whether Holy Trinity, a Protestant Episcopal Church in the city of New York, had violated the Contract Labor Act of 1885. In 1887 Holy Trinity had employed Reverend E. Walpole Warren, an English Christian minister. The United States Attorney General challenged that employment and the case eventually arrived at the Supreme Court.

The Contract Labor Act made it illegal for a corporation, among others, "to prepay the transportation, or in any way encourage the importation or migration of any alien . . . into the United States . . . to perform labor or service of any kind."[97] The Circuit Court ruled that the statute prohibited the church's contract with Reverend Warren.

Justice Brewer relied on two arguments to reverse the Circuit Court's decision. First, despite its broad language, he argued that the statute was not intended to prohibit the importation of members of the clergy to the United States for the purpose of serving as a pastor of a church. Second, after analyzing the significant role Christianity had played in our nation, Brewer argued that prohibiting a church from contracting for the services of a foreign pastor would be in complete contradiction to the overwhelming evidence that "this is a Christian nation."[98] As Brewer rhetorically asked, "In the face of all these [utterances that this is a Christian nation], shall it be believed that a Congress of the United States intended to make it a misdemeanor for a church of this country to contract for the services of a Christian minister residing in another nation?"[99]

Brewer's opinion in *Holy Trinity*, especially his famous statement that "this is a Christian nation," has engendered significant commentary within the legal community.[100] Efforts have been made to argue that Brewer used this phrase and related discussion merely to describe the history and culture of the nation. However, it seems more likely that Brewer thought the United States's status as a Christian nation had at least some legal significance.

Brewer's opinion in *Holy Trinity* is clearly based on such a rationale. It appears that he wrote about Christianity in the *Holy Trinity* opinion not only to describe the history or culture of the United States but also to offer a secondary rationale for overturning the application of the Contract Labor Act to the Holy Trinity Church and Reverend Warren. Indeed, it is a reasonable conclusion that Brewer included his lengthy discourse on Christianity to demonstrate that the Christian faith had, and should continue to have, an influence on the laws of the United States. In light of this influence, Brewer seemed to be arguing that the Contract Labor Act could not be construed to restrict the Christian religion.

Several aspects of Brewer's *Holy Trinity* opinion and his extrajudicial commentary on it support this characterization of the purpose behind Brewer's "Christian nation" maxim. In both his opinion and his *Christian Nation* speech, Brewer mentioned several state and national Supreme Court cases that used this nation's Christian heritage to support their decisions. In his *Holy Trinity* opinion, Brewer cited two decisions in which the courts stressed that Christianity was the professed religion of the people of their respective states.[101] He also cited *Vidal v. Girard* and approvingly quoted Justice Joseph Story's acknowledgment that "the Christian religion is a part of the common law of Pennsylvania."[102] To Brewer, these decisions "affirm[ed] and reaffirm[ed]" that the United States is "a religious nation."[103]

Brewer touched on other state court decisions that supported the outcome of *Holy Trinity* in his *Christian Nation* speech. He referred to a Louisiana case, decided in 1900, where the court was presented with the question whether Sunday should be included in determining whether the governor's veto was returned within the appropriate time. The court noted that the most recent version of the Louisiana Constitution had excluded the "Sundays excepted" language that had appeared in previous versions of that state's constitution. Despite this fact, the court decided that Sundays should still be excepted. The court recognized that "in the Christian world Sunday is regarded as the 'Lord's Day,' and a holiday—a day of cessation from labor."[104] Brewer also mentioned a South Carolina Supreme Court case decided in 1846 that recognized the sacred nature of Sunday. In this case, the court said it was not necessary for the purposes of the case before it to hold that Christianity was part of the common law. However, it notably stated that Christianity "lies at the foundation of even the article of the [state] constitution under consideration," and that upon Christianity "rest[s] many of the principles and usages, constantly acknowledged and enforced, in the courts of justice."[105]

Brewer's likely purpose for citing and discussing these cases was to show that other courts used this nation's Christian heritage as a rationale to support their decisions. Like those courts, Brewer used this nation's Christian heritage to support his decision in *Holy Trinity*. Indeed, he explicitly relied on our nation's religious heritage to defend his narrow interpretation of the Contract Labor Act, "[N]o purpose of action against religion can be imputed to any legislation, state or national, because this is a religious people."[106]

That Brewer believed the "Christian nation" maxim had legal significance is also supported by his subsequent discussion of *Holy Trinity* in his speeches and writings. In his *Christian Nation* speech, Brewer analyzed the impact Christianity had on our nation's history, culture, and laws in more depth and concluded:

> I could show how largely our laws and customs are based upon the laws of Moses and the teachings of Christ; how constantly the Bible is appealed to as the guide of life and the authority in questions of morals; how the Christian doctrines are accepted as the great comfort in times of sorrow and affliction, and fill with the light of hope the services for the dead.[107]

Here, Brewer clearly indicates that the laws of our country are based upon biblical laws and teachings. He ended his discussion of our nation's Christian heritage by saying that not only did Christianity have a powerful influence on this nation historically but "to-day exists as a mighty factor in the life of the republic."[108] Brewer appears to be declaring not only an historical fact but also a present reality, regarding the role of Christianity in America.

Brewer demonstrated the continued impact of Christianity on our nation's laws and governmental practices by discussing Sabbath laws and the provision of military and legislative chaplains. He noted both the pervasiveness of Sabbath laws among the states and, more importantly, the religious rationale for them: "[T]hrough a large majority of them, there runs the thought of [Sunday] being a religious day, consecrated by the [Fourth] Commandment."[109] Regarding chaplains, Brewer declared, "Their whole range of service, whether in prayer or preaching, is an *official recognition of Christianity*" [emphasis added].[110] These laws and practices, and others similarly inspired by Christianity, demonstrate Brewer's belief that the "Christian nation" maxim had legal, not just historical, significance.

Our previous examination of Brewer's Christian-based constitutional philosophy helps to shed light on how Brewer likely viewed his *Holy Trinity* opinion. Brewer derived his entire philosophy from his Christian convictions. Each time Brewer struck down a law that infringed upon the right to property or conscience, he was enforcing the Christian principles of natural law he believed were protected by the Declaration of Independence and the Constitution. Thus, the idea that Christianity would provide the basis for some of our nation's laws and practices would hardly be objectionable to him. Laws based generally on Christian teachings were simply the natural result of a nation heavily influenced by the Christian religion.

Brewer's view of church-state separation was far narrower than either the Blaine proposals or that of the Liberal League. For Brewer, the Sabbath laws, the Bible in schools, military and legislative chaplains, and other government accommodations of religion were all consistent with his notion of church and state separation. Thus, the implication of his "Christian nation" declaration—that our nation's laws can be and are based on Christianity—did not offend his conception of the proper relationship between church and state. Brewer would object to laws that established Christianity as the national church or that compelled people to support it, but he accepted the validity of laws generally based on Christian teachings as mere reflections of the predominant religious values of the nation.

Moreover, Brewer clearly believed that Christianity and its teachings provided the basis for our nation's commitment to church-state relations. Commenting on the Christian character of state constitutions, Brewer said:

> While the separation of church and state is often affirmed, there is nowhere a repudiation of Christianity as one of the institutions as well as benedictions of society. In short, there is no charter or constitution that is either infidel, agnostic or anti-Christian. Wherever there is a declaration in favor of any religion, it is of the Christian. In view of the multitude of expressions in its favor, the avowed separation between church and state is a most satisfactory testimonial that it is the religion of this country, for a peculiar thought of Christianity is of a personal relation between man and his Maker, uncontrolled by and independent of human government.[111]

Finally, Justice Brewer's personal religious beliefs provide a basis for understanding his decision in *Holy Trinity*. He sincerely believed that the spread of Christianity was essential to the future success and vitality of America. It must have satisfied Brewer greatly to overturn the decision of the lower court applying the Contract Labor Act to Reverend Warren. By interpreting the Contract Labor Act so as to render it inapplicable to Christian ministers, Brewer took an active role in ensuring the future freedom and expansion of religious liberty in the United States.

Justice Brewer never explicitly addressed the cultural debate regarding the nature of religious liberty that was being waged prior to and during his time on the Court by the National Reform Association, the National Liberal League, and the Republican Party and James Blaine. Nevertheless, Brewer's decision in *Holy Trinity* and his extrajudicial writings and speeches reveal volumes about where he stood in this debate.

Brewer delivered his most direct, though still implicit, commentary on the debate in his *American Citizenship* speech. Just after explicating his views that our country's disestablishmentarian stance was the best evidence of our status as a Christian nation and his belief that our country was indebted to Christianity for its commitment to freedom of conscience, Brewer remarked: "The very tolerance which some over-sensitive people deprecate is one of the best evidences that in the framing of our Constitution and the foundation of our nation there was recognized that truth which underlies [C]hristianity, to wit, that love not law is the supreme thing."[112] Brewer's remark could clearly be read so as to undercut the cause of an organization like the National Reform Association. Their desire to amend the Constitution to include references to Christianity would have been anathema to Brewer's belief that one of the "highest credentials" of a Christian nation is that it establishes no religion and protects freedom of conscience.

Some debate exists over precisely where Brewer would land in the debate between the Republican Party, the NRA, and the Liberal League. In his article, Steven Green notes Brewer's relative silence amidst the cultural battle over separation.[113] He suggests this silence demonstrates that Brewer objected to attempts by organizations like the NRA to employ his *Holy Trinity* opinion to further their goals. Based in large part on this conclusion, Green also subtly argues that Brewer favored a position on separation that had more in common with the Liberal League than with the NRA. In fact, after noting that some organizations "relied on *Holy Trinity* to argue for greater government support of religion and for morally-based legislation," Green asserts: "Brewer would not likely have agreed with such use of [*Holy Trinity*], especially if it resulted in government sponsorship of Christianity. Brewer believed strongly that two important attributes of a Christian nation were a respect for religious diversity and separation of church and state."[114]

Brewer's silence, however, is a weak foundation upon which to build a case that Brewer favored strict separation of church and state of the type being advocated by the Liberal League. Brewer's numerous extrajudicial writings and his *Holy Trinity* opinion, if anything, suggest that he had much more in common with the NRA than with the Liberal League.

The NRA promoted more than its Christian Amendment to the Constitution. It also existed to preserve the "Christian Institutions" of the United States, including civil observation of the Sabbath, the inclusion of the Bible in schools, the retention of the oath in courts, and the employment of chaplains by the military and Congress. Brewer, as outlined above, supported the continuation of all of these practices in his off-the-Court writings. He also implicitly threw his support behind them in *Holy Trinity*:

> If we pass beyond these matters [court decisions expressing support for Christianity] to a view of American life as expressed by its laws, its business, its customs and its society, we find everywhere a clear recognition [that this is a religious nation]. Among other matters note the following: The form of oath universally prevailing, concluding with an appeal to the Almighty; the custom of opening sessions of all deliberative bodies and most conventions with prayer; . . . the laws respecting the observance of the Sabbath, with the general cessation of all secular business, and the closing of courts, legislatures, and other similar public assemblies on that day.[115]

One of the striking similarities between Brewer and the NRA was their mutual espousal of the belief that the United States owed its commitments to freedom of conscience and religious liberty to Christianity. Brewer, as noted above, tied these concepts directly to the teachings of Christ. Felix Brunot, president of the NRA in the mid-1870s, made a similar point: "To Christianity, and to Christianity alone, is the world of the nineteenth century indebted for religious liberty. Destroy this, and you destroy Christianity—destroy Christianity, and you destroy religious liberty."[116]

Brewer spoke often about the ineffectiveness of statutes in changing men's hearts. The NRA espoused a similar position. President Brunot announced the NRA's opposition to statutes passed with the purpose "to compel men's consciences in their relation to God."[117] Brunot explained that Protestant Christianity "appeals to men's hearts to effect men's conduct. Its function is to work from within, outwardly. No human law can make a man religious, or a Christian; and no one knows this so well as the Christian."[118] Brewer said nearly the same thing in his *Twentieth Century* speech when he declared, "No man is reformed by a statute—made good by an ordinance. The Master taught a more excellent way. . . . It is only by filling [the empty chambers of the soul] with a new and better spirit that anything like reformation is possible."[119]

A final rhetorical point Brewer was fond of making was that the United States owed its prominence among nations to its close connection to the Christian religion. As Brewer explained in his *American Citizenship* speech, "[W]hatever else may be said of Christianity one thing is undisputed and indisputable—that Christian nations manifest the highest forms of civilized life, and that among professedly Christian nations those in which the principles of Christianity have the utmost freedom and power occupy the first place."[120]

In a similar vein, Justice Brewer argued in 1904 that the Bible was our nation's sacred book: "No nation has a sacred book comparable with ours. Above all the writings of [other religions] is this Bible that we believe in. It is our Nation's sacred Book."[121] NRA president Brunot made a similar pronouncement when he declared, "No nation has ever existed without a religion, and the religion of our nation is Christian."

While Brewer was clearly in agreement with many of the NRA's positions, he was just as clearly not in agreement with the National Liberal League's agenda. Francis Abbot, the founder of the Liberal League, produced a document titled *Demands of Liberalism* that summarized the major goals of the organization. Those goals included: (1) the abolishment of the employment of chaplains by the military, the Congress, state legislatures, and any other government entities, (2) a prohibition on the use of the Bible in public schools, (3) the ceasing of presidential proclamations of prayer and religious festivals, and (4) the discontinuance of judicial oaths in the courts, among others.[122] Brewer had, both in his *Holy Trinity* decision and in his extrajudicial writings, supported the continuance of all of these practices. Clearly, then, the National Liberal League's agenda did not express the views or beliefs of Justice Brewer.

Even more revealing of the divergence between Brewer and the Liberal League is the vast difference between Brewer's Christian statements and the secular, anti-Christian rhetoric the Liberal League employed for its purposes. The rhetorical flourishes of Robert Ingersoll present the starkest example of this disparity. Ingersoll unflinchingly argued the secularist's view of our nation. As mentioned previously, he proposed that the Founding Fathers had renounced God and all things religious in the Declaration of Independence. Ingersoll carried this argument further: "The government of the United States is secular. . . . It is a government with which God has nothing whatever to do—and all forms and customs, inconsistent with the fundamental fact that the people are the source of authority, should be abandoned."[123] Brewer thought completely the opposite. As outlined above, Brewer believed the Declaration of Independence embodied Christian principles of natural law and that the Constitution permitted the enforcement of those God-based principles. Moreover, Brewer explicitly recognized and praised the involvement of Christianity in the formation of our nation. He placed Christianity at the center of the development of civilizations. In his mind, only in nations in which Christianity was free and influential could there be hope of societal growth and betterment. Justice David Josiah Brewer personified what modern thought has either failed or refused to recognize about most nineteenth-century jurists—that religion and the law were intimately connected in their minds. Brewer's declaration in *Holy Trinity* that America is a Christian nation was a product of this belief. It embodied the recognition that our nation, from its very beginnings, was permeated by the Christian religion. His claim of Christian nationhood was not merely the statement of a sociological or cultural fact; it had legal significance. While Brewer would not have countenanced legal enforcement of the Christian religion, he certainly supported laws that were based on Christian teachings and laws that furthered the cause of Christianity.

Justice Brewer served twenty critical years on the Supreme Court of the United States, walking over the bridge from the nineteenth to the twentieth century. In all, he wrote 719 opinions, doing all that was in his power to honor President Abraham Lincoln's fervent hope at Gettysburg "that this nation, under God, shall have a new birth of freedom." He was seventy-three years old when he died on March 28, 1910, while still a Supreme Court justice.

NOTES

1. James McPherson, *Battle Cry of Freedom* (New York: Ballantine Books, 1989), 859.

2. Richard N. Current et al., *American History: A Survey*, 956; text of these three amendments.

3. Anthony A. Cowley, "From Whence We Came: A Background of the National Reform Association," in *Explicitly Christian Politics: The Vision of the National Reform Association*, ed. William O. Einwechter (Pittsburgh, Pa.: Christian Statesman Press, 1997), 1, 4.

4. David McAllister, "Introduction" to *Proceedings of the National Convention to Secure the Religious Amendment of the Constitution of the United States* (Philadelphia: Christian Statesman Association, 1874), 1, 5; hereafter McAllister, "Introduction to Proceedings," in reference to McAllister, and *Proceedings* in reference to the Proceedings of the Convention.

5. The NRA started a publication in 1867, called *The Christian Statesman*, that is still in print today. Cowley, "From Whence We Came," 6.

6. McAllister, "Introduction to Proceedings," 2–3.

7. "Constitution of the National Reform Association," reprinted in William Addison Blakely, *American State Papers Bearing on Sunday Legislation* (1911), [Willard Allen Colcord, ed., photo. reprint, 1970], 342 n1.

8. *Proceedings*, 22–25.

9. *Church of the Holy Trinity v. United States*, 143 U.S. 471 (1892).

10. Cowley, *From Whence We Came*, 6; quoting David McAllister, *Christian Civil Government in America*, 6th ed. (Pittsburgh, Pa.: National Reform Association, 1927), 23.

11. McAllister, "Introduction to Proceedings," 1.

12. McAllister, "Introduction to Proceedings," 1.

13. McAllister, "Introduction to Proceedings," 1.

14. McAllister, "Introduction to Proceedings," 1.

15. McAllister, "Introduction to Proceedings," 32.

16. McAllister, "Introduction to Proceedings," 3.

17. "National Liberal Platform" (14 September 1879), reprinted in Blakely, *American State Papers*, 170.

18. Philip Hamburger, *Separation of Church and State* (Cambridge: Harvard University Press, 2002), 338. Ingersoll, a liberal Republican, delivered a speech supporting James G. Blaine at the 1876 Republican National Convention that has been considered a masterpiece of the extravagant rhetoric of the Gilded Age. Known as "The Plumed Knight" speech, Ingersoll told his fellow Republicans that "'they demand a man who believes in the eternal separation and divorcement of church and school' and 'that man is James G. Blaine.'" Hamburger, *Separation of Church and State*, 324; quoting *Proceedings of the National Republican Convention, Held in Cincinnati, Ohio* (1876), 74.

19. Mark A. Plummer, "Robert Green Ingersoll," in *American National Biography*, vol. 11, ed. John A. Garraty and Mark C. Carnes (New York: Oxford University Press, 1999), 560–61. Toward the end of his life, Ingersoll's "extended speaking tours attracted thousands of listeners."

20. Edward Garstin Smith, *The Life and Reminiscences of Robert G. Ingersoll* (New York: National Weekly, 1904), 125–26. Smith averred: "If he had been willing to let religion alone, he could have had anything in the gift of the American people. He could have walked in and out of the White House to suit himself. He could have taken the Goddess of Liberty off the dome of the Capitol, and installed the old lady in his own family."

21. Robert G. Ingersoll, "God in the Constitution," *The Arena* (January 1890): 119, 121.

22. 4 *Cong. Rec.*, 44th Congress, 1st Session, 205 (1875).

23. Russell Herman Conwell, *The Life and Public Services of James G. Blaine with Incidents, Anecdotes, and Romantic Events Connected with His Early Life; Containing Also His Speeches and Important Historical Documents Relating to His Later Years* (Augusta, Ga.: E. C. Allen & Co., 1884), 51.

24. Sister Marie Klinkhamer, "The Blaine Amendment of 1876: Private Motives for Political Gain," *Cath. Hist. Rev.* 42 (1956): 31.

25. "The President's Speech at Des Moines," *Catholic World* 22 (1876): 433.

26. "President's Speech at Des Moines," 434.

27. "President's Speech at Des Moines," 434.

28. Mark Edward DeForrest, "An Overview and Analysis of State Blaine Amendments: Origins, Scope, and First Amendment Concerns," 26 *Harv. J. L & Pub. Pol'y* (2003): 558; citing Steven K. Green, "The Blaine Amendment Reconsidered," 36 *Am. J. Legal Hist.* (1992): 49–50.

29. DeForrest, "State Blaine Amendments," 559.

30. As discussed in chapter 1, reading from the King James Bible and singing from Protestant hymnals were common practices in public schools during the nineteenth century. An editorial in the *Presbyterian Q. & Princeton Rev.* provided the typical argument justifying the teaching of religion in state schools: "Education, therefore, divorced from morality and religion, becomes shrunken, distorted and monstrous." Green, "Blaine Amendment Reconsidered," 41–45.

31. DeForrest, "State Blaine Amendments," 560.

32. 4 *Cong. Rec.* 5189, 5192, 44th Congress, 1st Session (1876).

33. 4 *Cong. Rec.* 5580, 44th Congress, 1st Session.

34. Joseph P. Viteritti, "Blaine's Wake: School Choice, The First Amendment, and State Constitutional Law," *Harv. J. L. & Pub. Pol'y* 21 (1998): 675; citing Act of 22 February 1889, ch. 180, 25 Stat. 676 (1889), and Frank R. Kemerer, "State Constitutions and School Vouchers," *Educ. L. Rep.* (2 October 1997): 1, 37.

35. Robert F. Utter and Edward J. Larson, "Church and State on the Frontier: The History of the Establishment Clauses in the Washington State Constitution," *Hastings Const. L. Q.* 15 (1988): 468–69.

36. Utter and Larson, "Church and State," 473 n.111; quoting *Wash. Const.* of 1878, art. V, § 4.

37. Utter and Larson, "Church and State," 473; quoting *The Oregonian*, 19 July 1889, 4.

38. Utter and Larson, "Church and State," 647; quoting B. Rosenow, ed., *Journal of the Washington State Constitutional Convention of 1889* (Seattle: Book Pub. Co., 1962), 500.

39. *Wash. Const.* art. I, § 11 (1889, amended 1958).

40. Howard B. Furer, *The Supreme Court in American Life: The Fuller Court, 1888–1910* (Millwood, N.Y.: Associated Faculty Press, 1986), 244.

41. Michael J. Brodhead, *David J. Brewer: The Life of a Supreme Court Justice, 1837–1910* (Carbondale: Southern Illinois University Press, 1994), 1–2.

42. David J. Brewer, "The Estimate of Life: A Criterion of the State of Civilization, Commencement Speech at Yale University" (1856), 5, 6; transcript available from the Yale University Manuscript and Archives division.

43. Alvin M. Josephy Jr., *War on the Frontier: The Trans-Mississippi West* (Alexandria, Va.: Time-Life Books, 1986), 10.

44. Brodhead, *David J. Brewer*, 9.

45. David J. Brewer, "One Way of Conducting a Bible Class," *Sunday School Times* (Philadelphia), 17 July 1897, 39.

46. Brodhead, *David J. Brewer*, 129.

47. Linda Przybyszewski, "The Religion of a Jurist: Justice David J. Brewer and the Christian Nation," *J. Sup. Ct. Hist.* 25 (2001): 233.

48. Przybyszewski, "The Religion of a Jurist." This is typically referred to as a "post-Millenialist" view of Jesus' second coming.

49. David J. Brewer, *The Twentieth Century from Another Viewpoint* (New York: Fleming H. Revell Co., 1899), 34, 36–37, 44.

50. Brewer, *The Twentieth Century*, 38.

51. Brewer, *The Twentieth Century*, 54.

52. Przybyszewski, "The Religion of a Jurist," 237; quoting David J. Brewer, *Address on a Federation of Christian Denominations, Social Responsibilities of the Christian Church* (1905), 2.

53. Brewer, *The Twentieth Century*, 38.

54. Brewer, *The Twentieth Century*, 35.

55. David J. Brewer, *The Pew to the Pulpit: Suggestions to the Ministry from the Viewpoint of a Layman* (New York: Fleming H. Revell Co., 1897), 47.

56. Brewer, *The Twentieth Century*, 36.

57. David J. Brewer, "Address to the YMCA" (16 October 1904), 6; transcript available from the Yale University Manuscript and Archives division.

58. Przybyszewski, "The Religion of a Jurist," 238; quoting David J. Brewer, "Address on the Home to the Sons of the Pilgrims" (22 December 1897).

59. Steven K. Green, "Justice David Josiah Brewer and the 'Christian Nation' Maxim," *Alb. L. Rev.* 63 (1999): 458.

60. David J. Brewer, *The Twentieth Century*, 39.

61. David J. Brewer, "A Plea for the Bible," *The Ram's Horn* (10 September 1904): 27; transcript available from Yale University Manuscript and Archives division.

62. David J. Brewer, "The Religion of a Jurist," *Outlook* 80 (1905): 534; and Przybyszewski, "The Religion of a Jurist," 233–34, noting Brewer's views on the failure of temporal justice and the perfection of eternal justice.

63. Brewer, "The Religion of a Jurist," 536.

64. Brewer, "Address to the YMCA," 7. On another occasion, Brewer declared, "[T]he more [the] Bible enters into the national life, the grander and purer and better becomes that life." Accordingly, Brewer advocated the circulation "of copies of the Bible everywhere. . . . [I]f it were possible to put into the hand of every citizen of this Republic . . . a copy of the Bible, it would be a great blessing." Brewer, "A Plea for the Bible," 27.

65. Przybyszewski, "The Religion of a Jurist," 231, 238; Joseph Gordon Hylton,

"David Josiah Brewer and the Christian Constitution," *Marq. L. Rev.* 81 (1998): 424–25; hereafter "Christian Constitution"; Joseph Gordon Hylton, "David Josiah Brewer: A Conservative Justice Reconsidered," *J. Sup. Ct. Hist.* (1994): 45, 54–57; hereafter "Conservative Justice"; and Brodhead, *David J. Brewer*, xiii.

66. Hylton, "Christian Constitution," 424–25.

67. Brodhead, *David J. Brewer*, xiii.

68. Brodhead, *David J. Brewer*, 128; quoting from the text of Brewer's speech on the occasion of the "Celebration of the Twenty-fifth Anniversary of the First Congregational Church, of Washington, D.C., November 9th to 16th, 1890."

69. Brewer, "A Plea for the Bible," 27.

70. Brewer, *American Citizenship* (New York: Scribner 1902), 21–22.

71. Hylton, "Conservative Justice," 56; quoting David J. Brewer, "The Scholar in Politics," *Topeka Daily Capital*, 13 June 1883, in Lynford A. Lardner, "The Constitutional Doctrines of Justice David Josiah Brewer" (Ph.D. dissertation, Princeton University, 1938), 59.

72. Hylton, "Conservative Justice," 56; quoting David J. Brewer, "Some Thoughts about Kansas," *Kan. Bar Ass'n Reports* 12 (1895): 70.

73. David J. Brewer, "Protection to Private Property from Public Attack," an Address to the Graduating Class of the Yale Law School, 23 June 1891, 4; transcript available from the Yale University Manuscript and Archives division.

74. David J. Brewer, "Address to the Association of Agents of the Northwestern Mutual Life Insurance Company," 16 July 1908, 6; transcript available from the Yale University Manuscript and Archives division.

75. Owen M. Fiss, "David J. Brewer: The Judge as Missionary," in *The Fields and the Law* (San Francisco: United States District Court for the Northern District of California Historical Society; New York: Federal Bar Council, 1986), 63.

76. Brewer, "Protection to Private Property," 4–5.

77. Brewer, "Protection to Private Property," 22.

78. Brewer, *American Citizenship*, 21.

79. David J. Brewer, *The United States A Christian Nation* (Philadelphia: J. C. Winston, 1905), 32; hereafter *Christian Nation*.

80. *Wyandotte v. First Presbyterian Church of Wyandotte*, 30 Kan. 620 (1883).

81. *Wyandotte*, 637.

82. Brewer, *Christian Nation*, 56.

83. Brewer, *Christian Nation*, 55.

84. Brewer, *Christian Nation*, 61.

85. Brewer, *Christian Nation*, 61.

86. Brewer, *Christian Nation*, 56.

87. Brewer, *The Pew to the Pulpit*, 23–24.

88. Green, "Justice David Josiah Brewer and the 'Christian Nation' Maxim," 461.

89. Brewer, *The Pew to the Pulpit*, 16.

90. Brewer, *The Pew to the Pulpit*, 19.

91. Green, "Justice David Josiah Brewer and the 'Christian Nation' Maxim," 459.

92. Brewer, *The Twentieth Century*, 48–51.

93. Brewer, *The Twentieth Century*, 51–52.

94. Hoylton, "Christian Constitution," 422.

95. Hoylton, "Christian Constitution," 422.

96. Hoylton, "Christian Constitution," 424.

97. *Church of the Holy Trinity v. United States*, 458; quoting 23 Stat. 332 (1885).

98. *Church of the Holy Trinity v. United States*, 471.

99. *Church of the Holy Trinity v. United States*, 471.

100. Green, "Justice David Josiah Brewer and the 'Christian Nation' Maxim," 427–29 and nn4–19.

101. *Church of the Holy Trinity v. United States*, 470–71; citing *Updegraph v. Commonwealth*, 11 Serg. & Rawle 394, 400 (Pa. 1824), stating that Christianity is "part of the common law of Pennsylvania," and *People v. Ruggles*, 8 Johns. 290, 294–95 (N.Y. Sup. Ct. 1811), stating that the people of New York, "in common with the people of this country, profess the general doctrines of Christianity" and that "the morality of the country is deeply ingrafted upon Christianity."

102. *Church of the Holy Trinity v. United States*, 471; quoting *Vidal*, 198.

103. *Church of the Holy Trinity v. United States*, 471.

104. *Church of the Holy Trinity v. United States*, 471.

105. *City Council of Charleston v. Benjamin*, 33 S.C.L. 508, 509, 2 Strob. 508 (1846).

106. *Church of the Holy Trinity v. United States*, 465.

107. Brewer, *Christian Nation*, 11–40; analyzing numerous examples of organic law, judicial decisions, and individual and corporate acceptance, including universities such as Harvard, Yale, and William & Mary, that undeniably proved to Brewer that the United States is a Christian nation.

108. Brewer, *Christian Nation*, 40.

109. Brewer, *Christian Nation*, 30.

110. Brewer, *Christian Nation*, 32.

111. Brewer, *Christian Nation*, 32.

112. Brewer, *American Citizenship*, 22.

113. Green, "Justice David Josiah Brewer and the 'Christian Nation' Maxim," 467–68. Green notes that Brewer was undoubtedly aware of the cultural controversy yet failed to adopt a public position on the matter.

114. Green, "Justice David Josiah Brewer and the 'Christian Nation' Maxim," 457–58.

115. *Church of the Holy Trinity v. United States*, 471.

116. *Proceedings*, 33.

117. *Proceedings*, 32.

118. *Proceedings*, 32.

119. Brewer, *The Twentieth Century*, 51–52.

120. Brewer, *American Citizenship*, 22–23.

121. Brewer, "A Plea for the Bible," 27.

122. Hamburger, *Separation of Church and State*, 294 n21; quoting Francis Abbot, *The Demands of Liberalism* (1872); republished in *Equal Rights in Religion: Report of the Centennial Congress of Liberals* (1876), 7–8.

123. Ingersoll, "God in the Constitution," 124.

II

RELIGIOUS FREEDOM IN THE TWENTIETH CENTURY

A Matter of Conscience:
God and Country

We are a Christian people.

—Justice George Sutherland
United States v. Macintosh, 1931

The essence of religion is belief in a relation to God involving duties superior to those arising from any human relation.

—Chief Justice Charles Evans Hughes
United States. v. Macintosh, 1931

In the third year of the twentieth century, without fanfare or publicity, one of the most enduring changes occurred to the towering Statue of Liberty on Bedloe's Island in New York harbor when a bronze tablet was fastened to an interior wall of the pedestal. On it was inscribed the last five lines of Emma Lazarus's 1883 poem, *The New Colossus*:

> Give me your tired, your poor,
> Your huddled masses yearning to breathe free,
> The wretched refuse of your teeming shore,
> Send these, the homeless, tempest-tost to me,
> I lift my lamp beside the golden door!

For millions of immigrants of all ages and from many countries who left their homelands for America in the first three decades of the twentieth century, the Statue of Liberty and the poem became inseparable as the most unforgettable welcome to the United States of America and the hope of a future in the land of the free. From 1905 to 1914 over one million immigrants entered the United States every year. A new century, a new country, a new life.

One of those immigrants was a young Canadian named Douglas Macintosh. At the same time, George Sutherland was serving his first term as a Republican United States senator from Utah and Charles Evans Hughes had just taken office as the Republican governor of New York. Twenty-four years later and World War I in between, Sutherland and Hughes, both sons of English immigrant fathers, were justices of the Supreme Court of the United States and Macintosh was an ordained Baptist minister teaching at Yale. It was Macintosh's desire to become a citizen that brought the three men together in an historic freedom of religion case.

Macintosh's application for American citizenship had been going through the lower courts since 1926; the first court ruled that he could not become a citizen because of his answer to a question on his application and the second court ruled that he could. In 1931 his case reached the Supreme Court of the United States for final decision. Macintosh had openly and honestly declared in his application that his allegiance to God and his religious conscience would supersede allegiance to country in matters of future wars. In a close 5–4 decision, Macintosh was denied citizenship.

United States v. Macintosh, much forgotten today, "was one of the most famous cases of its era."[1] Justice Sutherland, writing for the majority, invoked Justice David Brewer's opinion in *Holy Trinity*. But where Brewer had utilized "we are a Christian nation" to allow a foreign-born clergyman access to the country, Sutherland used it to keep a foreign-born minister out. Chief Justice Charles Evans Hughes wrote a vehement dissent, outlining what a terrible injustice it was to deny Macintosh citizenship on the basis of the constitutional guarantee of freedom of religious liberty and conscience in the United States of America.

The *Macintosh* case provides a unique opportunity to compare the religious beliefs and influences of two Supreme Court justices whose lives spanned the end of the nineteenth and the beginning of the twentieth centuries. Sutherland and Hughes were born within a month of each other in 1862 and were thus representative of the first post–Civil War generation. Sutherland was raised in frontier Utah Territory and was impacted by the teachings of Mormonism. Hughes was raised in the cultured East under the strict instructions of his father, a Baptist minister. Both of them were distinguished lawyers and Republicans whose entire adult lives were dedicated to public service to their country. And yet they held completely opposite points of view regarding the definition of religious liberty. Their stances in their *Macintosh* opinions reflected two divergent strains of thought that emerged in the late nineteenth century and flowed into the twentieth: nationalism and religious pluralism.

What had happened to America in the forty years between *Holy Trinity* and *Macintosh* that caused such dramatic changes in the relationship between the federal government and the religious freedom of its people?

THE CULTURAL/HISTORICAL CONTEXT

Throughout the nineteenth century Europe experienced a population explosion of massive proportions that was to have profound effects on the United States as well. One of the first thinkers to probe the meaning of the phenomenon was the Spanish philosopher José Ortega y Gasset (1883–1955) in his 1930 work *The Revolt of the Masses*. From the time European history begins in the sixth century up to 1800, Ortega y Gasset points out, "Europe does not succeed in reaching a total population greater than 180 million inhabitants. Now from 1800 to 1914—the population of Europe mounts from 180 to 460 millions! . . . In three generations it produces a gigantic mass of humanity which, launched like a torrent over the historic area, has inundated it."[2] The dynasties of the Old Order in Europe simply could not sustain their people. In the last quarter of the century, Europe was embroiled in cycles of revolution and reaction, ethnic conflicts, and increasing numbers of starving people seeking a way out. As Gasset concludes, "America has been formed from the overflow of Europe."

Indeed, the policy of the government for most of the nineteenth century was to keep the newcomers moving to the United States. Statutes were passed to facilitate the flow, and the population rose from just over two million at the beginning of the century to thirty-one million by 1860. Until 1870, the largest number of immigrants came from England, Ireland, and northwestern Europe, and most had the advantage of speaking English. A wave of German Catholics emigrated after Prince Otto von Bismarck instituted a crackdown on Catholics. Then a dramatic shift took place as hundreds of thousands of immigrants arrived annually from southern European countries, speaking many different languages. The peasant masses from Italy fled from the cholera epidemic of 1887. From the east came eight million Poles, Jews, Hungarians, Bohemians, Slovaks,

Ukranians, and Ruthenians.³ By 1900, America's population had swelled to seventy-six million. The pressure put on the large northeastern cities in terms of housing, jobs, and schooling was intense. Nativist resentment of these strange-looking and -speaking people, especially those from the Catholic countries of southern Europe, grew stronger with each passing decade.

Congressional acts in 1875, 1882, and 1892 provided for the examination of immigrants. These restriction laws barred criminals, the insane, and others who might become public charges. In 1891, the list of excluded undesirables was extended to include believers in anarchism and polygamy. These were minimal controls, and the flow of immigrants continued into the first decade of the twentieth century.

Citizenship for males twenty-one years of age had been set out in the Fourteenth Amendment to the Constitution in 1868: "All persons born or naturalized in the United States, and subject to the jurisdiction thereof, are citizens of the United States and of the State wherein they reside." Generally, immigrants desiring to become naturalized citizens had to be residents for five years and prove to be productive members of society and of good character. Once naturalized, they could vote. The children of immigrants born in the United States were citizens by birth. The sheer numbers, especially the rise in the Catholic population, was increasingly of concern to Protestants, who had for so long held a position of political and population majority. There was also a growing concern on racial grounds that America might become "a melting pot." The Immigration Restriction League formed in Boston in 1894 to urge setting limits on the number of admissions and to develop "some device to select from among the potential applicants only the superior stocks related to the American Aryan."⁴

At the dawn of the twentieth century, the United States had become an economic, industrial, and military world power. In 1901, Buffalo, New York, hosted the Pan American Exhibition that showcased new technological, scientific, architectural, and cultural innovations from many countries. President William McKinley had arrived on Friday, September 6, to greet visitors and dignitaries to the exhibition. As the president stood in the receiving line in the Hall of Music, a man came up with his hand wrapped in a handkerchief. Two shots rang out and the president fell to the floor. The assassin was seized immediately and taken to jail.⁵

This was the third assassination of a president in the thirty-nine-year lives of future justices George Sutherland and Charles Evans Hughes. John Wilkes Booth, a proslavery fanatic, shot Abraham Lincoln in Washington, D.C., at Ford's Theater on April 14, 1865. Charles Guiteau, an unstable Chicago attorney whose application to be ambassador to France was denied, shot James A. Garfield on July 2, 1881, as the president waited to board a train with his good friend James G. Blaine at the Baltimore and Potomac railroad depot in Washington, D.C.[6] President McKinley's assassin was an ominous creature of a different sort whose life story, photograph, and trial proceedings filled the newspapers for months, fueling the fears of the American public on several counts.

Twenty-eight-year-old Leon Frank Czolgosz (pronounced "Choalgosh") was born in Detroit, one of the seven children of Catholic, Polish-Russian, immigrant parents. His family moved to a farm near Cleveland, Ohio, but Leon could not tolerate the Catholicism of his parents, and at the age of ten, when his mother died in childbirth, he left with two brothers to work at the American Steel and Wire Company. They became involved with a labor union and participated in a strike and were consequently fired.

Returning home, Leon became a recluse who spent much time reading socialist and anarchist newspapers. He attended a lecture given by Emma Goldman, the prominent American socialist, and was very affected by it. He had lived in brutal poverty most of his life and became fanatical in his belief that there was a great injustice in American society that allowed the wealthy to exploit the poor. He had read about the anarchist who assassinated King Umberto I of Italy in 1900. Leon made his way to the Pan American Exposition to kill the president because, he said, McKinley was the enemy of good working people.[7] At his trial, which lasted two days, witnesses to the shooting gave testimony and evidence was produced. The jury was out thirty minutes and rendered a guilty verdict; Czolgosz was sentenced to death and was executed shortly thereafter.

This event and the details of it cast a long, dark shadow over the mood of the country. Policymakers began to address seriously a change in qualifications for naturalization. Congress passed the Naturalization Act of June 29, 1906, which required:

> He (the applicant for naturalization) shall, before he is admitted to citizenship, declare on oath in open court . . . that he will support and defend the Constitution and laws of the United States against all enemies, foreign and domestic, and bear true faith and allegiance to the same.
>
> It shall be made to appear to the satisfaction of the court . . . that

during that time (at least five years preceding the application) he has behaved as a man of good moral character, attached to the principles of the Constitution of the United States, and well disposed to the good order and happiness of the same.[8]

This gave the district courts the ability to probe more fully into an immigrant's beliefs and thoughts in order to render judgment. With the 1905 revolution in czarist Russia, explosive conflicts in the Balkan region, and the entangling alliances among European governments that could trigger a chain reaction to global war, America's immigration laws were increasingly framed in terms of internal and external national defense. If the United States became involved in a foreign war, where would the immigrant's national loyalty lie—with his country of origin or the United States?

Theodore Roosevelt, who had brought America into the dangerous business of power politics by wresting Cuba and the Philippines from Spain in 1898, and, as president, purchased the rights for the Panama Canal Zone in 1903, was fond of moralizing about the position of the United States in the world. His most often repeated theme was: "The just war is a war for the integrity of high ideals. The only safe motto for the individual citizen of a democracy fit to play a great part in the world is service—service through the high gallantry of entire indifference to life, if war comes on land."[9]

As a military power with economic interests around the globe, America joined the arms race as Europe divided into two hostile alliances. But the American public held to the time-honored idea of keeping out of Europe's quarrels.

Finally, on June 28, 1914, in the little Balkan town of Sarajevo, an assassin fired two shots killing Archduke Francis Ferdinand of Hapsburg and his wife. This was the spark that ignited the great conflagration that was to become a brutal four years of trench warfare and sea battles.[10] By August, England, Russia, and France were at war with Germany and Austria-Hungary. World War I brought the greatest challenge to America's one-hundred-year policy of neutrality and diplomatic independence.

President Woodrow Wilson and his secretaries of state and the navy, William Jennings Bryan and Josephus Daniels, respectively, were all devoutly religious men who espoused pacifism. Wilson had said in a 1913 speech: "The United States will never again seek one additional foot of territory by conquest." He sought "the development of constitutional liberty in the world."[11] Bryan developed a scheme for "cooling off treaties" to stave off wars between nations. This was in keeping with the progressive theory that war was unthinkable and disputes could be settled with reasonable discussion. He negotiated thirty such treaties between small and large nations.[12]

When the war broke out in Europe, Americans were generally confident that at least the New World was secure and the explosion would not reach their shores. At the same time the vast majority with economic, educational, or sentimental ties to England and France were outraged by the German invasion of Belgium and thus were pro-Allied. German-Americans initially saw the war as an honorable German struggle against the cruel despotism of czarist Russia. Hardly anyone envisioned America having to go to war, and there was no clear call for a democratic crusade. The government kept a watchful eye on the Orient, as Japan declared war on Germany and seized German holdings in China's Shantung Peninsula.[13]

President Wilson issued a proclamation of neutrality in 1914 and appealed to Americans to be impartial in thought and deed. As the war progressed, however, it became clear that United States's merchant ships at sea were at risk because no country in Europe would accept neutral trade with their enemy. Blockades at sea to conduct economic warfare combined with trench warfare on land were the strategies of both the British and the Germans. In 1915, Germany announced that it would use submarines to sink merchant vessels without warning in a broad zone around England. On May 7, a German submarine torpedoed the *Lusitania*; 1,198 people were drowned, including 128 Americans. A few weeks earlier, Germany launched poison gas at the Allied soldiers at Ypres, Belgium.

The American press began a steady stream of stories highlighting alleged German atrocities in Belgium and by this time most people were willing to believe almost anything against Germany but were not ready to fight. In the ensuing two years, Wilson faced the choice between preparedness for war, advocated by his generals and admirals, and pacifism, supported by the majority of the country. In 1916, the presidential campaigns of the Democrats and Republicans were waged over the issue of foreign policy before a seriously divided people. Wilson's support came from Democrats, whose slogan was "We didn't go to war." The Republican, Charles Evans Hughes, had a distinguished progressive record but was supported by Theodore Roosevelt and others whose warlike speeches made voters think that Hughes would be likely to adopt a militant policy. Wilson won by a narrow margin in the popular vote to continue on the path of peace.

In January 1917, Wilson unveiled his proposal for a lasting peace that America would help maintain through a league of nations. Two weeks later, the German ambassador announced that submarines would begin to sink all ships, neutral or enemy, in a broad zone around the British Isles. On March 18, German submarines torpedoed three American ships. Wilson had no choice but to prepare the country for war. On April 2, he delivered his message to Congress: "It is a fearful thing to lead this great peaceful people into war, into the most terrible . . . of all wars." He told the nation that "we shall fight for the things which we have always carried nearest our hearts—for democracy . . . for the rights and liberties of small nations, for a universal dominion of right by such a concert of free peoples as shall bring peace and safety to all nations and make the world itself at last free." On April 6, Congress passed the declaration of war against Germany.[14] The whole country engaged in building a gigantic war machine. In the process, deep changes occurred in the fabric of what had been, prior to the war, a progressive America.

One of the most difficult tasks the government had to deal with was indoctrinating the public toward conformity to necessary legislation for national security and mobilization for war without that conformity spilling over into hatred for Germans and other groups. But throughout the war, as the government passed measures for the protection of the nation, a hysterical wartime hatred of all that did not seem to conform spread across the country. The Espionage Act, Trading-with-the-Enemy Act, Sabotage Act, and Sedition Act of 1917 and 1918 contained severe penalties for disloyal individuals. With the Russian Revolution of 1917 and the takeover of the government by Vladimir Lenin and the Communists, another category was added to the disloyal list.

In the minds of many people influenced by the sensationalism of the tabloid press, pacifists were pro-Germany; union members were Bolshevists or radical socialists, Italians were anarchists, and so on. What before the war had been friendly relations with your neighbor of German ancestry now became suspect. "Sauerkraut" was renamed "liberty cabbage" and "hamburger" became "liberty sausage." As millions of Americans fought for freedom overseas in the cause to liberate Europe, to many at home it seemed that the First Amendment to the Constitution had been suspended.

Historian Oscar Handlin describes the atmosphere: "The war of 1914 brought all the forces of xenophobia together and cast over them the aura of patriotic necessity. In the years when every citizen faced a running demand for proof of his '100 per cent Americanism,' it was dangerous to champion the cause of the foreign-born."[15]

In 1917 (over Wilson's veto) Congress took a decisive turn away from the long-accepted policy of free immigration. The new law enlarged the classes of aliens excludable from the United States to include an Asian barred zone to shut out Asians. The law also imposed a literacy test that had to be passed before admission. Handlin suggests that the sponsors of the test were interested in using it as "a means of barring the southern and eastern Europeans without excluding those from the northern and western parts of the continent where the facilities for elementary education had become common by 1917."[16] The Anarchist Act of 1918 expanded the provisions for the exclusion of subversive aliens.

After the war, there was a growing fear of the "red scare" as a wave of strikes occurred in 1919 at the same time that race riots broke out in major cities. Isolationist sentiment led to demands for more restrictive measures. In 1921 a congressional statute provided for a quota system in which the number of aliens of any nationality admitted to the United States in a year could not exceed 3 percent of the number of foreign-born residents of that nationality living in America in 1910. This applied to nations of Europe, the Middle East, Africa, Australia, New Zealand, Asia, Russia, and some islands in the Atlantic and Pacific. An even more restrictionist law was enacted in 1924. The National Origins Act set quotas for all countries based on the desirability of various nationalities. Aliens from northern and western Europe were considered more desirable than those from southern and eastern Europe. The number of immigrants admitted in 1921 was 800,000; twelve months later it had dropped to 300,000. By the decade of the 1930s, immigration had trickled down to a total of 70,000 for the whole period.[17]

It was in these historical and cultural contexts that Douglas Macintosh was examined to determine if he would be a loyal American citizen. George Sutherland and Charles Evans Hughes would participate in deciding his fate.

THE JUSTICE FOR THE MAJORITY:
GEORGE SUTHERLAND (1862–1942)

George Sutherland was born on March 25, 1862, at Stoney Stratford in Buckinghamshire, England.[18] His father, George Alexander Sutherland, a recent convert to the Church of Jesus Christ of Latter-Day Saints, moved his family to the Utah Territory less than two years after his son's birth. Sutherland's father was not a committed convert. Indeed, shortly after arriving in Utah the elder Sutherland renounced his faith in Joseph Smith's new revelations and moved to Montana to try his hand at mining. This venture failed, and the Sutherland family soon returned to Utah. They lived in Utah for the remainder of George's youth, yet never returned to the Mormon Church.

The Sutherland family's move to Utah was instrumental in the development of the character and mind of young Sutherland. The exposure to the hard realities of frontier-style living was the most significant influence of his youth. Reflecting on these experiences in a speech delivered to the graduates of Brigham Young University years later, Sutherland described life in the Utah Territory as "very hard as measured by present-day standards."[19] This was a modest statement considering the description of his childhood Sutherland provided to his audience:

> Nobody worried about child labor. The average boy of ten worked—and often worked very hard—along with the other members to support the family. He milked, cut and carried the night's wood, carried swill to the pigs, curried the horses, hoed the corn, guided the plow or, if not, followed it in the task of picking up potatoes which had been upturned, until his young vertebrae approached dislocation and he was ready to consider a bid to surrender his hopes of salvation in exchange for the comfort of a hinge in the small of his back.[20]

Sutherland also remarked on the scarcity of food, saying that "[a]t meals the platter was licked clean. Nothing was wasted." There was no distinction between rich and poor, either, since "everybody was poor and everybody worked."

As these descriptions suggest, the lessons of childhood were learned from the hard work Sutherland's circumstances required of him, not from the classroom. Indeed, his early education was rudimentary and short-lived. He learned little more than reading, writing, and arithmetic at small, single-room schoolhouses from teachers who "lacked much in the way of education." In addition, he was forced to leave school prematurely at the age of twelve because the family's poor financial state necessitated that he earn his own living.

Leaving school and working allowed Sutherland to learn yet another important lesson—the benefits of individual thrift and responsibility. He worked from age twelve through age sixteen as a clerk in a Salt Lake City clothing store and later as an employee of the Wells-Fargo Company in their mining recorder's office. As a result, he earned and saved enough money to pay for his entire college education at Brigham Young Academy. When he entered school, the values of hard work and individual responsibility had already been ingrained into his character.

What the tough, frontier experiences of Sutherland's youth had begun in laying the foundation for a conservative, individualistic political philosophy, his college education would complete by providing a theoretical basis for that philosophy. Two separate biographers have proposed drastically different explanations of the theoretical basis for Sutherland's political philosophy. Joel Francis Paschal, in his 1951 book titled *Mr. Justice Sutherland: A Man against the State*, argues that Sutherland was most heavily influenced by the evolution-inspired writings of Herbert Spencer, which he encountered at both Brigham Young Academy and the University of Michigan Law School. Hadley Arkes, in his 1994 book titled *The Return of George Sutherland: Restoring a Jurisprudence of Natural Rights*, argues that Sutherland espoused a theory of natural rights, which he learned while under the tutelage of Thomas Cooley and James Campbell at the University of Michigan.[21]

Sutherland's introduction to Herbert Spencer began upon his admission to Brigham Young Academy (which eventually became Brigham Young University) in 1879 at the age of sixteen.[22] The head of Brigham Young Academy at that time was a devout Mormon named Karl Maeser. Sutherland had a great deal of respect for Maeser, a fact confirmed in a letter Sutherland wrote memorializing Maeser's death: "Dr. Maeser was not only a scholar of great, and varied learning, with an exceptional ability to impart what he knew to others, but he was a man of such transparent and natural goodness that his students gained not only knowledge, but character, which is better than knowledge."[23] Sutherland's admiration of Maeser never diminished; he "carried with him for the remainder of his days a vivid and grateful memory of Maeser," and always acknowledged the influence Maeser had exerted over his "whole life."[24]

Maeser imparted the ideas of Herbert Spencer to his young pupil.[25] Spencer's theories were based on two fundamental concepts: evolution and liberty. Spencer relied on evolutionary theory to propound that "man, society, and the state were all results of an immeasurably lengthy growth, and that this process was to be continued to the end of time."[26] He called the force behind this evolutionary process "the principle of adaptation."[27] This principle contemplated that "every organism contains within itself an undeniable impulse urging the establishment of harmony with its environment."[28] Adaptation was so essential that Spencer considered it "the sole criterion of good and evil."[29] Thus, that which promoted adaptation was good, and that which inhibited adaptation was evil. Liberty, the second key concept of Spencer's philosophy, "proclaimed the freedom of the individual to effect the adaptation which nature demands."[30] In other words, liberty was essential because it allowed man to follow, unhindered, the dictates of his innate adaptive process. Following this process yielded the most important goal of man, personal perfection.[31]

Spencer's evolutionary theories had serious implications for the role of civil government. He considered the state an unnatural "deviation from the law of liberty" that presented great danger to the process of adaptation.[32] Spencer believed the state's activities should be limited to making society possible "by retaining men in the circumstances to which they are to be adapted."[33] According to Spencer, the state, once it succeeded in "securing the adaptive process," would "wither away and . . . appear ultimately as the crude expedient of a primitive age."[34] Within such a philosophy, government powers clearly needed to be aggressively circumscribed.

As Paschal explains, Spencer conceived of the state as "a wholly negative force of police, limiting its activities to enforcing contracts, suppressing insurrection, and repelling foreign invasion."[35] Paschal argues that this Spencerian philosophy explained why Sutherland repeatedly denounced the encroachments on individual liberty proposed by the progressive lawmakers of his day.

On the other hand, Hadley Arkes proposes that Sutherland's resistance to the New Deal program and similar state legislative programs was inspired by his jurisprudential foundation in natural rights, not his belief in the evolutionary theories of Herbert Spencer. Arkes attributes Sutherland's introduction to this theory to two of his professors at the University of Michigan, Thomas Cooley and James Campbell. The University of Michigan Law School placed a great deal of emphasis on teaching the tradition of natural rights. According to Arkes, both Cooley and Campbell based their theories of limited government on the moral foundation provided by the natural law.[36]

Arkes explains that the theory of natural rights Sutherland studied was based on the idea that men were "moral agents." By using this term, natural rights theorists were recognizing that human beings were by nature separate from "beings that did not have the competence" to weigh matters of morality and to make decisions. This difference was significant because it meant that certain rights, such as life, liberty, property, and contract, were inherent in human nature. Importantly, these natural rights were "moral truths holding in all places" and that they therefore existed prior to and exclusive of human government and laws.[37] Under Arkes's theory, Sutherland's statement in *Powell v. Alabama* (1932) that "there are certain immutable principles of justice that inhere in the very idea of free government," indicates his acceptance of this essential principle of natural rights.[38]

Powell further supports Arkes's assertion. For example, Sutherland argued that the right implicated in *Powell*, the Sixth Amendment right to counsel, could not be denied "without violating 'those fundamental principles of liberty and justice which lie at the base of all our civil and political institutions.'"[39] Even more, Sutherland quoted his former mentor, Thomas Cooley, to support his position that the right to counsel is a fundamental right:

> Judge Cooley refers to the right of a person accused of crime to have counsel as perhaps his most important privilege, and after discussing the development of the English law upon that subject, says: "With us it is a universal principle of constitutional law, that the prisoner shall be allowed a defense by counsel."[40]

Finally, Sutherland cited the numerous statutes and court decisions, both federal and state, that "make it a duty of the trial judge, where the accused is unable to employ counsel, to appoint counsel for him," buttressing his conclusion that the right to counsel is an "inherent" and "fundamental" right.[41]

Another point strongly suggests that Sutherland was more a student of natural rights than of Spencerian philosophy. Arkes argues that if Sutherland truly adhered unequivocally to Spencerian philosophy, he would have rejected many of the "layers of regulation [he] accepted with conviction."[42] Indeed, if Paschal's presentation of Spencerian philosophy is accurate, and if he is correct that Sutherland adhered to that philosophy, Sutherland would have had no choice but to strike down zoning ordinances and other novel governmental regulations aimed at solving social problems. A political philosophy based on Spencer's theories would countenance no other result. Yet, as Arkes notes, Sutherland accepted many forms of governmental regulation.[43]

Sutherland's appointment to the Supreme Court was the result of high-profile professional and political successes. He rode the wave of success, generated by his law practices in both Provo and Salt Lake City and the visible role he played in the establishment and leadership of the Utah State Bar Association and the Utah Republican Party, to positions in both the state and national legislatures.[44] Sutherland attained his first elected office in 1896, the year Utah became a state. He was elected to serve as a senator in the historic first session of the Utah state legislature. He also served as the chairman of the state's Senate Judiciary Committee, which gave him the opportunity to shape much of Utah's court structure and procedures. He championed other important measures while in the state Senate, including a bill requiring an eight-hour day for miners.[45] By the end of four years of distinguished service in that body, Sutherland had cultivated a respectable reputation in Utah.

A discussion of Sutherland's political success would be incomplete without a brief word concerning his opposition to the practice of polygamy. Yet, surprisingly, Sutherland's many political victories in Utah were achieved because the predominantly Mormon population supported him.[46] This support seems odd since his stance against polygamy would presumably offend and alienate many Mormon voters. But Sutherland secured their unwavering support by successfully defending a polygamist against prosecution by the United States.

In 1886 the United States decided to begin enforcing, after a period of reprieve, the territorial statute criminalizing polygamy, called the Edmunds Act. A man named Grosbeck was indicted and charged with two counts of unlawful cohabitation.[47] Grosbeck hired Sutherland as his defense attorney. In the course of defending Grosbeck, Sutherland argued that the statute outlawed the continuing offense of cohabitation, not each separate instance of polygamy; thus, "Grosbeck was amenable to but one conviction and one sentence."[48] This unique argument was later adopted by the Supreme Court in *In re Snow*.[49] In Utah, Sutherland was credited with "originating the argument that brought some relief to the harassed

Saints." Utah newspapers published Sutherland's Grosbeck brief, and he became "something of a hero to the Faithful."[50]

The assistance Sutherland provided the "harassed Saints" strongly suggests that his opposition to polygamy was not compelled by moral repugnance. Hadley Arkes corroborates this point, saying that Sutherland's political stance against the practice never "bore the stamp of moralistic posturing." Sutherland's service in the U.S. House of Representatives confirms this analysis. While a member of that body, he was given the opportunity to testify regarding whether sterner legislation was needed in order to ensure the complete cessation of polygamy within the newly added state. Instead of denouncing polygamy and supporting harsher laws, Sutherland seized the opportunity to "make the case for tolerance."

In his testimony, Sutherland hinted at the absence of a moral basis for his objection to polygamy: "the Gentiles fought polygamy with a bitterness that can hardly be understood." Sutherland also praised the moral qualities of the wives of polygamous marriages and shared personal anecdotes of his interaction with polygamous families.[51] Calling the complexities of dismantling polygamy "a difficult question to manage by law," he counseled adopting a policy that would allow time to work out the details and heal the wounds.[52]

Having gained a solid base of political support in his home state, Sutherland was ready to begin his journey to national prominence. This journey began in 1900 when he captured Utah's only seat in the House of Representatives. He served just one term in the House; his eyes were set on the higher goal of becoming a senator. In furtherance of this ambition, he left the House and returned to his home state to develop support among the members of the Utah state legislature, since in the early 1900s U.S. senators were still elected by the legislatures of the states. Sutherland's decision to go home, along with his previously established credibility and popularity in Utah, culminated in his triumph over the incumbent, Senator Thomas Kearns, in 1905.[53]

Sutherland served in the Senate until 1916, when the momentum of the Progressive movement, which had ushered Woodrow Wilson into office, pushed out conservatives like Sutherland. Nevertheless, Sutherland championed many important causes during his years in the Senate. One important cause was women's suffrage. As the recognized leader of the women's suffrage movement in the Senate, in 1915, he introduced the women's suffrage amendment. He counseled women's groups on tactics, received numerous delegations from women's organizations in his Senate office, and was recognized by various women's groups as their "powerful ally" in the Senate.[54]

Sutherland also played a prominent role in denouncing much of the Progressive movement's experimental legislation. Predictably, he was most concerned with legislative attempts to enhance the size and reach of the federal government. Consequently, he "condemned the Federal Reserve Act, the Federal Trade Commission, the Clayton Anti-Trust Act, and the constitutional amendment providing for an income tax."[55] The threat these programs posed to the natural rights of the individual left him no choice but to oppose them.

A speech Sutherland delivered in 1914 to the Cleveland Chamber of Commerce is an excellent summary of his reasons for opposing the numerous legislative proposals of the Progressive era. In that speech he lamented: "We are creating an army of official agents, governmental bureaus and all sorts of Commissions to pry into our affairs, smell out our shortcomings and tell us what we may and what we may not do."[56] He proposed that the better solution to the social and economic problems facing the nation was to allow "individual conduct . . . to be regulated and governed by moral restraint rather than by statutory enactment." Statutes motivated by an "excess of sentiment" could never make "everybody perfect." Instead, they simply encouraged the "idle and profligate." Sutherland concluded his speech with a concise statement of his essential political philosophy: "[Government] must not be allowed to wander too far from the sphere of its normal and traditional functions or interfere overmuch with the liberty of the individual to work out his destiny here and his salvation hereafter in his own way."[57]

This conservative philosophy restricted Sutherland's effectiveness as a legislator and likely contributed to his ouster from the Senate. Yet this defeat did not end his involvement in the nation's affairs. Shortly after leaving the Senate, Sutherland opened a law practice in Washington, D.C., was elected president of the American Bar Association, and argued several cases before the Supreme Court of the United States. Then, in 1920, Sutherland became a confidential advisor to Warren Harding in his bid for the presidency. It has been argued that Sutherland originated the famous and ultimately successful "front-porch" strategy employed by Harding during the election. Harding would eventually reward Sutherland for his faithful service with an appointment to the Supreme Court on September 5, 1922.

A key aspect of Sutherland's judicial philosophy was his belief in the supremacy of the judiciary. Among the three branches of government in the American constitutional system, he believed that the judiciary could best guarantee liberty.[58] As he said in an address written for the annual dinner of the Pennsylvania Society on December 13, 1913, the history of mankind's struggle to overcome oppression and injustice illuminated "at least this one basic principle. . . . That liberty to be secure must rest upon a foundation of preestablished law, administered by upright, impartial, and independent judges, to the end that there shall be a government of laws and not of men."[59] Sutherland's idealistic view of the judiciary shines through clearly when he claimed that judges are "stainless as virtue and incorruptible as the everlasting truth," capable of *"compelling* justice between the rich and the poor, the powerful and the weak, the multitude and the man."[60]

Sutherland's belief that the Supreme Court can enforce natural rights against government action has made him one of the most maligned justices in Supreme Court history. Franklin Roosevelt, whose New Deal program was constantly harassed by Sutherland and his conservative colleagues, began history's indictment of Sutherland with his harsh criticisms of the Court. Historians and critics have almost universally laid the responsibility for the Court's decisions against the New Deal program squarely at Sutherland's feet.[61] In doing so, they have minimized his jurisprudential basis in natural rights, instead choosing to call him a reactionary justice with no basis for his opposition to the New Deal except his anachronistic ideas about society and economics.[62] But as the analysis above demonstrates, Sutherland had developed his commitment to natural law theory during the course of his personal experiences and education. He did not conjure this theory up in his own mind. The natural rights tradition is steeped in this nation's history and is supported by Supreme Court precedent.[63] Sutherland simply applied that tradition to the cases that came before him during his many years on the Court.

While the basis of Sutherland's political philosophy can be determined by analyzing his speeches and Court opinions, the foundation of his religious beliefs is not as readily accessible. Sutherland rejected Mormonism, saying in his address to the graduating class of Brigham Young that his religious opinions were "at variance" with the faith that pervaded his youth and education.[64] A brief look at some of his speeches and writings will help illuminate his core religious beliefs.

The first clear evidence regarding Sutherland's religious beliefs is contained in his speech to the graduating class of Brigham Young University in 1941. In this address, Sutherland revealed that God had occupied a prominent position in his mind during his youth in Utah. He remarked that the trials and tribulations of life in the territory were met with "courage and faith in God." He spoke about the nature of God and the need for prayer:

> I have always believed . . . in the power and goodness of God and the efficacy of prayer. And by prayer I do not mean that empty recital of pious words which is a mere movement of the lips, signifying nothing. I mean the form of prayer which finds its source in the innermost self—whether it be a simple prayer expressing devotion to God and asking his guidance and aid in respect of our everyday affairs . . . or that supreme appeal for help in some dire extremity, when we can no longer summon powers of our own to help ourselves.[65]

According to Sutherland, when the pioneers of Utah faced dire, life-threatening circumstances, they prayed for "Divine intervention to avert disaster against which human power was of no avail."[66]

Clearly, Sutherland believed in God and found prayer to be a beneficial and worshipful endeavor. Yet amid these comments are intertwined lines of thought indicating that his belief in God was subordinate to an even more fundamental belief. For example, he said that when the impoverished Utah families asked God to "'[g]ive us this day our daily bread,' they did not seek an abnormal exercise of God's power as they stood idly by." Instead, "[t]hey looked for the answer in their own efforts, strengthened by prayer and a renewed faith."[67] This comment hints at Sutherland's deepest religious belief—the inevitable progress of man through his own strengths and abilities, independent of God's intervention.

Sutherland expounded upon this belief in a speech he delivered before Congress in 1907. This speech demonstrated that Sutherland's esteem of man was largely based on his rejection of the biblical teaching of the Fall and on his professed belief in the "law of evolution."[68] He made this point explicit:

> I am no believer in the doctrine of the fall of man. Man has not fallen. He has risen and will rise. In the process of evolution he has so far progressed that he is able to stand erect and look upward, but his feet are still upon the earth, and so while he sees the heights he ascends them only with slow and toilsome effort. But he does ascend.[69]

Sutherland consistently rejected the Fall throughout his life, as language from his Brigham Young address some thirty-four years later demonstrates:

> The new-born babe has neither good nor bad character, for it has no character at all. It reacts to physical stimuli, but cannot react to any moral appeal because its state is one of entire innocence, a purely passive quality, which connotes the absence of ability to distinguish good from evil, as we are told was the state of our first parents before the fall. But as the child grows, the difference between good and evil must be taught.[70]

Clearly, such a view of man's nature suggests that Sutherland likely rejected the Christian teaching that sinful man must be reconciled to God through Christ's atoning sacrifice. It also lays the philosophical foundation for Sutherland's utopian belief that man is ever-progressing to a higher state of existence.[71]

Sutherland's belief in evolution did not require a complete repudiation of God. While he characterized himself as "not religious in the ordinary acceptation of the term," and disavowed religious forms, creeds, and ceremonies, he nevertheless believed "with all the strength of [his] soul that 'there is a power in the universe, not ourselves, which makes for righteousness.'"[72] Thus, Sutherland's belief in the inevitable progress of man was predicated on a belief that some power, neither of man nor within man, was responsible for the "mighty power which silently and surely . . . works for the exaltation and uplifting of all mankind."[73] In this sense, Sutherland's adherence to the law of evolution appears to have been less categorical, and less anthropocentric, than Herbert Spencer's philosophy.

In addition, Sutherland believed in a final judgment of man by God. He referred to God's judgment when encouraging the graduating class of Brigham Young that character matters far more than scholastic or professional achievements: "The inquiry which God will make in passing judgment upon you, I imagine, will not be, how far have you gone in higher mathematics, how many languages you have mastered; but what is your character."[74]

It is interesting to note that Sutherland's beliefs, despite his protestations to the contrary, resemble certain teachings of the Mormon Church. The first and most apparent similarity between Sutherland's religious views and Mormonism is that Mormons also reject the orthodox doctrine

of original sin.[75] Mormons believe that the Fall simply introduced spiritual
and physical death into the world. Under this theory of the Fall, Christ's
atonement is robbed of its significance:

> [T]he atonement of Christ is designed to ransom men from the effects
> of the fall of Adam in that both spiritual and temporal death are con-
> quered; their lasting effect is nullified. The spiritual death of the fall is
> replaced by the spiritual life of atonement, in that all who believe and
> obey the gospel law gain spiritual or eternal life.[76]

This statement contains the second, less apparent, yet still intriguing,
similarity between Sutherland's religious beliefs and Mormon theology.
Mormons believe that salvation is based upon man's ability to progress
toward God-hood while on earth. The more faithfully the believer follows
the moral teachings of both the Bible and the Mormon Scriptures, the
greater inheritance he will receive upon death. The Mormon teaching
that progress up the path to salvation is based upon performing good
works during life on earth is reminiscent of Sutherland's belief that God
will judge man by his character. This teaching also resembles his belief
that man is continually progressing to a higher state of existence. Thus,
while Sutherland did not accept the Mormon faith, it is arguable that
Mormon thought and theology influenced some of his core beliefs.

Sutherland did, however, adopt one teaching of the Mormon Church
without reservation—the United States Constitution was "divinely
inspired."[77] While in college at Brigham Young Academy, Karl Maeser
introduced Sutherland to many Mormon Scriptures that proved this
point. Included among those Scriptures was the *Doctrine and Covenants*,
a foundational Mormon text, which quotes God as saying,

> 79. Therefore, it is not right that any man should be in bondage one
> to another.
> 80. And for this purpose have I established the Constitution of this
> land, by the hands of wise men whom I raised up unto this very pur-
> pose and redeemed the land by the shedding of blood.[78]

Later in life Sutherland would confirm his acceptance of this particular Mormon teaching in a letter to a friend: "I can recall, as far back as
1879 and 1880, the words of Professor Maesar, who declared that [the
Constitution] was a divinely inspired instrument—as I truly think it is."[79]
This may explain why Sutherland so vigorously protected constitutional

rights and liberties, which he must have considered sacred given his belief in the divine nature of the document securing those rights.

This brief review of Sutherland's writings and speeches paints a clearer picture of the main tenets of his religious beliefs. He appears to have been a humanist who made room for God within his ontological framework. He rejected the doctrine of the Fall of man, which set a foundation for his humanistic belief in the inevitable progression and betterment of man. Yet he also retained a belief in a Supreme Being who gave guidance and comfort in times of need and ultimately judged each individual for his or her actions during life.

THE JUSTICE IN DISSENT:
CHARLES EVAN HUGHES (1862–1948)

Charles Evans Hughes was born on April 11, 1862, in Glens Falls, New York.[80] His father was a Baptist minister, who, like Sutherland's father, had emigrated from England. His mother was an American whose family had Baptist roots going back to the colonial period. Young Charles was precocious from the start, as many examples from his childhood demonstrate. He was able to read at the tender age of three and a half and also had a knack for memorization, which, coupled with his intense religious training, resulted in his possessing "a fairly large repertoire of biblical lore" at a very young age.

Charles was educated almost entirely by his parents until he went to college. He had been home-schooled during the first few years of his life but was sent away for school at the age of six. He grew weary and bored after just three weeks and begged his parents to allow him to resume his studies at home. In support of this request, Hughes devised a document titled *Charles E. Hughes' Plan of Study*. This meticulously drafted document listed all of his proposed subjects of study in separate columns and allotted the time of day in which they would be studied. His father could not help but grant his request. Hughes prepared similarly for the entrance examinations to Madison University (now Colgate University). He obtained a Madison catalogue and set out to prove that he could fully prepare for the exams by diligently studying at home for one year. Hughes was successful, and entered college at the young age of fourteen.

After study at Madison, Hughes went on to Brown University and then attended Columbia Law School, where he excelled. He started his distinguished legal career with Walter S. Carter's New York firm, which was a leader in the newly developing and lucrative area of corporate law at the end of the nineteenth century. Hughes married Carter's daughter, Antoinette.

Hughes's childhood was a strong indicator of the success he would enjoy in life. His most conspicuous achievements would be in the area of public service. His initial foray into public service came when he was elected governor of New York in 1906, a position that he held until 1910. When his term as governor ended, President William Howard Taft nominated him to replace David Brewer on the Supreme Court of the United States. Hughes remained on the Court for six years, but in 1916 the Republican Party nominated him as their presidential candidate. Hughes resigned his position on the Court to pursue the presidency. Despite optimistic predictions of his inevitable victory, even as late as when he went to bed on election night, he lost the 1916 election to Woodrow Wilson by the slim electoral margin of 277 to 254.

As a result of this defeat, Hughes found himself out of public service for the first time in many years, and thus turned his attention to developing a private law practice. Four years later, however, another chance for public service presented itself again, as the Republicans were clamoring for Hughes to make another run at the presidency. He declined these overtures, however, choosing instead to throw his support behind Warren Harding. Harding, upon assuming office in 1921, rewarded Hughes by appointing him secretary of state. Hughes served faithfully in that position for four years, but eventually resigned in March 1925, eager to return to the calm of private life, especially now that he was approaching his sixty-third birthday. But public service would continue to pursue him. In 1930, upon the death of Chief Justice William Howard Taft, President Hoover appointed Hughes as chief justice; thus, he replaced the very man who had appointed him to the Court in 1910. Hughes finally ended his life of public service on July 1, 1941, when he tendered his resignation as chief justice to President Franklin Roosevelt.

Chief Justice Hughes regarded religion highly throughout his life, largely as a by-product of the faith of his parents, both of whom were deeply religious. In his autobiographical notes, Hughes described them as "alike in the depth of their religious feeling, in their acceptance of the evangelical conceptions of Christian truth and in their unselfish devotion to the Church."[81] Hughes also remarked of his parents that he never encountered anyone in his life more sincere in his or her faith and "more constantly dominated by a sense of religious duty" than they.

Christian orthodoxy and teaching pervaded Hughes's childhood as a result of his parents' faith and his father's position as a Baptist minister. In his autobiographical notes, Hughes expressed that his early years were not only subject to "an exceptional intellectual stimulus but also to a constant and rigorous religious discipline." Examples of this religious discipline abound. Hughes started attending church at a very young age, a family friend having provided a small rocking chair for him to use while his father preached and his mother sang in the choir. Sundays were strictly observed for church "services and devotions. Anything resembling sport or even pleasure was tabooed." Beyond these strict observances, he was taught early on that his "childish peccadilloes were evidence" of his sinful nature and that he needed to subdue his "evil inclinations." He was also drilled from a young age in the doctrines of the Baptist Church, which supplied him with a "'mastery' . . . of the tenets of the denomination." This mastery served him well when he was examined for membership in his father's church; the deacons were amazed at his extensive knowledge of church doctrine.

The purpose of the intense religious instruction of Hughes's youth was to prepare him for what his parents assumed would be a lifetime of work in the ministry. But despite their intentions, the intensity and rigidity of that instruction, according to Hughes, "defeated its own purpose by creating . . . a distaste for religious formalities." As a consequence, Hughes rejected his parents' overtures for him to pursue the ministry. Nevertheless, the nature of Hughes's "distaste" for religion should not be misunderstood. He had not developed a dislike of religious pursuits in general, but merely for the legalistic doctrines and dogmas of his youth. The following comment regarding his lifetime association with the Baptist Church confirms that Hughes's distaste was directed toward denominationalism, not Christianity:

> While I maintained my Baptist connection, I had long since ceased to attach any importance to what many regard as the distinctive tenets of the denomination. . . . I wished to throw what influence I had to the support of Christian institutions, and so far as the dogmas of the creeds were concerned I saw nothing to be gained by leaving the Church in which I had been brought up and joining another denomination.[82]

This quotation indicates two important things. First, it shows that Hughes attached little significance to the unique doctrines of the Baptist Church, or to any other denomination for that matter. Yet it also shows his respect for Christianity and his commitment to its institutions.

While Hughes rejected the formalism of his parent's faith, he still maintained strong religious beliefs throughout his lifetime that largely reflected the Christian teachings of his youth. Merlo Pusey, Hughes's official biographer, presented the following remarks made by Hughes to the Vaughan class of the Calvary Baptist Church in Washington as the essence of Hughes's religious beliefs:

> We need to cultivate the spiritual life, not by centering our attention upon dogma, or by sacrificing intellectual honesty, but by reflection upon the spiritual verities of the Sermon on the Mount.
>
> A truly Christian character is revealed in a balanced life. . . . What does the Christian character or balanced life mean? It is this:
>
> Faith without credulity; conviction without bigotry; charity without condescension; courage without pugnacity; self-respect without vanity; humility without obsequiousness; love of humanity without sentimentality; and meekness with power.
>
> That is our ideal.[83]

Missing from what Pusey presents as Hughes's "creed" is any mention of Christ's life, death, and resurrection. In fact, references to orthodox Christian doctrines are conspicuously absent from Hughes's many letters and writings on religion. It appears that what Hughes valued most about the Christian religion was its advice and guidance on how to develop Christian character, what Hughes called the "balanced life," and not its more fundamental message of salvation.

Hughes's rejection of religious rituals and Christian orthodoxy constantly agitated and saddened his mother, who often reminded him of this fact.[84] On one occasion, after receiving a particularly reproachful letter from his mother, Hughes set out to explain his religious beliefs. Not surprisingly, the letter focused on Hughes's disdain for religious formalism. Regarding prayer, he explained to his mother, "it is too wonderful and mysterious and sacred to be cheapened by formalism and vain repetitions."[85] Hughes called "prayers before meals and the so-called family prayers . . . a wretched business," finding such practices stifling to a meaningful prayer life.[86] Despite this attack on formalism, Hughes concluded his letter to his mother by assuring her that they had "the same desire to serve God" even though their methods of serving Him may have differed.[87]

A key personality trait that significantly influenced how he approached the formalism of his parents was intimately related to Hughes's religious beliefs: tolerance. While Hughes personally deplored religious creeds and doctrines, he nevertheless displayed patience and respect for them because he knew they were very important to others.[88]

Hughes's tolerant nature is also evident from the stand he took as a member of a committee selected in 1908 to reexamine the charter of his alma mater, Brown University. The school was still operating under its original 1764 charter, which gave "the Baptists substantial majorities among the trustees and fellows and requir[ed] the president to be a Baptist." Hughes viewed such requirements as expressions of the religious intolerance of a less enlightened time and took the lead in recommending that the charter be stripped of all denominational requirements. His recommendations were rejected at first, but over the next thirty-two years were adopted piecemeal. Finally, in 1940, the original vision of the 1908 committee was realized as all denominational requirements were removed from Brown's charter.[89]

Consistent with his promotion of religious tolerance and his connection with the Baptists, Hughes staunchly advocated religious liberty. His regard for religious freedom is captured in his words explaining why he associated with the Baptist denomination throughout his life. As Hughes said, it was not the "distinctive tenets of the denomination," but instead "the noble tradition of the Baptists as protagonists in the struggle for religious liberty" that kept him in the Baptist fold.[90]

Hughes expressed his appreciation for the Baptist commitment to religious liberty in a speech he gave in 1922 at the laying of the cornerstone of the National Baptist Memorial to Religious Liberty in Washington, D.C.[91] In that speech, he said that the Baptists' storied history of battling for religious liberty was "the glory of the Baptist heritage, more distinctive than any other characteristic of belief or practice. To this militant leadership all sects and faiths are debtors."[92]

In addition to pointing out America's indebtedness to the Baptists, Hughes proclaimed his understanding of what the Establishment and Free Exercise Clauses of the First Amendment meant:

> These Constitutional declarations are not forms of words conveying an abstract idea. They have definite and well-understood practical

implications. Men of all religious beliefs stand equal before the law. They are not to be punished by reason of their creeds or forms of worship so long as they respect the public peace and the equal rights of others. No one is exposed to civil disability either as a witness in our courts or with respect to qualification for any public office by reason of his religious faith. Nor are the people to be taxed and public moneys to be used for the support of any sort of religion.[93]

Numerous times Hughes stressed the point that true religious liberty demanded "the absolute freedom of religion from civil control." As Hughes stated, "The kingdom of God was not of this world and was not within the keeping of any prince."[94] Clearly, Hughes cherished religious liberty and espoused a separationist view of the religion clauses.

This brief analysis of Hughes's upbringing and his letters and writings regarding religion helps to clarify his religious beliefs. First, Hughes rejected any attachment to religious creeds or doctrines. He believed that a formalistic approach to Christianity robbed it of its deeper life and meaning. Yet despite his rejection of forms and creeds, he remained committed to the Christian religion and its institutions throughout his lifetime. Second, Hughes believed in religious tolerance. His respect for the denominational creeds he found so objectionable and the work he did to liberalize Brown University's charter exemplify his commitment to this ideal. Third, and most important, Hughes believed strongly in religious liberty. His regard for this bedrock principle of America's national experience was demonstrated both in his reasons for continuing to align himself with the Baptist Church and in his 1922 address at the future site of the Baptist National Memorial to Religious Liberty.

THE CASE: *UNITED STATES V. MACINTOSH* (1931)

Justice Sutherland's and Chief Justice Hughes's religious beliefs and experiences had a direct impact in their respective opinions in *United States v. Macintosh*.[95] Both justices' core philosophies and beliefs appear to have impacted their decisions. As between the two opinions, however, Justice Hughes's dissent offers the most obvious example of how religious beliefs can impact a justice's religious liberty jurisprudence.

The facts of *Macintosh* are straightforward.[96] Douglas Clyde Macintosh first came to the United States as a young graduate student at the

University of Chicago. In 1907 he was ordained as a Baptist minister and two years later began to teach at Yale University. After the outbreak of World War I in 1914, Macintosh volunteered to join the Canadian Army and served as chaplain to Allied soldiers at the front. He returned to the United States in 1917 and a year later went back to France where he had charge of an American Y.M.C.A. hut serving the soldiers until the end of the war in November 1918. Upon his return, Macintosh resumed his teaching duties at Yale. In 1926 he made application to become a naturalized citizen of the United States. At the time that his case reached the Supreme Court in 1931, Macintosh was a member of the Yale faculty of the Divinity School, chaplain of the Graduate School, and Dwight Professor of Theology.

The Naturalization Act of 1906 provided that an agent of the United States government had the right to appear at final naturalization hearings and cross-examine the petitioner on "any matter touching or in any way affecting his right to admission to citizenship."[97] Under the authority granted by this statute to inquire after matters touching or affecting one's fitness for citizenship, the United States's representative asked the question that would ultimately undermine Macintosh's bid for citizenship. The question was whether Macintosh would be "willing to take up arms in defense of this country."[98] Macintosh answered that he would take up arms to defend the country only if he regarded the war as morally justified, based upon his understanding of the moral principles of Christianity.

Justice Sutherland, in a 5 to 4 decision, prohibited Macintosh from becoming a United States citizen because of this answer. Sutherland justified his decision by arguing that the right of a conscientious religious objector to be exempted from the duty to bear arms was a right dependent on congressional prerogative. Such a right, according to Sutherland, had no basis in the Constitution. In essence, Sutherland believed that granting Macintosh citizenship would be tantamount to granting a naturalized citizen more rights than a native-born citizen enjoys. He couched his decision in terms at least relying on the concept of religious liberty. Nevertheless, he concluded that Macintosh's personal interpretation of the will of God could not be allowed to overcome Congress's power to declare war and raise armies. Taking this proposition one step further, Sutherland provocatively suggested that our government relies on the assumption that "unqualified allegiance to the Nation and submission and obedience to the laws of the land, as well those made for war as those made for peace, are not inconsistent with the will of God."[99]

The dissent took umbrage at this suggestion. Chief Justice Hughes argued that the Constitution recognizes that "in the forum of conscience, duty to a moral power higher than the State has always been maintained."[100] As to the majority's suggestion that the religious scruples of the individual had to acquiesce to Congress's war powers, Hughes answered that "[t]here is abundant room for enforcing the requisite authority of law . . . and for maintaining the conception of the supremacy of law . . . without demanding that either citizens or applicants for citizenship shall assume by oath an obligation to regard allegiance to God as subordinate to allegiance to civil power."[101] Hughes believed that such a requirement would not only be inimical to our constitutional heritage but also would be contrary to Congress's historic practice of exempting conscientious objectors from the duty to bear arms.

In expounding on his religious liberty argument, Hughes offered a definition of religion that envisioned "one's views of his relations to his Creator, and to the obligations they impose of reverence for his being and character, and of obedience to his will."[102] Loosely applying this definition to Macintosh's beliefs, Hughes concluded that Macintosh believed in what was "axiomatic in religious doctrine," namely, a belief in "allegiance to the will of God."[103] To Hughes, the religious nature of Macintosh's belief, the nation's historic practice of exempting conscientious objectors from the duty to bear arms, and the constitutional commitment to religious liberty and conscience, entitled him to become a naturalized citizen of the United States despite his stipulation that he would not take up arms in defense of country unless he believed the war was morally justified.[104] Macintosh's religious beliefs were simply more important to him than the nation's interest in conducting a war.

Sutherland's and Hughes's opinions in *Macintosh* are historically significant from the perspective of the First Amendment religion clauses for two reasons. First, Sutherland's opinion indicated that the Supreme Court, as late as 1931, was willing to at least recognize to some extent the Christian heritage of this nation.[105] Second, both the majority opinion and the dissent demonstrated that the Court was still defining religion in a way that was consistent with the Founders' understanding of that term. In addition, *Macintosh* is significant because it foreshadowed Justice Sutherland's greatest and most enduring contribution to constitutional law—his outlining of the war and foreign powers of the United States government.

The first reason *Macintosh* is historically significant is because it recognized our nation's Christian heritage. Sutherland's statement in *Macintosh* affirming that heritage was certainly not as categorical as that of Justice David Brewer in *Church of the Holy Trinity v. United States*.[106] In that case, Brewer analyzed the Christian character of our laws and institutions in depth and concluded from that analysis that the United States was "a Christian nation."[107] Sutherland did not conduct any such analysis but simply asserted that "[w]e are a Christian people."[108] But he cited Brewer's *Holy Trinity* decision as authority for this assertion; in doing so, he sanctioned Justice Brewer's conclusions in *Holy Trinity*.[109]

The second reason *United States v. Macintosh* is historically significant is that both the majority opinion, written by Sutherland, and the dissent, written by Chief Justice Hughes, define religion in a way that is faithful to the Founders' understanding of that term.[110] Several commentators on the religion clauses have remarked that the term "religion" was defined in theistic terms by both the Founders[111] and the nineteenth-century Supreme Court on the limited occasions where it had the opportunity to address the subject.[112] Sutherland's words in *Macintosh* echo this traditional, theistic sentiment: "We are a Christian people . . . according to one another the equal right of religious freedom, and acknowledging with reverence the duty of obedience to the will of God."[113] Chief Justice Hughes's dissent joined in a tribute to theism with these words: "The essence of religion is belief in a relation to God involving duties superior to those arising from any human relation. . . . One cannot speak of religious liberty, with proper appreciation for its essential and historic significance, without assuming the existence of a belief in supreme allegiance to the will of God."[114] Thus *Macintosh*, in addition to marking the last time the Supreme Court of the United States officially recognized that this nation has a uniquely Christian heritage, also marked the last time the Supreme Court defined religion in theistic terms.

Finally, Sutherland's decision in *Macintosh* hinted at his most important contribution to this nation's constitutional heritage, the outlining of the plenary nature of both the Congress's war powers and the president's power over foreign affairs. As mentioned, Sutherland paid homage to this nation's commitment to religious freedom in *Macintosh*, but he found that this commitment is subordinate to an "even more fundamental" power, Congress's war powers.[115] He demonstrated his belief in the expansiveness of these powers by listing permissible government actions during wartime:

> To the end that war may not result in defeat, freedom of speech may, by act of Congress, be curtailed or denied so that the morale of the

people and the spirit of the army may not be broken by seditious utterances; freedom of the press curtailed to preserve our military plans and movements from the knowledge of the enemy; deserters and spies put to death without indictment or trial by jury; ships and supplies requisitioned; property of alien enemies, theretofore under the protection of the Constitution, seized without process and converted to the public use without compensation and without due process of law in the ordinary sense of that term; prices of food and other necessities of life fixed or regulated; railways taken over and operated by the government; and other drastic powers, wholly inadmissible in time of peace, exercised to meet the emergencies of war.[116]

As this sweeping statement demonstrates, it was Sutherland's conviction that "[n]ational survival is a supreme duty to which not only scruples of conscience, but even the great organizational principles of the Constitution must yield."[117] This conviction is especially surprising in light of the reputation Sutherland garnered as a protector of the very rights he was now saying Congress could abridge with impunity during times of war. Later, in *United States v. Curtiss-Wright Export Corp.* (1936), Sutherland argued that the president's power over foreign affairs was equally as expansive as Congress's power to make war. Sutherland's work in outlining the war and foreign powers of the United States Government has had a lasting impact on the development of constitutional law.[118]

Sutherland's opinion in *Macintosh*, above all else, embodies his belief that the United States Government had the responsibility to ensure the nation's survival. While he is remembered as a justice who "considered the limits of the Constitution to be absolute and inflexible," his decision in *Macintosh* demonstrates his willingness to depart from this "absolute" position when personal rights conflicted with the nation's duty to survive.[119]

Sutherland's statement in *Macintosh* that "we are a Christian people" was not the product of an intense Christian upbringing, or the expression of a personal predilection in favor of the Christian religion. Indeed, he eschewed all religious doctrines and creeds and flatly rejected the orthodox Christian doctrine of the Fall. Hence, it appears that when he paid homage to the Christian heritage of this nation in *Macintosh*, he was simply affirming a fact about this nation's history that had previously been attested to by Justice Brewer in his 1892 *Holy Trinity* decision. Even more, it testifies to his intellectual and historical honesty. Despite professing beliefs contrary to the Christian faith, Sutherland was intellectually and historically honest enough to recognize the Christian heritage of our nation.

Hughes's dissent in *Macintosh* strongly resembles his religious beliefs. First and foremost, it reflects his deep devotion to religious liberty. For example, in his address at the National Baptist Memorial in 1922 Hughes declared that religious liberty requires "absolute freedom of religion from civil control" and "the emancipation of the spirit of man from the fetters of civil rule."[120] He also argued that "[m]en of all religious beliefs . . . are not to be punished by reason of their creeds or forms of worship so long as they respect the public peace and the equal rights of others."[121] Hughes's belief that the dictates of conscience are superior to the dictates of civil government, expressed so clearly in the above quotations, found voice in his *Macintosh* dissent:

> The battle for religious liberty has been fought and won with respect to religious beliefs and practices, which are not in conflict with good order, upon the very ground of the supremacy of conscience within its proper field. . . . The attempt to exact . . . a promise [to regard allegiance to God as subordinate to allegiance to civil power], and thus to bind one's conscience by the taking of oaths or the submission to tests, has been the cause of many deplorable conflicts. . . . [There is no] ground . . . for the exclusion of Professor Macintosh because his conscientious scruples have particular reference to wars believed to be unjust.[122]

Further statements from Hughes's *Macintosh* dissent also strongly reflect his personal beliefs regarding religious liberty. He declared that "[t]he essence of religion is belief in a relation to God involving duties superior to those arising from any human relation" and that, "in the forum of conscience, duty to a moral power higher than the State has always been maintained." Both of these statements evince his desire to protect the conscience from government intrusion.

Hughes's dissent manifested other aspects of his religious beliefs, including his disdain for religious creeds and tests and related advocacy of religious tolerance. For example, Hughes argued that when inquiring into the religious beliefs of a citizen one should put aside "dogmas with their particular conceptions of deity," and instead recognize that "freedom of conscience itself implies respect for an innate conviction of paramount duty."[123] Even more, just as Hughes found it offensive to subject someone to tests in order to determine their acceptability as a Christian, he found it offensive to subject applicants for citizenship to oaths or tests in order to determine their acceptability as a citizen, at least where those tests obligated the applicant to regard civil authority as superior to their sincere religious beliefs.

In conclusion, it would appear that the key aspects of Hughes's religious beliefs influenced his *Macintosh* dissent. He deplored religious tests and doctrines, was tolerant toward differing religious beliefs and practices, and cherished religious liberty. All three of these aspects of his religious beliefs, and especially his esteem for religious liberty, are apparent in the language of his *Macintosh* dissent.

The cultural reaction to the Court's decision in *Macintosh* was immediate. Secular and religious newspapers and periodicals expressed the mood of the country. Generally speaking, the mainstream press was evenly divided, supporting both majority and dissenting opinions. The religious press, however, universally deplored the decision.

The Christian Century vehemently denounced the Court's decision. It found most objectionable Sutherland's "equation of the will of the government with the will of God."[124] One *Christian Century* author wrote that Sutherland's suggestion represented "the most clear-cut enunciation of the doctrine of the supremacy of the state over the individual conscience—or in other words of the Cult of the Omnipotent State—ever formulated."[125] For its part, *The Christian Century* formulated a document entitled "Declaration of an American Citizen" and encouraged all Americans to sign it and send it to Congress and the president. The following paragraph of this document fairly sums up the reaction of *The Christian Century* and most other religious periodicals to *Macintosh*:

> Therefore, I, a native-born citizen of the United States, solemnly refuse to acknowledge the obligation which the supreme court [*sic*] declares to be binding upon native-born citizens. I have not promised, expressly or tacitly, to accept an act of Congress as the final interpretation of the will of God, and I will not do so. In my allegiance to my country I withhold nothing, not even my life. But I cannot give my conscience. That belongs to God. I repudiate the obligation which the Supreme Court's decision would impose upon me, and declare that the imposition of such an obligation is the essence of tyranny. I refuse to be bound by it.[126]

Other religious publications issued similar denunciations. A Northern Baptist newspaper said that "in the event of another war," the Court's decision would result in the nation's jails being "filled to overflowing. There may come a time when it will be a disgrace for a Baptist, with his spiritual heritage, to be out of jail."[127] *Gospel Messenger*, a Church of the Brethren publication, argued that the Court's decision marked the beginning of "the suicidal business of refusing to accept the sort of people who have made civilization possible."[128] And the Seventh-Day Adventist publication, *Liberty*, noted that: "The decision of the Court puts the government in the position of attempting to coerce the conscientious convictions of citizens rather than to punish them for outright violations of the law."[129] On top of this, several denominations passed resolutions condemning the decision and supporting Reverend Macintosh.

Besides religious publications, individual religious leaders condemned *Macintosh*, sometimes even from the pulpit on Sunday morning. The pastor of Riverside Church in New York City, the Reverend Dr. Harry Fosdick, criticized the Court's decision in a sermon one Sunday morning:

> [*Macintosh*] announces in a particularly obnoxious form the doctrine of the nation's right to conscript conscience. Such is the duress and necessity of war that we have gradually surrendered practically all our rights in the presence of it. The nation in wartime will conscript our children, conscript our property, conscript our business. There is no doubt of that now, and no one of us will be able to prevent it. Has the nation, however, so taken the place of God Almighty that it can conscript our consciences?[130]

Reverend George Crapullo, pastor of Irvin Square Presbyterian Church in Brooklyn, also addressed *Macintosh* in a sermon: "If Jesus were here today and applied for American citizenship, he would be politely informed that he was not eligible. On the basis of the Supreme Court decision he would be denied citizenship because he recognized loyalty to God and humanity as being higher than loyalty to the State."[131] A chorus of religious voices condemned *Macintosh* as an egregious violation of our nation's commitment to religious freedom.

The religious community's reaction to *Macintosh* shows that groups and individuals generally embraced Hughes's dissent. Hughes's plea for religious liberty and freedom of conscience permeated many of the commentaries on *Macintosh*. On some occasions, those commentaries specifically affirmed the chief justice's dissent. Dr. Fosdick referred to Hughes's dissent as "representative of true religion and true Americanism."[132] *The Christian Century* heaped glowing praise on Hughes's stand, saying his "dissenting opinion . . . may in time come to be regarded as a charter of liberty for the individual conscience comparable in importance to the Mayflower pact, the Virginia bill of rights, or the first ten amendments to the federal constitution."[133]

This connection is significant. Hughes's beliefs regarding religious liberty, described earlier, embodied what most Protestant denominations gradually advocated during the twentieth century as they became more aware of and involved in national issues pertaining to religious liberty. Hughes, a member and sometimes officer of the National Baptist Church, espoused a relatively strict separationist view of religious liberty. He argued that the First Amendment religion clauses prohibited the government from taxing and using public funds "for the support of any sort of religion."[134] They also embodied the principle "that no one should seek through political action to promote the activities of religious organizations, or should intrude differences of religious faith or practice into our political controversies."[135] This broad view that not just the church but also *religion* should be separate from government was increasingly advocated throughout the twentieth century by Protestant denominations and will be discussed at length in the next chapter.

The opinions of Justice Sutherland and Chief Justice Hughes in *United States v. Macintosh* have contributed to the ongoing discussion of the meaning of the First Amendment religion clauses. Sutherland and Hughes wrote the last opinions representative of the understanding that the United States has its deepest roots in the Christian religion, an understanding that was common throughout at least the first century of our country's existence.

Even more, this case demonstrates how the core philosophies and beliefs of Supreme Court justices can impact their decision-making in the area of religious liberty. Justice Sutherland believed in the duty of the nation to survive and, concomitantly, the need to subordinate other important rights to that duty. Hence his willingness to subjugate Macintosh's religious liberty claim to the need of the United States Government to ensure that its citizens would be willing to take up arms in defense of the nation. Hughes, who once famously declared during World War I his allegiance to Sutherland's proposition that the nation's paramount duty is to survive, nevertheless believed strongly in religious liberty and, unlike Sutherland, believed that conscience, "within its proper field," was supreme.[136] As far as Hughes was concerned, Macintosh's claim was one of conscience "within its proper field" and demanded recognition by the Court.

To understand the different outcomes these justices advocated in their respective opinions, it is helpful to recall the stark difference in their upbringings and experiences. Sutherland grew up in the territory of Utah, where Mormonism prevailed. He apparently had little instruction in any religion as a youth and young man. Even more, Sutherland's years in Utah came during the federal government's most aggressive attempts to curtail the Mormon practice of polygamy. Sutherland assisted the government in that endeavor, joining a political party in Utah whose main purpose was to dismantle the practice. While he did defend polygamists against prosecution as an attorney, he did so only to lessen the severity of their convictions, not to defend their odious practice. Thus, one of Justice Sutherland's most defining experiences in Utah, both politically and legally, was his involvement in assisting the federal government in ending the religious practice of polygamy.

Hughes grew up in a home dominated by Christian orthodoxy. Even more, he was brought up a Baptist, and therefore was the product of a Christian denomination that prided itself for its storied history in the battle for religious liberty. Hughes was clearly aware and intensely proud of the leadership of his Baptist ancestors in this struggle, on one occasion calling "[t]heir demand for the absolute freedom of religion from civil control" the "glory of the Baptist heritage."[137] His beliefs regarding religious liberty were wrought in a religion and a culture that highly esteemed religious freedom. Sutherland's upbringing conspicuously lacked such an influence. This stark contrast in upbringings and life experiences helps to explain the equally stark contrast between Justice Sutherland's and Chief Justice Hughes's opinions in *United States v. Macintosh*.

Justice Sutherland retired from the Supreme Court in 1938. He died on July 18, 1942, in Stockbridge, Massachusetts. Chief Justice Hughes retired from the Supreme Court in 1941 as the United States geared up for another horrific world war. Five years later, the Supreme Court of the United States overruled the *Macintosh* decision in *Girouard v. United States*.[138] Hughes's dissent was finally embraced and the uplifted torch on the Statue of Liberty burned brightly once again, welcoming millions of survivors of the war to their new home. Hughes died two years later on August 27, 1948.

NOTES

1. *United States v. Macintosh*, 283 U.S. 605 (1931); Ronald B. Flowers, "The Naturalization of Douglas Clyde Macintosh, Alien Theologian," *J. Sup. Ct. Hist.* 25 (2000): 243.

2. José Ortega y Gasset, *The Revolt of the Masses*, excerpt reprinted in *The Development of Civilization: A Documentary History of Politics, Society, and Thought* (Chicago: Scott, Foresman & Company, 1962), 253.

3. Oscar Handlin, *The Uprooted* (New York: Grosset & Dunlap, 1951), 35–36, 287.

4. Handlin, *The Uprooted*, 288.

5. "Lights Out in the City of Light," http://www.ublib.buffalo.edu/libraries/exhibits/panam/law/trial.html.

6. http://www.jamesgarfield.org/.

7. http://www.bartleby.com/65/cz/czolgosz.html.

8. U. S. C. tit. 8, 381 (8 USCA 381).

9. Current, Richard Nelson, T. Harry Williams, and Frank Burt Freidel, *American History: A Survey*, New York: Knopf, 1974, 666–67.

10. Edmund Taylor, *The Fall of the Dynasties: The Collapse of the Old Order 1905–1922* (New York: Dorset Press, 1963), 1.

11. Current et al., *American History: A Survey*, 674–75.

12. Current et al., *American History: A Survey*, 675.

13. Current et al., *American History: A Survey*, 677–78.

14. Current et al., *American History: A Survey*, 685.

15. Handlin, *The Uprooted*, 290.

16. Handlin, *The Uprooted*, 290.

17. Current et al., *American History: A Survey*, 729.

18. Joel Francis Paschal, *Mr. Justice Sutherland: A Man against the State* (1951), 3–4; David Burner, "George Sutherland," in *The Justices of the United States Supreme Court 1789-1969: Their Lives and Major Opinions*, vol. 3, Leon Friedman and Fred L. Israel, eds. (New York: Chelsea House and Bowker, 1969), 2133.

19. Paschal, *Mr. Justice Sutherland*; quoting George Sutherland's "A Message to the 1941 Graduating Class of Brigham Young University," 4 June 1941, 3.

20. Paschal, *Mr. Justice Sutherland*, 4–5.

21. Hadley Arkes, *The Return of George Sutherland: Restoring a Jurisprudence of Natural Rights* (Princeton, N.J.: Princeton University Press, 1994). Sutherland studied at the University of Michigan Law School for one term in 1882. Paschal, *Mr. Justice Sutherland*, 17, 20.

22. Burner, "George Sutherland," 2134.

23. Paschal, *Mr. Justice Sutherland*, 9.

24. Paschal, *Mr. Justice Sutherland*, 6–7; quoting a letter from George Sutherland to Reinhard Maeser, 26 February 1923.

25. Burner, "George Sutherland," 2134.

26. Paschal, *Mr. Justice Sutherland*, 10.

27. Paschal, *Mr. Justice Sutherland*, 10.

28. Paschal, *Mr. Justice Sutherland*, 10.

29. Paschal, *Mr. Justice Sutherland*, 10.

30. Paschal, *Mr. Justice Sutherland*, 10.

31. Paschal, *Mr. Justice Sutherland*, 11; citing Herbert Spencer, *Social Statics* (New York: D. Appleton, 1881), 80.

32. Paschal, *Mr. Justice Sutherland*, 12, 14.

33. Paschal, *Mr. Justice Sutherland*, 12.

34. Paschal, *Mr. Justice Sutherland*, 12.

35. Paschal, *Mr. Justice Sutherland*, 14.

36. Arkes, *The Return of George Sutherland*, 42–43, 276.

37. Arkes, *The Return of George Sutherland*, 43.

38. *Powell v. Alabama*, 287 U.S. 45, 71–72 (1932); quoting *Holden v. Hardy*, 169 U.S. 366, 389 (1898), and Arkes, *The Return of George Sutherland*, 272 n52.

39. *Powell*, 67; quoting *Hebert v. Louisiana*, 272 U.S. 312, 316 (1926).

40. *Powell*, 70; quoting Thomas M. Cooley, *A Treatise on the Constitutional Limitations Which Rest Upon the Legislative Power of the States of the American Union*, vol. 1, 8th ed. (New York: Da Capo Press, 1927), 700.

41. *Powell*, 73.

42. Arkes, *The Return of George Sutherland*, 42.

43. As a Supreme Court justice, Sutherland upheld the constitutionality of zoning ordinances. *Village of Euclid v. Ambler Realty Co.*, 272 U.S. 365 (1926).

44. *Village of Euclid*, 26–27.

45. Arkes, *The Return of George Sutherland*, 48.

46. Arkes, *The Return of George Sutherland*, 44.

47. Paschal, *Mr. Justice Sutherland*, 22–23.

48. Paschal, *Mr. Justice Sutherland*, 22–23.

49. *In re* Snow, 120 U.S. 274 (1887).

50. Paschal, *Mr. Justice Sutherland*, 23.

51. Arkes, *The Return of George Sutherland*, 46.

52. Arkes, *The Return of George Sutherland*, 47.

53. Paschal, *Mr. Justice Sutherland*, 48.

54. Paschal, *Mr. Justice Sutherland*, 92–98.

55. Burner, "George Sutherland," 2136.

56. Paschal, *Mr. Justice Sutherland*, 90; quoting George Sutherland, *Superfluous Government* (1914).

57. Paschal, *Mr. Justice Sutherland*, 91.

58. Paschal, *Mr. Justice Sutherland*, 89.

59. Paschal, *Mr. Justice Sutherland*, 89; quoting George Sutherland, *The Law and the People*, S. Doc. No. 63-328 (2d Sess. 1913), 5.

60. Paschal, *Mr. Justice Sutherland*, 89–90; quoting George Sutherland, *The Law and the People*, 8.

61. Robert P. George, "Natural Law, The Constitution, and the Theory and Practice of Judicial Review," *Fordham L. Rev.* 69 (2001): 2271–72. George states: "Roosevelt and other critics excoriated the Court for its rulings in cases involving economic regulation and

social welfare legislation, suggesting that the Justices were, without the slightest constitutional warrant, substituting their personal political and economic opinions for the contrary judgments of the elected representatives of the people." See also Gary C. Leedes, "An Unsuccessful Attempt to Restore Justice George Sutherland's Tarnished Reputation: A Review Essay," *U. Rich. L. Rev.* 30 (1996): 821–22; and Burner, "George Sutherland," 2133: "George Sutherland was the intellectual spokesman of the four reactionary Supreme Court Justices who opposed the New Deal."

62. Leedes, "An Unsuccessful Attempt," 816: "When the Great Depression arrived in the 1930s, Sutherland was known to be a Justice who wanted to take the nation back to the horse and buggy days."

63. "We hold these truths to be self-evident, that all Men are created equal, that they are endowed by their Creator with certain unalienable Rights, that among these are Life, Liberty, and the Pursuit of Happiness." *Declaration of Independence*, para. 2 (U.S. 1776).

64. Paschal, *Mr. Justice Sutherland*, 10.

65. Paschal, *Mr. Justice Sutherland*, 5.

66. Paschal, *Mr. Justice Sutherland*, 6.

67. Paschal, *Mr. Justice Sutherland*, 6.

68. 41 *Cong. Rec.* 1499 (1907).

69. 41 *Cong. Rec.* 1499 (1907).

70. Paschal, *Mr. Justice Sutherland*, 11.

71. 41 *Cong. Rec.* 1499 (1907).

72. 41 *Cong. Rec.* 1499 (1907).

73. 41 *Cong. Rec.* 1499 (1907).

74. Paschal, *Mr. Justice Sutherland*, 12.

75. Bruce R. McConkie, *Mormon Doctrine*, 2d ed. (Salt Lake City: Bookcraft, 1966), 550.

76. McConkie, *Mormon Doctrine*, 62.

77. Burner, "George Sutherland," 2134; Paschal, *Mr. Justice Sutherland*, 7–8 (discussing several Mormon scriptural texts confirming that the Constitution was a divinely inspired document); see also McConkie, *Mormon Doctrine*, 159–60.

78. Paschal, *Mr. Justice Sutherland*, 7 (quoting *Doctrine and Covenants* § 101:79-80).

79. Paschal, *Mr. Justice Sutherland*, 8; quoting a letter from George Sutherland to Mrs. Jeanette A. Hyde, 28 May 1936.

80. The biographical sketch of Hughes is based on Merlo J. Pusey, *Charles Evans Hughes*, vols. 1–2 (New York: Columbia University Press, 1963), unless otherwise noted.

81. David J. Danelski and Joseph S. Tulchin, eds., *The Autobiographical Notes of Charles Evans Hughes* (Cambridge, Mass.: Harvard University Press, 1973), 1–26. Unless otherwise noted, all following Hughes autobiographical quotations and information derive from this source.

82. Hughes, in Pusey, *Charles Evans Hughes*, vol. 1, 113.

83. Hughes, in Pusey, *Charles Evans Hughes*, vol. 1, 111; quoting Charles Evans Hughes, "Address to the Vaughan Class of the Calvary Baptist Church," 20 February 1925.

84. Hughes, in Pusey, *Charles Evans Hughes*, vol. 1, 111.

85. Hughes, in Pusey, *Charles Evans Hughes*, vol. 1, 112; quoting a letter from Charles Evans Hughes to Mary Hughes, 30 November 1893.

86. Hughes, in Pusey, *Charles Evans Hughes*, vol. 1, 112–13.

87. Hughes, in Pusey, *Charles Evans Hughes*, vol. 1, 113.

88. Hughes, in Pusey, *Charles Evans Hughes*, vol. 1, 25.

89. Pusey, *Charles Evans Hughes*, vol. 2, 621.

90. Pusey, *Charles Evans Hughes*, vol. 2, 110. For a discussion of the involvement of the Baptists in America's struggle for religious liberty, see Daniel L. Dreisbach, *Thomas Jefferson and the Wall of Separation Between Church and State* (New York: New York University Press, 2002), 7. See also Peter S. Field, *The Crisis of the Standing Order: Clerical Intellectuals and Cultural Authority in Massachusetts, 1780–1833* (Amherst: University of Massachusetts Press, 1998).

91. Charles E. Hughes, "Address at the Laying of the Corner-Stone of the National Baptist Memorial to Religious Liberty," 22 April 1922. The National Baptist Memorial was a joint venture between the Northern and Southern Baptist Conventions.

92. Hughes, "Address at the Laying of the Corner-Stone," 10.

93. Hughes, "Address at the Laying of the Corner-Stone," 12–13.

94. Hughes, "Address at the Laying of the Corner-Stone," 10. Later in his speech, Hughes again declared that religious liberty "demanded the emancipation of the spirit of man from the fetters of civil rule."

95. *United States v. Macintosh*, 283 U.S. 605 (1931), overruled by *Girouard v. United States*, 328 U.S. 61 (1946).

96. *Macintosh*, 628–29 (Hughes, C.J., dissenting).

97. *Macintosh*, 615 (quoting 8 U.S.C. § 399).

98. *Macintosh*, 617.

99. *Macintosh*, 625.

100. *Macintosh*, 633 (Hughes, C.J., dissenting).

101. *Macintosh*, 634.

102. *Macintosh*, 634; quoting *Davis v. Beason*, 133 U.S. 333, 342 (1890).

103. *Macintosh*, 634.

104. The Supreme Court adopted this reasoning fifteen years later to overrule *United States v. Macintosh;* see *Girouard v. United States*, 328 U.S. 61, 64–66 (1946).

105. The Supreme Court expressed a much more critical view of the Christian heritage of our nation just fifty-two years after *Macintosh* was decided. In *Lynch v. Donnelly*, 465 U.S. 668 (1984), 718, Justice Brennan referred to Brewer's statement that the United States was a Christian nation as an arrogant declaration.

106. *Holy Trinity*.

107. *Holy Trinity*, 465–71.

108. *Macintosh*, 625.

109. Several commentators have remarked that *Macintosh* represents the Supreme Court's recognition of this nation's Christian heritage. Harold J. Berman, "Religion and Law: The First Amendment in Historical Perspective," *Emory L.J.* 35 (1986): 779 n4; Daniel O. Conkle, "The Path of American Religious Liberty: From the Original Theology to Formal Neutrality and an Uncertain Future," *Ind. L.J.* 75 (2000): 5; E. Gregory

Wallace, "When Government Speaks Religiously," *Fla. St. U. L. Rev.* 21 (1994): 1203–1204.

110. Note: "Toward a Constitutional Definition of Religion," *Harv. L. Rev.* 91 (1978): 1060: "There is no doubt that to the Framers religion entailed a relationship of man to some Supreme Being." James Madison defined religion as "the duty which we owe to our Creator, and the manner of discharging it." James Madison, *Memorial and Remonstrance against Religious Assessments*, in Jack N. Rakove, ed., *Madison: Writings* (New York: Library of America, 1999), 29–30. In writing the "Virginia Bill for Establishing Religious Freedom," Thomas Jefferson demonstrated his theistic outlook by stating: "Almighty God hath created the mind free." Thomas Jefferson, *A Bill for Establishing Religious Freedom*, in *Jefferson: Writings*, ed. Merrill D. Peterson (New York: Viking Press, 1984), 346.

111. "Toward a Constitutional Definition of Religion," 1060–61; see also Richard O. Frame, "Belief in a Nonmaterial Reality—A Proposed First Amendment Definition of Religion," *U. Ill. L. Rev.* (1992): 819, 821–23; George C. Freeman III, "The Misguided Search for the Constitutional Definition of 'Religion'," *Geo. L.J.* 71 (1983): 1520–25; Roy S. Moore, "Religion in the Public Square," *Cumb. L. Rev.* 29 (1999): 352–56.

112. *Davis v. Beason*: "The term 'religion' has reference to one's views of his relations to his Creator, and to the obligations they impose of reverence for his being and character, and of obedience to his will."

113. *Macintosh*, 625.

114. *Macintosh*, 633–34.

115. Paschal, *Mr. Justice Sutherland*, 221.

116. *Macintosh*, 622.

117. Paschal, *Mr. Justice Sutherland*, 221.

118. *United States v. Curtiss-Wright Export Corp.*, 299 U.S. 304 (1936). Sutherland won "the approval of his brethren for the notion that the power of the government in the field of foreign relations does not depend for its existence on the Constitution. Rather, it is an inherent power arising by virtue of the United States' membership in the family of nations." Paschal, *Mr. Justice Sutherland*, 221. For a thorough discussion of Sutherland's contribution to these areas of law, see Paschal, *Mr. Justice Sutherland*, 221–32; and Arkes, *The Return of George Sutherland*, 196–241.

119. Paschal, *Mr. Justice Sutherland*, 217.

120. Hughes, in Pusey, *Charles Evans Hughes*, vol. 1, 10–11.

121. Hughes, in Pusey, *Charles Evans Hughes*, vol. 1, 12.

122. *Macintosh*, 634.

123. *Macintosh*, 634.

124. See Flowers, *The Naturalization of Douglas Clyde Macintosh*, 257–60, noting the divergent opinions, both for and against the *Macintosh* majority, in the national press.

125. Flowers, *Naturalization of Douglas Clyde Macintosh*; quoting "An Astounding Decision," *The Christian Century*, 10 June 1931, 766–67.

126. Flowers, *Naturalization of Douglas Clyde Macintosh*, 261: quoting "Declaration of an American Citizen," *The Christian Century*, 20 January 1932, 75.

127. Flowers, *Naturalization of Douglas Clyde Macintosh*, 260; quoting Heber H.

Votaw, "The Religious Press on the Macintosh Case," *Liberty* (First Quarter, 1932): 6–7, 22–23.

128. Flowers, *Naturalization of Douglas Clyde Macintosh*, 260.

129. Flowers, *Naturalization, of Douglas Clyde Macintosh*, 260.

130. "Preachers Assail Citizenship Ruling," *New York Times*, 1 June 1931, 16.

131. "Preachers Assail Citizenship Ruling," 16.

132. "Preachers Assail Citizenship Ruling," 16.

133. Flowers, *Naturalization of Douglas Clyde Macintosh*, 269 n82 (quoting "The Office Notebook," *The Christian Century* [20 January 1932]: 76).

134. Hughes, in Pusey, *Charles Evans Hughes*, vol. 1, 13.

135. Hughes, in Pusey, *Charles Evans Hughes*, vol. 1, 13.

136. In an address titled "War Powers Under the Constitution," Hughes declared, "The power to wage war is the power to wage war successfully." *Lichter v. United States*, 334 U.S. 742, 780 (1948) quoting Charles Evans Hughes, "War Powers Under the Constitution," *A.B.A. Rep.* 42 (1917): 238–39.

137. Paschal, *Mr. Justice Sutherland*, 10.

138. *Girouard v. United States*, 328 U.S. 61 (1946).

·6·

The Rise of the Church-State Separation Movement

> In the words of Jefferson, the clause against establishment of religion by law was intended to erect a wall of separation between church and state.
>
> —Justice Hugo Black
> *Everson v. Board. of Education*, 1947

The overall number of church-going Protestants from the 1920s through the 1960s remained fairly stable, but within the denominations an important shift in Protestant religious affiliation occurred during those forty years. Episcopalianism, Congregationalism, Presbyterianism, and northern Methodism, which had dominated the nineteenth century, were being rapidly outnumbered by affective, evangelical, working-class religions, and the emotional center of Protestantism was shifting to rural areas and the South.[1]

In particular, followers of the Baptist faith increased as a result of an absolutist, vocal, political stance calling for strict separation between church and state to thwart what they perceived as a threat from the ever-powerful influence of the Catholic Church. This was especially true on issues related to public schools. As we will see, other Protestant denominations joined in the southern effort to become a united voice against encroachments on the Establishment Clause of the First Amendment.

The Supreme Court's enshrinement of strict separation as the primary principle of the Establishment Clause in the 1947 *Everson v. Board of Education* opinion may very well have had its foundation in theological as much as secular thought.

This assertion becomes tantalizingly clear when one views the life of

Justice Hugo Black, who wrote the *Everson* opinion. As seen here, Black was one of the initial members of the Southern Baptist "Committee on Public Relations," a group that eventually birthed Protestants and Others United for Separation of Church and State. This organization continues even today advocating strict separation of church and state.

This chapter will discuss Black's close affiliation with the Southern Baptist Church and will show that he undoubtedly agreed with his denomination's official declarations advocating strict separation of church and state. While several factors influenced Black's personal preference for strict separation, none was as compelling as the religious influences in his life.

The Supreme Court's twentieth-century religious liberty decisions were reflections of the theological climate that pervaded the times. The Southern Baptist, more than any other denomination, took strong stands on church-state separation. Ultimately, their view prevailed at the Supreme Court. Justice Hugo Black's judicial approach to the issue of religious liberty clearly reflected the Southern Baptists' anti-Catholic views and their strict model of church-state separation. Justice Black wrote the majority opinion in *Everson v. Board of Education* that invoked Thomas Jefferson's famous "wall of separation" metaphor.[2] His position on the issue of church-state relations mirrored the denominational stance advocated by the Southern Baptist Convention.

THE CULTURAL/HISTORICAL CONTEXT

The Southern Baptist Convention (SBC) was by far the most active denomination of the twentieth century in expressing its views regarding church-state separation. The SBC provided the first resolution and the first official declaration of any denomination in the twentieth century concerning the relationship between church and state. At their convention in 1913 the Baptists adopted a general resolution on religious liberty. The issue that prompted it centered on religious schools. It read:

> RESOLVED, That the Southern Baptist Convention reaffirms its unalterable belief in the absolute separation of church and State and hereby expresses its sympathy with all who are having to fight efforts of any who would try to violate the holy principle of the absolute separation of church and State.[3]

In 1914, the Southern Baptists reacted to the presence of a papal representative in Washington, D.C., as a further threat to church and state separation and issued the following resolution:

> RESOLVED, That we view with serious alarm and vigorous protest the efforts of the Roman Catholic hierarchy to gain control of our government, and thereby be in a position to fasten either its faith or fallacies upon the consciences of a free and sovereign people.
> RESOLVED, That we deeply deplore the presence of a papal legate as the representative of the Vatican at our national capitol for the purpose of influencing governmental affairs.[4]

In 1920, the Southern Baptist Convention held its annual meeting in Washington, D.C. At the request of the churches of the Washington Baptist Association, Dr. George W. Truett, pastor of the First Baptist Church of Dallas, Texas, delivered an address from the east steps of the Capitol building on May 16, 1920, at three o'clock in the afternoon. The title of his address was *Baptists and Religious Liberty*. While only about five thousand messengers (delegates) were registered for the convention, over fifteen thousand people turned out to hear this historic address. Truett declared unequivocally the Baptist position in favor of strict separation of church and state:

> Every state church on the earth is a spiritual tyranny. And just as long as there is left upon this earth any state church, in any land, the task of Baptists will that long remain unfinished. . . .

> That utterance of Jesus, "Render therefore unto Caesar the things which are Caesar's, and unto God the things that are God's," is one of the most revolutionary and history-making utterances that ever fell from those lips divine. That utterance, once and for all, marked the divorcement of church and state.[5]

In 1925, the Southern Baptist Convention, for the first time in its history, adopted a statement of faith, called the "Baptist Faith and Message." It went further than historic Baptist confessions and included cultural and social issues in the statement rather than simply theological issues. Section XVIII was titled "Religious Liberty" and championed separation of church and state:

God alone is Lord of the conscience, and he has left it free from the doctrines and commandments of men which are contrary to his Word or not contained in it. Church and state should be separate . . . The state has no right to impose penalties for religious opinions of any kind.[6]

The Lutheran Church–Missouri Synod also adopted "A Brief Statement of Doctrinal Position" in 1932 concerning religious liberty with a section titled, "Of Church and State." This statement declared that church and state "must not be commingled" and condemned both "the policy of those who would have the power of the State employed 'in the interest of the Church'" and the policy "of those who, aiming to govern the State by the Word of God, seek to turn the State into a Church."[7]

As the nation was in the grip of the Great Depression in the mid-1930s, President Roosevelt created the Works Project Administration (WPA), approved by Congress in 1935. The purpose was to relieve economic hardship by providing jobs created and funded by the federal government, including the National Youth Administration (NYA). This program helped those who were between the ages of sixteen and twenty-five to obtain part-time jobs in order to allow them to continue their college education. More than seven hundred thousand students enrolled in this program. Federal funds were offered to church colleges and seminaries to employ students part-time as they continued their theological education.

The Southern Baptist Convention passed a resolution in 1935 denouncing this program as a violation of the separation of church and state. In the resolution, they reaffirmed their "devotion to the fundamental New Testament doctrine and fundamental principle of the American government, the separation of church and state."[8] They went on to urge Baptist pastors, churches, and institutions to "maintain this doctrine in all of their activities and relationships and at all costs to abstain from borrowing money from the government, receiving the financial endorsement of the government and receiving appropriations of funds from the public treasury, whether national or state."[9]

The Baptists' concern over the Roosevelt administration's involvement with the Vatican hit a new high in early 1939 when Pope Pius XI died on February 10. Cardinal Eugenio Pacelli, who had made an unprecedented visit throughout the United States in 1936 as the Vatican's secretary of state and had met with Roosevelt at Hyde Park, was elected Pope

Pius XII on March 2. For the traditional public coronation ceremonies at the Vatican on March 12, President Roosevelt sent Joseph P. Kennedy, the American ambassador to the Court of St. James in London (a Catholic and father of the future president John F. Kennedy) as his personal representative to Rome. It was the first time an American president had sent an official representative to such an occasion.[10] Kennedy, always eager for publicity for himself and his family, made sure his role at the historic occasion received the widest photo-news coverage possible.[11]

The Southern Baptists responded publicly to this event two months later by passing a resolution condemning Roosevelt's action. They declared that sending an "Ambassador of the United States . . . to honor the crowning of an ecclesiastical head . . . was an obvious violation of the traditions of this Republic and of the spirit of the First Amendment of our Constitution." The resolution admonished the "Congress and the President to adhere strictly to the principle . . . of separation of church and state so plainly taught in the first section of the bill of rights in our constitution."[12]

With Hitler's invasion of Poland on September 1, 1939, and France and Britain's declarations of war against Germany two days later, Roosevelt sought to strengthen European communication ties that would not cross the line of American neutrality. On Christmas Eve the president announced his intention to name a representative of the United States Government to the Vatican with the rank of ambassador. This was the final step in what many had feared would be the outcome of more and more involvement with the Vatican and was viewed by most Protestant denominations as a gross violation of church and state separation. For example, the United Lutheran Church in America adopted a resolution in which it denounced the president's plan as "*Un-American*, since it gives official recognition to a combination of Church and State (the Vatican) which is contrary to American principles" [emphasis in original].[13] The resolution further declared the United Lutheran Church in America "unalterably opposed to the establishment or maintenance of any relationship to the Vatican by the United States Government or its chief executive, which might in any sense be construed as diplomatic or official."[14]

In the same year, an unprecedented document was developed by the three largest Baptist denominations in the United States. The Southern Baptist Convention, the Northern Baptist Convention, and the National Baptist Convention, in their respective meetings that year, unanimously passed what they called "The American Baptist Bill of Rights." This was the first joint declaration of any type between the Southern and Northern Baptists since their separation in 1845. The document did not express any specific issues that animated the adoption of this joint declaration on religious liberty. Nevertheless, the main reason behind the issuance of it was to express a unified Baptist voice regarding the proper relationship between church and state:

> Since every session of the Congress considers legislation that raises the question as to the relation of the Federal Government to the institutions and the agencies of religion, and since recently many tendencies have appeared that involve the freedom of religion and con- science, and furthermore, since there are some state constitutions which do not have embodied in them the Bill of Rights of the Federal Constitution, American Baptists feel constrained to declare their posi- tion and their convictions.[15]

With this document, all three major Baptist denominations in the United States came out in favor of strict separation between church and state.

Protestant fear of the Catholic Church continued during the 1940s and was well expressed in a book by Paul Blanshard titled *American Free- dom and Catholic Power*. In his chapter, "The Catholic Plan for America," Blanshard outlines what might take place if Catholics became the pre- dominant denomination in the United States. His analysis did nothing to ease the fears of Protestants. He relied on what had happened in other countries dominated by the Catholic Church, especially Spain, Portugal, and Argentina, as a model of how it might work out in the United States. Blanshard outlined three areas where the United States Constitution might be amended to reflect Catholic beliefs:

1. Repealing of First Amendment to the Constitution and making the Roman Catholic Church the only religion publicly recognized by the state. Non-Catholic faiths would be tolerated, but public cere- monies and manifestations other than those of the Roman Catholic religion will not be permitted. These groups will be allowed to wor- ship privately only.
2. Amending the Constitution with a "Christian Education Amend- ment." This would give the Catholic Church the "inalienable right" to supervise the entire education of her children—making public schools lawful for them only when Catholic piety permeates all the instruction. The Federal government and the states will assist the

Catholic Church in its educational responsibility by appropriate measures—financial support being implied.

3. The third amendment that might be proposed would be the "Christian Family Amendment." This amendment would call for marriage and family relations to be in accordance with the canons of the Catholic Church. This would declare mixed marriages (with non-Catholics) as null and void and would declare that all marriages are indissoluble and divorce would be prohibited. Birth control and any form of sterilization would be forbidden.[16]

Blanshard's characterization of what "Catholic America" would look like, while far-fetched to the twenty-first century mind, fairly captured the general sentiment of mid-twentieth-century Americans toward Catholicism.

Probably the most significant event of the twentieth century related to church-state separation from a theological perspective happened at the Southern Baptists' 1936 meeting at St. Louis, Missouri, when they renamed their "Committee on Chaplains of the Army and Navy" as the "Committee on Public Relations." This was the denomination's first attempt to establish a vehicle for expressing their views concerning religious liberty, especially in the nation's capital.

This committee was to consist of "the President of the Southern Baptist Convention, the Executive Secretaries of the four Boards of the Convention, and later, the Chairman of the Social Service Commission as ex-officio members, with five others, all residing in or adjacent to the City of Washington [D.C.], one of whom being a competent lawyer."[17] In 1937 at their annual meeting in New Orleans, the SBC elected Alabama senator Hugo Black to serve on the Committee on Public Relations.[18] He served only part of this year, resigning when he was appointed by President Franklin Roosevelt to the Supreme Court of the United States.

Following the adoption of the "American Baptist Bill of Rights," the various Baptist denominations began to work more closely on church-state issues. In 1941, after some concessions whereby the Southern Baptists were assured that they would not forfeit their separate identity, the SBC finally agreed to a Joint Conference Committee.[19] By 1950, the name was changed from the Joint Conference Committee on Public Relations to the Baptist Joint Committee on Public Affairs (BJCPA).[20]

J. M. Dawson, a Southern Baptist pastor from Waco, Texas, serving as executive director of the Joint Conference Committee, was pleased with the cooperative work of Baptists in the nation's capital. Ultimately, the organization would include all Protestant denominations and would be a "larger organization which could speak on behalf of a wider segment of the citizenry concerned about the principles of religious freedom and separation of church and state."[21]

Two meetings were held in Washington in May and October of 1947. At the second meeting on October 13, a motion was made by Louie D. Newton, president of the Southern Baptist Convention, to create a national organization "devoted to the single issue of maintenance of separation of church and state as provided in the First Amendment."[22]

In the same year (some six months after the Supreme Court's decision in *Everson*) the new organization, "Protestants and Other Americans United for Separation of Church and State" (POAU), was formed. The main motivation for its creation was the fear of many Protestant leaders that "the Roman Catholic Church was entering upon a campaign which if not checked might lead to the demand that parochial schools be supported by the State and other infringements of Constitutional Church-State separation might take place."[23] POAU's raison d'être was the preservation of strict separation between church and state.

Shortly after the establishment of POAU, the Southern Baptist Convention passed a resolution in support of the organization. The resolution recognized POAU's purpose as "the maintenance of the principle of separation of church and state, upon which the Federal Constitution guarantees religious liberty to all the people and all churches of this republic."[24]

The United Lutheran Church of America shared the Southern Baptists' concern over preserving the wall of separation between church and state. At their Biennial convention in 1950, the United Lutheran Church reported that in 1946 President Truman gave assurance to their church leaders that the appointment of a special representative to the Vatican would be terminated at an early date and would certainly terminate when the peace treaty to end the war was signed.[25] By their 1950 convention, however, this had not taken place. In response, the church adopted a resolution affirming its allegiance to the principle of separation and condemning the establishment of diplomatic relations with the Vatican. The resolution reads as follows:

> That The United Lutheran Church in America in convention assembled emphatically reaffirm its belief in the absolute separation of

Church and State and record its unalterable opposition to the establishment of any kind of diplomatic relations, or resemblance thereto,
between the United States Government and the Vatican or any other
religious group.[26]

The United Lutherans also passed a resolution regarding parochial
schools, which further demonstrates their commitment to strict separation. It recognized "the separation of church and state" as one of the "high
privileges of democratic life."[27] The resolution then stated that "certain
influences [i.e., Catholics] have been at work to vitiate the principle of
separation of church and state [through] attempts to secure authorization
for the use of public funds for the support of private parochial schools."[28]
Such use of public funds, the United Lutherans averred, "constitutes a
preferment inimical to the very impartial nature of a democracy."[29]

The smaller Augustana Lutheran Church combined the issues of
diplomatic relations with the Vatican and aid to parochial schools into a
single condemnatory resolution adopted in 1952:

In the light of the First Amendment to the Constitution of the United
States we continue to protest every attempt to give preference to any
particular church or group of churches by our Government, such as an
appointment of an ambassador to the Vatican or the use of public
funds for parochial schools.[30]

These sketches of Protestant denominational declarations regarding
church-state relations suggest much about the general cultural-theological
climate during the first half of the twentieth century. Most notably, they
show that Protestant denominations have had significant influence on the
development of a strict separationist model in church-state relations.
Protestant fear of Catholic power was the driving force behind their advocacy of church-state separation. Indeed, through their opposition to the
establishment of official diplomatic relations with the Vatican and public
funds for parochial schools, Protestants unequivocally promoted an absolutist version of church and state separation.

As we can readily see, the evolution of this general commitment
among Protestant denominations predated the development of the
Supreme Court's Establishment Clause jurisprudence. In fact, the recognized Protestant position on church-state separation was adopted in large
part by the Supreme Court in its very first Establishment Clause case,
Everson v. Board of Education, written by Justice Hugo Black.

THE JUSTICE: HUGO LAFAYETTE BLACK
(1886–1971)

"I'm just a Clay County hillbilly." This saying, one of Black's favorites, wonderfully captures the truly provincial and unremarkable beginnings of this future Supreme Court justice.[31] Hugo Lafayette Black was born on February 27, 1886, to William and Della Black, who lived in the Alabama wilderness hamlet of Harlan, nestled in the Appalachian foothills of Clay County. Harlan was composed of the Black household, a general store owned by William, and two cabins.

Despite their frontier-like home and surroundings, the Black family achieved a good standard of living by late nineteenth-century Alabama standards. When Hugo was three years old, the family moved to the county seat of Ashland, which contributed greatly to the financial success and relatively high societal position they would attain. While William's main reason for relocating to Ashland was to give his children access to better schools, it also provided him the opportunity to enter into a partnership in a highly successful general merchandise store.

Given his status in the community and business savvy, it would be natural to assume that Hugo learned a great deal from his father, but that was not the case. Tragically, the most significant lesson he derived from his relationship with his father was to avoid his most obvious moral failing, excessive drinking. The growing young son observed his father's ignoble conduct and concluded that "sobriety" was "essential." In his 1975 book, Hugo Black Jr. revealed that his father had nothing but "cold indifference" for William because of his lifestyle.[32]

William's sincere desire to provide better schooling for his children, however, was a point in his favor. Ashland was well known for its country high school, called Ashland College, which offered an impressive program with classes in twenty different subjects. More importantly, a degree from Ashland virtually guaranteed admission to the University of Alabama. But Hugo had different ideas forming in his mind. He enrolled in Ashland College but soon dropped out to pursue the lofty and seemingly unrealistic goal of gaining acceptance to another Alabama university. Following the advice of his mother and the footsteps of his brother, Orlando, who by this time had a budding medical practice, Black entered Birmingham Medical College in 1903.[33] He excelled there, finishing the first two years of medical school in just one year. During that year he worked relentlessly, taking "time out only for Sunday school and church."[34] During his summer break Hugo assisted his brother in his medical practice. Orlando soon realized that his brother's heart was not in medicine and encouraged him to go to law school. Black agreed, for "the pull of the remembrances of all those fascinating trials he had attended [as a boy] was just too strong."[35]

Black had always been enamored of the legal profession. From age six, Hugo attended almost every session of court held. He was fascinated by trials. He would sit in the back row and critique the attorneys he watched, thinking to himself how he would have asked a question differently. In his short and unfortunately incomplete autobiography, Black commented that while at these trials he often found himself thinking that "lawyers, frequently good ones, were just throwing away their cases by making stupid mistakes."[36]

Finally, in 1904, Black was able to act on that childhood dream. In September of that year he gained acceptance to the University of Alabama Law School at Tuscaloosa despite lacking a high school degree. His time there was generally unremarkable. He cherished his education and greatly revered the two professors who comprised the law department as men who not only "taught me how to get a diploma but did their dead-level best to teach me how to think and to challenge."[37]

The most important aspect of Black's education at the University of Alabama was his introduction to the writings of Thomas Jefferson. Recognizing the gaps in his educational background, Black decided to take courses in history, literature, and political economy in addition to his law classes. He was first exposed to Jefferson's writings in his history class and found the appeal of Jeffersonian idealism immediate and irresistible. Black became a devoted follower of Jefferson and his political theories throughout his life, and that influence would inform many of the stances he took as a Supreme Court justice.

Upon graduation from law school and admittance to the Alabama bar in 1906, Black returned to Ashland to open a law practice. His first year was a resounding failure. His total income from legal business was a mere $150, and his tiny law office was destroyed by fire. Some years later Black jokingly reminisced about his first year, saying that it was "rather a relief when the office burned down" as it gave him an incentive to move to Birmingham. Black could not have made a better decision; Birmingham would provide him the opportunity to fulfill his lifelong dream of a career in public office. Reminiscing about his youthful enthusiasms in a letter dated January 20, 1948, to his friend John P. Frank, Black wrote, "I expected to go to Congress, become a governor, and probably a senator."

Black's many activities and achievements during his Birmingham years, 1907 to1926, were strongly motivated by his desire to be elected to office. Besides his law practice, he served as police court judge in Birmingham and prosecutor for Jefferson County. Endowed with an expansive, generous, and engaging personality, Black befriended as many people as he could from the minute of his arrival in Birmingham and kept it up for the next two decades. Integral to this process was joining every conceivable civic organization that existed. He joined the Masons, Woodmen of the World, Redmen, Civitan Club, Eagles, Elks and Dokies, Ku Klux Klan, and the Knights of Pythias. For this last group, Black recruited over one thousand members. He also took on the responsibility of teaching the men's Sunday School class at the Birmingham First Baptist Church, which he continued for twenty years. These memberships and activities not only helped bring in business for his fledgling law practice but also gave him a grassroots foundation upon which to build a future political career as a Democrat.

During World War I, the thirty-two-year-old Black responded to the call of his country by serving as a captain of the Eighty-First Field Artillery and as company regimental adjutant in the Nineteenth Artillery Brigade from 1917 to the end of the war in 1918.

A review of the religious beliefs of Hugo Black is a study in regression. During his childhood Black was heavily involved in his parents' local Baptist church. These early years seemingly left their mark; Black remained committed to the Baptist denomination throughout his many years in Alabama. Yet despite an outward appearance of religious devotion, Black's involvement in the church sprang predominantly from his overwhelming sense of obligation to his mother and, to some degree, political opportunism. When Black arrived in Washington in 1927, he had lost nearly all inclination toward religion. Biographer Roger Newman could confidently declare of Black's approach to religion during his Washington years, "[a] more formally irreligious man would have been hard to find."[38]

The Primitive Baptist Church Black attended with his family as a young boy served as his introduction to organized religion and its dangers. The Primitive Baptists engaged in many practices that Black found highly embarrassing and offensive. One common practice he found particularly embarrassing was when members stood up and "witness[ed] to the Lord

Jesus Christ when the spirit hit them."[39] During these times church members would relate how the spirit had convicted them just after they had committed adultery or woken up from a drinking binge, or they would stand up and speak in tongues.

Even more, Black found offensive the church's "New England Puritan" approach to the sins of its parishioners. Drunkenness often led to expulsion, but not until the individual accused was subjected to the embarrassment of a "trial" and a vote by the congregation. Black was alienated by these practices. He thought the "trials" inflicted "punishment without justice."[40] He felt that the public accusations and confessions that were extracted embarrassed and humiliated the accused church member. Tragically, Black had to watch his own father and uncle be expelled from the church because of their drinking problems. For Black, the Primitive Baptist Church of his youth provided vivid examples of the dangers and excesses of organized religion. Undoubtedly, these early experiences soured Black's attitude toward Christianity in general and contributed to his lifelong distrust of organized religion.

Notwithstanding these negative events, Black's early years did provide some positive religious experiences. Black's mother, Della, introduced him to the Bible. She read the Scriptures devoutly every night, frequently read them to her son, and made him study them. Della's insistence that Black read and study the Bible and attend church left a deep impression. Indeed, in his autobiographical sketch Black admitted that the Bible was always one of his favorite books. Later in life Black instructed his son in the meaning of Jesus' parables and on occasion utilized the Bible as a source of inspiration. Even more, he admitted that his main reason for joining the Ashland Baptist Church after graduating law school was out of obligation to his mother. It is clear that Della's religious example made an impression that had a lasting impact on her young son.

Surprisingly, especially considering the ill effects his drinking problem had on his relationship with his son, Black's father also role-modeled an important lesson on religious tolerance. One Sunday afternoon the Blacks had their pastor over for dinner.[41] While Black, his father, and their pastor were sitting on the porch, a man who was not affiliated with any church and generally regarded by the community as a worldly sinner came walking down the street. Black's father, "not the least embarrassed by the pastor's presence, greeted the man, engaged him in conversation at the front gate and urged" him to stay for dinner. His father's conduct was a serious departure from the typical religious intolerance of the members of the Primitive Baptist Church. Newman explained that William was of the opinion that "a man's soul was his own business, nobody else's."[42] This sentiment was remarkably similar to one Black would impress upon his son a generation later. Mirroring his father's point of view, Black told his son that "[p]rayer ought to be a private thing, just like religion for a truly religious person."[43]

Black's early church experiences planted the seeds for many of his future attitudes about religion. His mother's devotion to the Bible and religious example laid the groundwork for Black's lifelong love of the Bible. His belief that religion was an intensely personal matter quite possibly found its root in his father's similar view. But most importantly his experiences at the Primitive Baptist Church set a foundation for his lifelong suspicion of organized religion.

Black's less-than-devout approach to religion was signified by more than just the obligatory nature of his reasons for joining church and attending Sunday School. Also indicative of his growing disaffection from religion was the condition Black placed on his membership in the Ashland Baptist Church:

> [A]s an applicant for church membership I did not want to be publicly required to confess a religious faith greater than I had, nor did I intend to follow the custom of pretending that I had been a heavy sinner simply because I had sometimes played cards or danced. The preacher and I easily agreed, and I became a member of the church.[44]

Clearly, Black had become disillusioned with the Christian faith. Perhaps the memories of his experiences at the Primitive Baptist Church of his youth had taught him never to submit completely to church authority. His son reported that his father was always outraged by "any church's attempt to encourage belief by compulsion."[45] Black probably viewed his conditional membership as a protective measure against church excesses.

When Black moved to Birmingham he joined the First Baptist Church and its men's Baraca Sunday School class on his first Sunday in town. He soon became the teacher of the Baraca class, a position he would hold for sixteen years, as well as a superintendent of the Sunday school. Black was held in high regard by his many pupils during the years he taught the class. While one might conclude that Black's long tenure as a Sunday school teacher was motivated by a newly found religious devotion, two aspects of his service indicate otherwise. First, it is quite likely the politically motivated Black saw the Baraca class as an expedient to greater visibility in the Birmingham area since nearly one thousand men attended his weekly lectures. Even more illuminating, however, is how Black viewed his highly visible teaching position. Years later in Washington, Hugo Jr. asked his father how he could reconcile being a renowned Sunday school teacher in Alabama and yet not attend church in Washington. Black responded, revealingly, "All I did was teach the Bible in Alabama; those parts I selected, I taught. I didn't have to go to listen to the preacher."[46]

This comment once again underscores Black's growing lack of religious devotion. In Birmingham, just as in Ashland, Black attended church on his own conditions, avoiding any unwanted or excessive contact with its doctrines, practices, or pastor. His comment also reveals that he adopted a selective approach to the Christian faith. As Hugo Jr. explained, "To him the Bible wasn't a profession of faith but, rather, a book that had more lessons to give for a constructive life than any other work."[47] This remark from Black's son contains the key to understanding the religious beliefs of Hugo Black. For him, "ethical conduct" was the only "real religion." This was very much within the theological framework of Thomas Jefferson.

By the time he reached Washington in 1927, Black had developed an apathetic attitude toward formal religion. He immediately discontinued his relationship with the Baptist Church, and he rarely attended church during his more than forty years in the nation's capital.[48] On the few occasions when he did attend, he went to the All Souls Unitarian Church, providing further confirmation of his dislike for religious formalism and dogma. Nevertheless, he retained his love of the Bible and interest in religious matters during this time. Indeed, throughout his life, he derived comfort and meaning from his favorite chapter, 1 Corinthians 13, which teaches that one's gifts profit nothing unless they are governed by love, as summarized in verse 13: "And now abideth faith, hope, love, these three; but the greatest of these is love." Hugo Jr. said his father believed that I Corinthians 13 taught "the most important lesson in life" and must have read that chapter to him "a thousand times" while he was growing up. He also instructed his son in religious matters and looked to the Bible for inspiration and direction. Thus it seems that although Black rejected formal religion, he never ceased seeking religious meaning in his own personal way. His son reported that his father "passionately wanted to believe" in God, the divinity of Jesus, life after death, and Heaven and

Hell but "just could not." However, Black once told his son, "Understand, . . . I cannot believe. But I can't not believe either." In the end the only thing he could bring himself to believe in was the Bible's ethical and moral teachings, and to those "he had a profound commitment" throughout his life.[49]

Two of Black's convictions regarding the role of religion in our society are somewhat surprising considering his genuine lack of interest in and distrust of organized religion. First, Black believed that our nation had a uniquely Christian heritage. Second, despite finding no place for it in his own life, he believed the cause of organized religion was essential for maintaining civil society. Several times during his life Black publicly declared his beliefs that religion, and especially Christianity, was largely responsible for the founding of our nation, and that religion needed to continue to be a force in the lives of the people in order for the nation to endure. A lecture Black gave to the Baraca Sunday school class at First Baptist Church in Birmingham, testifies to these beliefs:

> Religion . . . is a vital part of the warp and woof of our national existence. Its glowing burning truths inspired the hearts of American pioneers. Its sacred precepts established our home life; shaped our infant institutions and nourished a spirit of equality and democracy. The voice of Roger Williams and his followers played no small part in impressing the principles and policies that molded our institutions and crystallized our sentiments into [a] written Constitution and laws. The Bible penetrated the trackless forests with the pioneers and strengthened the sturdy characters of our early settlers. In the name of Religion and Freedom of Religion laws were resisted to cross a tempestuous ocean to an unknown land. Our country has grown great, wealthy and prosperous beyond the wildest dreams of avarice, under a government instituted by readers and lovers of the Bible.
>
> Today, there are those who say that no longer do we need religion; no longer is the Bible essential. Like an ungrateful and overgrown child, we are urged by some to renounce the old-time religion to which many attribute the stability of our institutions and therefore the cause of our greatness. With the pride and boastfulness of the Prodigal Son, we are asked to leave the safety of our Father's House to wander in search of Happiness and glory into distant lands and other climes.[50]

Evidence of Black's belief in the primacy of religion to our national experience is not limited to occasional references in speeches delivered to his Sunday school class. He made similar statements in his capacity as a United States senator. In an address to an audience in Birmingham in 1931, Black declared: "Our country is Christian. It is not infidel. It can never be so until it departs from the foundation stone. The great [Daniel] Webster [the early nineteenth-century senator from Massachusetts] spoke right when he said that Christianity is the common law of the United States."[51] This is a startling statement coming from the man who later in life wrote the Supreme Court opinion that adopted strict separation as the constitutional rule embodied in the Establishment Clause.

Also surprising was Black's remark to a Montgomery audience that "[s]ubject to God's laws, man rules the world, and the kind of rulership depends on the kind of thoughts that abide in his mind."[52] These comments may simply represent attempts by a shrewd politician to curry favor with a religiously devout audience. Yet they may also demonstrate that Black believed that this country owed at least its founding, and maybe even its continued vitality, to the healthful influences of religion.

Black's words to his son regarding organized religion corroborate this conclusion. As Hugo Jr. reported, one day in the 1930s when he was a teenager, his father surprised him by voicing "his concern about the decline in popularity of organized religion."[53] Black told his son:

> This stuff's been a great foundation for doing right. Some people got to be scared into doing the right thing, some others got to be given blind hope you gonna find it better somewhere else by doing right on this earth. You pull out faith in God and these incentives to do good disappear.[54]

With these words Black rightly places his finger on the danger of removing religion from society. Religion inspires people to do good, live moral lives, and think of the needs of others before their own. Black understood that as the popularity of organized religion waned in our society, so would the motivation to do good.

Despite these words of approbation, Black never lost his fear of and hostility toward organized religion. More than anything, he feared the natural inclination of churches to seek out a close relationship with the state. He was especially suspicious of the Catholic Church whose politically powerful archbishops, he believed, made no secret in the twentieth century of the fact that their mission was to grow Catholicism into the de facto established religion in the United States. The excesses of the churches of Black's youth and the irrefutable historical record of established churches abusing political and legal power dominated his thoughts in the context of church-state relations. In a telling comment to his wife, he pointed to the Catholic Church's blemished history to explain his opinion in *Engel v. Vitale* (1962), saying that he decided the case as he did because "people had been tortured, their ears lopped off, and sometimes their tongues cut or their eyes gouged out, all in the name of religion."[55] Therefore, he ruled that compulsory prayers at a state-run school were unconstitutional.

Philip Hamburger points out in his book, *Separation of Church and State*, that Black's thoughts on religion were the result of a "confluence of Protestant, nativist and progressive anti-Catholic forces," which cultivated in him an extreme distaste for the Catholic Church.[56] Black spent the first half of his life in the Baptist Church, a denomination which at the time was renowned for its vilification of Catholicism. According to Wayne Flynt, a historian of the Baptist denomination in Alabama, by 1894 "anti-Catholicism . . . had become a sustained and major element" in Baptist thought.[57]

After World War I and, more significantly, during the time Black attended and taught Sunday school at First Baptist Church of Birmingham, "Catholicism became an obsession" for the Baptists. Black's own pastor, A. J. Dickinson, organized a semi-secret, anti-Catholic society called the "True American Society," whose main goal was to prevent Catholics from winning public office in Birmingham. The *Alabama Baptist* declared that the postwar world would present a struggle between "Baptist democracy and Catholic Tyranny. Every denomination would have to choose one or the other because neutrality was no longer possible."[58] While many of the theological doctrines and practices of the Baptist denomination did not appeal to Black, their separationist and anti-Catholic declarations found a deep resonance within him.

Any treatment of Hugo Black would be incomplete without discussing the nature of his association with the infamous Ku Klux Klan. This secret society had its origins in the Deep South during the Reconstruction decade following the Civil War among virulent white supremacists who used intimidation and terrorist tactics against former slaves who could now vote and hold political office.[59] That outrage, in the Klan's view, coupled with Union military occupation and northern "carpetbag" provisional governments, was exacerbated further by the fact that hundreds of thousands of southern white males who had fought for or supported the Confederacy were stripped of all political rights by the Fourteenth Amendment (1868, section 3).

Fortified with all the oaths, signs, symbols, secret handshakes, and hyperbolic titles for their leaders, Klan members felt a sense of brotherhood and mission reminiscent of the medieval Crusaders against the infidels. Outfitted in their signature white hoods to hide their identity, these gangs of torch-wielding nightriders set fire to churches and homes, conducted kidnappings and lynchings against blacks and northern provisional politicians, and generally terrorized the countryside. In 1871 Congress passed the Ku Klux Klan Act authorizing the president to use military force and martial law in areas where the Klan was active. The violent activities of the secret order diminished in subsequent years, replaced in the late nineteenth century and early twentieth by state and local legal passage and enforcement of "Black Codes." These laws systematically and effectively separated the white and black races in every aspect of life, and made it virtually impossible for blacks to exercise their right to vote—in both the North and the South. In 1896 the Supreme Court validated the system of segregation in its landmark *Plessy v. Ferguson* decision upholding the "separate but equal" theory of rights. By 1910, segregation was a way of life throughout America. Southern racism spread to the North and West as their urban black populations increased, and the Klan became a faded memory. This was the world in which young Hugo Black grew up.

And then came D. W. Griffith's full-length silent film, *The Birth of a Nation*, in 1915. A deplorable glorification of the Ku Klux Klan after the Civil War, Griffith luridly "portrayed ex-slaves as sex-crazed subhumans."[60] Distributed nationwide with great fanfare, it was the "must see" for moviegoers and generated much reaction in the press—praise and condemnation—because it reignited all the primeval sexual fears of the white man against the black. The film has been linked to the sudden rebirth of an old organization. In that very year, the new Ku Klux Klan was organized in Georgia as a highly regimented form of racism against blacks and other racial and religious minorities (Jews and Catholics). With its expanded mission, the Klan spread nationwide and garnered a larger following outside the South than within. Lynchings rose from thirty in 1917 to seventy in 1919; many of the victims were black veterans in uniform returning from World War I. There were twenty-five race riots in cities across the country in 1919 (the worst in Chicago), and by the mid-1920s Klan membership peaked at around five million. When Al

Smith, the New York Catholic governor, ran for president of the United States on the Democratic ticket in 1928, he was greeted by ominous Klan cross-burnings lining Southern and Midwestern roads along his campaign trail. Smith was soundly defeated by the landslide victory of Herbert Hoover, and in the following few years the Klan diminished in violent activities, membership numbers, and visibility.

Joining millions of others in the early 1920s from all parts of the country, Black became a member of this infamous organization on September 13, 1923. "It was a decision he did not make lightly."[61] He was first approached to join in 1920, but declined. Yet as time wore on and more and more of his friends and colleagues became members the pressure on Black to join became unbearable. But peer pressure was not the main reason he joined the Klan; it was a calculated political move. By 1923 the Klan was one of the most powerful political forces in Alabama. As biographer Roger Newman explained, Black recognized that "[w]ithout this well-disciplined bloc of voters . . . no candidate could hope to get elected to any office in Alabama in the foreseeable future. The Klan offered Black a ready-made base for political advancement. It was a vehicle he had to ride, to whatever destination would be his."[62]

While there clearly was a powerful political motivation for Black's decision to join the Klan, it is also important to note that he identified with a large portion of the Klan's platform. The Klan supported prohibition of alcohol under the 1919 Volstead Act, the "common man," and the rights of organized labor; and opposed corporations, immigration, and the Catholic Church. All of these issues appealed to Black to some degree or another. The Klan's anti-Catholic stance certainly did. A conspicuous example of Black's anti-Catholicism was his involvement in one of the most famous murder trials in Alabama history, *State v. Stephenson* (1921). In this case, a Methodist minister, Reverend Stephenson, was charged with the murder of a Catholic priest, Father Coyle. Stephenson believed Coyle was responsible for his daughter's conversion to Catholicism and marriage to a Catholic. In representing Stephenson, Black exploited the jury members' anti-Catholic sentiments on cross-examination of witnesses and during his closing remarks. He wrapped up his summation with a flourish:

> Because a man becomes a priest does not mean that he is divine. He has no more right to protection than a Protestant minister. Who believes Ruth Stephenson has not been proselytized? A child of a

Methodist does not suddenly depart from her religion unless someone has planted in her mind the seeds of influence. . . . When you find a girl who has been reared well persuaded from her parents by some cause or person, that cause or person is wrong.[63]

In short order, Stephenson was acquitted of the murder charge.

Black's attempts to distance himself from the more virulent and out-right illegal activities of the Klan supports the conclusion that Black did not embrace the Klan's extreme racism. For instance, on one occasion the Klan was debating a resolution to whip a man. Black declared, perhaps a little naively, "[t]his is a law-abiding organization and if you whip him, I leave the Klan."[64] The resolution passed and Black left the meeting in protest, yet still maintained his membership. On another occasion the Klan attempted to strip a Jewish man, Chester Bandman, of his job as a high school principal simply because he was Jewish. Bandman happened to be one of Black's friends. He fought the Klan's proposed course of action by exhorting other community organizations to protest the princi-pal's dismissal. Bandman's job was saved by Black's efforts.

The intimacy of Black's relationship with the Klan increased expo-nentially when he announced his intention to run for the Senate in 1925. Klan members played crucial roles in his campaign. The Exalted Cyclops of Birmingham's Lee Klan, Crampton Harris, acted as Black's finance chairman. James Esdale, Grand Dragon and head of the Alabama Ku Klux Klan, was Black's "campaign manager in everything but name."[65] Esdale and other Klan members chauffeured Black to local Klaverns (secret organizational units) to deliver speeches. The Grand Dragon typi-cally instructed Black to deliver talks against Catholicism at these clandes-tine gatherings, and Black did not disappoint him: "Hugo could make the best anti-Catholic speech you ever heard," Esdale recounted proudly.[66] It is undeniable that the support of the Alabama Klan accounted for Black's success in winning his U.S. Senate seat in 1926.

Black's membership in the Klan accounts for the "nativist" influence on the development of his anti-Catholicism. Indeed, Klan pamphlets, cir-culated about the time Black was a member, declared that the Founding Fathers had "wisely provided for the absolute divorce of Church and State."[67] When members recited the "Klansmen's Creed," they declared their belief "in the eternal Separation of Church and State."[68]

As a consequence of his affiliation with the Baptists and the Klan, Black's views regarding Catholicism and separation of church and state were well developed by the time he arrived in Washington. But it was Black's own admission at an Alabama Klan convention held a month after his victory that foreclosed any meaningful dispute as to whether he owed his victory to the Klan. When it was his turn to address the convention, Black expressed his gratitude to his fellow Klansmen: "I know that without the support of the members of this organization I would not have been called, even by my enemies, 'the junior Senator from Alabama.'"[69]

Black spent the next eleven years in the Senate. He was reelected in 1932, this time without any help from the Klan, whose power had substantially diminished in Alabama. Black's Senate years were significant in many ways, but most importantly in that they placed him on President Roosevelt's radar screen as a potential candidate for the Supreme Court. Black ingratiated himself to the new president through his tireless support of Roosevelt's New Deal economic package and "court-packing" proposal, which attempted, in effect, to reorganize the entire federal judiciary with Roosevelt appointees. His position on these two issues supplied Roosevelt with confidence in appointing Black to the Court. First, he knew Black was a dependable liberal who would work to clear the legal obstacles to New Deal legislation. Second, Black was a perfect vehicle for retaliation against a Senate that invited Roosevelt's vengeance for scuttling his court-packing plan. Thus, on August 12, 1937, Roosevelt nominated Hugo Black to the Supreme Court.

Black's nomination to the Court had its intended effect. When the announcement of Roosevelt's choice was read to the Senate "[a] gasp went through the chamber."[70] After the initial shock had subsided, Senator Ashurst, chairman of the Judiciary Committee, called for the Senate to follow the immemorial rule of confirming one of its members selected to serve on the Court "without reference to a committee."[71] Two senators objected and "[f]or the first time since 1888 a committee would consider a colleague's confirmation."[72] Just five days later the Senate confirmed Black's appointment 63 to 16, with 17 abstentions.[73]

The progressive, liberal culture Black encountered in the capital probably served more to fortify his beliefs than to develop them. According to Hugo Black Jr., Paul Blanshard's anti-Catholic books probably had the greatest fortifying effect upon Black's beliefs.[74] Blanshard was the prototypical religious liberal and humanist. On one occasion he expressed his disdain for the devoutly religious, saying he was pleased "that 'the new movement against Catholic aggression is rising not on . . . the lunatic fringes of religion and fanaticism, but right in the hearts of American

University leaders.'"[75] Liberals like Blanshard feared the Catholic Church because they perceived its authoritarian structure as a threat to American democracy.[76] In his 1949 book, *American Freedom and Catholic Power*, Blanshard expressed the solution to this threat that most liberals were advocating: "In the field of politics and law, the platform should favor 'a wall of separation between church and state,' and make it real with no compromise."[77]

Another probable liberal influence on Black's anti-Catholic and separationist beliefs was his friend and pastor A. Powell Davies. Davies was the pastor of All Souls Unitarian Church, which Black infrequently attended during his years in Washington, and officiated, upon Black's request, at his second marriage.[78] Davies was a leading figure in the liberal movement who "frequently used the pulpit to warn of the danger posed to American society by an aggressive Catholicism."[79] In a speech delivered at the Fourth National Conference on Church and State, Davies expressed his fear that the authoritarian principles taught at Catholic schools, if allowed into public schools, could undermine American unity, "without which [our] democratic society can[not] long endure." Davies argued that parochial schools undermined unity by preparing "its students . . . for life in an *exclusive* society ruled by authoritarian principles, namely, the Catholic Church" [emphasis in original]. He also admonished Protestants not to make any concessions to the Roman Catholic hierarchy in the realm of public education for fear that such concessions could enable the Catholics to "demolish the entire case for separation of church and state." He closed his speech by encouraging his listeners to "go back and learn what the Founding Fathers intended by the separation of church and state" and to be vigilant against attempts by the Catholic Church to "rewrite this phase of our history to give it an aspect more favorable to their aims."[80]

It is interesting to note that just as Black's constitutional philosophy resembled Thomas Jefferson's, so did his religious beliefs. Barbara Perry pointed out in a 1989 article that Jefferson believed that "religion was an intensely private matter between the individual and 'his maker.'"[81] Similarly, Jefferson extracted Christianity's ethical and moral teachings as the true essence of that religion and rejected its supernatural aspects.[82] Moreover, Jefferson, like Black, was suspicious of organized religion and believed that its tendency toward "ecclesiastical tyranny was just as despicable as the political variety."[83]

Jefferson's belief that religion was an intensely personal matter led him to conclude that government should hold no power over personal religious beliefs. Jefferson expressed this sentiment in his Bill for Establishing Religious Liberty, a document that Black quoted from frequently, declaring "Almighty God hath created the mind free."[84] The similarity between Black's and Jefferson's views regarding religion ineluctably brings to mind Black's remark of Jefferson: "In practically everything . . . he said, I agree with him."[85]

Black's religious experiences help to explain why he favored a policy of complete separation in matters of church and state. His lifelong suspicion of organized religion was a major tenet of all the cultural forces with which he aligned himself. The Baptists, the Ku Klux Klan, and mid-century religious liberals and humanists all advocated separation of church and state and fanned the flames of Black's preexisting suspicion of organized religion with their anti-Catholic rhetoric. The ultimate lesson Black's religious experiences taught him was that religious beliefs should "remain in the private realm of a person's conscience . . . free from ecclesiastical, societal, or governmental coercion."[86] In *Everson*, Black was afforded an opportunity to act on this core belief.

THE CASE: *EVERSON V. BOARD OF EDUCATION* (1947)

Hugo Black has achieved a place of historical preeminence in the realm of Establishment Clause jurisprudence by crafting the majority opinion in *Everson v. Board of Education*.[87] *Everson* was the first Supreme Court decision to make the First Amendment Establishment Clause of the U.S. Constitution binding upon the states. Ironically, the most significant legacy *Everson* contributed to the debate over church-state relations was Black's injection of Thomas Jefferson's "wall of separation" metaphor in the dicta portion of the opinion that seemed to completely contradict the actual holding in the case. Nevertheless, the metaphor became shorthand for communicating a whole concept of interpreting the First Amendment religion clauses in subsequent cases. *Everson*, in no small measure, marks the line of demarcation between the Christian world of *Holy Trinity* at the end of the nineteenth century and the secular humanist world of the twentieth century.

The adoption of Jefferson's strict separationist metaphor as the meaning of the Establishment Clause has remarkably affected our culture.

Daniel Dreisbach has commented on the ubiquity of the phrase since 1947, saying that "the Jeffersonian metaphor has eclipsed and supplanted constitutional text in the minds of many jurists, scholars, and the American public."[88] Though the metaphor has not been invoked explicitly on a regular basis by the Supreme Court in recent years and has been soundly criticized on occasion, its obvious separationist implications continue to dominate the analysis of any church-state issue that comes before the Court.

Everson presented the question whether a New Jersey school board could reimburse parents for the cost of transporting their children to Catholic parochial schools without violating the Establishment Clause. Essentially, the school board was using public funds to pay for the transportation of children to sectarian schools. Considering everything in Justice Black's background, replete with lifelong anti-Catholic sentiments and speeches, it was surprising that he ruled in favor of the school board and found that its policy to assist Catholic parents did not violate the Establishment Clause. The close 5–4 decision by the Court engendered much confusion from all quarters. Why build a high solid brick wall and then immediately drive a Mack truck through it?

In this first opportunity for the Supreme Court to construe the Establishment Clause, Black wrote a lengthy historical rationale in the same vein as Justice David Brewer had in *Holy Trinity* fifty-five years earlier, but this time from a secularist point of view on religion and the First Amendment. Consistent with his theory of constitutional interpretation, Black turned to the history surrounding that clause to divine its meaning. He recounted that the early American settlers were religious dissenters who came to America's shores to flee the persecution they had experienced at the hand of religious establishments in their home countries. Unfortunately, these settlers, carrying with them their own peculiar religious beliefs, established similar practices in the New World. Thus the bondage the settlers sought to escape became an intimate part of their lives in the colonies. As examples of the persecutions that existed during colonial times, Black highlighted the hounding and jailing of religious minorities at the hands of the Puritans, who also compelled dissenters to pay tithes and taxes to support their established churches.

According to Black, the practices of these colonial establishments shocked the "freedom-loving colonials into a feeling of abhorrence" and "aroused their indignation."[89] Black turned exclusively to the battle for religious liberty in the colony of Virginia to unfold the meaning of the

Establishment Clause. He asserted that the people of Virginia "reached the conviction that individual religious liberty could be achieved best under a government which was stripped of all power to tax, to support, or otherwise to assist any or all religions, or to interfere with the beliefs of any religious individual or group."[90]

Black specifically relied on a cursory examination of James Madison's *Memorial and Remonstrance* and a more thorough review of Thomas Jefferson's *Virginia Bill for Religious Liberty* in arriving at this conclusion. (It may be recalled from chapter 3 that Chief Justice Morrison Waite had done the same review in his 1878 *Reynold's* opinion to define "religious belief" and separate it from "conduct.") Black defended his dependence on the Virginia experience by asserting that previous Supreme Court decisions had recognized that the aim of the First Amendment was to secure "the same protection against governmental intrusion on religious liberty as the Virginia statute [Jefferson's *Bill for Religious Liberty*]."[91]

Against this historical backdrop, Black announced his now famous interpretation of the Establishment Clause:

> The "establishment of religion" clause of the First Amendment means at least this: Neither a state nor the Federal Government can set up a church. Neither can pass laws which aid one religion, aid all religions, or prefer one religion over another. Neither can force nor influence a person to go to or to remain away from church against his will or force him to profess a belief or disbelief in any religion. No person can be punished for entertaining or professing religious beliefs or disbeliefs, for church attendance or non-attendance. No tax in any amount, large or small, can be levied to support any religious activities or institutions, whatever they may be called, or whatever form they may adopt to teach or practice religion. Neither a state nor the Federal Government can, openly or secretly, participate in the affairs of any religious organizations or groups and *vice versa*. In the words of Jefferson, the clause against establishment of religion by law was intended to erect a "wall of separation between church and State."[92]

Black's interpretation of the Establishment Clause seemed to allow no aid to religion whatsoever, and adopted Jefferson's wall metaphor as its true intent. This strict view raises the question of how he found it constitutional for public funds to be dispersed to parents who sent their children to Catholic schools. It would seem such an arrangement would be a direct violation of the newly interpreted clause. Yet Black scaled the wall he had just so emphatically and unapologetically constructed by classifying the school board's reimbursement policy as "general welfare legislation," similar to police, fire and sewage services also provided by the state. According to Black, this kind of legislation was "so indisputably marked off from the religious function" that allowing religious institutions to avail themselves of its benefits did not violate the First Amendment. Even more, "[t]he state contribute[d] no money to the schools. It d[id] not support them."[93] It simply established "a general program to help parents get their children, regardless of their religion, safely and expeditiously to and from accredited schools."[94] Thus, surprisingly, an opinion filled with separationist rhetoric ended with a decidedly accommodationist result.

The *Everson* decision injected several important and enduring concepts into Establishment Clause jurisprudence. Among them are a strict separationist approach to church-state relations, the secular purpose doctrine, and neutrality.

Black's majority opinion, while failing to provide any concrete legal rules for analysis of church-state issues, did provide the strict separationist framework within which many subsequent Establishment Clause cases would be analyzed. Black's adoption of the wall metaphor from Jefferson's letter to the Danbury Baptists effectively made separation of church and state the "ultimate principle in the first amendment."[95] Such unequivocal separationist language would appear to prohibit government programs that provide any benefit to religion whatsoever, even incidental and indirect ones.

Despite adopting strict separation of church and state as the ultimate principle of the Establishment Clause, Black developed several ideas in *Everson* that mitigated the harshness of its application. One such idea was the "secular purpose" doctrine. Legal researcher and writer Paul Kauper explained this doctrine in these terms: "[T]he government, in pursuing secular purposes, may properly afford aid to religious institutions so long as the aid to religion and the institution is simply incidental to the achievement of a secular purpose."[96] This doctrine has become a staple in Establishment Clause jurisprudence for almost sixty years. It was adopted in *School District v. Schempp* (1963) as the proper test to determine whether the Establishment Clause had been violated, relied upon in *Board of Education v. Allen* (1968) to sidestep the strict separationist thrust of the *Everson* opinion, and later emerged as prongs one and two of the *Lemon* test articulated in *Lemon v. Kurtzman* (1971).[97] (This case is the subject of chapter 8.)

Black developed another enduring idea that mitigated the impact of his separationist rhetoric—neutrality. He asserted that the First Amendment "requires the state to be a neutral in its relations with groups of religious believers and nonbelievers; it does not require the state to be their adversary. State power is no more to be used so as to handicap religions than it is to favor them."[98] In speaking of separation and neutrality, Black seemed to be advocating two diametrically opposed ideas. The no-aid doctrine is decidedly separationist in that it calls for any government program providing aid to religion to be struck down. In contrast, the neutrality doctrine is decidedly accommodationist in nature, implying that government aid policies can pass constitutional muster so long as they treat religion and non-religion equally.[99] Significantly, Black relied on the concept of neutrality when he gave the Court's approval to the reimbursement policy in question in *Everson*, noting that the reimbursements were provided to the parents "regardless of their religion."[100] Thus, Black found no violation of the Establishment Clause partly because the school board reimbursed parents regardless of their religious affiliation.

Due to its watershed status, the *Everson* decision has engendered a mountain of scholarly research. Significant for present purposes is the scholarship focusing on the factors that influenced how Black formulated the *Everson* opinion. The two elements that most conspicuously impacted the formulation of his opinion were his personal religious beliefs and his approach to constitutional interpretation.

Barbara Perry makes a compelling argument that Black's religious beliefs figured prominently in his decision. After conducting a brief examination of Black's core religious and political beliefs and noting his near perfect separationist voting record on Establishment Clause cases, Perry concludes that "Black's personal religious heritage and attitudes may well have served as the most formative components of his nearly unanimous record in religious establishment cases."[101]

Black's poor analysis of the history of the First Amendment also tends to indicate that something other than that history influenced the formulation of his opinion. In his recounting of the historical context within which the Establishment Clause was crafted and adopted, Black focused narrowly on the history of the religious liberty battle in Virginia and on the contributions of Madison and Jefferson. In so doing, Black completely ignored other more appropriate and obvious sources of historical information concerning the meaning of the Establishment Clause, such as the approaches the other twelve colonies took toward religion, the

House and Senate debates regarding the First Amendment, the debates in the state ratifying conventions, and the practices of the early Congresses of the Republic.[102]

What accounts for such conspicuous historical ignorance from a man who espoused "originalism" as the proper method of constitutional interpretation? In his book *A Constitutional Faith*, Justice Black defined his originalist approach to constitutional interpretation:

> I strongly believe that this history [of our Nation's founding] shows that the basic purpose and plan of the Constitution is that the federal government should have no powers except those that are expressly or impliedly granted, and that no department of government—executive, legislative, or judicial—has authority to add to or take from the powers granted it or the powers denied it by the Constitution. Our written Constitution means to me that where a power is not in terms granted or not necessary and proper to exercise a power that is granted, no such power exists in any branch of the government—executive, legislative, or judicial. Thus, it is the language and history that are crucial factors which influence me in interpreting the Constitution.[103]

Some preeminent constitutional scholars, and even one Supreme Court justice involved in the *Everson* opinion, would say it was Black's own personal religious predilections. Law professor Daniel L. Dreisbach has written that "[T]he Court recounted American history 'not in order to tell accurately the story of the past, but in order to legitimate its own judgment of policy.'"[104] Edward S. Corwin, McCormack Professor of Jurisprudence at Princeton, wittily remarked, "Undoubtedly the Court has the right to make history, as it has often done in the past; but it has no right to make it up."[105] Just one year after *Everson*, Justice Robert Jackson, who dissented in *Everson*, issued a concurring opinion in *Illinois ex rel. McCollum v. Board of Education*, in which he candidly declared that, in matters of church and state, the justices were ultimately governed by "no law but our own prepossessions."[106]

The situation would be different if the historical evidence Black used to prove that the Establishment Clause erected a wall of separation between church and state actually supported that interpretation. But it does not. In fact, Black did not even review the debates of the First Congress, which discussed the religion amendments, until after he announced his decision in *Everson*.[107] The superficial and incomplete nature of

Black's historical analysis leads one inexorably to conclude that something other than history played the most important role in his decision.

On several separate occasions and to different family members, Black remarked that his decisions regarding church-state issues were influenced by his religious experiences and attitudes. For instance, Black told his son that the people protesting his decision in *Engel v. Vitale* outlawing prayer in school were "pure hypocrites who never pray anywhere but in public for the credit of it. Prayer ought to be a private thing, just like religion for a truly religious person."[108] Regarding the same case, Black told his wife that "people had been tortured, their ears lopped off, and sometimes their tongues cut or their eyes gouged out, all in the name of religion."[109] Of her husband's religious beliefs, Mrs. Black said, "He advocated many religions of a diverse nature, because, as he said, when one religion gets predominance, they [*sic*] immediately try to suppress others."[110] In a comment encompassing all of his Establishment Clause decisions, he once told a nephew, "All of my religious decisions are influenced by what happened to our Toland ancestors in Ireland."[111] Black was referring to the political and religious persecution his Scot-Irish ancestors had suffered at the hands of the government.[112]

Philip Hamburger presents a compelling argument that Black's decision in *Everson* was the product of his personal beliefs rather than a fair reading of constitutional history. Hamburger tracks a broad-based movement that developed between the mid-nineteenth and early twentieth centuries composed of evangelical Protestants, nativists, theological liberals, and secularists that advocated separation of church and state.[113] As we have seen, Black was, at one time or another during his life, associated with each one of these cultural groups.

This overview of Black's religious experiences and opinions yields several insights into the nature of his religious beliefs. On the personal level, Black was brought up in a nominally Christian home, attended church, taught Sunday school, and maintained a genuine interest in religious matters throughout his life. But despite his years of membership in and service to the Christian religion, he could never bring himself to believe in its supernatural aspects. In the end, Black's religion was comprised of a code of ethical conduct based primarily on Christianity's moral teachings as expressed in the New Testament and taught to him by his mother.

More importantly, Black's religious experiences help to explain why he favored a policy of complete separation in matters of church and state.

At a young age, Black was introduced to the dangers of religious devotion running amok at his parent's Primitive Baptist Church. The resultant suspicion for organized religion that Black developed was a major tenet of all the cultural forces he aligned himself with throughout the rest of his life. The Baptists, the Ku Klux Klan, and mid-century religious liberals and humanists all advocated separation of church and state and fanned the flames of Black's preexisting suspicion of organized religion with their anti-Catholic rhetoric. The ultimate lesson Black's religious experiences taught him was that religious beliefs should "remain in the private realm of a person's conscience . . . free from ecclesiastical, societal, or governmental coercion."[114] In *Everson*, Black was afforded an opportunity to act on this core belief.

Justice Black served on the Supreme Court of the United States for thirty-four years until he resigned on September 17, 1971. He died nine days later and is buried in Arlington National Cemetery. In the 1950s and 1960s, this former Alabama Klansman was a major judicial force in achieving the desegregation of schools in the South. The legacy of his *Everson* opinion grew a life of its own as the Court continued to struggle with how to apply it to cases concerning the constitutionality of long-standing traditions of prayer in the public schools.

NOTES

1. Morris, *American Catholic*, 155.

2. *Everson v. Board of Education*, 330 U.S. 1 (1947).

3. *Resolution on Religious Liberty*, Southern Baptist Convention, May 1913; full text available at http://www.sbc.net.

4. *Resolution on Religious Liberty*, Southern Baptist Convention, May 1914; full text available at http://www.sbc.net.

5. George W. Truett, sermon preached on the U.S. Capitol steps during the annual meeting of the Southern Baptist Convention, 16 May 1920 (Southern Baptist Historical Library and Archives).

6. *Baptist Faith & Message*, Section XVIII, adopted by the Southern Baptist Convention, May 1925; full text available at http://www.sbc.net/bfm/bfmcomparison.asp.

7. *A Brief Statement of the Doctrinal Position of the Lutheran Church—Missouri Synod*, § 34 (St. Louis: Concordia Publishing, 1932); full text available at http://www.lcms.org/pages/internal.asp?NavID = 575.

8. *Resolution Concerning Freedom of Religion*, Southern Baptist Convention, May 1935; full text available at http://www.sbc.net.

9. *Resolution Concerning Freedom of Religion*.

10. To illustrate the sea change in American attitudes and policies regarding the Vatican from the 1930s to the present, on 8 April 2005, President George W. Bush, accompanied by former presidents George H. W. Bush and William Jefferson Clinton, represented the United States at the funeral of Pope John Paul II held in Vatican Square. It is the first time in history that an American president, let alone three, all devout Protestants, attended such a formally religious occasion at the Vatican to honor the life of a pope.

11. Timothy G. McCarthy, *The Catholic Tradition in the Twentieth Century*, rev. and expanded 2nd ed. (Chicago: Loyola Press, 1998), 9; Rose Fitzgerald Kennedy, *Times to Remember* (New York: Doubleday & Company, 1974), 244, and formal photograph of the Kennedy family in front of the Vatican at the coronation, facing page 204.

12. *Resolution Urging Care in Safeguarding the Principle of the Separation of Church and State*, Southern Baptist Convention, May 1939; full text available at http://www.sbc.net.

13. *Vatican Relations*, Minutes of the 12th Biennial Convention, United Lutheran Church in America, 1940, 34; full text available at www.elca.org.

14. *Vatican Relations*, 34.

15. *The American Baptist Bill of Rights: A Pronouncement upon Religious Liberty* (1939), 3; reprinted in *Baptist Life and Thought, 1600–1980*, ed. William H. Brackney (Valley Forge, Pa.: Judson Press, 1983).

16. Paul Blanshard, *American Freedom and Catholic Power* (Boston: Beacon Press, 1949), 266–88.

17. *Report of the Committee on Public Relations*, Minutes of the Southern Baptist Convention, 1937, 101; full text available at www.sbc.net.

18. *Report of the Committee on Committees*, Minutes of the Southern Baptist Convention, 1937, C8.

19. Stanley L. Hastey, "A History of the Baptist Joint Committee on Public Affairs, 1946-1971" (1973), 24; (unpublished Ph.D. dissertation, Southern Baptist Theological Seminary, on file with the Southern Baptist Theological Seminary library).

20. *1950 Annual of the Southern Baptist Convention*, 393.

21. Hastey, "A History of the Baptist Committee," 62.

22. Hastey, "A History of the Baptist Committee," 63.

23. Anson Phelps Stokes, *Church and State*, vol. 2, 464.

24. *Resolution on Protestants and Other Americans United for Separation of Church and State*, Southern Baptist Convention, May 1948; full text available at http://www.sbc.net.

25. *Minutes, 15th Biennial Convention* (1946), United Lutheran Church in America, 258; full text available at www.elca.org/jle/ulca/ulca.church_state.html.

26. *Minutes, 17th Biennial Convention* (1950), United Lutheran Church in America, 877; full text available at www.elca.org/jle/ulca/ulca.church_state.html.

27. *Minutes*, Adopted by the Executive Board, United Lutheran Church in America (1950); full text available at www.elca.org/jle/ulca/ulca.church_state.html.

28. *Minutes*, United Lutheran Church in America (1950).

29. *Minutes*, United Lutheran Church in America (1950).

30. *Minutes*, Augustana Lutheran Church (1952), 379; full text available at www.elca .org/jle/ulca/ ulca.church_state.html.

31. Roger K. Newman, *Hugo Black: A Biography* (New York: Fordham University Press, 1997), 3.

32. Hugo Black, Jr., *My Father: A Remembrance* (New York: Random House, 1975), 5–6. William's drinking problem, unfortunately, was inherited by some of Hugo's brothers. Pelham, whom Hugo looked to as a role model, died as a result of a night of excess. As the story went, Pelham was driving the family horse and buggy home after a night of heavy drinking and fell asleep. The horse veered right and threw Pelham into a pond. "Pelham, the best swimmer in Clay County, never awoke." This event solidified Hugo's already strong dislike of alcohol.

33. Hugo L. Black, "Reminiscences," *Ala. L. Rev.* 18 (1965): 4.

34. Newman, *Hugo Black*, 17. Black's allotment of time for Sunday school and church during this busy time of his life should not be viewed as an indication of a genuine interest in religious matters. Instead, he likely went to church and Sunday school out of obligation to his mother.

35. Newman, *Hugo Black*, 17.

36. Hugo L. Black and Elizabeth Black, *Mr. Justice and Mrs. Black: The Memoirs of Hugo L. Black and Elizabeth Black* (New York: Random House, 1986), 15.

37. Hugo and Elizabeth Black, *Mr. Justice and Mrs. Black*, 10.

38. Newman, *Hugo Black*, 521.

39. Black, Jr., *My Father*, 11.

40. Black, Jr., *My Father*, 11.

41. Newman, *Hugo Black*, 10.

42. Newman, *Hugo Black*, 10.

43. Black, Jr., *My Father*, 176.

44. Black and Black, *Memoirs*, 21.

45. Black, Jr., *My Father*, 176.

46. Black, Jr., *My Father*, 173.

47. Black, Jr., *My Father*, 173.

48. Barbara A. Perry, "Justice Hugo Black and the 'Wall of Separation between Church and State,'" *J. Church & St.* 31 (1989): 58.

49. Black, Jr., *My Father*, 172–74.

50. Newman, *Hugo Black*, 68; quoting Hugo L. Black, First Baptist Church Sermon, (no date).

51. Newman, *Hugo Black*, 146; quoting Hugo L. Black, Memorial Speech, Auditorium, Birmingham, 1931 (alteration in original).

52. Newman, *Hugo Black*, 146 n3; quoting Hugo L. Black, "As a Man Thinketh," speech to Judge Leon McCord's Bible Class, Montgomery, 1931.

53. Black, Jr., *My Father*, 175.

54. Black, Jr., *My Father*, 175.

55. Black and Black, *Memoirs*, 95.

56. Hamburger, *Separation of Church and State*, 423.

57. Wayne Flynt, *Alabama Baptists: Southern Baptists in the Heart of Dixie* (Tuscaloosa: University of Alabama Press, 1998), 232.

58. Flynt, *Alabama Baptists*, 302.

59. The discussion of the Ku Klux Klan's early beginnings and reappearance in the twentieth century is based on: Current, *American History*, 466–67; Morris, *American Catholic*, 147, 201; and C. Vann Woodward, *The Strange Career of Jim Crow*, (New York: Oxford University Press, 1966), 114–15. For the impact of D.W. Griffith's 1915 film, *Birth of a Nation: The Clansman*, see websites: http://www.pbs.org/americanmasters/data base/griffith_d.html; and http://www.imdb.com/title/H0004927/news.

60. Morris, *American Catholic*, 201.

61. Newman, *Hugo Black*, 92.

62. Newman, *Hugo Black*, 93.

63. Newman, *Hugo Black*, 76, 83–84.

64. Newman, *Hugo Black*, 93.

65. Newman, *Hugo Black* 104.

66. Newman, *Hugo Black*, 104.

67. Hamburger, *Separation of Church and State*, 408; quoting C. Lewis Fowler, *The Ku Klux Klan: Its Origin, Meaning and Scope of Operation* (Atlanta, Ga., 1922), 33–34.

68. Hamburger, *Separation of Church and State*, 408.

69. Newman, *Hugo Black*, 116.

70. Newman, *Hugo Black*, 237.

71. Newman, *Hugo Black*, 238; quoting 81 *Cong. Rec.* 8732 (75th Cong., 1st Session, 1937).

72. Newman, *Hugo Black*, 238.

73. Newman, *Hugo Black*. 242.

74. Black, Jr., *My Father*, 104.

75. John T. McGreevy, "Thinking on One's Own: Catholicism in the American Intellectual Imagination, 1928–1960," *J. Am. Hist.* 84 (1997): 98; quoting Harvard Law School Forum, *The Catholic Church and Politics: A Transcript of a Discussion of a Vital Issue* (Cambridge, Mass.: Harvard University Press, 1950).

76. McGreevy, "Thinking on One's Own," 106–107.

77. Blanshard, *American Freedom*, 305.

78. William O. Douglas, ed., foreword to *The Mind and Faith of A. Powell Davies* (Garden City, N.Y.: Doubleday, 1959), 11, 21, 28; Newman, *Hugo Black*, 466. Davies was pastor of All Souls from 1944 until his death in 1957.

79. McGreevy, "Thinking on One's Own," 124.

80. A. Powell Davies, "Separation of Church and State," in *The Mind and Faith of A. Powell Davies*, 126, 128, 130.

81. Barbara Perry, "Justice Hugo Black and the 'Wall of Separation between Church and State," *J. of Church & St.* 31(1989): 69.

82. Perry, "Justice Hugo Black and the 'Wall,'" 69. Perry quotes Dumas Malone, a renowned Jefferson biographer, as saying that "in the ripeness of 'his years he [Jefferson] found in the teachings of Jesus the purest system of morals ever before preached to man.'" Dumas Malone, *Jefferson the Virginian* (Boston: Little, Brown, 1948), 107.

83. Perry, "Justice Hugo Black and the 'Wall,'" 69.

84. Thomas Jefferson, *A Bill for Establishing Religious Freedom*; reprinted in Merrill D. Peterson, ed., *Thomas Jefferson, Writings* (New York: Viking Press, 1984), 346.

85. Newman, *Hugo Black*, 143; quoting 75 *Cong. Rec.* 3516 (72nd Cong., 1st Session, 1932).

86. Perry, "Justice Hugo Black and the 'Wall,'" 59.

87. *Everson v. Board of Education*, 1.

88. Daniel L. Dreisbach, *Thomas Jefferson and the Wall of Separation between Church and State* (New York: New York University Press, 2002), 2, 5. Dreisbach explains why the use of Jefferson's metaphor has persisted: "Occasionally, a figure of speech is thought to encapsulate so thoroughly an idea or concept that it passes into the language as the standard expression of that idea. Such is the case with the graphic phrase, 'wall of separation between church and state.'"

89. *Everson v. Board of Education*, 11.

90. *Everson v. Board of Education*, 11.

91. *Everson v. Board of Education*, 13. Paul Kauper's 1973 analysis of Black's historical review of previous cases is most instructive: none of the decisions Black referred to, *Davis v. Beason*, 133 U.S. 33 (1890), *Reynolds v. United States*, 98 U.S. 145 (1878), and *Watson v. Jones*, 80 U.S. 679 (1871), elaborated on the Establishment Clause in any way whatsoever. *Davis* and *Reynolds* dealt with the Free Exercise Clause, and *Watson* was a diversity case largely dependent on the common law. Paul G. Kauper, "*Everson v. Board of Education:* A Product of the Judicial Will," *Ariz. L. Rev.* 15 (1973): 312 n25.

92. *Everson v. Board of Education*, 15–16.

93. *Everson v. Board of Education*, 18.

94. *Everson v. Board of Education*, 18

95. Kauper, "A Product of Judicial Will," 322.

96. Kauper, "A Product of Judicial Will," 320 n54.

97. *Abington v. Schempp*, 374 U.S. 203 (1963), 222; *Bd. of Educ. v. Allen*, 392 U.S. 236 (1968), 241–44, and *Lemon v. Kurtzman*, 403 U.S. 602 (1971), 612–13. Citing *Everson* as authority, the *Schempp* Court said:

> The test may be stated as follows: what are the purpose and primary effect of the enactment? If either is the advancement or inhibition of religion then the enactment exceeds the scope of legislative power as circumscribed by the Constitution. That is to say that to withstand the strictures of the Establishment Clause there must be a secular legislative purpose and a primary effect that neither advances nor inhibits religion.

In the *Allen* case, the Court upheld a New York law that made schoolbooks available free of charge to children, including those who attended parochial schools. The Court, depending on the rationale of *Everson*, found that the law had a secular legislative purpose and did not have the primary effect of advancing or inhibiting religion.

98. *Everson v. Board of Education*, 1, 18.

99. For a useful discussion of the competing concepts of separation and neutrality as outlined in *Everson*, see Kauper, "A Product of Judicial Will," 322–24.

100. *Everson v. Board of Education*, 18.

101. Perry, "Justice Hugo Black and the 'Wall,'" 60.

102. Gerard V. Bradley, *Church-State Relationships in America* (New York: Greenwood Press, 1987), 12–13.

103. Hugo L. Black, *A Constitutional Faith* (New York: Knopf, 1968), 8.

104. Daniel L. Dreisbach, "A Lively and Fair Experiment: Religion and the American Constitutional Tradition," *Emory L.J.* 49 (2000): 232; quoting Mark DeWolfe Howe, *The Garden and the Wilderness*, (Chicago: University of Chicago Press, 1965), 168.

105. Dreisbach, "A Lively and Fair Experiment," 232.

106. *Illinois ex rel. McCollum v. Board of Education*, 333 U.S. 203 (1948), 238; Jackson, J., concurring.

107. Newman, *Hugo Black*, 365.

108. Black, Jr., *My Father*, 176.

109. Black and Black, *Memoirs*, 95.

110. Black and Black, *Memoirs*, 95.

111. Newman, *Hugo Black*, 365.

112. Newman, *Hugo Black*, 4; discussing briefly Toland's revolutionary activities in Ireland.

113. Newman, *Hugo Black*, 10–11, 14–16; outlining the role Protestants, theological liberals, and secularists played in the rise of the principle of separation.

114. Perry, "Justice Hugo Black and the 'Wall,'" 59.

The School Prayer Controversy

In the relationship between man and religion, the State is
firmly committed to a position of neutrality.

—Associate Justice Tom Clark
School District v. Schempp, 1963

*E*mboldened by success in the *Everson* case, both because of its incorporation of the Establishment Clause to state governments as well as its
adoption of the "wall of separation" metaphor, a growing movement
developed around the country to remove state-sanctioned religious exercises. Nothing was as prevalent as the issue of prayer and Bible reading in
public schools. As may be recalled, this controversy had been present in
the United States since the 1820s and now reached its zenith in the 1960s.
When the issue came before the Supreme Court of the United States in
the case of *School District v. Schempp* in 1962, the political and theological
ramifications crystallized. One need only look at the briefs filed in the case
to understand the theological positions being advocated by the denominations.

The American Jewish Committee as well as the American Ethics
Union (AEU) both filed briefs in the case. The AEU was founded by
secularists and Unitarians in the 1870s. Not one brief was filed on behalf
of any Christian denomination in support of the challenged practices.
Also, the author of the opinion, Associate Justice Tom Clark, was a
devout Presbyterian, who was actually in favor of greater religious influence in American public life. In fact, Justice Clark's position was that
mandatory prayer at school trivialized the importance of religious influences.

THE CULTURAL/HISTORICAL CONTEXT

In the 1960s, many states still had statutes or school board rules requiring the reading of the Bible in public schools. These statutes dated from the mid-1850s, just a few years after Justice Story's opinion in the *Vidal v. Girard* case. Typical of these laws were the statutes at issue in *Schempp*.

Thirteen state courts heard challenges to these statutes from 1854 through 1935; most courts upheld the statutes. The states listed below upheld the reading of the King James version of the Bible in public schools without comment and/or the recitation of prayer or the singing of hymns, often on the ground that the teaching of "morality" was a valid state concern:[1]

1854—Maine	1908—Texas
1859—Massachusetts	1922—Georgia
1884—Iowa	1924—California
1891—Illinois	1927—Colorado[2]
1898—Michigan	1927—Minnesota
1902—Nebraska	1935—New York; this policy
1905—Kentucky	dated back to 1851[3]

The "without comment" language derives, of course, from Justice Story's opinion in *Vidal*, where he states that the Bible can be taught "without note or comment" in the public schools as part of a discussion of morality. Yet there were some state court opinions which held that the reading of the Bible in the public schools, especially when combined with prayers or hymn singing, constituted sectarian instruction and violated the state constitution's Establishment Clause:

1872—Ohio (a somewhat conflicting opinion was issued in 1894)
1890—Wisconsin
1910—Illinois (a somewhat conflicting opinion was issued in 1880)
1915—Louisiana
1918—Washington
1929—South Dakota

In a span of only two terms (1962 and 1963) the Supreme Court declared unconstitutional two public school practices which were perhaps the last remaining vestige of the "de facto Protestant establishment." In

Engel v. Vitale (1962) the Court determined that the practice of the recitation of a prayer at the beginning of the school day was unconstitutional.
Engel was followed up a year later by the Court's opinion in *Schempp*,
which banned the reading of the Bible and the recitation of the Lord's
Prayer at the commencement of the school day.

The Pennsylvania statute was typical of the school district policies
involving school prayer. The statute was passed on May 20, 1913, and
provided that:

> Whereas, It is in the interest of good moral training, of a life of honor-
> able thought and of good citizenship, that the public school children
> should have lessons of morality brought to their attention during their
> school-days; therefore, be it resolved:
> . . . At least ten verses from the Holy Bible shall be read, or caused to
> be read, without comment, at the opening of each public school on
> each school day, by the teacher in charge: Provided, That where any
> teacher has other teachers under and subject to direction, then the
> teacher exercising such authority shall read the Holy Bible, or cause it
> to be read, as herein directed.
>
> If any school teacher, whose duty it shall be to read the Holy
> Bible, or cause it to be read, shall fail or omit so to do, said school
> teacher shall, upon charges preferred for such failure or omission, and
> proof of the same, before the board of school directors of the school
> district, be discharged.

In 1905, the Board of School Commissioners of Baltimore City,
Maryland, enacted a statute regarding opening exercises that provided
that:

> Each school, either collectively or in classes, shall be opened by the
> reading, without comment, of a chapter in the Holy Bible and/or the
> use of the Lord's Prayer. The Douay version may be used by those
> pupils who prefer it. Appropriate patriotic exercises should [also] be
> held as a part of the general opening exercise of the school or class.

In keeping with Maryland's historical roots and large Catholic population, this version of opening exercises allowed for the Catholic version,
the Douay Bible, to be used by those students who preferred it. Maryland
was the only colonial charter granted by the English crown to a Catholic,
George Calvert (Lord Baltimore), in the 1630s. He determined to establish a refuge for English Catholics in the New World. It will be recalled

that the Philadelphia riots and the uprising in New York concerned utilization of different versions of the Bible in public schools.

The time leading up to the *Schempp* case had already seen challenges to long-standing traditions in the public school systems. The most pronounced of these were the matters of Bible reading and prayer at the beginning of the school day. These challenges began in the mid-1950s. By 1963, the Supreme Court ruled that these traditions violated the Establishment Clause.[4] Protestant denominations struggled to understand how something that had been a vital part of public school programs for so long could now be considered unconstitutional. Yet most came to recognize that the eradication of prayer and Bible reading in public schools was simply a natural corollary of the separation they had been advocating for most of the century.

Reaction to the Supreme Court's decision was swift. After the Supreme Court's decision in 1962 in *Engel v. Vitale*, which held unconstitutional prayer in public school, and prior to the Supreme Court's decision in *Schempp*, Congressman Frank J. Becker called for a constitutional amendment to overrule the Court's decisions. Over 160 congressmen eventually threw their support behind the so-called Becker Amendment. There is no doubt that the decision in *Engel* fueled the move for a constitutional amendment, and the Court's decision one year later in *Schempp* added more fuel to that fire. The Becker Amendment was officially introduced in 1962 after *Engel* and before *Schempp*. It read as follows:

> Nothing in this Constitution shall be deemed to prohibit the offering, reading from, or listening to prayers or biblical Scriptures, if participation therein is on a voluntary basis, in any governmental or public school institution, or place.
>
> Nothing in this Constitution shall be deemed to prohibit making reference to belief in, reliance upon, or invoking the aid of God or a Supreme Being in any governmental or public document, proceeding, activity, ceremony, school, institution, or place, or upon any coinage, currency, or obligation of the United States.
>
> Nothing in this article shall constitute an establishment of religion.

The Episcopal Church was vocal in both supporting the decisions of the Court and opposing the proposed constitutional amendment. The Rt.

Reverend Arthur Lichtenberger, presiding bishop of the Protestant Episcopal Church, said in a press release concerning the Court's decisions that "it is not the task of public schools to inculcate religious beliefs or habits of worship. This is the task of our homes and churches and synagogues. . . . [O]ur varied beliefs are embodied in institutions which are not governmental and are not dependent on majority votes."[5]

Reverend Halbert, in his letter to the Episcopal bishop of Washington, summarized the general view of the Episcopal Church regarding the Becker Amendment:

> Episcopalians are divided on the question and the Church has no official position. We in the Department of Christian Social Relations feel that the arguments against changing the Constitution are more cogent than those for the change. For instance, what translation of the Bible is to be read, what prayers are to be said? We feel that not only our freedom *of* religion but freedom *from* religion is protected by the First Amendment as it now stands. We believe that we should inform our Congressmen that they can oppose the Becker Amendment and not be hostile to religion nor to their churches.[6]

On April 16, 1964, New York Democratic congressman William F. Ryan, in a speech before the House of Representatives, read into the record statements by various religious groups opposed to the effort to amend the Constitution. These statements illuminate the broad consensus among Protestant denominations in favor of the Court's decisions forbidding prayer and Bible reading in schools.

The Lutheran Church in America, for instance, said the Court's decisions did "not stem from any hostility to religion or to the churches," but instead were "premised on the assumption that due regard for the necessity of freeing religion from the compulsion of government and of freeing government from the domination of religious forces, serves the best interest of both religion and government."[7]

Representatives of the Presbyterian Church asserted that teaching children the beliefs and practices of the Christian faith was the responsibility and privilege of the church and the family, and that these things were not to be provided by the state or by any agency of the state, including the public schools. The Baptist Joint Committee on Public Affairs concurred by declaring: "[L]aws and regulations prescribing prayers or devotional exercise do not contribute to a free exercise of religion and should not be encouraged."[8] The committee asserted that such laws were in bad taste and violated the principles of separation of church and state.

The Southern Baptist Convention issued further statements concerning the Becker Amendment. At their meeting in Atlantic City, New Jersey, in June of 1964, the SBC passed a resolution opposing the amendment. After declaring their dedication to the principle of separation, the resolution appealed to Congress not to amend the Constitution:

> We appeal to the Congress of the United States to allow the First Amendment of the Constitution of the United States to stand as our guarantee of religious liberty, and we oppose the adoption of any further amendment to that Constitution respecting establishment of religion or free exercise thereof.[9]

The Lutheran Church in America passed an official statement on *Prayer and Bible Reading in the Public Schools*. In this document they affirmed the Supreme Court's decisions and opposed any constitutional amendment aimed at permitting prayer or Bible reading in public schools. The statement noted that the Court's decisions

> open[ed] an era in which Christianity is kept separate from the state in a way that was foreign and would have been repugnant to the minds of our ancestors at the time when the Constitution was written and ever since. They signalize the fact that the United States of America, like many other nations, is past the place where underlying Christian culture and beliefs are assumed in its life.[10]

After making this stark declaration, the Lutheran Church stated its opposition to the Becker Amendment. Specifically, the resolution declared, "The Constitution should not be amended except to achieve large and important public needs and purposes consistent with the basic nature of our constitutional system. The current proposals for constitutional amendment do not meet these standards."[11]

A document produced by the National Council of Churches (NCC) in 1964 fairly depicted the general theological mood among Protestants during the middle of the century regarding church-state relations. In February of 1964, the NCC commissioned a Study Conference on Church and State. Delegates from twenty-four Protestant and Orthodox Communions met in Columbus, Ohio, to develop a paper on "Separation and Interaction of Church and State."[12] This paper recognized that the functions of church and state were distinct, but often overlapped; and in this country, there had been separation and interaction, as well as harmony and tension. The paper also acknowledged that our nation had changed since its birth from a predominantly Protestant society to a pluralistic society. It stated:

> The nation which adopted the First Amendment . . . considered itself both Christian and Protestant and saw no contradiction in passing laws which required Sunday observance, prayer and Bible reading in public schools. . . .
>
> In recent decades . . . a predominately Protestant society developed into a pluralistic society. This has raised crucial questions concerning both separation and interaction between church and state.[13]

The NCC's study group, while acknowledging that the issues facing the church and the state were complex, came to agreement on the following matters:

(1) a strong commitment to religious liberty as man's natural right and indispensable condition of a free society;

(2) recognition that ours is a pluralistic and not simply a Protestant society;

(3) acceptance and support of Supreme Court decisions insofar as they prohibit officially prescribed prayers and required devotional reading of the Bible in public schools;

(4) recognition that the Court's decision underscores the primary responsibility of the family and the church for religious education;

(5) opposition to any proposal such as the so-called Christian Amendment which seeks to commit our government to official identification with a particular religious tradition;

(6) rejection of the over-simplified formulations such as that which seeks to make religion exclusively a private matter or to make all public matters secular; and

(7) awareness that the functions of church and state must be clearly defined as separate, yet relationships should be flexible enough to encompass the increasing areas of interaction.[14]

The NCC study conference demonstrated a willingness to accept public monies for religious-based work. This openness was especially seen in the conference's discussion of programs dealing with health and welfare. The conferees accepted that although it was not government's business to promote or support religion, it was government's role and duty to further religious liberty. Accordingly, the paper issued by the conference allowed that "[u]nder some well-defined circumstances, government may legitimately support specific programs of church-affiliated health and welfare agencies. The sole purpose of any governmental policy in this respect must be the promotion of a clearly identifiable public interest as against a private interest of an individual or religious group."[15]

Nevertheless, the paper distinguished between health and welfare programs and education programs, arguing that the use of government funds to support religiously affiliated primary and secondary educational enterprises raised more questions about health and welfare enterprises. It also said that government funds should not be used to support religious teaching.

Southern Baptists continued their unqualified support for the separation of church and state throughout the 1960s. At their 1967 meeting, they took the unusual step of calling on Congress to enact legislation which would help clarify the responsibility of the judiciary in interpreting the concept of separation of church and state. The resolution began with a reaffirmation of Baptist devotion to separation and concluded by urging Congress "to enact legislation which would help clarify responsibility of the judiciary to interpret the meaning of the United States Constitution for separation of Church and State, including constitutionality of federal funds in church-sponsored programs."[16]

There can be little argument that *Schempp* offers the most conspicuous example of how Clark's religious beliefs impacted his Establishment Clause jurisprudence. Before discussing *Schempp*, however, it is important to note the cultural climate within which it was decided. A year before *Schempp*, the Court decided *Engel v. Vitale*.[17] The Court's ruling in *Engel* banning public school prayer elicited a vociferous and acrimonious response from much of America. "In the first few weeks after *Engel*, the Supreme Court received five thousand letters denouncing the Court's decision."[18] A Gallup poll taken shortly after the decision showed that "nearly eighty percent favored prayers in public schools."[19]

Religious leaders condemned the decision as well. For instance, famed evangelist Billy Graham declared that he was "shocked and disappointed" by the decision and that "[f]ollowed to its logical conclusion . . . prayers cannot be said in Congress, chaplains will be taken from the armed forces and the President will not place his hand on the Bible when he takes the oath of office."[20] Francis Cardinal Spellman from New York denounced the decision even more vehemently: "I am shocked and frightened that the Supreme Court has declared unconstitutional a simple and voluntary declaration of belief in God by public school children. . . . The decision strikes at the very heart of the Godly tradition in which America's children have for so long been raised."[21] And James Francis Cardinal McIntyre of Los Angeles said, "The decision is positively shocking and scandalizing to one of American blood and principles. It is not a decision according to law, but a decision of license."[22] While not all religious groups deplored *Engel*, a vast majority of them lined up to condemn it.

Congressmen and senators uttered similar denunciations. Senator Herman Talmadge of Georgia branded the decision "unconscionable" and "an outrageous edict."[23] Congressman Haley of Florida "offered an amendment to a judiciary appropriations bill to earmark out of the Supreme Court's appropriations funds to purchase 'for the personal use of each justice a copy of the Holy Bible.'"[24] Senator Sam Ervin of North Carolina, "widely regarded as an authority on constitutional law, insisted that 'the Supreme Court has made God unconstitutional.'"[25] Congressman Frank Becker of New York expressed his dissent, as did some seventy-five other congressmen and senators, by proposing the constitutional amendment that would have legitimized prayer in public schools, prior to the Court's decision in *Schempp*.[26]

This vituperative backdrop led one commentator to conclude that Justice Clark's conciliatory words concerning religion in *Schempp* were "consciously addressed" to the "ordinary citizen" in order to dispel the country's concern that the Supreme Court "was undermining religion in America."[27] From this standpoint, Justice Clark's encomium to religion in *Schempp* was simply a matter of public relations, of getting the Supreme Court back in right relationship with the people. This view, however, ignores what appears to have been the critical role Clark's personal religious belief had on the formulation of his opinion in *Schempp*. This influence is not overt in Clark's opinion; however, when one looks at *Schempp* through the lens of Clark's numerous extrajudicial writings and addresses on church-state relations, the impact of his religious beliefs becomes evident.

The issue of the role of religion in politics was also a factor in the Supreme Court's school prayer cases. As the controversies over school prayer and Bible reading were developing in the lower court, Senator John F. Kennedy's bid for the presidency was under way. Kennedy was Roman Catholic, and it was feared that his allegiance to the pope would override his allegiance to the Constitution. Protestant denominations, while not wanting to appear biased, did address Kennedy's faith in resolutions at their conventions.

The Augustana Lutheran Church issued a lengthy position paper in 1960, and while affirming that "a Roman Catholic should not as such be legally barred from the presidency," they gave guidelines that at least implied that their members should be very cautious in the upcoming election. At the end of the position paper they concluded:

1. That ideological beliefs and affiliations are valid grounds for judging candidates for public office, and that it is a misuse of the concept of intolerance to exclude them for consideration.
2. That the Roman Church, because of its unique institutional claims, poses special problems in relation to the questions of religion and public office.
3. That there are grounds for reasonable doubt that a Roman Catholic president would be free of institutional control and from desires to promote in special ways the ends of the Roman Church.
4. That in turn this doubt raises the question of a potential threat to the work of the Church, the conscience of its members, and the traditional ideals and sense of justice of American society.[28]

The Augustana Lutheran Church concluded its resolution by encouraging its members "to give special consideration to these problems and to the use of their voting privilege should a Roman Catholic candidate be nominated for President."[29]

The Southern Baptists passed a *Resolution on Christian Citizenship* at their 1960 convention in Miami Beach, Florida. Though not mentioning either the Roman Catholic Church or John Kennedy by name, the resolution left little doubt that they had serious concerns about Kennedy being elected president. Specifically, the resolution stated that "a candidate's affiliations, including his church, are of concern to the voters in every election."[30] An elected official, the resolution said, must "be free from sectarian pressures" so he can "make independent decisions consistent with the rights and privileges of all citizens."[31] The clear implication was that Kennedy should be carefully considered given his connection to the Catholic Church. Despite these concerns, John Fitzgerald Kennedy was elected the first Catholic president of the United States in 1960, by a narrow margin over Richard M. Nixon.

The unique circumstances of the school prayer case, a Roman Catholic running for the presidency, and a proposed constitutional amendment on religion all served as the backdrop for the removal of a long-held practice in America's public schools. This last vestige of the de facto Protestant establishment of religion in the public schools was declared unconstitutional in an opinion issued by a devout Presbyterian, Justice Thomas C. Clark.

THE JUSTICE: THOMAS C. CLARK
(1899–1977)

Thomas C. Clark was born in Dallas, Texas, on September 23, 1899. He grew up in what his son, Ramsey, called "religious America."[32] His home life reflected America's religious atmosphere at the beginning of the twentieth century. He was born into an Episcopalian family and was regularly exposed to religious influences such as Sunday school, worship services, and mealtime prayers. In his reflections on the *Schempp* decision, Clark reminisced about his family's little prayer rug that they would kneel down on and saying grace at their meals. His son asserted that Clark had perfect Sunday school records and that he was a very religious person. Clark remained in the Episcopal Church until he married Mary Jane Ramsey in 1924, after which he joined her denomination, the Central Presbyterian Church.

Clark's father, William Henry Clark, was a prominent attorney who had been elected the youngest president of the Texas Bar Association. His family was firmly established in both the Democratic Party and the legal profession, thus setting the stage for Clark's successful career in the legal and political realms.

Little has been written of Clark's early years. Perhaps the most notable aspect of his childhood was the effect his father's addiction to alcohol had on the Clark family. Once a prominent figure in Dallas's social structure, Clark's father, because of his addiction, lost his stature in the community as well as the financial security of the Clark family. Thus, at a young age Clark was forced to work in order to mitigate the family's financial woes. Yet despite these difficult circumstances, Clark excelled as a young boy. He became one of the first Boy Scouts to achieve the level of Eagle Scout, discovered and developed his oratorical skill, and even won several debate competitions while in high school.

Clark graduated from high school in 1917 and dutifully enrolled at Virginia Military Institute (VMI) to prepare for service in World War I. His family could not afford VMI's tuition, however, so Clark returned to Texas and served his country in the Texas National Guard. Soon thereafter Clark enrolled at the University of Texas to pursue college studies and, remarkably, earned his undergraduate and law degrees in just three years. Clark was admitted to the Texas bar in 1922 and joined his father's and brother's law firm.[33]

Clark practiced law and was active in Democratic politics in Texas from 1922 through 1937. He pursued private practice predominantly, but also spent six years serving as "civil district attorney in his home county."[34] More important, Clark worked tirelessly on the political campaigns of many prominent Texas Democrats, including Senator Tom Connally and Congressman Sam Rayburn. With his political associations and success as an attorney, he was ultimately offered a position in the Department of Justice in 1937, which he readily accepted.

Clark moved up through this department with amazing speed. Between 1937 and 1945, the year in which he was appointed attorney general by President Harry Truman, Clark filled many different roles in the Justice Department. He was deeply involved in the department's antitrust activities, helped coordinate the relocation of Japanese Americans during World War II, and served as assistant attorney general of the department's Criminal Division.

During his years at the Justice Department, Clark had the good fortune of being able to develop a close relationship with then senator Harry Truman.[35] This acquaintance would be the most significant of Clark's many political relationships—Truman was responsible for Clark's appointments both as attorney general and as a Supreme Court justice.

The moment that permanently solidified Clark's and Truman's friendship came in 1944 when the Democrats were battling over who would be their vice presidential candidate. Initially, Clark threw his support behind his friend and fellow Texan Sam Rayburn, but difficulties within the Texas Democratic Party prevented Rayburn from becoming a serious candidate. Clark then transferred his support to Truman, who won the nomination; with the death of Franklin Roosevelt one year later, Truman became president. Truman immediately replaced Roosevelt's attorney general, Francis Biddle, with Clark. Biddle had refused to support Truman for the Democratic vice presidential nomination.

Clark served as attorney general from 1944 through 1949, when Truman elevated him to the Supreme Court. Clark's most significant work as attorney general was in the development of the country's anticommunist programs. According to Richard Kirkendall, Clark believed that subversive activity was increasing and that even one disloyal government employee constituted a serious threat to security. In this regard, Clark worked to obtain greater investigative authority for his department and the FBI, and advocated the establishment of loyalty programs for federal employees. Truman followed Clark's advice and set up such a program. At Clark's request, the FBI was given control over the investigative phase of the loyalty programs, and Clark's department drafted the first Attorney General's List of dangerous political organizations. In 1948, at Clark's direction, the Justice Department began proceedings against the leaders of the American Communist Party for violating the Smith Act of 1940, which made it illegal to advocate the overthrow or destruction of the United States Government through violence or assassination. Once elevated to the Court, Clark frequently found himself defending the loyalty programs he helped to create as attorney general.

Clark's record on the Court places him outside the civil libertarian camp of fellow justices Hugo Black and William O. Douglas, as his creation and defense of loyalty programs suggest. One commentator called Clark "the only dependable 'conservative' member of the Court."[36] In an article he wrote two years after retiring from the Supreme Court, Clark explicitly disassociated himself from his absolutist brethren:

> I do not believe that the first amendment's commands are absolutes. . . . I submit that the Constitution is not a suicide pact; the preservation of the government that it creates is its paramount concern and all individual rights are subservient to the necessity of its self-preservation. . . .
>
> . . . .

Moreover, I do not subscribe to the conclusion that "Freedom of press, freedom of speech, [and] freedom of religion are in a preferred position" in the constitutional constellation, if that means that these are "preferred freedoms."[37]

Despite rejecting the core premises of civil libertarianism, Clark embraced certain critical theories spawned by that legal philosophy.[38]

Clark's opinions in *United States v. Seeger* (1965) and *Schempp* demonstrate both acceptance and rejection of civil libertarianism. *Seeger* demonstrates his acceptance of the civil libertarian proposition that the religion clauses protected the broader realm of conscience, not just theistic religions. In addition to his decision in *Seeger*, Clark spelled out his allegiance to this principle in his article on minority rights: "The first amendment withholds from the State any authority to compel belief or expression of it where that expression violates conviction."[39]

In contrast, *Schempp* demonstrates Clark's rejection of the civil libertarian proposition that the First Amendment should be protected absolutely. In his written opinion, Clark disavowed the "high and impregnable" wall of separation between church and state, and implicitly argued for accommodation between these two realms.[40] He showed his disdain for the wall metaphor in an address to the 25th National Conference on Church and State, saying that the wall of separation between church and state the Supreme Court had built had "many huge cracks in it." Later in the same speech, Clark said that many of the Court's decisions since *Everson* had "reduced the wall to a brick pile."[41] As discussed below, Clark was much more direct in his off-the-Court writings and speeches than in *Schempp* about his belief in accommodation between church and state.

Clark served on the Court for eighteen years. At the time of his retirement in 1967, he was still mentally and physically strong enough to serve for several more years. He retired not out of fatigue, or out of a loss of interest in the work of the Court, but in order to clear the path for his son, Ramsey Clark, to be appointed as United States Attorney General by President Lyndon Johnson. Clark knew from his own experience as attorney general that his son would be responsible for many of the cases that came before the Court. Thus, in an act of self-sacrifice, Clark relinquished his seat on the Court to help his son advance his own career.

The emphasis placed on religion in Clark's early life never left him and eventually matured into a sincere and deep devotion to his faith. He was an active member and leader in the Presbyterian Church throughout his adulthood. He served as a trustee and an elder of the National Presbyterian Church in Washington, D.C., while he served on the Court and even after his retirement. Clark also served on the board of the Presbyterian Home for the District of Columbia and was the honorary chairman of a major fund-raising endeavor for the Presbytery of Washington, D.C. In a March 12, 1976, letter from Rev. Edward Elson, chaplain of the United States Senate and former pastor of the National Presbyterian Church, Clark was praised for serving faithfully and effectively on committees and for being one of two men in public life in Washington to whom Rev. Elson would go for counsel on matters of crucial importance in the life of the church. This testimony indicates that Clark was sincere about his Christian faith and duties throughout his life.

Perhaps reflecting the sincerity of his faith, Clark, in an address delivered to the Tennessee Law School, encouraged his audience to adopt the biblical phrase, "Justice ye shall pursue," as the motto for their approach to the law. Clark elaborated on this phrase in his closing remarks:

> I hope you, as the Bible says, will "pursue justice." Daniel Webster said . . . that "justice is the great interest of man on earth." And he went further: "He who works to improve the foundations of justice and to raise its mighty spires higher into the sky will be blessed not only by that great Judge who looks down upon all of us, but likewise be called blessed by his fellow man."[42]

Clark's words suggest that he viewed the legal profession's pursuit of justice as a calling from God.

Justice Clark wrote and spoke extensively about the issue of religious freedom before and after his retirement from the Court. His opinions, coupled with his extrajudicial writings, reveal that his religious beliefs and experiences impacted his decisions in both cases. The influence of Justice Clark's religious beliefs is overwhelmingly apparent in his *Schempp* opinion.

One of Justice Clark's opinions in an unrelated case dealt extensively with the impact that theologian Paul Tillich had on Clark's judicial philosophy. Clark's opinion in *United States v. Seeger* demonstrates his commitment to protecting conscience, not merely religion, from the inroads of government.

Seeger concerned three challenges to the conscientious objector exemption provision of the Universal Military Training and Service Act.[43] This provision exempted individuals from combat training and service in the armed forces of the United States who, by reason of their religious training and belief, were conscientiously opposed to participation in any form of war. Congress defined the phrase "religious training and belief" as "an individual's belief in a relation to a Supreme Being involving duties superior to those arising from any human relation, but [not including] essentially political, sociological, or philosophical views or a merely personal moral code."[44] The question presented to the Court was the constitutionality of this definition.

Clark avoided the constitutional question by construing "Supreme Being" in the broadest possible terms. In so doing, he adopted a test that deviated from what appeared to be the clear intent of Congress to grant exemptions to a narrow set of traditional religions.[45] Clark set forth his latitudinarian test with these words: "[T]he test of belief 'in a relation to a Supreme Being' is whether a given belief that is sincere and meaningful occupies a place in the life of its possessor parallel to that filled by the orthodox belief in God of one who clearly qualifies for the exemption."[46] A belief that occupied such a position in the objector's life, according to Clark, comes within the statutory definition. By adopting a broad test, Clark managed to qualify all three of the challenger's religious beliefs for conscientious exemption status under the act. The challengers offered varying "religious" rationales for their exemption requests. Clark's opinion in *Seeger* did not expressly avow a belief in a Supreme Being, yet he did state "the cosmic order does, perhaps, suggest a creative being." In light of this admission and the unquestioned sincerity of his conviction against war, Clark found that Seeger's beliefs occupied the same place in his life as the belief in a traditional deity holds in the life of others. Jakobson and Peter, the other challengers, explicitly affirmed belief in a Supreme Being, and thus Clark granted exemptions to them as well.

Clark offered several rationales to support his decision. First, he argued that a broad construction of the term "Supreme Being" "avoids imputing to Congress an intent to classify different religious beliefs, exempting some and excluding others, and is in accord with the well-established congressional policy of equal treatment for those whose opposition to service is grounded in their religious tenets." Earlier in his opinion, Clark said that Congress's use of the term "Supreme Being" instead of "God" demonstrated that Congress intended to "embrace *all* religions and to exclude essentially political, sociological, or philosophical views."[47] Clearly, Clark believed that without this imputation, the act would have been unconstitutional.

Clark supplied an additional rationale to support his broad interpretation of the statute, namely, that his construction of the term "Supreme Being" embraced the ever-broadening understanding of the modern religious community. To demonstrate this point, Clark quoted several eminent theologians, including Paul Tillich, and church councils to support his proposition that within the religious community there were diverse manners in which beliefs, equally paramount in the lives of their possessors, could be articulated. Clark apparently found the following words from Tillich's book *Systematic Theology* particularly compelling:

> I have written of the God above the God of theism. . . . In such a state [of self-affirmation] the God of both religious and theological language disappears. But something remains, namely, the seriousness of that doubt in which meaning within meaninglessness is affirmed. The source of this affirmation of meaning within meaninglessness, of certitude within doubt, is not the God of traditional theism but the "God above God," the power of being, which works through those who have no name for it, not even the name God.[48]

The similarity between the test Clark enunciated for the Court in *Seeger* and Tillich's description of the "God above the God of theism" is difficult to ignore.

Clark himself made the connection between his decision and Tillich's theories in his reflections on *Seeger*. He admitted that he was reading Tillich at the time he decided *Seeger* and that the theologian's views had a keen influence on the reasoning of his opinion. In fact, he said he wrote *Seeger* based on Dr. Tillich. Clark elaborated:

> [S]ince I was reading Tillich, I decided that, perhaps we could read that concept into the statute. And that [concept] was that some people's supreme being is not the supreme being of other people. In other words, your supreme being might be the one God; another supreme being might be [a] bronze image; another one might be a beautiful tree. . . . And if this is sincere, that would be in so far as that individual is concerned, in the eyes of Tillich, a religion.[49]

The above discussion strongly suggests that Clark's understanding of the religious pluralism of our society and, even more, his own personal readings in theology were the primary influences in the formulation of his *Seeger* opinion. Clark's concern over the pluralistic nature of American society was a common theme in his off-the-Court writings. One year before he decided *Seeger*, he declared:

> [W]e are a pluralistic society whose members follow over a hundred separate religions. We also have among us agnostics, atheists and "unchurched" people. It is elemental that each of these people is equal before the law. These religious guarantees protect not only freedom *of* religion but freedom *from* religion. In short, each of us has a free choice of whatever religion we wish to follow; or if we choose none, the law still affords us complete protection in that choice. This has been the hallmark of our society since its organization.[50]

As this shows, Clark believed the protections of the religion clauses should be extended to atheists as well.

THE CASE: *SCHOOL DISTRICT V. SCHEMPP* (1963)

Schempp was a consolidation of two cases, one from Pennsylvania and the other from Maryland. The Pennsylvania claimants, the Schempps, who attended a Unitarian church, were challenging a Pennsylvania statute that required "[a]t least ten verses from the Holy Bible shall be read, without comment, at the opening of each public school on each school day. Any child shall be excused from such Bible reading, or attending such Bible reading, upon the written request of his parent or guardian."[51] The Maryland claimants, the renowned atheist Madalyn Murray and her son, were challenging a Baltimore City School Board policy that "provided for the holding of opening exercises in the schools of the city, consisting primarily of the 'reading, without comment, of a chapter in the Holy Bible and/or the use of the Lord's Prayer.'"[52]

Clark found that both of these practices violated the First Amendment's prohibition against laws "respecting an establishment of religion." As Clark said in his opinion,

> we find that the States are requiring the selection and reading at the opening of the school day of verses from the Holy Bible and the recitation of the Lord's Prayer by the students in unison. These exercises are

prescribed as part of the curricular activities of students who are required by law to attend school. They are held in the school buildings under the supervision and with the participation of teachers employed in those schools.[53]

Based on these findings Clark concluded: "in both cases the laws require religious exercises and such exercises are being conducted in direct violation of the rights of the appellees and petitioners."[54]

Significantly, Clark came to this conclusion without once uttering the phrase "wall of separation between church and state." Clark did quote separationist language from previous church-state cases, including *Everson*, but managed effectively to move the Court away from separation as the overriding principle of the Establishment Clause by adopting "neutrality" as the proper principle to guide the government in its relationship with religion. As he said in *Schempp*, "In the relationship between man and religion, the State is firmly committed to a position of neutrality."[55]

At least one commentator has suggested that Clark's avoidance of Jefferson's wall metaphor was "deliberate," since he found it inconsistent with his own view of the proper relationship between church and state.[56] Clark's remarks in a law review article he wrote the same year in which the *Schempp* decision came down lend credence to this observation. In this article, Clark revealed his disdain for the wall metaphor, declaring, "As I read our history no such wall has ever existed."[57] Instead, Clark argued that the First Amendment demanded a "wholesome separation of a concordant nature" between church and state.[58] These comments clearly indicate that Clark did not agree with the absolute separation of church and state advocated by members of the Court like Justices Black and Douglas. Indeed, in his speech at Wartburg College, Clark advised his audience, "Whether the constitutional standard of separation is met is *one of degree*."[59] Someone who believed in absolute separation between church and state could hardly utter this comment.

In later speeches and writings Justice Clark expounded on his belief that the proper relationship between church and state was one of accommodation. In a lecture at the National Conference on Church and State in 1973, Clark again attacked the Court's use of Jefferson's separationist metaphor:

I rather suspect that Jefferson rued the day that he coined this metaphor. It was he who later said that the "want of instruction in the various creeds of religious faith existing among our citizens presents . . . a chasm in a general institution of the useful sciences." And, he proposed that the University of Virginia, a state institution, entertain courses in religion for its students.[60]

Clark pointed to Robert Frost's saying, "good fences make good neighbors," instead of Jefferson's "wall" metaphor, as the expression that best captures the kind of relationship that should prevail between church and state. Clark went on to say that between walls and good fences, "I am one to believe that the 'good fences' of Robert Frost will prevail."[61]

In a 1971 lecture delivered in Austin, Texas, titled "The Needs of Society—Religion and Education: The Place of Religion in the Public Schools," Clark made his allegiance to accommodation explicit:

> Americans generally agree that there must be a separation between church and state. . . . But Americans believe also that there can be an accommodation between church and state. Since there is an area of moral concern shared by church and state, every effort should be made to work out an accommodation within the permissible areas under the First Amendment.[62]

Clark's opinion for the Court in *Schempp* reflected his belief that "every effort should be made" to accommodate church and state. Indeed, he listed numerous examples of permissible accommodations, including the country's practice of concluding oaths of office with the phrase "So help me God," the chaplaincy program for the House and Senate, and the Supreme Court's practice of opening each session with a "short ceremony, the final phrase of which invokes the grace of God."[63] Clark also mentioned the provision of chaplains for the military, and explained in a footnote that the Court's holding in *Schempp* did not impact the constitutionality of this program. In this footnote, Clark stated:

> We are not of course presented with and therefore do not pass upon a situation such as military service, where the Government regulates the temporal and geographic environment of individuals to a point that, unless it permits voluntary religious services to be conducted with the use of government facilities, military personnel would be unable to engage in the practice of their faiths.[64]

In a draft opinion in *Schempp*, Clark also penned these words dealing with the constitutionality of both military and congressional chaplaincy pro-

grams more affirmatively and in the body of the text rather than in a footnote:

> We take it that the Chaplain service is in a different category. There,
> only adults are involved and the service is purely voluntary. The soldier
> often has no service available and being under command would be
> deprived of his religious activity had the government not made a
> Chaplain available. In the Congress the Chaplain's prayer is not by law
> but by action of each body independently.[65]

Clark's adoption of the "purpose and effect" test in *Schempp* also
reflected his allegiance to accommodation and disdain for the absolutism
of Jefferson's metaphor. Clark described his test for determining whether
the Establishment Clause had been violated with these words:

> The test may be stated as follows: what are the purpose and the pri-
> mary effect of the enactment? If either is the advancement or inhibi-
> tion of religion then the enactment exceeds the scope of legislative
> power as circumscribed by the Constitution. That is to say that to
> withstand the strictures of the Establishment Clause there must be a
> secular legislative purpose and a primary effect that neither advances
> nor inhibits religion.[66]

This test (which later became the first two prongs of the tripartite "*Lemon*
test" discussed in the next chapter) was far less stringent than the "no-aid"
language of *Everson*.[67] As one commentator suggested, Clark's purpose
and effect test "does not prohibit laws whose secondary or indirect impact
is the advancement or inhibition of religion."[68] In adopting this test, Clark
was attempting to undercut the momentum of the separation juggernaut
created by the Court's previous Establishment Clause decisions, thus
clearing the path for reasonable accommodation between church and
state.

Clark's views regarding church and state naturally led him to argue
that the principle of neutrality, not separation, was the proper way to conceive of the relationship between government and religion. Clark viewed
the neutrality principle as requiring "absolute equality before the law, of
all religious opinions and sects."[69] The main justification Clark provided
for his neutrality principle was the dual and at times overlapping commands of the Establishment and Free Exercise Clauses. He explained that
the Establishment Clause protects against "powerful sects or groups"

bringing about a "fusion of governmental and religious functions" so as to procure "official support of the State or Federal Government" for "the tenets of one or of all orthodoxies."[70] The protections of the Establishment Clause, however, are not absolute. They need to be balanced against the religious freedom guaranteed by the Free Exercise Clause. That clause "recognize[s] the value of religious training, teaching and observance and, more particularly, the right of every person to choose his or her own course with reference thereto, free of any compulsion from the state."[71] The natural tension that exists between these two guarantees requires a governmental stance of neutrality toward religion. In Clark's mind, a separationist stance would allow the Establishment Clause to swallow up the freedom of religion guaranteed by the Free Exercise Clause.

Another key aspect of Justice Clark's *Schempp* opinion was his discussion of the rich religious heritage of our country. Clark began his opinion, aside from reciting the facts of the two cases involved, by asserting that "religion has been closely identified with our history and government."[72] He quoted language from previous Supreme Court cases that emphasized this point, including Justice Douglas's accommodationist paean from *Zorach v. Clauson* (1952): "We are a religious people whose institutions presuppose a Supreme Being."[73] And, after paying homage to the sincerity of the religious faith of our Founding Fathers, Clark declared, "today, as in the beginning, our national life reflects a religious people who, in the words of Madison, are 'earnestly praying, as . . . in duty bound, that the Supreme Lawgiver of the Universe . . . guide them into every measure which may be worthy of his [blessing].'"[74]

Clearly, Clark appreciated the importance of religion to American culture, both in the past and in the present. Reiterating this appreciation, Clark concluded his opinion by asserting that "the place of religion in our society is an exalted one."[75]

Clark's high regard for religion was manifested in his rejoinder to Justice Stewart's charge that the Court's holding in *Schempp* would establish a "religion of secularism" in public schools.[76] In rejecting this charge, Clark declared:

> [I]t might well be said that one's education is not complete without a study of comparative religion or the history of religion and its relationship to the advancement of civilization. It certainly may be said that the Bible is worthy of study for its literary and historic qualities. Nothing we have said here indicates that such study of the Bible or of reli-

gion, when presented objectively as part of a secular program of education, may not be effected consistently with the First Amendment.[77]

As this quote demonstrates, Clark went out of his way to demonstrate how *Schempp* did not stand for the absolute secularization of the schools.

In fact, Clark's opinion and subsequent writings indicate how limited he believed the holding of *Schempp* was. In his opinion, he declared the challenged practices unconstitutional because they constituted "religious exercises, required by the States in violation of the command of the First Amendment."[78] In his article defending and explaining the Court's decision in *Schempp*, Clark once again used the words "religious exercise" to describe what the Court had outlawed.[79] By stressing "religious exercises" Clark was trying to point out that the Court's holding was limited and that a plethora of other religious activities and courses of study could be pursued in the public schools.

Clark's clearest declaration on this point came in his address to the Texas Conference of Churches in 1971. He explained the intended effect of *Schempp* by saying,

all that has been held unconstitutional is the practice of having a required mini-worship service at the beginning of each school day. . . . [T]he Court went out of its way to point out that our history was steeped in religious tradition. . . . [Even more,] the Court has emphasized that there is no constitutional objection to the use of the Bible as a reference work, its study for its literary and historic values, the teaching of comparative religion and the study of the history of religion and its place in the development of present civilizations.[80]

Clark made a similar argument seven years earlier in an address at Wartburg College. In his speech, Clark relayed to his audience that a "noted author" had charged the Court with prohibiting "Christianity" from being "taught in the public schools of a Christian nation." Clark repudiated this charge, saying that its decisions have not "held that Christianity shall not be taught in public schools. All that we have held is that required prayers violate the First Amendment."[81] Clearly, Justice Clark saw his decision in *Schempp* as having a very limited effect.

The question of what influence Justice Clark's religious beliefs exercised over his religious liberty opinions has already been the subject of some scholarly research. In his article on the subject, Ellis West concluded that Clark's religious beliefs "may have had a decisive influence on" his *Schempp* opinion.[82] West argued that Clark's main "reason for . . . opposing officially prescribed prayer and Bible-reading . . . [was] his desire to protect the integrity of the religious experience."[83] West's argument stands up under scrutiny.

In nearly every article he wrote or address he gave about his *Schempp* decision, Clark voiced his concern for maintaining the "integrity of the religious experience." In his article defending *Schempp*, Clark noted that Wilbur Katz, in a commentary he wrote regarding *Schempp*, recalled that "one of the lawyers . . . argued that 'public school recitation of the Lord's Prayer is not a religious act but a mere exercise in civic morality.'"[84] Katz argued that the diminution of prayer to a mere civic duty was dangerous because "children might regard all prayer in this light."[85] Clark agreed with this sentiment and expressed concern that a decline in respect for religion had already occurred among school children. He observed: "Young people today do not seem to practice prayer. . . . [T]heir average make-up seems devoid of religious background and training."[86]

Clark's criticism of mandatory school prayer continued throughout the remainder of his life. In his address at Wartburg College a year after the *Schempp* decision, Clark referred to prayers chosen and conducted by school officials pejoratively as the mere "intoning of words."[87] Clark more plainly expressed his aversion to such prayers in his address at the National Conference on Church and State: "[T]he stricken prayer [in *Engel*] was nothing more than ceremony, the actual thrust of which was the daily chanting by the students of a common rote prepared by school authorities. It was but a hollow conformity which unfortunately is increasingly manifested in our contemporary life."[88] Clark went so far as to assert that striking down the Regents' Prayer in *Engel* proved constructive because it "led to a re-examination of the school board's practice and the realization that it promoted more irreverence than moral rectitude."[89]

Clark's criticism of school prayer was simply a component of his broader concern over the state of religion in contemporary American culture. He often deplored the state of religion in the homes and churches of America. In one of his lectures, Clark asserted that if churches "perform[ed] their function properly" there would "be no crisis over the religion clause of the First Amendment."[90] Churches, Clark argued, were failing both in teaching young people to pray and in instructing them in "what prayer is all about."[91] Clark also criticized parents: "There are few homes that religion ever enters. The parents either will not let it or do not have time for it. We use to have prayer rugs in the poorer homes and small altars in the more affluent. But not now."[92] One of the main points Clark was trying to drive home in making this argument was that it was not the Supreme Court that was at fault for kicking "God out of the front door of the school house"; it was the parents and the churches.[93] Their failure to stress the importance of religion outside the schoolhouse doors was merely reflected within the public schools.

Clark's belief that a religious people were essential for a society to flourish motivated his concern over the culture's growing apathy toward religion. Clark expressed this point of view by praising the following words of the great statesman and philosopher Edmund Burke: "We know, and what is better, we feel inwardly, that religion is the basis of civil society and the source of all good and all comfort."[94] Clark certainly believed that prayer and religion, if practiced at home, would have a beneficial impact on our children and our society. He argued that prayers conducted at home, as opposed to at school, "would have much greater weight with children, bring the family into a closer and more intimate circle and be extremely good for parents as well." It is especially effective when the child is taught to lead the prayer. "A juvenile prayer leader can hardly become a problem child."[95]

While Clark thought it imperative for parents and churches to develop a religious atmosphere for children outside of the schoolhouse, he also envisioned an active role for the public schools in the realm of religion. In fact, Justice Clark admitted that he wrote *Schempp* the way he did in order to provide schools a method by which they could promote religion without violating the Constitution:

> What I was trying to do was point in another direction that we might go, rather than striking down all directions; I was trying to point out a direction we might follow in an effort to try to reach the same goal but go through a constitutional route rather than an unconstitutional one.[96]

As this quote shows, Clark thought it was a proper function of the public schools to promote the interests of religion. Despite his position that schools could and should promote religion, Clark never recanted his decision striking down school prayer and Bible reading. In fact, he adopted a rather extreme position on school prayer, advising attendees at one of the many church-state conferences he spoke at that even voluntary prayer at school would likely be unconstitutional:

[A]ny regularly scheduled [public school] ceremony, whether called an assembly or by any other name, might well be a required exercise. A prayer or scripture reading chosen and offered even by a volunteer at such an assembly might well be met with objection on the grounds of being violative of the free exercise clause. Prayer is the conversation of religion and it is impossible to separate the two, which means that it would be difficult to prove that such an exercise had a secular purpose, neither advancing nor inhibiting religion.[97]

Advocating an active role for schools in the religious realm was certainly consistent with Clark's views regarding the proper relationship between church and state. As noted previously, Clark believed that "every effort should be made to work out an accommodation" between church and state since both shared an interest in cultivating morality among the nation's youth.[98] In applying this philosophy to the public schools with regard to religion, Clark said that "the role of the public school in a free society" is "the teaching of subjects that will bring respect and integrity to the place of religion in every day life."[99] The public schools, in Clark's mind, could best fulfill the government's obligation to bring "respect and integrity" to the religious experience, not by writing meaningless and hollow nondenominational prayers for students to recite, but by adopting a program of study in religion. As Clark said himself,

[W]hy not inaugurate a course of study on religion in the public school—its background—its part in the advancement of civilization—a comparison of the various tenets of the sects—the story of the Bible—the Koran—and others of the great books—the biographies of great churchmen and the like. I dare say such a course would do more to strengthen religion than all the present exercises combined. Through such an awareness the value of true religion will be found by the student himself.[100]

Justice Clark not only believed that courses about religion would be found constitutional but also that they would likely help students discover or revitalize their religious beliefs. Even more, Clark believed that adopting a system of instruction about religion in the public schools "would bring a high moral fiber to the people of our country" and help to make "the whole nation a better place to live morally and spiritually."[101]

Despite Clark's obvious approval of an active role for public schools in furthering the interests of religion, he nevertheless believed that religion was ultimately the responsibility of the home, the church, and the individual. Clark advocated this position both in *Schempp* and in his off-the-Court writings. For example, in the conclusion to his *Schempp* opinion Clark stated that "[t]he place of religion in our society is an exalted one, achieved through a long tradition of reliance on the home, the church and the inviolable citadel of the individual heart and mind."[102] Clark reiterated this argument in his law review article, "Religion and the Law," stating,

> There is no better place to develop religion than in the home, at the church and in the Sunday School. In my day it was the job of the parents and the preachers and Sunday School teachers to inculcate and develop a religious atmosphere among children. What we need is more people doing this and fewer passing the buck onto the public schools.[103]

Yet until the families and churches of America accepted the responsibility of teaching the nation's children about religion, an outcome Clark seriously doubted would occur, he would continue to advocate the public schools as "possibly [the] next best [institution to teach religion] . . . because it could reach so many thousands in one swoop."[104]

A final intriguing aspect of Clark's position on matters of church and state is its similarity to the Presbyterian Church's historical position on religious liberty. Clark himself specifically adverted to this tradition in his "Religion and the Law" article and embraced the words of a memorial issued by the Presbyterian Church against the Virginia general assessment bill in 1776 as an accurate expression of his beliefs:

> As one church trustee, who was born an Episcopalian and for some 39 years has by marriage been a Presbyterian, I stand foursquare on the 'Presbyterian Memorial' of June 12, 1776, which was enunciated by much wiser and more religious men than I.
>
> It said in part:
>
> > Neither can it be made to appear that the gospel needs any such civil aid; [we] rather conceive that, when our blessed Savior declares his kingdom is not of this world, he renounces all dependence on State power, and . . . [we] are persuaded that, if mankind were left in the quiet possession of their unalienable religious privileges, Christianity . . . would . . . flourish in the greatest purity by its own native excellence, and under the all-disposing providence of God.[105]

Clark's position also resembled that of his Presbyterian contemporaries. As Ellis West points out, the General Assembly of the Presbyterian Church adopted a "major report on church-state relations" in 1963 which "condemned state aid to religion as 'dangerous to the purity of religion,' approved the policy of state 'neutrality' with respect to faith and dogma, condemned religious observances in the public schools, and recommended concerted action to prevent the state from becoming amoral and demonic."[106] Presbyterian ministers and officials who spoke out were making similar statements. Reverends Silas Kessler and Eugene Blake declared that "[t]he Court's decision [in *Schempp*] underscores our firm belief that religious instruction is the sacred responsibility of the family and the churches. It is both mistaken and dangerous to assume the spiritual needs of our youth are met by formal recitation of prayers or the casual learning of words taken from the Holy Writ."[107] These comments from Presbyterian leaders express sentiments similar to those of Justice Clark—that the home and the church were the best vehicle for cultivating religion and public school prayers undermined the integrity of religion.

Justice Clark's personal religious beliefs, experiences, and observations were the primary motivation behind his decision in *School District v. Schempp*. In fact, nearly every major aspect of Clark's decision can be attributed to his sincere view of the Christian faith and his genuine distress over the decline of religion in American culture. His laudatory words regarding the religious heritage of our nation likely sprang from his being immersed in that heritage while growing up. As Ramsey Clark said of his father, he grew up in religious America.

Clark's decision striking down school prayer and Bible reading was apparently based upon his sense that religious exercises conducted by school officials undermined the integrity of religion and diminished its importance in the eyes of school children. Furthermore, his rejection of the Court's use of Jefferson's wall metaphor was likely influenced by his concern that a rigid separationist stance could damage the cause of religion.

Above all else, however, Clark's overwhelming concern that religion's "exalted" position in our society was slipping led him to advocate accommodation between church and state and to encourage public schools to adopt courses of study in religion.[108] In advocating accommodation and the study of the Bible in schools, Clark was attempting to point out a way in which the states could constitutionally incorporate religion into their curricula. Clark thought it was the duty of public schools to teach subjects that would "bring respect and integrity to the place of religion in every day life"; he just did not believe conducting religious exercises in the schools achieved that goal.[109] Yet despite Clark's commitment to a role for public schools in the promotion of the interests of religion, it should be remembered that he ultimately believed the solution to the degradation of religion in our society was a revitalization of religion in America's homes and churches.

Justice Clark's view of church-state relations laid the foundation for the Court's next major engagement in *Lemon v. Kurtzman*, the subject of the next chapter. In fact, when Chief Justice Burger wrote the opinion in *Lemon* declaring unconstitutional the teacher salary supplements provided by Rhode Island and Pennsylvania, he relied on Justice Clark's legal analysis. Like Clark, Burger was a Presbyterian and adopted the denomination's stance on government funding of religious institutions.

NOTES

1. Opinion issued by the Pennsylvania Department of Justice in 1948 in light of *McCollum v. Board of Education*, 333 U.S. 203 (1948) entitled "Religious Education." 1948 Pa. D. & C. LEXIS 259, * 14.

2. *People ex rel. Vollmar v. Stanley*, 255 P. 610, 618 (Col. 1927), overruled by *Conrad v. City & County of Denver*, 656 P.2d 662 (Col. 1982).

3. *Lewis v. Board of Education*, 285 N.Y.S. 164 (1935).

4. *Engel v. Vitale*, 370 U.S. 421 (1962) (outlawing prayer in public schools); *School District v. Schempp*, 374 U.S. 203 (1963) (outlawing the Lord's prayer and Bible reading in public schools).

5. Press Release, National Council/Episcopal Church, Division of Christian Citizenship (19 June 1963). (On file in the Archives of the Episcopal Diocese of Washington, D.C.).

6. Letter from Rev. Herschel Halbert, of the Division of Christian Citizenship, to the Rt. Rev. William Creighton, bishop of Washington, located in the Archives of the Episcopal Diocese of Washington, D.C. These are the same questions that were asked in the 1830s and 1840s and referenced to in *Vidal*.

7. 110 *Cong. Rec.* 1 (88th Cong., 2nd Session, 1964).

8. 110 *Cong. Rec.* 1 (88th Cong., 2nd Session, 1964), 4; quoting Baptist Joint Committee on Public Affairs, 10 March 1964.

9. *Resolution on Religious Liberty*, Southern Baptist Convention, (June 1964); available at http://www.sbc.net.

10. *Prayer and Bible Reading in the Public Schools*, Adopted by the Second Biennial

Convention, Lutheran Church in America (July 1964); available at www.elca.org/jle/lca/lca.prayer_public_schools.html.

11. *Prayer and Bible Reading in the Public Schools.*

12. National Council of Churches, "Separation and Interaction of Church and State," *J. of Church and State* 6 (1964): 147.

13. NCC, "Separation and Interaction of Church and State," at 147–48.

14. NCC, "Separation and Interaction of Church and State," 148.

15. NCC, "Separation and Interaction of Church and State," 148.

16. *Resolution on Separation of Church and State*, Southern Baptist Convention (June 1967); available at http://www.sbc.net.

17. *Engel v. Vitale*, 421.

18. Thomas M. Mengler, "Public Relations in the Supreme Court: Justice Tom Clark's Opinion in the School Prayer Case," *Const. Comment.* 6 (1989): 331, 337; citing David L. Grey, *The Supreme Court and the News Media* (1968), 83.

19. Mengler, "Public Relations in the Supreme Court"; citing William A. Hatchen, "Journalism and the Prayer Decision," *Colum. Journalism Rev.* (Fall 1962): 4, 7.

20. Alexander Burnham, "Edict Is Called a Setback by Christian Clerics—Rabbis Praise It," *New York Times,* 26 June 1962, 1.

21. Burnham, "Edict Is Called a Setback," 1.

22. Burnham, "Edict Is Called a Setback," 1.

23. Mengler, "Public Relations in the Supreme Court," 336; quoting 108 *Cong. Rec.* 11675 (1962).

24. William M. Beaney and Edward N. Beiser, "Prayer and Politics: The Impact of *Engel* and *Schempp* on the Political Process," *J. Pub. L.* 13 (1964): 475, 478; quoting 108 *Cong. Rec.* 14360 (1962).

25. Beaney and Beiser, "Prayer and Politics," 478; quoting Dr. Leo Pfeffer, *Information Bulletin No. 6*, Commission on Law and Social Action of the American Jewish Congress, 15 August 1962, 2.

26. William M. Beaney and Edward N. Beiser, *Prayer and Politics: The Impact of* Engel *and* Schempp *on the Political Process*, 13 J. Pub Law 475 (1964), 479; Thomas M. Mengler, *Public Relations in the Supreme Court: Justice Tom Clark's Opinions in the School Prayer Case*, 6 Constitutional Commentary 331 (1989), 336–37. Becker's proposed amendment read: "Prayers may be offered in the course of any program in any public school or other public place in the United States." Beaney and Beiser, "Prayer and Politics," 337; quoting *Hearings on Prayer in Public Schools and Other Matters Before the Senate Committee on the Judiciary*, 87th Cong. 71 (1962).

27. Beaney and Beiser, "Prayer and Politics," 331, 334.

28. *Minutes*, Augustana Lutheran Church (1960), 255; available at www.elca.org/jle/ulca/ulca.church_state.html.

29. *Minutes*, Augustana Lutheran Church, 255.

30. *Resolution on Christian Citizenship*, Southern Baptist Convention (June, 1960); available at http://www.sbc.net.

31. *Resolution on Christian Citizenship.*

32. Richard Kirkendall, "Tom C. Clark," in Leon Freidman and Fred L. Israel, eds.,

The Justices of the United States Supreme Court 1789–1969: Their Lives and Major Opinions, vol. 4 (New York: Chelsea House and Bowker, 1969), 2665; Ramsey Clark, Remarks, in *A Symposium on the Tom C. Clark Papers: Tarlton Law Library, University of Texas Law School* (1987), 32.

33. C. B. Dutton, "Mr. Justice Tom C. Clark," *Ind. L.J.* 26 (1951): 169, 170.

34. Kirkendall, "Tom C. Clark," 2665. It was during this time that Justice Clark developed one of his personal axioms, "A good lawyer doesn't file a case unless he's sure he'll win." Dutton, "Mr. Justice Tom C. Clark," 170; quoting Tom C. Clark, "Cautious Trust Buster," *Business Week*, 26 May 1945, 5. Apparently Clark strictly adhered to this adage during his years as district attorney, as he was "reputed never to have lost a case."

35. Kirkendall, "Tom C. Clark," 2665–66. Truman was in charge of a Senate investigatory committee that referred its findings to the Justice Department. Clark handled the findings of Truman's committee. Clark and Truman first met through this process, and "quickly became friends." Kirkendall, "Tom C. Clark," 2665–66.

36. Kirkendall, "Tom C. Clark," 2672; quoting *U.S. News & World Report*, 13 July 1969.

37. Tom C. Clark, "The First Amendment and Minority Rights," *U. Chi. L. Rev.* 36 (1969): 257, 259–60 (footnote omitted).

38. One key theory of civil libertarianism Clark did accept was Justice Douglas's penumbral right of privacy. In an article Clark wrote after retirement, he embraced Douglas's privacy theory and argued that abortion was included in that right. See Tom C. Clark, "Religion, Morality, and Abortion: A Constitutional Appraisal," *Loy. U. Chi. L. Rev.* 2 (1969): 1. In contrast, Clark's disagreement with civil libertarianism is evident in his rejection of strict separation of church and state as the guiding principle of the Establishment Clause.

39. Clark, "The First Amendment and Minority Rights," 265–66.

40. *Everson v. Board of Education*, 18.

41. Tom C. Clark, "The Fourth R," *Address at the 25th National Conference on Church and State*, 5 February 1973, 4, 6; transcript available at University of Texas at Austin School of Law Tarlton Law Library.

42. Tom C. Clark, "Justice Ye Shall Pursue," *Tenn. L. Rev.* 38 (1971): 487–88.

43. *United States v. Seeger*, 380 U.S. 163-64 (1965); citing 50 U.S.C. App. § 456(j) (1958 ed.).

44. *United States v. Seeger*, 165 (alteration in original).

45. Abner Brodie and Harold P. Southerland, "Conscience, The Constitution, and the Supreme Court: The Riddle of *United States v. Seeger*," *Wis. L. Rev.* (1966):306, 311–14; discussing that the Congress, in adopting the 1948 Military Service Act, had intended to foreclose a liberal interpretation of previous conscientious objector provisions by the Circuit Courts. The liberal interpretation Congress was attempting to thwart was essentially that adopted by Clark in *Seeger*.

46. *United States v. Seeger*, 166.

47. *United States v. Seeger*, 165, 176.

48. *United States v. Seeger*, 180; quoting Paul Tillich, *Systematic Theology*, vol. 2 (New York: Scribner's, 1957), 12. Clark also quoted this passage from another of Dr. Tillich's books:

And if that word [God] has not much meaning for you, translate it, and speak of the depths of your life, of the source of your being, of your ultimate concern, *of what you take seriously without any reservation*. Perhaps, in order to do so, you must forget everything traditional that you have learned about God. . . .

Seeger, 187; quoting Paul Tillich, *The Shaking of the Foundations* (New York: Scribner's, 1948), 57; emphasis added by Clark (alteration in original).

    49. Tom C. Clark, "Personal Reflections on the *Schempp* Decision," in Peter Bracher et al., eds., *Religion Studies in the Curriculum: Retrospect and Prospect, 1963–1983* (Dayton, Ohio: Public Education Religion Studies Center, Wright State University, 1974), 20.

    50. Tom C. Clark, "The Church and the State—Its History and Relationship," Lecture at Wartburg College, 4–5 November 1964, 2; transcript available at University of Texas School of Law Tarlton Law Library.

    51. *School District v. Schempp*, 374 U.S. 203 (1963), 205; quoting 24 Pa. Stat. § 15-1516, as amended, Pub. Law 1928 (Supp. 1960).

    52. *Schempp*, 211.

    53. *Schempp*, 223.

    54. *Schempp*, 224.

    55. *Schempp*, 226.

    56. Ellis M. West, "Justice Tom Clark and American Church-State Law," *J. Pres. Hist.* 54 (1976): 397. West quotes another author who argued that Clark's disdain for the wall metaphor was motivated by his fear that it could make the Court "so rigidly separationist as to be detrimental to religion." West, "Justice Tom Clark and American Church-State Law," 398; quoting Arthur Gilbert, "Religious Freedom and Social Change in a Pluralistic Society: A Historical Review," in *Religion and the Public Order* (Chicago: University of Chicago Press, 1964), 117.

    57. Tom C. Clark, "Religion and the Law," *S.C. L. Rev.* 15 (1963): 855.

    58. Clark, "Religion and the Law," 855.

    59. Clark, "The Church and the State," 31 (emphasis added).

    60. Clark, "The Fourth R," 4; quoting *The Writings of Thomas Jefferson*, vol. 19 (Washington, D.C.: Thomas Jefferson Memorial association of the United States, 1903 ed.), 414.

    61. Tom C. Clark, "The Needs of Society—Religion and Education: The Place of Religion in the Public Schools," Address to the Texas Conference of Churches, 7 November 1971, 5; transcript available at University of Texas School of Law Tarlton Law Library.

    62. Clark, "The Needs of Society," 5.

    63. *Schempp*, 203, 213.

    64. *Schempp*, 226 n10.

    65. Mengler, "Public Relations in the Supreme Court," 344–45; quoting Tom C. Clark, Draft Opinion 20 (exact date unknown, probably April 1963); manuscript available at University of Texas School of Law Tarlton Law Library.

66. *Schempp*, 222.

67. In *Everson*, the Court said, "Neither a state nor the Federal Government can set up a church. Neither can pass laws which aid one religion, aid all religions, or prefer one religion over another." *Everson v. Board of Education*, 1, 15.

68. West, "Justice Tom Clark," 398. For a thorough discussion of Clark's neutrality principle and its implications, see Paul G. Kauper, "*Schempp* and *Sherbert*: Studies in Neutrality and Accommodation," in Donald A. Giannella, ed., *Religion and the Public Order: An Annual Review of Church and State and of Religion, Law, and Society* (Chicago: University of Chicago Press, 1964), 3.

69. *Schempp*, 215; quoting *Minor v. Board of Education of Cincinnati*, in *The Bible in the Common Schools* (Cincinnati: Robert Clarke & Co., 1870). Justice Clark's reference to the neutrality language of *Minor v. Board of Education* lends a sense of historical continuity to our study of religious liberty.

70. *Schempp*, 222.

71. *Schempp*, 222.

72. *Schempp*, 212.

73. *Schempp*, 213; quoting *Zorach v. Clauson*, 343 U.S. 306, 313 (1952).

74. *Schempp* 213; quoting James Madison, *Memorial and Remonstrance against Religious Assessments* (alteration in original).

75. *Schempp* 226.

76. *Schempp*, 225. Of this charge, Clark said, "We agree of course that the State may not establish a 'religion of secularism' in the sense of affirmatively opposing or showing hostility to religion, thus 'preferring those who believe in no religion over those who do believe.' We do not agree, however, that this decision in any sense has that effect." *Schempp*, 225; quoting *Zorach*, 314.

77. *Schempp*, 225. It is important to note that the program on religion Clark envisioned was not sectarian in any sense. He wanted a program that merely taught about religions. He said the program's "instruction would be . . . *about* religion. . . . After you get through with all this study *about* religion, then you can pick out a particular one for yourself that you like, and you can worship that in any way you wish." Consistent with his concern for protecting conscience and respecting the diverse religious viewpoints of our pluralistic communities, Clark said he would include a study of atheism within a religious studies program. Clark, "Personal Reflections on *Schempp*," 18–19.

78. *Schempp*, 225.

79. Clark, "Religion and the Law," 856. Clark said the Court had merely ruled that "religious exercises in public schools are illegal."

80. Clark, "The Needs of Society," 5–6.

81. Clark, "The Church and the State," 2.

82. West, "Justice Tom Clark," 394.

83. West, "Justice Tom Clark," 400.

84. Clark, "Religion and the Law," 864.

85. Clark, "Religion and the Law," 864.

86. Clark, "Religion and the Law," 864.

87. Clark, "The Church and the State," 32.

88. Clark, "The Fourth R," 2. In the same address Clark disparaged school prayers as "forcing young people to mumble in unison." Clark, "The Fourth R," 11.

89. Clark, "The Fourth R," 2.

90. Clark, "The Fourth R," 11.

91. Clark, "The Fourth R," 11.

92. Clark, "The Fourth R," 11. Clark expressed the same sentiments in his Wartburg College lectures: "You must agree that our homes have changed since our childhood. With both parents working there is little family life there. Spiritual training is nil—delinquency at an all-time high. Only a handful of children attend Sunday School and fewer go to church." Clark, "The Church and the State," 33.

93. Clark, "The Fourth R," 11.

94. Clark, "The Needs of Sociey," 6.

95. Clark, "The Church and the State," 32, 33. Clark echoed these sentiments in another address, arguing that "a child that prepares and gives grace at the family dinner receives more benefit from those few words of his own than all the prayers that others write and he chants at school." Clark, "The Fourth R," 11.

96. Clark, "Personal Reflections," 19–20.

97. Clark, "The Fourth R," 31.

98. Clark, "The Needs of Society," 5.

99. Clark, "The Needs of Society," 6.

100. Clark, "The Church and the State," 33.

101. Clark, "Personal Reflections," 17, 18.

102. *Schempp*, 203, 226.

103. Clark, "Religion and the Law," 866. Clark made this point time and again. In his Wartburg lecture, for instance, Clark said, "I submit that more private prayers in the home and public worship in the church . . . is what the American people need." Clark, "The Church and the State," 32.

104. Clark, "Personal Reflections," 21. Clark viewed America's reliance on the public schools to teach about religion as a "sad commentary" on the state of religion in our culture. Nevertheless, he believed so strongly in the importance of religion to the lives of Americans that he was willing to accept an active role for the public schools in the dissemination of religious ideas and beliefs.

105. Clark, "Religion and the Law," 866; quoting Mark DeWolfe Howe, *Cases on Church and State in the United States* (Cambridge, Mass.: Harvard University Press, 1952), 5.

106. West, "Justice Tom Clark," 400 n89; quoting *Relations between Church and State in the United States of America* (Philadelphia: United Presbyterian Church in the U.S.A., n.d.), 4–7, 19*f*.

107. 110 *Cong. Rec.* 8118 (88th Cong., 2nd Session, 1964); statement of Congressman Ryan. Congressman Ryan read the statements of various religious bodies regarding school prayer into the record during his speech. He also read the following statement from a magazine for Presbyterian ministers called *Monday Morning*: "[T]he instruction of chil-

dren in the beliefs and practices of the Christian faith is the responsibility and privilege of the church and family; these things are not properly to be provided by the state or by any of the agencies of the state, including the public schools." 110 *Cong. Rec.* 8119.

108. *Schempp*, 203, 226.

109. Clark, "The Needs of Society," 6.

· 8 ·

Separation of Church and State:
The *Lemon* Test

First, the statute must have a secular legislative purpose; second, its principal or primary effect must be one that neither advances nor inhibits religion; finally, the statute must not foster "an excessive government entanglement with religion."

—Chief Justice Warren Burger
Lemon v. Kurtzman, 1971

*O*nce the Supreme Court declared prayer and Bible reading in the nation's public schools unconstitutional, a not-so-subtle shift began to occur within Christian denominations and the focus of litigation. As we have seen, the overwhelming negative reaction to the school prayer controversy in the *Schempp* case came from all sectors of American society: Evangelist Billy Graham, members of the United States Senate, the press, broadcast media covering the story, ordinary church-going citizens writing letters to the editor of their local papers—all shocked and surprised that the Supreme Court of the United States actually declared the time-honored practices of prayer and Bible reading effectively illegal in the nation's public schools.

With the issue of religious practices in public schools at least temporarily settled by the Supreme Court, the issue of funding of religiously affiliated institutions by government became significant. In fact, one of the most important Establishment Clause cases in Supreme Court history, *Lemon v. Kurtzman*, focused on the issue of funding of religiously affiliated private schools with government funds. Chief Justice Warren Burger wrote the opinion in *Lemon*. The opinion in *Lemon* generates controversy even today.

275

THE CULTURAL/HISTORICAL CONTEXT

Despite the initial and sustained public outcry, proposed school prayer amendments failed in Congress. These constitutional amendments in favor of school prayer were introduced in 1963 and, again, in 1964. Both amendments failed to garner the necessary support to be put into law.

In the decade after *Schempp*, a new focus on litigation began to emerge in the state and federal courts. President Lyndon Baines Johnson initiated his War on Poverty in 1964. One of President Johnson's primary concerns was the continued deterioration of inner-city schools. In order to improve the plight of inner-city students, Congress passed the Elementary and Secondary Education Act in 1965.[1] The act provided funding for special education programs in both public and private schools, including religiously affiliated institutions. It was "the first federal aid-to-education program authorizing assistance for private school children as well as for public school children."[2] The primary recipients of the private school portion of the funding were the inner-city Roman Catholic schools. Once the federal government took action, states soon followed. This was the first significant series of legislation at the federal and state levels that specifically authorized taxpayer funds to be used for private, religiously affiliated schools.

These programs were adopted primarily for two reasons. First, as a simple matter of fairness, parents who were sending their students to private schools were also paying state and federal tax dollars that were supporting the public school system. Thus, these parents were maintaining the double burden of tax and tuition in order to educate their children. By providing supplemental funding to private schools, including religiously affiliated schools, state and local governments were attempting to alleviate some of the burdens parents were facing.

Second, many states began providing financial assistance to private schools as a part of their educational programs during the 1960s as a way to ensure that all children in the state received at least a minimal quality of education. The policies were designed to help defray the rising costs of salaries, books, and materials in secular subjects. They were not an attempt to advance religious teachings or to raise the level of private school education above what was offered in public schools.

By the mid-1960s, a number of states had adopted programs to provide aid to private sectarian schools:

1965—New York: Local public school districts were required to lend textbooks for free to any public or nonpublic school student in 7th through 12th grade who lived in the district.[3]

1968—Pennsylvania: The state passed a statute to help private schools cope with the rising costs of education. The state reimbursed nonpublic schools for actual expenditures made for teacher salaries, textbooks, and materials.

1969—Rhode Island: The state enacted a statute to supplement teachers' salaries in private schools.[4]

1969—South Carolina: The state provided financing for public and private colleges by issuing revenue bonds.[5]

1970—New York: The state reimbursed all schools for the costs they incurred to administer and grade tests, keep student enrollment and health records, and send information to the state.[6]

1971—Maryland: The state provided money to private colleges, including sectarian ones, through grants.[7]

1971—Vermont: Two months before *Lemon,* state statutes were passed allowing public school districts to share aid with nonpublic schools for the cost of "providing teachers and educational materials for the teaching of physical sciences, modern languages, physical education and mathematics."[8]

These state statutes were significant revenue sources for private religiously affiliated schools. For instance, in 1968, the state of Pennsylvania authorized $5 million of state money to be given to hundreds of private elementary and secondary schools, the vast majority of which were affiliated with the Roman Catholic Church. The schools were required to show that the funds received were used only for certain courses that were also taught in public schools: math, modern foreign languages such as French and Spanish, science, and physical education.

The Rhode Island statute was enacted in 1969 to help nonpublic schools maintain a quality education by being able to recruit competent teachers in light of rising salaries. A unique aspect of the Rhode Island statute was that it actually authorized a direct payment to private school teachers of a salary supplement of up to 15 percent of their current salaries. The only eligible teachers were those who taught at private schools where the average expenditure per student was lower than the state average for public schools. Also, only teachers who taught subjects offered in public schools and used materials that were used in public schools could receive the funds.

In *Lemon v. Kurtzman* (1971), the Supreme Court was faced with a challenge to the constitutionality of the Pennsylvania and Rhode Island statutory schemes providing for supplemental education salaries of teachers.[9] While the case was being litigated in the lower courts, the Southern Baptist Convention passed a resolution in 1969 reiterating their "opposition to the use of public tax funds for religious functions or institutions."[10]

THE JUSTICE: CHIEF JUSTICE WARREN EARL BURGER (1907–1995)

Warren Burger's life epitomized the fulfillment of the American dream. Born on September 17, 1907, in St. Paul, Minnesota, this future chief justice of the Supreme Court began life in a nine-member family. His grandfather, Joseph Burger, had emigrated from Switzerland to the United States, joined the Union army, and served in the Civil War. His parents, Charles Joseph Burger and Katharine Schnittger, were of Swiss-German descent.

Warren Burger was an intensely private man who did not write about his personal life or upbringing. However, his Minnesota childhood friend, Harry Blackmun, who later served on the Supreme Court with Justice Burger, offered a glimpse of the religious practices of the Burger family. Young Warren and Harry were close friends from the time they first met at the local Presbyterian church, where their "respective mothers packed [them] off to Sunday School at five or six years of age."[11] This information suggests that the Burger household placed at least some emphasis on religion. The boys went to elementary school together, and Blackmun was also a groomsman in Burger's wedding. Although their relationship strained in later years, Blackmun was most familiar with Burger's childhood.

Tinsley E. Yarbrough's study of the justices and decisions of the Burger Court indicates that Burger was "raised in a Swiss-German Protestant family" and that his mother taught her children "respect for traditional values."[12]

The Burgers raised their nine children on modest financial means.[13] Warren learned the value of hard work at a young age and did his share to contribute to his family by taking a job as a newspaper delivery boy and, later, writing articles on high school sports and selling them to local St. Paul newspapers. He was an outstanding all-around high school student in academics, athletics, and leadership skills—lettering in four sports and serving as editor of the school newspaper and president of the student body. He graduated from John A. Johnson High School in 1925.

Burger's diligence during high school was rewarded with a scholarship to Princeton University. In a decision that must have been very difficult for him but reveals much about his character, Burger turned down the Princeton scholarship, opting instead to take a job in order to support his struggling family. His first post–high school job was as a construction worker; after a summer of this work, he was hired by the Mutual Life Insurance Company of New York as an insurance salesman. While holding down a full-time job, Burger enrolled in night courses at the University of Minnesota. After two years in the night division, Burger enrolled in evening law classes at the St. Paul College of Law (now William Mitchell College of Law). Indicative of his excellent work ethic and sense of responsibility for his family, Burger kept his insurance sales job throughout his undergraduate and legal studies. He graduated magna cum laude from St. Paul College of Law in 1931.

Burger joined the law firm of Otis & Faricy, located in St. Paul, immediately after graduating. He attained partner status in less than three years. He also began teaching contracts at his alma mater the year after his graduation and continued to do so for twelve years.

In addition to practicing and teaching law, Burger became active in local Republican politics. He supported Minnesota governor Harold Stassen's bids for the presidency in 1948 and 1952. Significantly, at the 1952 Republican National Convention, in his role as floor manager of the Minnesota delegation, Burger led his state's delegates to switch their support from Stassen to Eisenhower. As a result, Burger made a very important political acquaintance, Eisenhower's campaign manager, Herbert Brownell. This acquaintance paid dividends almost immediately. In 1953, Eisenhower appointed Brownell to the post of attorney general. Brownell, in turn, named Burger assistant attorney general for the Civil Division. Burger's many distinguished years of public service had begun.

Burger spent three years at the Justice Department. Upon completing his time there he planned to return to Minnesota, but he was in for a surprise. A vacancy opened on the District of Columbia Court of Appeals, and President Eisenhower seized the opportunity to appoint Burger to the court, where he served from 1956 to 1969. While on the Court of Appeals, Burger made a name for himself as a consistent conservative voice on a court that had been perceived as very liberal.

Burger's conservative record on the D.C. Court of Appeals brought him to the attention of newly inaugurated president Richard M. Nixon in 1969. Nixon had run primarily on a law-and-order platform. He openly criticized the Warren Court's decisions regarding criminal rights during his campaign and stressed that a principal way to resolve the law-and-order problem was to appoint justices who were strict constructionists in criminal procedure. Nixon found his "strict constructionist" in Warren Burger. Nixon explained that he appointed Burger to the Supreme Court because he viewed him as a judge "who would 'apply' the law, not broadly 'legislate' social policy. He told reporters that Burger had authored opinions . . . on criminal procedure that expressed 'the minority view of the Supreme Court. It happens to be my view.'"[14] Based largely on these criminal justice considerations, Nixon appointed Warren Burger as chief justice of the Supreme Court on May 21, 1969.

While Chief Justice Burger did not speak about his personal religious views in public, he did discuss his view of the role of religion in American public life. The most salient off-the-Court resource that sheds some light on the nature of Burger's religious beliefs was his 1990 speech titled *The Constitution and Religion* that he delivered during his tenure as the chairman of the Commission on the Bicentennial of the United States Constitution. In that speech, Burger declared:

> We have survived and prospered for 200 years because the strength of our Nation was not simply in the words of the Declaration and the Constitution—great as they are—but because of the strength of a free people, of personal integrity, of individual responsibility and accountability of the traditions of home and family, and of religious beliefs.[15]

Burger stressed the importance of religion to our nation's history throughout his speech, especially to those of the founding generation. He remarked how the "problems and burdens of those 3 million early Americans who began" our nation led them to "constantly [call] for Divine guidance for their efforts." Noting the "complexities of a nation grown to 240 million people and the world problems we share," Burger provocatively asked whether "we can survive without [Divine] help" today.

Burger then proceeded to list specific examples of leading men of the founding generation who had sought God's guidance and direction. He mentioned how "Washington, both as General and President, constantly called for Divine guidance and credited all progress to that Source." He referenced a letter John Adams wrote to his wife on the day the Declaration was signed, in which he declared "that the day of its signing 'ought to be commemorated as the day of deliverance, by solemn acts of devotion to Almighty God.'" And he noted that when the Constitution was approved, James Madison "observed that all people must 'perceive in [the Constitution] a finger of that Almighty hand which has been so frequently . . . extended to our relief in the critical states of the revolution.'"

Burger cited these deeply religious sentiments of our Founding Fathers and appeared to believe that such sincere religious conviction was not only integral to the successful founding of our nation but also necessary for our nation's continued vitality. This sentiment was best captured in his quotation of this famous passage from Alexis de Tocqueville's classic 1835 work, *Democracy in America*:

> I sought for the greatness and genius of America in her Commodious harbors and her ample rivers, and it was not there; in her fertile fields and boundless prairies, and it was not there; in her rich gold mines and her vast world commerce, and it was not there. Not until I went to the churches of America . . . did I understand the Secret of her genius and power. America is great because she is good, and if America ceases to be good, America will cease to be great.

The religious references Burger utilized in this speech should not be given more significance than they deserve. While his use of religious quotations may reflect some inner religious belief of his own, it would be far too speculative to draw a definitive conclusion. The speech was, after all, about the relationship between religion and the Constitution; general religious quotations from the pens and mouths of our founders were especially salient to the topic of his speech.

At best, then, his speech on the Constitution and religion demonstrates that Chief Justice Burger had a great deal of respect for the role religion had played in the development of our nation and still played in the closing decade of the twentieth century. Moreover, Burger's remarks indicate his dislike of a strict separationist reading of the First Amendment. Indeed, he scrupulously avoided discussing any Supreme Court Establishment Clause opinions that utilized a church-state-separation operating model. For example, he discussed *McDaniel v. Paty* (ministers serving in the legislature), *Marsh v. Chambers* (legislative prayer), and *Wisconsin v. Yoder* (involving accommodation of Amish practices), all of which could be said to stand more for religious freedom and accommodation than for the establishment of religion.[16]

In his discussion of *Marsh*, Burger made specific mention of our country's long-standing history of governmental acknowledgment and accommodation of religion. He outlined that:

> from the very beginning of the country the idea of opening public meetings and a legislative session with a prayer given by a chaplain and paid by government funds was not a violation of the establishment laws. The first Congress of the United States in 1789, passed a law creating the positions of Chaplain of the House of Representatives and Chaplain of the Senate, each paid out of public funds. Nothing was said in the statute limiting what denomination the chaplain should be. That was left by the Congress to the discretion of Congress.

Burger also noted that today nearly every court in the United States, state or federal, opens its sessions with a prayer. Burger even declared that the Supreme Court's practice of opening its sessions with the words, "God save the United States and this Honorable Court," amounted to the opening of Court sessions with a prayer.

Chief Justice Burger seems to have drawn a constitutional line of distinction between the acknowledgment of God and religion by government officials, which he favored, and direct funding of religious institutions and organizations, which early in his tenure as chief justice he appeared to oppose.

The Presbyterian Church to which Justice Burger belonged had a long history of advocating church-state separation when it came to funding issues. As early as June 12, 1776, the presbytery adopted a specific statement regarding the relationship between church and state. It said in part:

> Neither can it be made to appear that the Gospel needs any such civil aid; [we] rather conceive that, when our Blessed Savior declares His Kingdom is not of this world, He renounces all dependence on state power, and . . . [we] are persuaded that if mankind were left in the quiet possession of their unalienable religious privileges, Christianity . . . would . . . flourish in the greatest purity by its own native excellence, and under the all-disposing Providence of God.[17]

As late as 1963, the General Assembly of the Presbyterian Church "condemned state aid to religion as dangerous to the purity of religion."[18]

Burger's opinion in *Lemon v. Kurtzman* reflected this Presbyterian view of church-state relations.

In the final analysis, Burger's *The Constitution and Religion* speech embodied the chief justice's overarching beliefs in religious accommodation and freedom. As his speech indicated, Burger was more concerned with the advancement of religious freedom than with that of church-state separation. Unlike several of his colleagues, he did not view strict separation of church and state as the best guarantor of religious freedom. He preferred a pragmatic approach that often left room for reasonable accommodations of the religious traditions and practices of our nation.

Chief Justice Burger's Establishment Clause opinions largely reflected the view of church-state relations he outlined in his speech on religious liberty. While he did author opinions that fell on the separationist side of the church-state fence when it came to funding issues, a comprehensive review of his Establishment Clause jurisprudence supports the conclusion that Burger was a church-state accommodationist.[19]

THE CASE: *LEMON V. KURTZMAN* (1971)

The most appropriate place to begin a discussion of Chief Justice Burger's Establishment Clause jurisprudence is with *Lemon v. Kurtzman*. Of Burger's many religious liberty opinions, his *Lemon* opinion has had the most lasting impact because of its enunciation of what became known as "the *Lemon* test."

Lemon involved the statutes of two states, Pennsylvania and Rhode Island. Both statutes provided aid to nonpublic, religious schools. The Pennsylvania statute provided reimbursements directly to nonpublic schools "for the cost of teachers' salaries, textbooks, and instructional materials in specified secular subjects." The Rhode Island statute paid "directly to teachers in nonpublic elementary schools a supplement of 15% of their annual salary."

One of the most fascinating aspects of the litigation concerning funding was that for the first time in its history, Protestants and Other Americans United for Separation of Church and State (now known as Americans United for Separation of Church and State) filed amicus briefs with the Supreme Court opposing the funding at issue in *Lemon*. Interestingly, this same organization did not file briefs in the school prayer cases. Also arguing for the unconstitutionality of the government aid programs were United Americans for Public Schools, the Center for Law and Education, Harvard University; and the Connecticut State Conference of Branches of the NAACP. The position advocated by Americans United for Separation of Church and State ultimately was adopted by Justice Burger in *Lemon*.

The United States Department of Justice filed briefs in support of the states of Rhode Island and Pennsylvania in *Lemon* pursuant to President Nixon's directive of encouraging vouchers for education in private schools, including religiously affiliated ones. The attorney general of Ohio, the city of Philadelphia, the city of Pittsburgh, the city of Erie, the school district of the city of Scranton, the National Catholic Educational Association, the National Association of Independent Schools, Inc., and the Pennsylvania State AFL-CIO also filed briefs in favor of the reimbursement programs. The aforementioned cities all had majority Catholic populations.

Two prominent Jewish organizations took opposite positions in these funding cases. The National Jewish Commission on Law and Public Affairs filed briefs in favor of the financial assistance to public schools, while the American Jewish Committee filed briefs against the statutes.

An interesting fact concerning the plaintiff in *Lemon v. Kurtzman* is that Alton Lemon was a member of the American Civil Liberties Union (ACLU). In fact, the ACLU director at the time, Spencer Cox, asked Lemon to become the plaintiff in the case after an ACLU meeting occurred in Philadelphia. Based on the comments that Alton Lemon made during the meeting, the ACLU director thought that he would be the ideal plaintiff in the case. In a 2004 interview that was given to the First Amendment Center, Mr. Lemon, reflecting upon the significance of his case and his view of religion, noted that: "At this point in my life, I seriously wonder why we have religion."[20] He also acknowledged that while he was never a member of any formal religious organization, he was a member of the Ethical Culture Society, a humanist organization that has been in existence since the 1870s.

In *Lemon*, Chief Justice Burger struck down as unconstitutional both the Rhode Island and the Pennsylvania statutes.[21] He recognized that "[c]andor compels acknowledgment, moreover, that we can only dimly perceive the lines of demarcation in this extraordinarily sensitive area of constitutional law." He began his analysis by declaring the mandatory nature of the *Lemon* test, borrowing language from his fellow Presbyterian, Associate Justice Thomas Clark. Burger wrote:

Every analysis in this area must begin with consideration of the cumulative criteria developed by the Court over many years. Three such tests may be gleaned from our cases. First, the statute must have a secular legislative purpose; second, its principal or primary effect must be one that neither advances nor inhibits religion . . . ; finally, the statute must not foster "an excessive government entanglement with religion."

As to the first prong, Burger summarily concluded that neither the Pennsylvania nor the Rhode Island statute had the purpose of advancing religion. Burger saw the statutes as attempts "to enhance the quality of the secular education in all schools covered by the compulsory education laws." He sidestepped any analysis of the second prong, opting instead to strike the statutes down as violations of the Establishment Clause because they failed the excessive entanglement prong.

Burger provided three criteria that needed to be analyzed in order to determine whether a government program resulted in excessive entanglement: "the character and purposes of the institutions that are benefited, the nature of the aid that the State provides, and the resulting relationship between the government and the religious authority." Burger's analysis demonstrated that both the Rhode Island and the Pennsylvania statutes failed these criteria. Both statutes failed the first criterion because they predominantly benefited private, Catholic schools. The Rhode Island statute was especially problematic in view of Burger's third criterion because, in order to ensure that the "subsidized teachers d[id] not inculcate religion," the statute "carefully conditioned its aid with pervasive restrictions." These restrictions were aimed at ensuring that the aid received be utilized to teach only secular courses, thus avoiding a violation of the Establishment Clause. As Burger put it, the state needed to "be certain, given the Religion Clauses, that subsidized teachers do not inculcate religion—indeed the State here has undertaken to do so. To ensure that no trespass occurs, the State has . . . carefully conditioned its aid with pervasive restrictions."

According to Burger, the restrictions the Rhode Island statute placed on the schools receiving aid would require "comprehensive, discriminating, and continuing state surveillance" in order to ensure compliance. This type of surveillance violated the excessive entanglement prong and was the key flaw in the Rhode Island program. Distinguishing the Rhode Island program from the free textbook program validated in 1968 by the Court in *Board of Education v. Allen*, Burger said, "Unlike a book, a teacher cannot be inspected once so as to determine the extent and intent of his or her personal beliefs and subjective acceptance of the limitations imposed by the First Amendment. These prophylactic contacts will involve excessive and enduring entanglement between state and church."

The Pennsylvania statute was similarly flawed. Its restrictions limiting public funds to be used solely for the teaching of secular courses, like the Rhode Island statute, would inevitably lead to a pervasive system of state surveillance of private, religious schools. Even more, Burger pointed out, the Pennsylvania statute presented problems with his second criterion since it gave aid directly to the schools. In his mind, this fact distinguished the case from both *Everson* and *Allen*, where the aid "was provided to the student and his parents—not to the church-related school."

While Burger's opinion in *Lemon* did have a separationist thrust and outcome, this case was not characteristic of the position Burger would adopt in subsequent Establishment Clause cases, although, as mentioned previously, the Presbyterian Church U.S.A. was on record as late as 1963 as opposing direct aid to religiously affiliated schools. Indeed, subsequently, Burger became an ardent proponent of government accommodation of religion. Not surprisingly, then, on the same day the decision in *Lemon* was announced, Burger issued an opinion in another Establishment Clause case that largely undermined the separationist implications of *Lemon*: that case was *Tilton v. Richardson*.[22]

In *Tilton*, Burger demonstrated his more conservative view of the dictates of the Establishment Clause. He also revealed, in the words of his former law clerk, Bruce Brown, his "immediate discomfort with a rigid application of the *Lemon* test."[23] *Tilton* presented the question whether a federal statute that provided direct financial assistance to private, religious colleges and universities for the construction of buildings dedicated to secular purposes violated the Establishment Clause. This statute seemingly violated the *Lemon* test, especially as Burger had defined it that very day. Burger's opinion concluded that the statute did not fail the *Lemon* test and thus did not violate the Establishment Clause.

In his *Tilton* opinion, Burger treated the *Lemon* test as a mere guideline in Establishment Clause cases. In *Lemon*, he had intimated that it was mandatory when he said that "*every* analysis in this area [the Establishment Clause] *must* begin with consideration of the cumulative criteria developed by the Court" and then announced the *Lemon* test. Yet in *Tilton*, Burger referred to the three parts of the *Lemon* test as mere "guidelines" and admitted that the Court could "only dimly perceive the boundaries of permissible government activity in this sensitive area of constitutional adjudication." More specifically, Burger said:

> There are always risks in treating criteria discussed by the Court from time to time as "tests" in any limiting sense of that term. Constitutional adjudication does not lend itself to the absolutes of the physical sciences or mathematics. The standards should rather be viewed as guidelines with which to identify instances in which the objectives of the Religion Clauses have been impaired.

Burger's immediate recantation in *Tilton* of a separationist reading of *Lemon* should come as no surprise. His first Establishment Clause opinion one year earlier in *Walz v. Tax Commission* strongly suggested that he would utilize an accommodationist approach concerning questions of church-state interaction.[24] In that case, which presented a challenge to the historically rooted practice of exempting churches from taxation, Burger expressed what commentator Joseph F. Kobylka considered Burger's essential "vision" of the Establishment Clause:[25]

> The course of constitutional neutrality in this area cannot be an absolutely straight line; rigidity could well defeat the basic purpose of these provisions, which is to insure that no religion be sponsored or favored, none commanded, and none inhibited. The general principle deducible from the First Amendment and all that has been said by the Court is this: that we will not tolerate either governmentally established religion or governmental interference with religion. Short of those expressly proscribed governmental acts there is room for play in the joints productive of a benevolent neutrality which will permit religious exercise to exist without sponsorship and without interference.

In later cases, Chief Justice Burger directly questioned the efficacy of the Court's continued reliance on *Lemon*. For instance, in *Wallace v. Jaffree*, in dealing with Alabama's moment of silence statute, Burger wrote that:

> The Court's extended treatment of the "test" of *Lemon v. Kurtzman* suggests a naive preoccupation with an easy, bright-line approach for addressing constitutional issues. We have repeatedly cautioned that *Lemon* did not establish a rigid caliper capable of resolving every Establishment Clause issue, but that it sought only to provide "sign-

posts." "In each [Establishment Clause] case, the inquiry calls for line-drawing; no fixed, *per se* rule can be framed." In any event, our responsibility is not to apply tidy formulas by rote; our duty is to determine whether the statute or practice at issue is a step toward establishing a state religion. Given today's decision, however, perhaps it is understandable that the opinions in support of the judgment all but ignore the Establishment Clause itself and the concerns that underlie it.[26]

Burger echoed this sentiment in other opinions. For example, in *Aguilar v. Felton* Burger said the Court harbored an "obsession with the criteria identified in *Lemon v. Kurtzman*" that had "led to results that are 'contrary to the long-range interests of the country.'"[27] And in *Lynch v. Donnelly*, a case involving a nativity scene display, Burger undermined the authority of *Lemon* by asserting that "we [the Court] have repeatedly emphasized our unwillingness to be confined to any single test or criterion in this sensitive area [government establishments of religion]."[28]

From the very beginning of the elucidation of his views regarding the Establishment Clause, Burger distanced himself from the absolutist approach and decisions of the Courts that had preceded him. Although Burger was probably not driven by a predetermined philosophy in the area of church-state relations, he was nevertheless more open to governmental accommodation and recognition of religion than most other justices on the Court during his tenure.

In a treatment of Burger's jurisprudence, James L. Volling asserted that Burger "came to each case before the Court without any rigid ideology or preconceived determination, but strove to decide correctly each case on its own merits and to decide no more than the case required." Volling argued that Burger's pragmatic approach led him to seek "reasoned balance" in the context of the religion clauses. Joseph Kobylka's analysis of Burger's conduct and writing in Establishment Clause cases led him to conclude that Burger was a justice "who sought to allow greater governmental accommodation of religion." Bruce Brown similarly concluded that "the tradition . . . of governmental acknowledgment and accommodation of religion in American life" was a "core value" of Burger's Establishment Clause opinions.[29]

An evolution began to occur almost immediately after the Court's decision in *Lemon* was announced. Burger's opinions in *Marsh v. Chambers* and *Lynch v. Donnelly* provide the best examples of the chief justice's tendency to advocate greater governmental accommodation of religion. In

Marsh, the constitutionality of the Nebraska state legislature's practice of employing a chaplain to open its legislative sessions with prayer was at issue. The most interesting aspect of Burger's *Marsh* opinion was his refusal to even apply the *Lemon* test to determine whether the practice of legislative prayer was unconstitutional. The only time Burger mentioned the *Lemon* test in his opinion was in his recital of the procedural history of the case, where he mentioned that the Eighth Circuit applied the *Lemon* test and found that Nebraska's chaplaincy program "violated all three elements of the test."

Perhaps the reason Burger refused to apply *Lemon* is that he knew doing so would almost certainly have resulted in the invalidation of Nebraska's chaplaincy program. Bruce Brown remarked that while the *Lemon* test may produce accommodationist results in the parochial aid setting, "when the subject changed to . . . state-sponsored prayer . . . the *Lemon* test had the potential of becoming dispositive."[30]

It is hard to imagine how a chaplain, employed by the state, whose job it is to open each legislative session with prayer, could not be a violation of the *Lemon* test. In his dissenting opinion in *Marsh*, Justice Brennan clearly expressed his view that if *Lemon* had been applied, Nebraska's chaplaincy program would have been struck down. After demonstrating how the practice failed the secular purpose, primary effect, and entanglement prongs, Brennan declared, "I have no doubt that, if any group of law students were asked to apply the principles of *Lemon* to the question of legislative prayer, they would nearly unanimously find the practice to be unconstitutional."

Instead of applying the *Lemon* test, Burger predominantly relied on historical evidence to justify Nebraska's chaplaincy program. He argued:

> The opening of sessions of legislative and other deliberative public bodies with prayer is deeply embedded in the history and tradition of this country. From colonial times through the founding of the Republic and ever since, the practice of legislative prayer has coexisted with the principles of disestablishment and religious freedom. In the very courtrooms in which the United States District Judge and later three Circuit Judges heard and decided this case, the proceedings opened with an announcement that concluded, "God save the United States and this Honorable Court." The same invocation occurs at all sessions of this Court.

In addition to the above evidence, Burger found it compelling that the members of the first Congress, who wrote the First Amendment religion clauses, contemporaneously authorized the appointment of paid chaplains. As Burger argued,

> It can hardly be thought that in the same week Members of the First Congress voted to appoint and to pay a chaplain for each House and also voted to approve the draft of the First Amendment for submission to the states, they intended the Establishment Clause of the Amendment to forbid what they had just declared acceptable.

Based on what Burger considered an "unambiguous and unbroken history" of legislative chaplaincy programs on the state and federal level, he concluded that

> there can be no doubt that the practice of opening legislative sessions with prayer has become part of the fabric of our society. To invoke Divine guidance on a public body entrusted with making the laws is not, in these circumstances, an "establishment" of religion or a step toward establishment; it is simply a tolerable acknowledgment of beliefs widely held among the people of this country.

Burger's appreciation of our country's historical practice of accommodating the religious needs of the people would be a recurrent theme in his subsequent Establishment Clause opinions. One commentator, the Honorable Kenneth F. Ripple, a judge on the Seventh Circuit Court of Appeals, noted the pivotal role history played in Burger's interpretation of the Constitution. Ripple said that for Burger,

> [c]areful study and contemplation of the values embodied in the Constitution were the first steps in interpreting the Constitution. Identifying and understanding those seminal constitutional values was not an exercise in abstract political theory. The Constitution, as he viewed it, was rooted in the history of our people. Only when he had an understanding of those roots did he feel comfortable looking forward.[31]

Ripple's words ring true in the context of Burger's Establishment Clause jurisprudence.

In *Lynch v. Donnelly*, the Court was presented with the question of whether the city of Pawtucket, Rhode Island, had violated the Establishment Clause by including a crèche in its annual Christmas display. The city of Pawtucket had included the crèche for over forty years. It consisted of the Infant Jesus, Mary and Joseph, angels, shepherds, kings, and animals. Chief Justice Burger, writing for the majority, upheld the practice; once again leaning heavily on our country's history of accommodating religion to support his decision.

Notably, at the outset of his opinion in *Lynch*, Burger endeavored to explain how "total separation" of church and state was "not possible." He referred to Jefferson's "wall" metaphor as a "useful figure of speech" that "served as a reminder that the Establishment Clause forbids an established church or anything approaching it." Nevertheless, according to Burger, the metaphor failed to provide "a wholly accurate description of the practical aspects of the relationship that . . . exists between church and state." In fact, Burger declared that the Constitution, far from requiring "complete separation of church and state," actually "mandates accommodation, not merely tolerance, of all religions, and forbids hostility toward any." "Anything less," Burger said, "would require the 'callous indifference' we have said was never intended by the Establishment Clause."

After this strong declaration of his accommodationist understanding of the Establishment Clause, Burger provided multiple examples of the "unbroken history of official acknowledgment by all three branches of government of the role of religion in American life" to support his position in *Lynch*. He once again pointed to the significance of the First Congress's adopting a chaplaincy program contemporaneously with adopting the First Amendment religion clauses. He wrote,

> A significant example of the contemporaneous understanding of that Clause is found in the events of the first week of the First Session of the First Congress in 1789. In the very week that Congress approved the Establishment Clause as part of the Bill of Rights for submission to the states, it enacted legislation providing for paid Chaplains for the House and Senate.

Burger also included in his list of government accommodations presidential proclamations of prayer and thanksgiving; government subsidization of religious holidays; our national motto "In God We Trust"; the inclusion of the phrase "one nation under God" in our Pledge; publicly supported art galleries that display artwork with religious themes; and the depiction of Moses with the Ten Commandments in the Supreme Court, among others. (The latter two issues would be litigated in the Supreme Court in 2000 and 2004, respectively, and are discussed in detail in chapter 9.)

The Supreme Court briefs filed in the *Lynch* case relied heavily on history to support the constitutionality of the practices. In pursuing these kinds of accommodations, Burger explained, "governmental action has '[followed] the best of our traditions' and '[respected] the religious nature of our people.'"

Burger proposed that this rich history of accommodations of religion "may help explain why the Court consistently has declined to take a rigid, absolutist view of the Establishment Clause." Historical evidence played a decisive role in Burger's decision in *Lynch* and other cases. Indeed, while Burger did apply the *Lemon* test in *Lynch*, he did so through the lens of the accommodationist history with which he began his opinion. It was on this historical evidence that his opinion ultimately hinged, not the *Lemon* test.

Burger's analysis of the secular purpose prong as applied to *Lynch* exemplified the importance of history to Burger's decision. He argued that the district court had "plainly erred" in ruling that the city's display had "no secular purpose" because the court failed to view the crèche "in the proper context of the Christmas Holiday season." He explained that the crèche was simply part of a display designed to celebrate a holiday that our country's civil institutions had officially recognized for over two hundred years.

Referring to the historical examples he had provided at the beginning of his opinion, Burger declared that the city of Pawtucket, "like the Congresses and Presidents, . . . has principally taken note of a significant historical religious event long celebrated in the Western World." He concluded that erecting a display "to celebrate the [Christmas] Holiday and to depict the origins of that Holiday" were "legitimate secular purposes."

Addressing the primary effect prong of *Lemon*, Burger argued that including a crèche in a Christmas display no more advanced religion than did the provision of free textbooks in *Board of Education v. Allen*, the reimbursement of bus fares in *Everson v. Board of Education*, the furnishing of construction grants in *Tilton v. Richardson*, or the bestowing of tax exemption on churches in *Walz v. Tax Comm'n*. He explained, "We are unable to discern a greater aid to religion deriving from inclusion of the crèche than from these benefits and endorsements previously held not violative of the Establishment Clause." Even more, if including a crèche in a Christmas display impermissibly advanced religion, Burger said the Court would have to "view it as more of an endorsement of religion than" Sunday closing laws, *Zorach*-like released-time programs, and legislative prayers. To Burger, such conclusions bordered on the ridiculous. Toward the conclusion of his opinion, Burger remarked:

> We are unable to perceive the Archbishop of Canterbury, the Bishop of Rome, or other powerful religious leaders behind every public acknowledgment of the religious heritage long officially recognized by the three constitutional branches of government. Any notion that these symbols [crèches] pose a real danger of establishment of a state church is farfetched indeed.

Burger's comments indicate that he did not suffer from the same suspicion of organized religion that some of his counterparts labored under. As to the third prong of *Lemon*, Burger affirmed the district court's finding that the inclusion of the crèche in the display did "not create excessive entanglement between religion and government."

Chief Justice Burger's concluding words in *Lynch* rested upon the history of governmental "acknowledgment . . . of the role of religion in American life":

> It would be ironic . . . if the inclusion of a single symbol of a particular historic religious event, as part of a celebration acknowledged in the Western World for 20 centuries, and in this country by the people, by the Executive Branch, by the Congress, and the courts for 2 centuries, would so "taint" the city's exhibit as to render it violative of the Establishment Clause. To forbid the use of this one passive symbol . . . would be a stilted overreaction contrary to our history and to our holdings. If the presence of the crèche in this display violates the Establishment Clause, a host of other forms of taking official note of Christmas, and of our religious heritage, are equally offensive to the Constitution.

From its very inception in *Walz* to its later formulation in *Lynch*, Burger emphasized the importance of our nation's historical traditions and practices in interpreting the religion clauses. Bruce Brown observed in his analysis of Burger's Establishment Clause opinions that the chief justice's reliance on "American history to determine whether particular governmental action respected an establishment of religion" was one of the major themes that dominated his Establishment Clause opinions.[32]

It should be recalled that in *Walz v. Tax Comm'n*, Burger depended heavily on our country's history of granting tax exemptions to churches to uphold the continuation of that practice in the face of an Establishment Clause challenge. Burger himself indirectly noted the consistency between his *Walz* and *Lynch* opinions when he quoted *Walz* to support his contention that the Court's less-than-rigid view of the Establishment Clause resulted from its refusal "'to construe the Religion Clauses with a literalness that would undermine the ultimate constitutional objective *as illuminated by history*'" [emphasis added].[33]

Chief Justice Burger presented his strongest case for accommodation of religion in *Wallace v. Jaffree*. In his dissenting opinion, he declared that the Court's decision striking down Alabama's minute of silence statute reflected "hostility toward religion." Borrowing the words of Justice Goldberg from *Schempp*, Burger said that the Court's decision evinced "a brooding and pervasive dedication to the secular and a passive, or even active, hostility to the religious." Writing with less decorum than one usually sees from the Supreme Court, Burger declared that "[t]he notion that the Alabama statute is a step toward creating an established church borders on, if is does not trespass into, the ridiculous." As he saw it, the statute "affirmatively furthers the values of religious freedom and tolerance" by accommodating "the purely private, voluntary religious choices of the individual pupils who wish to pray while at the same time creating a time for nonreligious reflection for those who do not choose to pray." Even more, the statute reinforced in the minds of children the "absolute constitutional right of each individual to worship and believe as the individual wishes." Burger favored the statute because it embraced the view that the "religious observances of others should be tolerated and, where possible, accommodated."

Brown observed that Burger's dissent in *Wallace* reflected "either a final evolution in Chief Justice Burger's Establishment Clause thinking or its most candid articulation."[34] Whichever it was, Burger's *Wallace* dissent leaves no doubt that he strongly favored accommodation between church and state wherever possible.

Other compelling evidence exists of Burger's preference for church-state accommodation. He quoted extensively from the Supreme Court's most ardently accommodationist opinion, *Zorach v. Clauson* (1952).[35] In *Walz v. Tax Comm'n*, for example, Burger favorably quoted Justice Douglas's *Zorach* opinion:

> In *Zorach v. Clauson*, after recalling that we "are a religious people whose institutions presuppose a Supreme Being," [Justice Douglas] went on to say:

"We make room for as wide a variety of beliefs and creeds as the spiritual needs of man deem necessary. . . . *When the state encourages religious instruction . . . it follows the best of our traditions.* For it then respects the religious nature of our people and accommodates the public service to their spiritual needs."[36]

Burger repeatedly quoted *Zorach*'s accommodationist language in his Establishment Clause opinions.[37]

Burger's critique of the test that he created should not be overlooked. For example, in *Wallace*, Burger asserted that the Court had "repeatedly cautioned that *Lemon* did not establish a rigid caliper capable of resolving every Establishment Clause issue, but that it sought only to provide 'signposts.'" And on one occasion, Burger went so far as to charge his colleagues with having an "obsession" with the test.

In addition to Burger's overall contributions to Establishment Clause jurisprudence, the chief justice also had a hand in developing the "private choice doctrine." This doctrine modified his approach in *Lemon*: Chief Justice Burger concluded that government funding of religious institutions would be constitutional if the choice as to funding actually vested in private individuals. Burger offered a concise articulation of his understanding of this doctrine in *Committee for Public Education and Religious Liberty v. Nyquist*:

While there is no straight line running through our decisions interpreting the Establishment and Free Exercise Clauses of the First Amendment, our cases do, it seems to me, lay down one solid, basic principle: that the Establishment Clause does not forbid governments, state or federal, to enact a program of general welfare under which benefits are distributed to private individuals, even though many of those individuals may elect to use those benefits in ways that "aid" religious instruction or worship.[38]

As he further explained, the Establishment Clause is not violated when a statute provides aid directly to individuals because it is ultimately the decision of those individuals, not the government, that results in public aid flowing to religious schools.

Burger's views regarding the private choice doctrine were grounded in his understanding of the relationship between the Establishment and Free Exercise Clauses. As he said in *Nyquist*,

The answer [to why the private choice doctrine is constitutional], I
believe, lies in the experienced judgment of various members of this
Court over the years that the balance between the policies of free exercise and establishment of religion tips in favor of the former when the
legislation moves away from direct aid to religious institutions and
takes on the character of general aid to individual families.

Burger's appreciation for the delicate balance that needed to be struck
between the Establishment and Free Exercise Clauses can be seen elsewhere in his opinions. In *Walz* he noted that "[t]he Court has struggled
to find a neutral course between the two Religion Clauses, both of which
are cast in absolute terms, and either of which, if expanded to a logical
extreme, would tend to clash with the other."

The private choice doctrine, to which Burger clearly subscribed, continues to influence Supreme Court decisions today. Most recently, the
Supreme Court evoked the private choice doctrine in *Zelman v. Simmons-
Harris* (2001) to uphold the state of Ohio's school-voucher program. Justice Rehnquist, writing for the *Zelman* majority, said,

> [W] here a government aid program is neutral with respect to religion,
> and provides assistance directly to a broad class of citizens who, in
> turn, direct government aid to religious schools wholly as a result of
> their own genuine and independent private choice, the program is not
> readily subject to challenge under the Establishment Clause. A pro-
> gram that shares these features permits government aid to reach reli-
> gious institutions only by way of the deliberate choices of numerous
> individual recipients. The incidental advancement of a religious mis-
> sion, or the perceived endorsement of a religious message, is reasonably
> attributable to the individual recipient, not to the government, whose
> role ends with the disbursement of benefits.[39]

Such a program of "true private choice," Chief Justice Rehnquist
said, has "never [been] found [by the Supreme Court] . . . to offend the
Establishment Clause." Rehnquist's description of the attributes of a program of "true private choice" was essentially a restatement of Burger's
articulation of the "one solid, basic principle" emanating from the Court's
Establishment Clause cases: that government aid that flows to religious
schools or institutions because of the choices of private individuals does
not violate the Constitution's prohibition against establishment of religion.[40]

Chief Justice Burger's writings both on and off the bench showed a healthy respect for the role of religion in the American experience. It can confidently be said that Chief Justice Burger left a lasting impression on Supreme Court Establishment Clause jurisprudence. His most conspicuous contribution, of course, was the *Lemon* test. This test has endured numerous assaults over the past thirty years, including from Burger himself, yet still looms large in the Establishment Clause context.

Burger's other, less recognized, yet no less important, contribution was the emphasis he placed on "the history of governmental acknowledgment and accommodation of religion in American life," and the important role that history should play in the interpretation of the First Amendment religion clauses. Burger's emphasis on history led him to oppose an absolutist approach to the Establishment Clause and advocate greater accommodation of church and state.

Chief Justice Burger clearly understood the important role that religious thought played in the development of the American Republic. This was reflected not only in the more than 250 opinions he authored but also in his off-the-Court statements as well. It is interesting that with regard to the specific issue of funding, Chief Justice Burger followed the Presbyterian view on the issue. However, when it came to the accommodation of religious practices by government, he clearly fell into the accommodationist model of church-state relations.

Chief Justice Warren Burger died on June 25, 1995, in Washington, D.C., from heart failure, and was buried in Arlington National Cemetery in Arlington, Virginia. Associate Justice Sandra Day O'Connor spoke at Chief Justice Burger's funeral, recalling that from her first day on the Court, he was "kind and considerate" to her. With admiration, she also observed that Chief Justice Burger "left his mark on every facet of our judicial system."

The legacy of Chief Justice Burger's *Lemon* test continues to draw criticism from members of the Court even today. The most stinging rebuke of the test came from the pen of Associate Justice Antonin Scalia in 1993, when he criticized the Court for applying *Lemon* to a First Amendment claim raised by a church that was denied access to church facilities. Although the Court was unanimous in concluding that the church's free speech rights were violated, to the displeasure of Scalia, Justice White applied *Lemon* to this case. Justice Scalia's response will probably go down in the annals of Supreme Court history as one of the most imaginative, humorous, and graphic reviews of *Lemon* ever to be offered to contemporary American audiences:

> Like some ghoul in a late-night horror movie that repeatedly sits up in its grave and shuffles abroad, after being repeatedly killed and buried, *Lemon* stalks our Establishment Clause jurisprudence once again, frightening the little children and school attorneys of Center Moriches Union Free School District. Its most recent burial, only last Term, was, to be sure, not fully six feet under: Our decision in *Lee v. Weisman* conspicuously avoided using the supposed "test" but also declined the invitation to repudiate it. Over the years, however, no fewer than five of the currently sitting Justices have, in their own opinions, personally driven pencils through the creature's heart (the author of today's opinion repeatedly), and a sixth has joined an opinion doing so.
>
> The secret of the *Lemon* test's survival, I think, is that it is so easy to kill. It is there to scare us (and our audience) when we wish it to do so, but we can command it to return to the tomb at will. When we wish to strike down a practice it forbids, we invoke it . . . when we wish to uphold a practice it forbids, we ignore it entirely. . . . Sometimes, we take a middle course, calling its three prongs "no more than helpful signposts" . . . Such a docile and useful monster is worth keeping around, at least in a somnolent state; one never knows when one might need him.

One of the most admirable aspects of Chief Justice Burger's tenure on the Supreme Court was his willingness to criticize tests that he had authored. This was certainly the case on the issue of the interpretation of the religion clauses.

NOTES

1. Title I of Elementary and Title I of Elementary and Secondary Education Act of 1965, 20 U.S.C. § 241a (LEXIS 2005) (repealed 1978).

2. *Wheeler v. Barrera*, 417 U.S. 402, 405 (1974).

3. *Board of Education v. Allen*, 392 U.S. 236, 238–39 (1968). All subsequent quotations from *Allen* are based on this reference.

4. Rhode Island Salary Supplement Act, 1969 R.I. Pub. Law 246.

5. *Hunt v. McNair*, 177 S.E.2d 362, 36364 (1970).

6. *Levitt v. Comm. for Pub. Educ. & Religious Liberty*, 413 U.S. 472, 474–76 (1973).

7. Md. Code Ann., Educ. § 17-101 (LEXIS 2005).

8. *Americans United for Separation of Church & State v. Oakey,* 339 F. Supp. 545, 546–48 (D. Vt. 1972).

9. *Lemon v. Kurtzman,* 403 U.S. 602 (1971). All subsequent quotations of *Lemon* are based on this reference.

10. *Resolution on Church–State Separation,* Southern Baptist Convention, June 1969; available at http://www.sbc.net.

11. Harry A. Blackmun, "A Tribute to Warren E. Burger," *Wm. Mitchell L. Rev.* 22 (1996): 15.

12. Tinsley E. Yarbrough, *The Burger Court: Justices, Rulings, and Legacy* (Santa Barbara, Calif.: ABC-CLIO, 2000), 78.

13. The biographical sketch of Warren Burger is based on Donn McLellan, "Biographical Profile," *Wm. Mitchell L. Rev.* 22 (1996): 3; James L. Volling, "Warren E. Burger: An Independent Pragmatist Remembered," *Wm. Mitchell L. Rev.* 22 (1996): 40; and Douglas D. McFarland, "Chief Justice Warren E. Burger: A Personal Tribute," *Hamline L. Rev.* 19 (1995): 2.

14. Charles M. Lamb, "Chief Justice Warren E. Burger," in *The Burger Court: Political and Judicial Profiles* (Urbana: University of Illinois Press, 1991), 130; quoting *Public Papers of the Presidents of the United States: Richard M. Nixon* (Washington, D.C.: U.S. Government Printing Office, 1971), 396.

15. All quotations from the speech are from Warren E. Burger, *The Constitution and Religion* (Washington, D.C.: Commission on the Bicentennial of the United States Constitution, 1990). See also Warren E. Burger, "We The People," *Case W. Res. L. Rev.* 37 (1987): 385: "My thesis is that the Declaration of Independence first, and then its articulation and implementation in the Constitution and the Bill of Rights, operated to release—to unleash—the talents, the energies, the abilities of a whole people in a way that had never before occurred in human history." It seems Chief Justice Burger was destined for his position as chairman of the Bicentennial Commission, because he shared his birthday with the birth of our nation: on September 17, 1987, when the Constitution turned two hundred, Warren Burger turned eighty. Cannon, "A Tribute to Chief Justice Warren E. Burger," 987.

16. *McDaniel v. Paty,* 435 U.S. 618 (1978); *Marsh v. Chambers,* 463 U.S. 783 (1983); and *Wisconsin v. Yoder,* 406 U.S. 205 (1972). All subsequent quotations from *Marsh* are based on its case reference cited here.

17. Mark DeWolfe Howe, *Cases on Church and State in the United States* (Cambridge, Mass.: Harvard University Press, 1952), 5.

18. United Presbyterian Church in the USA, *Relationships between Church and State in the United States of America* (Philadelphia: United Presbyterian Church in the USA, 1963), 4, 7.

19. See *Larkin v. Grendel's Den,* 459 U.S. 116 (1982); see also *Estate of Thornton v. Caldor,* 472 U.S. 703 (1985).

20. Alton Lemon, "Lemon Plaintiff, Out of Limelight, Still Tracks Church-State Issues," interview by David L. Hudson Jr., *First Amendment Center* (19 May 2004); full text available at http://www.firstamendmentcenter.org.

21. *Lemon v. Kurtzman*, All subsequent quotations from *Lemon* are based on this case citation.

22. *Tilton v. Richardson*, 403 U.S. 672 (1971). All subsequent quotations from *Tilton* are based on this case citation.

23. Bruce P. Brown, "The Establishment Clause Jurisprudence of Chief Justice Warren E. Burger," *Okla. L. Rev.* 45 (1992): 44. Brown clerked for Chief Justice Burger in 1985.

24. *Walz v. Tax Comm'n*, 397 U.S. 664 (1970). All subsequent quotations from *Walz* are based on this case citation.

25. Joseph F. Kobylka, "Leadership on the Supreme Court of the United States: Chief Justice Burger and the Establishment Clause," *W. Pol. Q.* 42 (1989): 552.

26. *Wallace v. Jaffree*, 472 U.S. 38 (1985).

27. *Aguilar v. Felton*, 473 U.S. 402 (1985).

28. *Lynch v. Donnelly*, 465 U.S. 668, 679 (1984).

29. Volling, "A Pragmatist Remembered," 60; Kobylka, "Chief Justice Burger and the Establishment Clause," 560; Brown, "The Establishment Clause Jurisprudence," 56.

30. Brown, "The Establishment Clause Jurisprudence," 50.

31. Kenneth F. Ripple, "In Memoriam: Warren E. Burger," *Harv. L. Rev.* 109 (1995): 7.

32. Brown, "The Establishment Clause Jurisprudence," 39.

33. *Lynch*, 678; quoting *Walz*, 671.

34. Brown, "The Establishment Clause Jurisprudence," 55.

35. *Zorach v. Clauson*, 343 U.S. 306 (1952). All subsequent quotations from *Zorach* are based on this case citation.

36. *Walz*, 672; quoting *Zorach*, 313–14 (emphasis added by Burger).

37. See *Meek v. Pittenger*, 421 U.S. 349, 386–87 (1975) (Burger, C.J., dissenting); see also *Marsh*, 792; *Lynch*, 673–75; *Aguilar*, 420 (Burger, C.J., dissenting).

38. *Committee for Pub. Educ. and Religious Liberty v. Nyquist*, 413 U.S. 756 (1973) (Burger, C.J., dissenting). All subsequent quotations from *Nyquist* are based on this case citation.

39. *Zelman v. Simmons-Harris*, 536 U.S. 639 (2001).

40. Burger viewed *Everson* (1947), *Allen* (1968), and *Quick Bear v. Leupp*, 210 U.S. 50 (1908), as prime examples of the application of the private choice doctrine. *Nyquist*, 799–802.

· 9 ·

Coming Full Circle

[N]othing in the Constitution as interpreted by this Court prohibits any public school student from voluntarily praying at any
time before, during, or after the schoolday.

—Justice John Paul Stevens
Santa Fe v. Doe, 2000

$\mathcal{I}$n the last decade, the Supreme Court has engaged the issue of church-
state relations more significantly than at any time since the school prayer
decision of the 1960s. Since 1990, in the context of America's public
schools, the Court has addressed prayer and Bible clubs, churches utiliz-
ing school facilities for its meetings, and prayer and Bible study groups
meeting in elementary schools. The Court has also delved back into the
issue that divided the country in the 1880s concerning the Blaine Amendment. As you will recall, this amendment prohibited states from funding
sectarian education in the school setting. In addition to the Blaine
Amendment cases, the Supreme Court has also reviewed the constitutionality of the posting of the Ten Commandments in public parks and
courthouses, as well as the constitutionality of the phrase "under God" in
the Pledge of Allegiance. The Court even found itself in the extraordinary
circumstance of having to determine the constitutionality of the phrase
"so help me God," which has been included in the oath of office by every
president since George Washington.

NEW PERSPECTIVES: THE
DENOMINATIONS, THE CONGRESS, THE
COURT, AND THE CATHOLICS

In the 1980s, a significant change occurred at the Supreme Court, in
Congress, and among the most prominent of the denominational voices,

the Southern Baptists, concerning issues of religious liberty and church-state separation. Specifically, by 1982 the conservatives within the Southern Baptists had gained control of the important committees and seminaries. This evidenced a significant shift in its stand on church-state separation. While the other denominations continued to back a strict version of separation of church and state, the Southern Baptists actually backed a constitutional amendment calling for voluntary school prayer.

Attempts to obtain the constitutional amendment for voluntary prayer in school continued to fail in Congress. Momentum was building, however, for a congressional response to perceived hostility toward religion in America's public schools. Such hostility was reflected in actual cases that were presented to Congress where student groups were denied access to public schools for after-school prayer and Bible club meetings. The Court's application of *Lemon* in a rigid, formulistic manner consistently resulted in their declaring unconstitutional any religious expression in the public school context, including after-school, student-led prayer, and Bible study groups.

Ten years after *Lemon*, the American Baptist Convention (formerly the Northern Baptist Convention) weighed in on the perennial issue of public funds flowing to religious schools. At their 1981 meeting, they passed a resolution affirming "that separation of church and state is central to our American heritage; that it has made possible a measure of freedom not previously achieved under any other system; that it is indispensable to our national policy of equal rights for all religions and special privileges for no religion."[1] This principle led the American Baptists to "object strenuously . . . to any proposal that taxes or borrowing power be used to make grants or loans to sectarian or church-related schools. We emphasize that the use of government finances in support of any sectarian purpose is a violation of basic religious liberties."

The Episcopal Church continued to focus on the practice of school prayer, which was still observed in many southern states, even though it had been declared unconstitutional twenty years earlier. The denomination denounced legislation aimed at permitting the government to compose or prescribe prayer in the public schools. In 1981, the church stated, "It is not and should not be the business of government to establish when people shall pray or the prayers which they shall use."[2] Accordingly, the church expressed strong opposition to "all government legislation which would prescribe means or methods of prayer in public schools or which is designed to encourage local authorities to prescribe such means or methods of prayer."

While the Episcopalians and American Baptists continued to maintain strict separation of church and state, the Southern Baptist Convention began a dramatic move concerning church-state relations. In fact, in a meeting in New Orleans, Louisiana, in 1982, at the height of a conservative shift in the Southern Baptist Convention, the denomination reversed its previous resolutions and called for a constitutional amendment to allow voluntary prayer in public schools. A detailed review of the resolution demonstrates clearly the significant change that occurred in the Southern Baptist Convention.

> WHEREAS, The first amendment to the Constitution of the United States of America clearly states that the Congress shall pass no law prohibiting the free exercise of religion, and

> WHEREAS, The same first amendment protects us against the establishment of religion, and

> WHEREAS, A constitutional amendment is pending wherein there is no violation of either of those ideals inherent in the separation of church and state, and

> WHEREAS, This proposed amendment neither requires nor restricts the vocal expression of individual or group prayer in public schools, and

> WHEREAS, Considerable confusion as to the rights and privileges guaranteed by the Constitution with regard to prayer in schools has been engendered by the Supreme Court decisions of 1962 and 1963, and

> WHEREAS, Public school officials and lower courts have frequently misinterpreted these Supreme Court decisions as a ban on voluntary prayer, and

> WHEREAS, For 170 years following the writing of the First Amendment, the right of prayer in public schools was a time-honored exercise and a cherished privilege, and

WHEREAS, Southern Baptists historically have affirmed the right of voluntary prayer in public places, and

WHEREAS, The proposed constitutional amendment reads simply, "Nothing in this Constitution shall be construed to prohibit individual or group prayer in public schools or other public institutions. No person shall be required by the United States or by any state to participate in prayer," and

WHEREAS, This proposed amendment does not constitute a call for government-written or government-mandated prayer.

Therefore, be it RESOLVED, That we the messengers of the Southern Baptist Convention in session, June 1982, New Orleans, Louisiana, declare our support of the aforementioned proposed constitutional amendment.[3]

Subsequent resolutions of the Southern Baptist Convention demonstrate a continued commitment to religious liberty but diminished concern over maintaining strict separation between church and state. At their meeting in Pittsburgh, Pennsylvania, in 1983, the Baptists passed a resolution on religious liberty that failed even to mention the concept of separation, instead choosing to discuss neutrality toward religion.[4] The Pittsburgh resolution did reiterate the denomination's concern over the use of public funds for religious purposes, yet objected to this practice in far less strident terms than in earlier resolutions.[5]

Although the Baptists' attempt to obtain a voluntary school prayer amendment failed, they were successful along with others in advocating for the Equal Access Act, which passed in 1984 with wide bipartisan support. For the first time in its history, Congress authorized prayer and Bible clubs to meet in our nation's public schools. This statute and the subsequent cases that interpreted it served as a marked departure from the Supreme Court's previous view of church-state relations within the public school context. Most importantly, Justice Sandra Day O'Connor, in her opinion in *Board of Education v. Mergens* (1990), which affirmed the constitutionality of the Equal Access Act, recognized that "there is a crucial difference between government speech endorsing religion, which the Establishment Clause forbids, and private speech endorsing religion, which the Free Speech and Free Exercise Clauses protect."[6] This was precisely the legal position advocated by the Southern Baptist Convention in its 1982 resolutions. It also focused on the Free Speech Clause rather than the Establishment Clause of the First Amendment.

What also became apparent was a thawing in the relationship between the Southern Baptists and the Catholic Church. While in 1986 and 1993 the Baptists again called on the United States to cease diplomatic relations with the Vatican, they also expressed an appreciation for the Catholic Church in the area of social, moral, and policy issues and their desire to work together in these areas of agreement.[7]

The shift to a free speech analysis in religious cases marked a significant change in litigation strategy. Free exercise cases, by and large, were not given a positive reception by the Supreme Court. By the early 1980s, a change in litigation strategy began to occur, relying on the argument that religious speech was protected under the First Amendment's Free Speech Clause. In fact, in 1981, the Supreme Court in *Widmar v. Vincent* held that religious prayer and worship on college campuses were "forms of speech and association protected by the First Amendment."[8] This position was later applied to the high schools in two significant Supreme Court cases, *Mergens* and *Lamb's Chapel.*[9] This same free speech principle was also applied to the elementary schools in *Good News Club v. Milford Central School* (2001).[10] Even in the Supreme Court's most recent school prayer case, *Santa Fe v. Doe* (2000), while striking down the school district's policy, Justice John Paul Stevens, nevertheless, noted that there is "nothing in the Constitution as interpreted by this Court" that "prohibits any public school student from voluntarily praying at any time before, during, or after the schoolday."[11] This was a marked departure from the prohibition of school prayer in the 1960s.

COLLEGES AND UNIVERSITIES:
WIDMAR V. VINCENT (1981)

In the late 1970s, a Christian group at the University of Missouri called "Cornerstone" sought to have prayer and Bible study meetings on campus. Their request was denied by university officials, citing church-state separation concerns. The case reached the Supreme Court of the United States in 1981, and the Court held that when colleges allow student groups to use their facilities, they could not discriminate against student religious groups. In other words, Christian students have to be allowed to use a meeting room on campus with the same rights and privileges that are applied to any other student group. The Court further held that the Establishment Clause of the First Amendment was not violated when a government entity, such as a public university, treats all groups the same, without attempting to censor religious speech. In essence, the Supreme Court in an 8–1 decision held that there was not a religious speech exception to the First Amendment of the United States Constitution.

HIGH SCHOOLS: CONGRESS PASSES THE EQUAL ACCESS ACT (1984); *BOARD OF EDUCATION V. MERGENS,* SUPREME COURT DECISION (1990)

In 1984, fifteen-year-old Bridget Mergens was denied the right to form a Bible club at her Nebraska high school. The principal denied Bridget's request on the basis of church-state separation. After an unsuccessful attempt to have the request granted by the school board, Bridget went to federal court, arguing that her right to form a Bible club was protected by both the Free Speech Clause and the Equal Access Act that had been passed by Congress the year before her litigation commenced.

The Equal Access Act, which was passed with wide bipartisan support, was intended to address the perceived widespread discrimination against religious groups and religious speech in our nation's public schools. In fact, in upholding the act, the Supreme Court harkened back to *Lemon* and concluded that "Congress' avowed purpose—to prevent discrimination against religious and other speech—is undeniably secular." It was the Southern Baptist Convention, along with members of Congress, who backed what was known as the "Equal Access Act."[12]

So significant was the shift in the litigation strategy that, when one looks at the briefs filed on behalf of Bridget Mergens, a fascinating alignment develops. The Baptist Joint Committee on Public Affairs, which was founded by the Southern Baptist Convention immediately after the Supreme Court's decision in *Everson* and which advocated a strict version of separation of church and state, joined with the Catholic League for Religious Civil Rights and the Christian Legal Society in support of allowing prayer and Bible clubs to meet on our nation's public school campuses. In addition to the United States Department of Justice, the Knights of Columbus, and the United States Catholic Conference also filed briefs in favor of religious expression in the public schools. This case marked a significant change in the working relationship between Protestants and Catholics in the United States. Some 150 years after the Supreme Court's decision in *Vidal*, for the first time, Catholic legal groups, the United States Catholic Conference, and evangelical organizations like Campus Crusade for Christ joined together to defend religious expression in the public schools. At long last, the Bible wars in America were over.

Opposing the Equal Access Act was the American Jewish Congress, People for the American Way, Anti-Defamation League, the National School Board Association, and Americans United for Separation of Church and State. This was also the first case in which a split in legal position took place between the Baptist Joint Committee on Public Affairs and Americans United for Separation of Church and State. As noted in previous chapters, these two organizations had worked very closely together for over fifty years.

While the United States Supreme Court in *Mergens* still applied the *Lemon* test, the Court had no problem dismissing the arguments made by the school board concerning the act's constitutionality. Justice O'Connor noted in her opinion that "if a state refused to let religious groups use the facilities open to others, then it would demonstrate not neutrality but hostility toward religion. The Establishment Clause does not license government to treat religion and those who teach or practice it, simply by virtue of their status as such, as subversive of American ideals and therefore subject to unique disabilities."

CHURCH UTILIZATION OF SCHOOL FACILITIES: *LAMB'S CHAPEL V. CENTER MORICHES UNION FREE SCHOOL DISTRICT* (1993)

As cases continued to develop in the 1990s, the Supreme Court again tackled the issue of religious expression in the public-school context in the *Lamb's Chapel v. Center Moriches Union Free School District* case.[13] A small evangelical church on Long Island requested access to a high school in the Center Moriches School District in order to show a film series on raising children. The school district denied a request to use the facility because the film series was from a "Christian perspective." The Supreme Court in *Lamb's Chapel* was unanimous in declaring that the prohibition targeting religious groups for exclusion from school facilities in the evenings was unconstitutional.

Similar to the *Mergens* case, another fascinating alignment developed at the Supreme Court in *Lamb's Chapel*. Briefs filed on behalf of the church included the United States Department of Justice, the American Civil Liberties Union, the AFL-CIO, the Christian Legal Society, and the National Jewish Commission on Law and Policy. The Court held that under the First Amendment, the church was entitled to access. Justice Byron White, writing for the Court, noted that "the government violates the First Amendment when it denies access to a speaker solely to suppress a point of view he espouses on an otherwise includible subject."

Justice Anthony Kennedy, in his concurring opinion, thought that the *Lemon* test should not have even been addressed. He wrote that "[g]iven the issues presented, as well as the apparent unanimity of our conclusion that this overt, viewpoint-based discrimination contradicts the Speech Clause of the First Amendment and that there has been no substantial showing of a potential Establishment Clause violation, I agree with Justice Scalia that the Court's citation of *Lemon v. Kurtzman* is unsettling and unnecessary."

A NEW MILLENNIUM: BACK TO THE FUTURE OF RELIGIOUS FREEDOM IN AMERICA

At the turn of the new millennium, some 160 years after Justice Story's opinion in *Vidal v. Girard*, the Court has once again found itself engaged in religion cases which have had significant impact on the citizenry. Interestingly, the Court has increasingly relied on its view of American history to support its judicial decisions. Two cases have arisen out of the U.S. Court of Appeals for the Ninth Circuit that have received a great deal of attention.

In October 2003, the Court decided to review a case involving the constitutionality of the phrase "under God" as contained in the Pledge of Allegiance. Without much fanfare, the U.S. Court of Appeals for the Ninth Circuit had previously struck the Pledge as violating church-state separation. The decision out of the Ninth Circuit declaring the Pledge unconstitutional garnered a firestorm of protests throughout the country. The second case out of the Ninth Circuit delved into history that we have covered at length in this book. The Court was called upon in 2004 to review a Blaine-like state constitutional amendment passed in 1889, prohibiting scholarships to students who desired to obtain an education preparing them for the ministry. (The full details of these cases are presented below.)

The very next year after deciding the Pledge and scholarship cases, the Court dove headfirst back into two major cases involving icons of law: the Ten Commandments and the phrase "so help me God," which is rendered at the presidential swearing-in as part of the oath of office. The challenge to the oath of office and the inaugural prayer was brought by the same party who challenged the Pledge of Allegiance. Dr. Michael Newdow, a medical doctor, lawyer, and self-avowed atheist, brought his request for injunctive relief that went from the United States District Court in Washington, D.C., to the Supreme Court of the United States in a matter of days just prior to the inauguration of President George W. Bush on January 20, 2005.

These cases collectively thrust the Court once more into raging debates on the proper role of the acknowledgment of religion by government. The history of our country, the thoughts of the Founders, and the views of the early justices of the Supreme Court of the United States all played a significant role in the outcome of each of these cases. An onslaught of aggressive litigation by groups like the American Civil Liberties Union (ACLU), People for the American Way, and Americans United for Separation of Church and State brought these cases to the forefront of national attention.

THE SCHOLARSHIP CASE: *LOCKE V. DAVEY* (2004)

In *Locke v. Davey*, the Supreme Court was faced with a free exercise challenge to a state statute that authorized scholarship funds to students with high grade point averages who could also establish economic need.[14] Joshua Davey qualified for the scholarship. Any student receiving a Promise Scholarship could utilize the approximately $2000-per-year fund to attend any accredited college or university in the state of Washington. Religiously affiliated colleges and universities, so long as they were accredited, also qualified as a recipient university. Students were allowed to major in any subject matter taught at such a college except theology taught from a religious perspective. For instance, students could attend state universities and major in theology and qualify for the Promise Scholarship. However, students like Joshua Davey, who attended Northwest College, a sectarian university, would not be able to obtain Promise Scholarship funds if he majored in theology taught from a religious perspective.

The prohibition on obtaining a degree in theology taught from a religious perspective was based upon a provision of the Washington State Constitution dating back to 1889. This constitutional provision, modeled after the Blaine Amendment (see chapter 4), was a requirement for statehood. Washington State's Blaine Amendment had been authoritatively interpreted by the Washington Supreme Court as prohibiting public funds to be utilized in any manner if the student was majoring in theology that was being taught from a religious perspective. The Ninth Circuit Court of Appeals ruled in favor of Joshua Davey and found that his free exercise rights had been violated. The Supreme Court, after granting review, reversed the decision of the lower court.

Chief Justice William Rehnquist, in his opinion, also relied on a view of history in supporting the state of Washington's ability to disqualify a theology student from obtaining scholarship funds. The chief justice acknowledged that "there is no doubt that the State could, consistent with the Federal Constitution, permit Promise Scholars to pursue a degree in devotional theology." The issue before the Court was "whether Washington, pursuant to its own constitution, which has been authoritatively interpreted as prohibiting even indirectly funding religious instruction that will prepare students for the ministry, can deny them such funding without violating the Free Exercise Clause."

The chief justice approached this case with his view of American history as the overriding principle. He concluded his opinion by noting that "[s]ince the founding of our country, there have been popular uprisings against procuring taxpayer funds to support church leaders, which was one of the hallmarks of an 'established' religion." The reference to the "popular uprisings" in the chief justice's analysis was based, in part, on the riots that took place in New York and Philadelphia concerning both the use of the Bible in public schools and the proposed use of funding sectarian education, specifically Catholic schools, advocated by the archbishops of New York City and Philadelphia.

In *Locke v. Davey*, the history issue was very contentious among members of the Court. The historical analysis provided by the chief justice served as the basis for the Court's opinion denying Joshua Davey's claim of a free exercise violation. Chief Justice Rehnquist is a Lutheran. The Lutheran Church had been on record since the 1950s as formally opposing "the use of public funds for the support of private parochial schools."[15]

Justice Antonin Scalia, a Roman Catholic, took issue with the chief justice's view of history. It will be recalled, as discussed in chapter 1, that the Roman Catholic bishops in New York and Philadelphia requested funding for parochial school education as early as the 1840s. Also, the aid program in *Lemon* was primarily benefiting parochial schools. Justice Scalia noted that "the Court's reference to historical popular uprising against procuring taxpayer funds to support church leaders is quite misplaced. That history involved not the inclusion of religious ministers in public benefit programs like the one at issue here, but laws that singled them out for financial aid." In fact, Justice Scalia went further in challenging the chief justice's view of history:

> Equally misplaced is the Court's reliance on founding-era state constitutional provisions that prohibited the use of tax funds to support the ministry. There is no doubt what these provisions were directed against: measures of the sort discussed earlier in the text, singling out the clergy for public support. The Court offers no historical support for the proposition that they were meant to exclude clergymen from general benefits available to all citizens.

It is not simply history that controls but, rather, the individual Supreme Court justices' view of American history that has had the overreaching impact. The use of history as a basis upon which Establishment and Free Exercise Clause cases are decided has now become the major theme in the Supreme Court's opinions. If history supports a particular practice, it is deemed to be constitutional. If there is no historical support for a given practice, it is declared unconstitutional. The historical ghost of the Blaine Amendment lives on in Supreme Court opinions some 130 years after they were introduced and with the same force and effect.

"ONE NATION UNDER GOD," THE PLEDGE OF ALLEGIANCE CASE: *ELK GROVE UNIFIED SCHOOL DISTRICT V. NEWDOW* (2004)

Medical doctor and lawyer Michael Newdow filed the challenge to the California statute authorizing the recitation of the Pledge of Allegiance because it contained the phrase "under God."[16] The original Pledge did not contain "under God" in the text. It was an act of Congress passed in 1954 that called for the inclusion of the phrase "one Nation under God." It was the view of Congress that the phrase needed to be inserted into our Pledge of Allegiance in order to draw a distinction between the United States's view of liberty and that of the Soviet Union. The Founders believed that freedom and liberty derived from the Creator to mankind. Thus, government could not take away the inalienable rights of life, liberty, and the pursuit of happiness. In contrast, the Soviet government believed that all rights derived from the state; and, therefore, the state could take them away. Although there had been several challenges to the Pledge of Allegiance over the past fifty years, none reached the high court until 2004.

It was Chief Justice Warren Burger who prophetically noted in 1985 the dangers posed by an absolutist interpretation of the Establishment Clause. In his dissent in *Wallace v. Jaffree,* Chief Justice Burger addressed specifically the issue of the constitutionality of the phrase "under God" as contained in the Pledge of Allegiance. Justice Burger wrote: "Congress amended the statutory Pledge of Allegiance 31 years ago to add the words 'under God.' Do the several opinions in support of the judgment today render the Pledge unconstitutional?"[17]

The government asserted that history controlled the case and supported the constitutionality of the phrase "under God." The phrase accurately reflects the historical fact that this nation was founded upon a belief in God. The Founders of this nation based a national philosophy on a belief in a Deity. The Declaration of Independence and the Bill of Rights locate inalienable rights in a Creator rather than in government, precisely so that such rights cannot be stripped away by government.[18] The Declaration of Independence recognizes that human liberties are a gift from God: "All men are created equal, that they are endowed by *their Creator* with certain unalienable Rights" [emphasis added]. In 1782, Thomas Jefferson wrote: "Can the liberties of a nation be thought secure when we have removed their only firm basis, a conviction in the minds of the people that these liberties are the gift of God? That they are not to be violated but with His wrath?"[19]

The Father of the Country, George Washington, used the phrase "under God" in several of his orders to the Continental Army. On one occasion he wrote: "The fate of unborn millions will now depend, under God, on the courage and conduct of this army."[20] Also, at other times during the Revolutionary War, Washington encouraged his army by declaring that "the peace and safety of this country depends, under God, solely on the success of our arms."[21]

Washington routinely acknowledged the role of Divine Providence in the nation's affairs. His first inaugural address is replete with references to God, including thanksgivings and supplications. He wrote that "[n]o people can be bound to acknowledge and adore the Invisible Hand which conducts the affairs of men more than those of the United States."[22] In Washington's Proclamation of a Day of National Thanksgiving, he wrote that it is the "duty of all nations to acknowledge the providence of Almighty God, to obey His will, to be grateful for His benefits, and humbly to implore His protection and favor."[23] The Founders may have differed over the contours of the relationship between religion and government, but they never deviated from the conviction that "there was a necessary and valuable moral connection between the two."[24] Thus, the phrase, "one nation under God" in the Pledge of Allegiance simply describes an indisputable historical fact.

As we have discussed elsewhere in this book, the Court has recognized the primacy of religion in the nation's heritage. In *Zorach v. Clauson* (1952), Justice Douglas wrote that "[w]e are a religious people whose institutions presuppose a Supreme Being."[25] Often overlooked in Justice Douglas's opinion in *Zorach* is where he focused on the importance of accommodating religious practices and beliefs:

> When the state encourages religious instruction or cooperates with religious authorities by adjusting the schedule of public events to sectarian needs, it follows the best of our traditions. For it then respects the religious nature of our people and accommodates the public service to their spiritual needs. To hold that it may not would be to find in the Constitution a requirement that the government show a callous indifference to religious groups. *That would be preferring those who believe in no religion over those who do believe.* [emphasis added]

In every instance in which the Court or individual justices have addressed patriotic exercises with religious references, including the Pledge of Allegiance, they have concluded unequivocally that those references pose no Establishment Clause problems. No member of the Court, past or current, has suggested otherwise. To the contrary, recognizing that certain of its precedents may create the impression that patriotic exercises with religious references would be constitutionally suspect, the Court has taken pains to assure that that is not the case.

Even in the school prayer cases, the Supreme Court has consistently distinguished between religious exercises, such as prayer and Bible reading, and patriotic exercises with religious references. In *Engel v. Vitale* (1962), which struck down New York State's law requiring school officials to open the school day with prayer, this Court explained:

> There is of course nothing in the decision reached here that is inconsistent with the fact that school children and others are officially encouraged to express love for our country by reciting historical documents such as the Declaration of Independence which contain references to the Deity or by singing officially espoused anthems which include the composer's professions of faith in a Supreme Being, or with the fact that there are many manifestations in our public life of belief in God. Such patriotic or ceremonial occasions bear no true resemblance to the unquestioned *religious exercise* that the State of New York has sponsored in this instance.[26] [emphasis added]

Justice William Brennan expressly opined in *Schempp* that although Bible reading and prayer at the commencement of the school day were unconstitutional, "reciting the pledge may be no more of a religious exercise than the reading aloud of Lincoln's Gettysburg Address, which contains an allusion to the same historical fact."[27] Again, Justice Kennedy in *Lee v. Weisman*, while striking down a school policy allowing for prayer to be given at a graduation ceremony, nevertheless pointed to the dangers of an attempt to remove references to the religious heritage of America:

> Our society would be less than true to its heritage if it lacked abiding concern for the values of its young people, and we acknowledge the profound belief of adherents to many faiths that there must be a place in the student's life for precepts of a morality higher even than the law we today enforce. We express no hostility to those aspirations, nor would our oath permit us to do so. A relentless and all-pervasive attempt to exclude religion from every aspect of public life could itself become inconsistent with the Constitution. We recognize that, at graduation time and throughout the course of the educational process, there will be instances when religious values, religious practices, and religious persons will have some interaction with the public schools and their students.[28]

In 1984, in *Lynch v. Donnelly*, while declaring a nativity scene display in a city park constitutional, the Supreme Court also recognized the "unbroken history of official acknowledgment by all three branches of government of the role of religion in American life."[29] "Our history is replete with official references to the value and invocation of Divine guidance in deliberations and pronouncements of the Founding Fathers and contemporary leaders." The Court listed many examples of our "government's acknowledgment of our religious heritage," and included among those examples Congress's addition of the words "under God" to the Pledge of Allegiance in 1954.

> [E]xamples of reference to our religious heritage are found in the statutorily prescribed national motto "In God We Trust," which Congress and the President mandated for our currency, and in the language "one nation under God," as part of the Pledge of Allegiance to the American flag. That pledge is recited by many thousands of public school children—and adults—every year.

In *Wallace* (1985), although striking down on church-state separation grounds Alabama's moment of silence law, Justice O'Connor stated explicitly that the words "under God" in the Pledge do not violate the Constitution because they "serve as an acknowledgment of religion with 'the legitimate secular purpose of solemnizing public occasions, and expressing confidence in the future.'"

In *Allegheny County v. American Civil Liberties Union* (1989), even Justices Blackmun, Marshall, Brennan, and Stevens, who supported a strict separation of church and state model, stated:

> Our previous opinions have considered in dicta the motto and the pledge, characterizing them as consistent with the proposition that government may not communicate an endorsement of religious belief. We need not return to the subject of "ceremonial deism" . . . because there is an obvious distinction between crèche displays and references to God in the motto and the pledge.[30]

The First Amendment does not compel the redaction of all references to God in the Pledge of Allegiance, patriotic music, and foundational documents just to suit atheistic preferences, even when such materials are taught in the public schools. If a public school district violated the Establishment Clause by requiring teachers to lead students in the voluntary recitation of the Pledge of Allegiance, it is difficult to conceive of a rationale by which compulsory study or recitation from the nation's founding documents would not also violate the Constitution. The Mayflower Compact and the Declaration of Independence contain religious references substantiating the fact that America's "institutions presuppose a Supreme Being."[31] Similarly, Lincoln's 1863 Gettysburg Address, though not a founding document, contains religious language and, historically, has been the subject of required recitations in public schools. President Lincoln declared "that this Nation, *under God*, shall have a new birth of freedom—and that Government of the people, by the people, for the people, shall not perish from the earth" [emphasis added].[32] Interestingly, transcriptions of the address, as given, include the phrase "under God," while earlier written drafts omit the phrase. Lincoln's inclusion of the phrase in his address is thoroughly consistent with his conviction, shared with Washington and Jefferson, that Divine Providence played an essential role in the rise of the nation.

Although the Ninth Circuit Court of Appeals answered Chief Justice Burger's question in *Wallace* in the affirmative by declaring the phrase "under God" unconstitutional, the Supreme Court reversed. Justice Sandra Day O'Connor placed great emphasis on the history of the founding of America in concluding that the Pledge of Allegiance with the phrase "under God" is constitutional. She wrote: "It is unsurprising that a Nation founded by religious refugees and dedicated to religious freedom should find references to divinity in its symbols, songs, mottoes, and oaths. Eradicating such references would sever ties to a history that sustains this Nation even today."

Justice O'Connor's reliance on history in her 2004 *Newdow* opinion is significant. Writing as to the importance of religious references, Justice O'Connor noted specifically that they serve valuable purposes in public life: "[S]uch references serve, in the only ways reasonably possible in our culture, the legitimate secular purposes of solemnizing public occasions, expressing confidence in the future, and encouraging the recognition of what is worthy of appreciation in society. For centuries, we have marked important occasions or pronouncements with references to God and invocations of divine assistance."

Justice O'Connor's reliance on history expressed in her opinion is significant concerning the role of religion in America's public life: "Certain ceremonial references to God and religion in our Nation are the inevitable consequence of the religious history that gave birth to our founding principles of liberty. It would be ironic indeed if this Court were to wield our constitutional commitment to religious freedom so as to sever our ties to the traditions developed to honor it."

While the majority of the Court did not reach the substantive Establishment Clause issue in the case, Justice O'Connor's analysis provides an important historical framework to evaluate further inevitable challenges to the Pledge of Allegiance.

PRESIDENTIAL OATH CASE "SO HELP ME GOD" AND INAUGURAL PRAYER: *NEWDOW V. GEORGE W. BUSH* (2005)

Days before the inauguration of President George W. Bush on January 20, 2005, Dr. Michael Newdow filed a challenge to the administration of the oath of office because of the inclusion of the phrase "so help me God" and raised concerns over the inclusion of the inaugural prayer, specifically because it referenced Jesus. Dr. Newdow is the same medical doctor and lawyer who brought the challenge to the Pledge of Allegiance. The oath of office as set forth in the United States Constitution does not actually include the phrase "so help me God." The oath reads: "I do solemnly swear (or affirm) that I will faithfully execute the office of President of the United States, and will to the best of my ability, preserve, protect and defend the Constitution of the United States."[33] However, every president, including George Washington, has utilized the phrase "so help me God," and it has become part of the ceremonial references of presidential inaugurals.

In his first inaugural address, President Washington proclaimed that "no people can be bound to acknowledge and adore the Invisible Hand which conducts the affairs of men more than those of the United States," because "every step by which they have advanced to the character of an independent nation seems to have been distinguished by some token of providential agency."[34] Thus, the inauguration of the man who was "first in war, first in peace, and first in the hearts of his countrymen" was blessed with an invocation of divine aid by the highest chief executive. Every subsequent inaugural has likewise afforded the chief executive the opportunity to expressly invoke divine aid, or to acknowledge the working of the divine hands in the enterprise that is America.

To justify the request for injunctive relief, Dr. Newdow patched together quotations from various Supreme Court cases. He relied principally upon contextually inapplicable quotations from Supreme Court decisions arising in the context of public schools. In essence, Newdow concluded that permitting any prayer at the presidential inauguration, including the phrase "so help me God" as part of the oath of office, offended the Constitution. Newdow's conclusion rested on a flawed premise that the Supreme Court's decision in *Marsh*, upholding the constitutionality of legislative chaplains, is no longer good law. In *Marsh*, the Supreme Court held that opening legislative sessions with a prayer did not violate the Establishment Clause.

The Court's decision in *Marsh* required that it affirm the district court's dismissal of Newdow's challenge. The United States District Court in Washington, D.C., ruled in favor of the president and allowed the inaugural events to go on as planned, including delivery of the phrase "so help me God." Dr. Newdow quickly filed an appeal and within hours of the filing, the U.S. Court of Appeals affirmed the district court's decision.

Then, in an unusual move, Dr. Newdow, on an emergency basis, took his case to the Supreme Court of the United States. He first petitioned the chief justice, William Rehnquist, to recuse himself, since he was scheduled to actually administer the oath of office to President Bush. The chief justice refused to issue a recusal and, instead, denied Dr. Newdow's request for injunctive relief.

Not satisfied with the chief justice's decision, Dr. Newdow, pursuant to Supreme Court rules, petitioned Justice Stevens to stop the oath of office from occurring with the phrase "so help me God." Within a matter of hours, Justice Stevens also denied the request. Dr. Newdow then continued to petition individual justices with the same request, and each time it was rebuffed. What was highly unusual about this case is that it went from the U.S. District Court to the Supreme Court of the United States in just a matter of days.

As noted, the Court of Appeals and the U.S. District Court relied on the Supreme Court's decision in *Marsh*. In that case, the Supreme Court conducted a searching examination of the nation's history when considering a challenge to the Nebraska state legislature's practice of opening its sessions with prayer by a paid chaplain. Upholding the practice, the Court rested its legal conclusion on the fact that the "opening of sessions of legislative and other deliberative public bodies with prayer is deeply embedded in the history and tradition of this country." As the Court reasoned, "[i]n this context, historical evidence sheds light not only on what the draftsmen intended the Establishment Clause to mean, but also on how they thought that Clause applied to the practice authorized by the First Congress—their actions reveal their intent."

The *Marsh* Court observed that the first Congress "did not consider opening prayers as a proselytizing activity or as symbolically placing the government's official seal of approval on one religious view"; rather, the Framers merely considered "invocations as conduct whose effect harmonized with the tenets of some or all religions."

In *Marsh*, the Court held further that there was no establishment of religion, even though the same Presbyterian minister had served as the chaplain for sixteen years and had his salary paid from public funds. "To invoke Divine guidance on a public body entrusted with making the laws is not, in these circumstances, an 'establishment' of religion or a step toward establishment; it is simply a tolerable acknowledgment of beliefs widely held among the people of this country."

Like the phrase "so help me God" being uttered as part of the oath of office, presidential inaugurations have included formal prayers by clergy since the inauguration of George Washington.[35] Moreover, the inaugural addresses of virtually every president have invoked assistance of the Divine to the enterprise of the presidency and for the blessing of the nation and its people.

Pursuant to a congressional resolution, after the oath of office was administered and President Washington had given his inaugural address, he, along with the vice president and members of Congress, proceeded to St. Paul's Chapel for the recitation of prayers by the chaplain of Congress. Although no longer conducted in a church, inaugural prayers remain integral to the inauguration ceremony to this day. In addition, every inaugural ceremony for the last sixty-five years has included explicit supplications to Jesus Christ. Moreover, inaugural prayers during the last two centuries have incorporated the Lord's Prayer found in the book of Matthew.[36]

Nevertheless, Dr. Newdow, having examined the Supreme Court public school religion cases, including *Santa Fe*, concluded that *Marsh* was constitutionally suspect. Although Dr. Newdow tried to ignore the historical approach of *Marsh*, no justice of the Supreme Court agreed with him.

No Supreme Court Establishment Clause case decided subsequent to *Marsh* undercuts its vitality. In *Lynch*, the Court listed many examples of our "government's acknowledgment of our religious heritage," leading off with the historic practice of employing congressional chaplains. The Court said:

> The interpretation of the Establishment Clause by Congress in 1789 takes on special significance in light of the Court's emphasis that the First Congress "was a Congress whose constitutional decisions have always been regarded, as they should be regarded, as of the greatest weight in the interpretation of that fundamental instrument." It is clear that neither the 17 draftsmen of the Constitution who were Members of the First Congress, nor the Congress of 1789, saw any establishment problem in the employment of congressional Chaplains to offer daily prayers in the Congress, a practice that has continued for nearly two centuries. It would be difficult to identify a more striking example of the accommodation of religious belief intended by the Framers.

The Supreme Court concluded that this history may help explain why it consistently has declined to take a rigid, absolutist view of the Establishment Clause. The courts have refused "to construe the Religion Clauses with a literalness that would undermine the ultimate constitutional objective as illuminated by history." In our modern, complex society whose traditions and constitutional underpinnings rest on and encourage diversity and pluralism in all areas, an absolutist approach in applying the Establishment Clause is simplistic and has been uniformly rejected by the Court.

Justice O'Connor, as recently as the *Wallace* case in 1985, repeated her approval of the Court's decision in *Marsh*. "The Court properly looked to history in upholding legislative prayer. . . . As Justice Holmes once observed, if a thing has been practiced for two hundred years by common consent, it will need a strong case for the Fourteenth Amendment to affect it."

The long-standing history of the inclusion of the phrase "so help me God," as well as prayers, at the inaugural events resulted in the Court denying Dr. Newdow's challenge and allowing the inauguration to go on in the same vein that it had for over two hundred years.

TEN COMMANDMENTS CASES[37] (2005)

Starting in the 1990s, dozens of lawsuits erupted across the country, primarily sponsored by the ACLU and Americans United for Separation of

Church and State, focusing on the display of the Ten Commandments in public locations. These cases are interesting because Ten Commandments displays have been in existence in cities and towns throughout the United States for over fifty years, with relatively few subject to constitutional challenge. The story behind the installation of thousands of these displays is fascinating.

In the 1950s, famed movie director Cecil B. Demille assisted the Fraternal Order of Eagles in erecting thousands of granite Ten Commandments monuments across the country. These displays coincided with the release of his movie, *The Ten Commandments*. In fact, in several larger cities, movie stars such as Charlton Heston and Yul Brynner actually attended the dedication of the monuments. The Fraternal Order of Eagles is a secular organization that believed the Ten Commandments would serve as an appropriate guide to help young people develop good moral standards.

These Ten Commandments monuments, by and large, sat quietly until a national controversy erupted involving the former chief justice of the Alabama Supreme Court. In the early 1990s, Judge Roy Moore placed a small wooden plaque of the Ten Commandments in his Superior Court courtroom in Alabama. This action by Judge Moore helped fuel the ensuing litigation. A few months after Moore was elevated to chief justice of the Alabama Supreme Court in November 2000, he placed a two-and-a-half ton Ten Commandments monument in the lobby of the Alabama Supreme Court building. This further fueled the Ten Commandments litigation that had already begun several years earlier.

By the mid-1990s, over thirty lawsuits were pending in district courts around the country challenging the constitutionality of Ten Commandments displays. The lower courts were split on the issue of whether the monuments violated the Establishment Clause. Ultimately, the Supreme Court of the United States took two cases involving the Ten Commandments in October 2004. Ironically, the Supreme Court building itself has incorporated artistic pictorials of the Ten Commandments, and more than once, members of the Court have pointed upward to the depiction of Moses and the Ten Commandments in the Court's own courtroom to illustrate acceptable accommodation by government of a religious practice or display. In fact, the Supreme Court building has no fewer than three depictions of Moses and/or the Ten Commandments: (1) as part of the courtroom frieze, (2) dominating the East Pediment, and, (3) as part of a depiction of Chief Justice John Marshall on the West Pediment.[38] The

East Pediment shows Moses holding the Tablets of the Law flanked by Solon of Athens and Confucius, the ancient Greek and Chinese wise men and lawgivers. The script on Moses's Tablets is in Hebrew.

In the various court cases, the arguments in favor of the Ten Commandments were based on history—as one court said, "History matters here."[39] In fact, the history and ubiquity of governmental recognition of the Decalogue's secular role ensures that public displays of the Ten Commandments convey a message that is predominantly secular. In the development of law, the influence of the Old Testament Ten Commandments cannot be overstated.

The constitutionality of the Ten Commandments cases cannot be properly evaluated without an understanding of the "history and ubiquity" of the Decalogue as both a source and symbol of law in American culture. In fact, an understanding of the Commandments' role in the development of Western law and a survey of judicial, executive, legislative, and other secular references to and depictions of the Ten Commandments demonstrate that symbolic use of the Decalogue—such as that exemplified by the Texas display of the Fraternal Order of Eagles monument—is at least as ubiquitous and as much a part of "our Nation's cultural landscape."

The portion of the Hebrew Scriptures called the Ten Commandments, or the Decalogue, is an integral part of the legal heritage of Western civilization. The argument in favor of the constitutionality of the displays is straightforward. To require its removal from the walls of American courthouses and other public settings because it refers to the God of Israel as a source of fundamental legal obligations would be similar to requiring the removal of the Declaration of Independence because it refers to "Nature's God" and to "the Creator" and to "divine providence" as the source of the equality of all persons and of the universal rights of life, liberty, and the pursuit of happiness. Indeed, if one were to eliminate religious references from our legal history, one would reduce the time frame of that history to very recent generations.

The founders of the American Republic, in carrying over to it many features of the English law inherited from the colonial period, were highly conscious of the historical sources of that law, including its source in biblical law and morals. The Founding Fathers were entirely familiar with, and strongly influenced by, the great treatise of William Blackstone titled *Commentaries on the Laws of England*, published in 1765, in which he wrote that there are two main sources of human law, namely, a law of nature, which "God has enabled human reason to discover," and a divine law, "whose doctrines are to be found only in holy scripture." "Upon these two foundations," Blackstone wrote, "depend all human laws; that is to say, no human laws should be suffered to contradict these."[40] As historian Daniel Boorstin puts it, "In the history of American institutions, no other book—except the Bible—has played so great a role."[41] Indeed, the first major book of English history, King Alfred's ninth-century collection of rules of Anglo-Saxon law, starts with the full text of Exodus 20:1–17 of the Old Testament, containing the Ten Commandments.[42]

The biblical commandments were also considered to be authoritative in English law throughout the Roman Catholic period of its history (twelfth to early sixteenth centuries) as well as throughout the Tudor-Stuart period of royal supremacy over the Church of England (sixteenth and seventeenth centuries). Sir John Fortescue's fifteenth-century political and legal treatise, *In Praise of the Laws of England*, which was republished and annotated by John Selden two centuries later, invoked Mosaic law in order to inspire the "Prince" to govern according to the rule of law. Fortescue's treatise is presented as a dialogue between a "Prince" and a "Chancellor" who advises the Prince on English law and good governance. "Moses, that greatest of legislators," Fortescue's Chancellor advises the Prince, "invites you to strive zealously in the study of the law." Furthermore, Fortescue urges the Prince to study the Mosaic law of Deuteronomy "all the days of his life."[43] Likewise, Sir Edward Coke considered natural law, "which predated and underlay the laws of England," to have "had its earliest written expression in Mosaic law."[44] William Welwood's 1636 commentary on maritime law twice cited precedents from Deuteronomy as authoritative, in the division of spoils and on letters of marque, respectively.[45] Under the influence of Calvinism in the late seventeenth and early eighteenth centuries, an even stronger emphasis was placed on Mosaic law, including the Decalogue, and on the biblical sources of English law.

Although Calvinism remained especially strong in the American colonies, it eventually had to compete with other forms of Protestantism and also with Deism and Catholicism. All these belief systems shared, however, a strong belief both in the religious foundation of moral values and in the moral foundations of legal principles found in the Decalogue. The Ten Commandments have also played a decisive role in Western legal scholarship. Protestant legal scholars of the sixteenth century, starting with Martin Luther and his lifelong aid Philip Melanchthon, faced with the task of synthesizing for Protestant princes the preexisting separate systems of canon law, Roman law, royal law, feudal law, and mercantile law, turned to the last six of the Commandments to identify "branches" or "fields" of law. They found the source of constitutional law expressed in the commandment to honor one's father and mother, which they interpreted as a command to respect higher authority; the source of criminal law in the commandment not to kill; the source of family law in the commandment not to commit adultery; the source of property law in the commandment not to steal; the source of contract law in the commandment not to bear false witness; and the source of the law of delict in the commandment not to covet, that is, not to seek to obtain what belongs to another. These categories, which are still preserved in our legal science, cut across the diverse jurisdictions of the earlier period, each of which had been autonomous but, with the rise of Protestantism, came to be combined under the authority of the monarch. Of particular importance legally was the separation, for the first time, of the category of property from the Roman law category of obligations.[46]

Not only the authors of the United States Constitution but also their successors who are authorized to interpret it have preserved the historical dimension of American law. The continuity of its development over generations and centuries, which is reflected in the doctrine of precedent as well as in legal scholarship, is symbolized in the display of the Ten Commandments, which for centuries have been considered to be the historical source of universal legal obligations.

On at least seven occasions, members of the Supreme Court of the United States have noted the foundational role of the Ten Commandments in the development of our legal system.[47] Chief Justice Earl Warren attributed such a role to the Bible in general when he stated, "I believe the entire Bill of Rights came into being because of the knowledge our forefathers had of the Bible and their belief in it." In *McGowan v. Maryland* (1961), Associate Justice Felix Frankfurter wrote: "Innumerable civil regulations enforce conduct which harmonizes with religious concerns. State prohibitions of murder, theft and adultery reinforce commands of the Decalogue."[48] Justice Potter Stewart, dissenting in *Griswold v. Connecticut* (1965), said that most criminal prohibitions coincide with the prohibitions contained in the Ten Commandments.[49] In *Stone v. Graham* (1980), Chief Justice William Rehnquist stated in his dissenting opinion that the Ten Commandments, undeniably, "have had a significant impact on the development of secular legal codes of the Western World."[50] Justice Warren Burger noted in *Lynch* his approval of the presence of the depiction of Moses and the Ten Commandments on the Supreme Court's wall.

In *Edwards v. Aguillard* (1987), Justice William Brennan noted that the Ten Commandments have played both a secular and a religious role in the history of Western civilization.[51] In *County of Allegheny,* Justice John Paul Stevens agreed that the carving of Moses with the Ten Commandments on the wall of the Supreme Court's courtroom alongside famous secular lawgivers was a fitting message for a courtroom. Again, Chief Justice William Rehnquist declared in *City of Elkhart v. Books* (2001) that it was undeniable that "the Commandments have secular significance as well, because they have made a substantial contribution to our secular legal codes."[52]

It should come as no surprise to find that, historically, the foundational role of the Commandments has found expression in legislation. It is no exaggeration to say that the Ten Commandments, *literally,* have been part of our legal system for over a millennium. The ubiquity of the Ten Commandments in our history also manifests itself in the legal codes of the thirteen original colonies. It may be fairly said that all of the colonies incorporated the Decalogue—in whole or in part—in their legal codes.[53]

Even Thomas Jefferson drew analogies from the Bible and, specifically, Moses. The imagery of Moses and the Israelites was apparently second nature to him. Jefferson's original design for the Great Seal of the United States was of Moses leading the people of Israel through the Red Sea while Pharaoh and his army drowned, with the following motto: "Rebellion to Tyrants is Obedience to God."[54] His Second Inaugural Address also evoked Exodus:

> I shall need, too, the favor of that Being in whose hands we are, who led our forefathers, as Israel of old, from their native land and planted them in a country flowing with all the necessities of life.[55]

The widespread and long-standing recognition by government and secular society of the Decalogue's foundational role is firmly embedded in American culture and, like other traditions and practices, are part of the fabric of our society. As Justice Arthur Goldberg put it in the 1960s: "[n]either government nor this Court can or should ignore the significance of the fact that many of our legal, political and personal values derive historically from religious teachings."

The Supreme Court of the United States accepted the Ten Commandments cases in October 2004 and oral arguments were presented on

March 26, 2005. On June 26, the Supreme Court rendered its decisions. As was widely expected, the Court split the two cases: one display was held to be constitutional, the other was not.

In the Texas case, *Van Orden v. Perry*, in a most unusual line-up, the Court held that the Fraternal Order of Eagles monument, which graced the lawn of the Texas state capitol grounds, was constitutional. Chief Justice Rehnquist wrote an opinion for the Court, which was joined by Justices Scalia, Thomas, and Kennedy. This opinion was only a plurality and did not constitute a majority opinion of the Court. It was Justice Breyer's concurring opinion that proved to be decisive for the outcome of this case. Justices O'Connor, Souter, Stevens, and Ginsburg dissented and would have ordered the removal of thousands of Fraternal Order of Eagles monuments throughout the country. In *McCreary County v. American Civil Liberties Union of Ky.*, the Court held that the evolving display in the county courthouse was unconstitutional. Justice Souter wrote the majority opinion of the Court, which was joined by Justices Stevens, Ginsburg, O'Connor, and Breyer. The *McCreary County* case was actually not a surprising result. The facts of *McCreary* were problematic. The display had evolved from one of only the Ten Commandments to a more complex freedom monument. The intent of this particular display in a government building also had an overriding religious theme, according to Justice Souter. In other words, this violated the Establishment Clause.

Although the opinions on the surface appear somewhat conflicting, which is no surprise with regard to the Court's Establishment Clause cases, there are some important principles that can be gleaned, especially from Justice Stevens's dissenting opinion and Justice Breyer's concurring opinion in the Texas case. First, Justice Stevens's dissent noted the issue of the role of the impact of the Ten Commandments on the development of law:

> Though this Court has subscribed to the view that the Ten Commandments influenced the development of Western legal thought, it has not officially endorsed the far more specific claim that the Ten Commandments played a significant role in the development of our Nation's foundational documents . . . at the very least the question is a matter of intense scholarly debate.

Justice Stevens cited the brief of the Legal Historians and Law Scholars and compared it to the brief filed by the American Center for Law and

Justice to point out this "intense scholarly debate." This fundamental issue, although not resolved in the case, once again points to the importance of history as it relates to the determination of the religion clauses cases at the Supreme Court of the United States.[56]

Justice Breyer incorporated the jurisprudence of Justice Arthur Goldberg, for whom Breyer had served as a law clerk, in holding "that there is 'no simple and clear measure which by precise application can readily and invariably demark the permissible from the impermissible'" regarding the Establishment Clause. In upholding the display, Justice Breyer carefully noted "the Establishment Clause does not compel the government to purge from the public sphere all that in any way partakes of the religious." Justice Breyer also warned of a "'brooding and pervasive devotion to the secular'" which can result in an active "'hostility to the religious.'"

Context matters here. Justice Breyer found that the Texas display of the Fraternal Order of Eagles, a secular group, with sixteen other monuments scattered over the Texas state capitol grounds, provided "a context of history and moral ideals" as represented in the Ten Commandments. For Justice Breyer, the monument communicated "moral principles, illustrating a relation between ethics and law that the State's citizens, historically speaking, have endorsed." This moral message component in the context of the other displays was decisive for Justice Breyer.

Justice Breyer distinguished the "40-year history" of the Fraternal Order of Eagles monument in Texas as compared with the "short (and stormy) history of the McCreary County courthouse Commandments' displays, [which] demonstrates the substantially religious objectives of those who mounted them." During the oral arguments, there was considerable discussion regarding the religious nature of the Ten Commandments and its impact on the outcome of the cases. There is no doubt that the Ten Commandments are a sacred text. The fact that the Ten Commandments have a religious component did not dissuade Justice Breyer. To remove the display because of the religious nature of the tablets' text would, according to Justice Breyer, "lead the law to exhibit a hostility toward religion that has no place in our Establishment Clause traditions." Justice Breyer was also concerned that monuments throughout the country would be impacted by the decision.

Second, it was not the sacred aspect of the Ten Commandments display that became decisive. It was the context and history of the display that served as a primary issue for Justice Breyer. During oral argument, Justice Breyer commented that the Texas display was not divisive. The

Texas monument has been in place for forty years without objection. On the other hand, the "stormy" history of the McCreary County, Kentucky, display was decisive in the outcome of that case for Justice Breyer.

We can be certain of one outcome: the issue of the public display of the Ten Commandments will continue to be litigated. In one sense, the Texas and Kentucky opinions may have added more reasons for litigation to take place since the history and context of the individual display is what is now the determinative factor. This surely guarantees a trajectory of analysis and decision on a case-by-case basis beginning in the lower courts.

Another critical factor in future cases that reach the Supreme Court is the composition of the Court itself. Just four days after the Supreme Court articulated its decisions in the Ten Commandments cases, Justice Sandra Day O'Connor announced her retirement after twenty-four years of service on the Court. Justice O'Connor's votes throughout her career on the Court were very often decisive in 5–4 decisions. She was the justice who made all the difference. On September 3, 2005, Chief Justice William H. Rehnquist passed away at home surrounded by his children. The chief justice served our country with honor and distinction and will be remembered for his great service to this nation. President Bush nominated John G. Roberts Jr. to be the seventeenth chief justice of the United States. Interestingly, John Roberts served as a law clerk for the late chief justice. With his judicial philosophy of interpreting the Constitution instead of legislating from the bench, John Roberts will set a tone that will resonate with the American people as the high court tackles some of the most challenging issues of the day. The successors of Justice O'Connor, and other Supreme Court justices as they occur, will impact the constitutional interpretation and adjudication of the First Amendment religion clauses for future generations.

There is no doubt that the Supreme Court will continue to delve into the difficult area of the appropriate relationship between church and state. What becomes self-evident is that the Court's reliance on history will serve as the overarching test to determine the constitutionality of a public religious acknowledgment or practice.

That history, as established in this study, illustrates that justice is never truly blind. The influence of the religious faith and practices of the justices on their opinions is significant. The backgrounds and faith of the justices and the religious controversies of their day are reflected in the opinions of the Court. In each case, the justices have, each in his or her own way, witnessed their faith through their opinions. The effectiveness of their witness persists for generations. The current Court and future Courts must continue to confront the witnesses of these justices from a previous time and draw conclusions faithful to the Constitution.

NOTES

1. *Separation of Church and State,* American Baptist Convention, September 1981; available at www.sbc.net. All subsequent quotations from *Separation of Church and State* are based on this source.

2. Executive Council Minutes, Episcopal Church, USA, *Opposition to U.S. Legislation on Prayer in Public Schools,* (November 1981), 13–14, 37–38; available at www.episcopal archives.org.

3. *Resolution on Prayer in Schools,* Southern Baptist Convention (June 1982) available at http://www.sbc.net.

4. *Resolution on Religious Liberty,* Southern Baptist Convention (June 1983) available at http://www.sbc.net.

5. Regarding aid to religious schools and institutions, the *Resolution on Religious Liberty* stated:

> Be it . . . RESOLVED, That we encourage Southern Baptists to oppose efforts to use governmental institutions and processes to promote the particular interests of a religious constituency or by favoring those who believe in no religion over those who have a faith commitment; and
>
> Be it further RESOLVED, That we encourage Southern Baptists to oppose the use of public monies for religious institutions and all unwarranted attempts by government to define "church."

6. *Board of Education of the Westside Community Schools v. Mergens,* 496 U.S. 226 (1990). All subsequent quotations from *Mergens* are based on this case citation.

7. *Resolution on Diplomatic Relations with the Vatican,* Southern Baptist Convention (June 1993); full text available at http://www.sbc.net.

8. *Widmar v. Vincent,* 454 U.S. 269 (1981). All subsequent quotations from *Widmar* are based on this case citation.

9. *Lamb's Chapel v. Center Moriches Union Free School District,* 508 U.S. 384 (1993). All subsequent quotations from *Lamb's Chapel* are based on this case citation.

10. *Good News Club v. Milford Central School,* 533 U.S. 98 (2001).

11. *Santa Fe Independent School District v. Doe,* 530 U.S. 290, 313 (2000). All subsequent quotations from *Santa Fe* are based on this case citation.

12. *Resolution on Equal Access,* Southern Baptist Convention (June 1985) full text available at http://www.sbc.net.

13. In the interest of full disclosure, the author of the present work argued the *Mergens*

and the *Lamb's Chapel* cases before the Supreme Court of the United States representing the students in *Mergens* and the church in *Lamb's Chapel.*

14. *Locke v. Davey*, 124 S.Ct. 1307 (2004). All subsequent quotations from *Davey* are based on this case citation.

15. Executive Board, United Lutheran Church in America, 1950; available at *Journal of Lutheran Ethics* at www.elca.org/jle/ucla/ucla.church_state.html.

16. *Elk Grove Unified School District v. Newdow*, 124 S. Ct. 2301 (2004). All subsequent quotations from *Newdow* are based on this case citation.

17. *Wallace v. Jaffree*, 472 U.S. 38 (1985). All subsequent quotations from *Wallace* are based on this case citation.

18. *The Declaration of Independence* para. 2 (U.S. 1776). Jefferson wrote further that the right to "dissolve the political bands" connecting the colonies to England derives from Natural Law and *"Nature's God."* Declaration, para. 1. The founders also believed that God holds man accountable for his actions as the signers of the Declaration "[appeal] to the *Supreme Judge of the world* to rectify their intentions." Declaration, para. 32. In 1774, Jefferson wrote that "The God who gave us life gave us liberty at the same time; the hand of force may destroy, but cannot disjoin them." Thomas Jefferson, *Rights of British America*, 1774. ME 1:211, Papers 1:135.

19. Thomas Jefferson, *Notes on Virginia* Q.XVIII (1782).

20. Kerby Anderson, *Pledge of Allegiance*, available at http://www.pointofview.net/ar_pledge1111.htm.

21. Edwin S. Davis, "The Religion of George Washington: A Bicentennial Report," *Air Univ. Rev.* (July–August 1976); available at http://www.airpower.maxwell.af.mil/air chronicles/aureview/1976/jul-aug/edavis.html; quoting John C. Fitzpatrick, ed., *The Writings of George Washington*, vol. 3 (1931–1944), 301.

22. George Washington, *First Inaugural Address*, full text available at http://www.archives.gov/exhibit_hall/american_originals/inaugtxt.html.

23. Jared Sparks, *The Writings of George Washington*, vol. 12 (1833–1837), T19.

24. Hamburger, *Separation of Church and State*, (Cambridge, Mass.: Harvard University Press, 2002), 480.

25. *Zorach v. Clauson*, 343 U.S. 306 (1952). All subsequent quotations from *Zorach* are based on this case citation.

26. *Engel v. Vitale*, 370 U.S. 421 (1962). All subsequent quotations from *Engel* are based on this case citation.

27. *School District of Abington Township v. Schempp*, 374 U.S. 304 (1963) (Brennan, J., concurring). All subsequent quotations from *Schempp* are based on this case citation.

28. *Lee v. Weisman*, 505 U.S. 577 (1992).

29. *Lynch v. Donnelly*, 465 U.S. 668 (1984). All subsequent quotations from *Lynch* are based on this case citation.

30. *Allegheny County v. American Civil Liberties Union*, 492 U.S. 573 (1989). All subsequent quotations from *Allegheny* are based on this case citation.

31. The Mayflower Compact, written by William Bradford in 1620, provides:

> We whose names are underwritten, the loyal subjects of our dread sovereign Lord, King James, by *the grace of God*, of Great Britain, France and Ireland

king, defender of the faith, etc., having undertaken, *for the glory of God, and advancement of the Christian faith*, and honor of our king and country, a voyage to plant the first colony in the Northern parts of Virginia, do by these presents solemnly and mutually *in the presence of God*, and one of another, covenant and combine ourselves together into a civil body politic, for our better ordering and preservation and furtherance of the ends aforesaid; and by virtue hereof to enact, constitute, and frame such just and equal laws, ordinances, acts, constitutions, and offices, from time to time, as shall be thought most meet and convenient for the general good of the colony, unto which we promise all due submission and obedience. [emphasis added]

Mayflower Compact, available at http://www
.project21.org/MayflowerCompact.html.

32. President Abraham Lincoln, *The Gettysburg Address* (19 November 1863). See also Allan Nevins, *Lincoln and the Gettysburg Address* (Urbana: University of Illinois Press, 1964); and William E. Barton and Edward Everett, *Lincoln at Gettysburg* (Indianapolis: Bobbs-Merrill Co., 1930, reprint 1971).

33. *U.S. Constitution*, art. II, § 1.

34. *Inaugural Addresses of the Presidents of the United States*, S. Doc. No. 10, 101st Cong., 1st Sess. 2 (1989). All subsequent quotations from *Inaugural Addresses* are based on this source.

35. Steven B. Epstein, "Rethinking the Constitutionality of Ceremonial Deism," *Colum. L. Rev.* 96 (1996): 2083; citing Martin Jay Medhurst, "'God Bless the President': The Rhetoric of Inaugural Prayer" (1980), 61 (unpublished Ph.D. dissertation, Pennsylvania State University; on file with the Pennsylvania State University Library).

36. Magistrate Judge Hollows found that under *Marsh* "presidential invocations to the Deity, i.e., prayers, at inaugurations were historical and commonplace" and that "[a]s such, the prayers in general did not offend the Establishment Clause of the First Amendment to the Constitution." See "Findings and Recommendations," No. CIV-01-0218 LKK GGH PS (28 December 2001), 2.

37. The author filed briefs on behalf of the state of Texas and McCreary County in the Ten Commandments cases, arguing in favor of the displays.

38. Office of the Curator, Supreme Court of the United States.

39. *Van Orden v. Perry*, 351 F. 3d 181 (5th Cir. 2003).

40. William Blackstone, *Commentaries on the Laws of England* (1765; facs. editions, 1979), 39–42. The American founding generation learned its law from Blackstone's *Commentaries on the Laws of England*. See Albert Altschuler, "Rediscovering Blackstone," *U. Pa. L. Rev.* 145 (1996): 1.

41. Daniel J. Boorstin, *The Mysterious Science of the Law* (Boston: Beacon Press, 1958).

42. J.A. Giles, *The Whole Works of King Alfred the Great*, vol. 3 (London: Bosworth & Harrison, ed., 1858), 120.

43. Sir John Fortescue, *De Laudibus Legum Anglie*, published in Sir John Fortescue, *On the Laws and Governance of England*, ed. Shelly Lockwood, in *Cambridge Texts in the History of Political Thought* (New York: Cambridge University Press, 1997), 4.

44. See Steven K. Green, "The Fount of Everything Just and Right? The Ten Commandments as a Source of American Law," *J.L. & Religion* 14 (1999): 534. Green denies that the Ten Commandments formed a significant part of eighteenth-century legal theory, although he acknowledges that prior to that century the Ten Commandments in general, and Mosaic law in particular, were often cited as part of the English legal tradition and constituted the moral foundation of common law, including the charters and laws of the American colonies.

45. William Welwood, *An Abridgement of All Sea-Laws Gathered Forth of all Writings and Monuments, Which Are to Be Found Among Any People or Nation* (1636), 179, 182.

46. Harold J. Berman, *Law and Revolution II: The Impact of the Protestant Reformations on the Western Legal Tradition* (Cambridge, Mass.: Belknap Press of Harvard University Press, 2003), 82–85, 117–18.

47. *Time*, 15 February 1954.

48. *McGowan v. Maryland*, 366 U.S. 420 (1961).

49. *Griswold v. Connecticut*, 381 U.S. 479, 529, n2 (1965) (Stewart, J., dissenting).

50. *Stone v. Graham*, 449 U.S. 39, 45 (1980) (Rehnquist, J. dissenting).

51. *Edwards v. Aguillard*, 482 U.S. 578, 593–94 (1987).

52. *City of Elkhart v. Books*, 532 U.S. 1058 (2001) (Rehnquist, C. J., with whom Scalia, J. and Thomas, J., join, dissenting from denial of certiorari).

53. See examples reprinted in Donald S. Lutz, ed., *Colonial Origins of the American Constitution: A Documentary History* (Indianapolis: Liberty Fund, 1998).

54. James H. Hutson, *Religion and the Founding of the American Republic* (Washington, D.C.: Library of Congress, 1998), 50–51.

55. *A Compilation of the Messages and Papers of the Presidents, 1789–1897*, 10 vols. (Washington, D.C.: U.S. Government Printing Office).

56. The author was counsel of record for the brief by the American Center for Law and Justice.

Index

About the Author

Jay Alan Sekulow is chief counsel for the American Center for Law and Justice (ACLJ) and the European Center for Law and Justice (ECLJ). An accomplished and respected judicial advocate, Sekulow has presented oral arguments before the Supreme Court in numerous cases in defense of constitutional freedoms, especially those involving religion. The *National Law Journal* has twice named Sekulow one of the "100 Most Influential Lawyers" in the United States, and *Time* magazine named him one of the top twenty-five most influential evangelicals in America. A popular guest on nationally televised news programs on ABC, CBS, NBC, CNN, FOX, MSNBC, CNBC, and PBS, Sekulow hosts the television program "ACLJ This Week," has his own call-in radio program which is broadcast throughout the country on more than 600 radio stations, and frequently contributes articles and commentary to national publications such as *USA Today*, the *New York Times*, *Washington Post*, and *Washington Times*.